Quetzalcoatl.

Dictionary of
Chicano Folklore

Quetzalcoatl.

Dictionary of Chicano Folklore

Rafaela G. Castro

ABC-CLIO

Santa Barbara, California
Denver, Colorado
Oxford, England

Copyright © 2000 by Rafaela G. Castro

Quetzalcoatl illustration based on the *Codex Barbonicus*.

Library of Congress Cataloging-in-Publication Data
Castro, Rafaela, 1943–
   Dictionary of Chicano folklore / Rafaela G. Castro.
     p. cm.
   Includes bibliographical references and index.
   ISBN 0-87436-953-3 (alk. paper)
   1. Mexican Americans—Folklore—Dictionaries.   2. Mexican Americans—Social life
and customs—Dictionaries.   I. Title
GR111.M49 C37   2000
398'.089'6872073—dc21   00-022477

06 05 04 03 02 01 00 10 9 8 7 6 5 4 3 2 1

ABC-CLIO, Inc.
130 Cremona Drive, P.O. Box 1911
Santa Barbara, California 93116-1911

This book is printed on acid-free paper ∞.

Manufactured in the United States of America

In memory of
Cipriana Aguilar Gonzales, 1898–1980
and
Enriqueta Duran Castro, 1902–1985

Quetzalcoatl.

Contents

Preface, xi
Introduction, xiii

DICTIONARY OF CHICANO FOLKLORE

Quetzalcoatl

Preface

The expansion of Chicano studies is an exciting development; it is a much more highly developed discipline now than it was thirty years ago when it first began, but it continues to require publication of new reference sources. Research in the field of Chicano folklore is growing, and university academic programs are developing new courses in Chicano folk narrative, folk drama, popular culture, and cultural studies. Teachers often present cultural concepts and folkloristic terms in the classroom, but the student must go to the library to find additional background and historical information for a research paper. Resources on a variety of genres are difficult to find in the library, since they are not all available in one source, and it may take an expert researcher considerable time to find even basic data.

This dictionary was developed to bring together folklore and cultural information from many sources, such as published books, journal and newspaper articles, and literary and historical works. It provides basic definitions of concepts such as *duendes*, *pintos*, *la llorona*, *la migra*, *Cinco de Mayo*, *pachucos*, low riders, zoot suits, *las posadas*, and other cultural phenomena. Reference sources for additional research are cited for each entry. The purpose of this reference work is to facilitate the student's research on Chicano folklore and culture; an alphabetically arranged bibliography of all the references cited is provided at the end of the book. The bibliography identifies a core body of literature, much of it written by Chicanos, and displays a cultural inventory of library and research resources on Chicano folklore.

The general rationale determining the inclusion of a term, genre, or concept was that it represent or describe a folk speech, folk narrative, folk artifact, cultural tradition, or ritual occurring in the United States that pertains to the Chicano, or Mexican American, population. Folklore genres usually fall into the categories of oral narrative, literature, material culture, folk customs and beliefs, and folk arts. All of the genres presented in this work are covered under the standard classifications of folklore and almost all have been written about in folklore or Chicano studies literature. Although some concepts have been well researched, many others have been explored very little. This dictionary will be helpful for librarians, students, and scholars studying Chicano literature, history, music, art, popular culture, and border studies.

Acknowledgments

I was very fortunate to receive much financial, emotional, intellectual, and spiritual support from many individuals and sources while I worked on this project. I'd like to thank the administration of Shields Library, University of California, Davis, for the personal encouragement, but especially for the release time granted me so I could focus complete attention on this project. Grateful thanks are also extended to the Academic Federation of UC Davis, which provided me with a Professional Development Award that allowed me to start this work five years ago. Also, I feel great appreciation and indebtedness to the Librarians Association of the University of California (LAUC) for granting me funds for two summers, which provided me with release time to continue this work. Ultimately, I owe everything to my personal devotees, who have been fantastic in encouragement, patience, and love: John, Solange, and Laura, my family. I also want to thank my two sisters, Elva and Linda, for being there.

Rafaela G. Castro

Quetzalcoatl

Introduction

Growing up Chicano in the United States is an unusual cultural experience. The Chicano population is a conglomeration of native-born Americans; recently arrived Mexican immigrants; long-term permanent residents; first-, second-, and third-generation families; and descendents of seventeenth-century Spanish settlers. Monolingual English-speaking Chicanos, with absolutely no ties to Mexico, may live side by side with immigrant Mexican families who speak only Spanish. Some Chicano families make annual trips to Mexico to visit relatives, while others have grandmothers who have never been outside of the United States and have never spoken English. Yet all may identify as *Mexicanos* or Chicanos; may speak Spanish, English, or a mixture of the two; and may feel culturally united and "different" from the rest of American society. Not all Mexican Americans identify as or call themselves Chicanos, but most Chicanos will also call themselves *Mexicanos*. The term Chicano has a controversial history and is accepted primarily by Mexican Americans who came of age in the 1960s. Today the term Latino is embraced by most Chicanos and Mexican Americans as a more encompassing term because it includes other groups that have descended from the Spanish encounter, such as Puerto Ricans and Cubans.

People of Spanish and Mexican descent have been living in what is now the Southwest of the United States since the Spanish first settled the area in the late 1500s. The Southwest was not conquered or settled all at once: New Mexico was the first region settled, in 1598; Texas was settled in 1682; Arizona in 1700; and California last, in 1769. In 1848, after the United States–Mexican War, most of this area, almost half of Mexico's northern territory, was ceded to the United States, and approximately 80,000 Spanish-Mexican-Indian people suddenly became inhabitants of the United States. After 300 years of Spanish being the dominant language in public and private, it was displaced in public by English, which became the official language of government and commerce.

The Chicano cultural experience in the United States has not always been positive, but it has been diverse and rich with multidimensional social, cultural, and linguistic dynamics. It has been different for those who migrated during the Mexican Revolution than for the *Mexicanos* who came in the 1950s, or for those living in Texas, New Mexico, Colorado, Arizona, or California at the turn of the century. There has always been migration to and from Mexico, with large waves occurring after the Mexican Revolution from 1910 to 1928. Since the United States–Mexican War this great movement of people has succeeded in reinforcing folk customs, traditions, rituals, and language permanency throughout "greater Mexico" (Paredes 1958, 129). Those who come to the United States from Mexico, unable to completely relinquish their Mexican cultural identity, tend to maintain their folkways, even if only in an adapted form. Many customs, rituals, and traditional cultural forms have been adapted to the culture of the United States, yet still maintain an unmistakable *Mexicano* character.

The study of a people's folklore provides one with a view of the intimate and meaningful aspects of their private and communal life. Folklore is the informal knowledge of a culture that circulates within and among families, groups, towns, and regions. The late Américo Paredes, the most influential scholar of Chicano folklore, defines folklore as "the unofficial heritage of a people" (1982, 1–11). That heritage is passed on from generation to generation, through word of mouth, through stories, songs, family histories, and humorous tales. But it is also passed on through nonverbal gestures, unwritten habits and customs, favorite foods, and religious and family beliefs that sometimes appear to have no historical basis yet have persisted for many generations.

Folklore, besides being the unofficial history of Chicanos, is important to a community for other reasons. Folklore provides a means of educating children about the acceptable social behavior and social norms of the community. It also allows individuals a vehicle for engaging in social protest against the established standards of the dominant Anglo culture. In a now famous article the prominent anthropologist William R. Bascom discussed the four basic functions of folklore. One obvious function is amusement, such as that derived from oral stories, jokes, riddles, and games. A second function of folklore is that it validates a community's culture by maintaining its rituals and institutions for those who participate in them. Third, it performs an instructional function by providing a means of passing on wisdom. The fourth function, mentioned by Bascom and many other folklorists as well, is folklore's role in maintaining conformity and exerting social pressure for social control. Bascom succinctly states this principle: "Here, indeed, is the basic paradox of folklore, that while it plays a vital role in transmitting and maintaining the institutions of a culture in forcing the individual to conform to them, at the same time it provides socially approved outlets for the repressions which these same institutions impose upon him" (1965, 298).

Some studies of ethnic folklore analyze it as a means of measuring acculturation and assimilation of an ethnic group into American society. But the process of Americanization has not been the same for all immigrant groups, and it has been very different from the norm for Mexicans. Linguistic acculturation has been slow because of the constant migration of new immigrants and the nearness of the Mexican border; this maintenance of the Spanish language has been a primary means of preserving *Mexicano* culture and folklore. New scholarly approaches to studying the folklore of ethnic groups now look at the creation of and participation in cultural rituals and customs as a means of maintaining cohesive ethnic identity and group consciousness. It is now believed that participation in folkloric cultural forms such as religious celebrations, social dances, ethnic festivals, and other shared traditions maintains ethnic group boundaries and solidifies ethnic identity.

Américo Paredes, in an essay titled "*El Folklore de los Grupos de Origen Mexicano en Estados Unidos*," proposes that one distinct characteristic of the folklore of Chicanos is related to the experience of "*choque de culturas y de pueblos*," the conflict of cultures experienced by the Mexican people in the United States (1966b, 154). He defines three population folk groups of Mexican American culture: immigrant, regionalist, and urban. He argues that folklore is generated when the *Mexicano* comes into conflict with the dominant Anglo American culture. He distinguishes Mexican American folklore from Mexican immigrant folklore found in the United States, and from colonial Spanish American regionalist folklore collected during the early twentieth century. That folklore is extremely significant to understanding the Chicano experience is undisputed, and Paredes emphasizes this by stating, "the Mexican American would do well to seek his identity in his folklore" (1982, 1).

Folk culture is often mistakenly considered to be the culture of primitive or peasant societies that have not yet become westernized or sophisticated. In the field of folklore studies, folk culture is a term used to designate culture that is transmitted among a group of people face-to-face on a daily basis, from generation to generation. The "folk" are any group of people that share something in common. It could be an occupational group such as firefighters, cowhands, students, or nurses; an age group such as children or the elderly; a family group; or an ethnic group. Folk culture is culture that is passed on among people who interact intimately and informally.

In contrast, high culture or elite culture is generally taught or conveyed through formal channels, such as music academies, universities, and other established institutions of society. In the realm of art or classical music or world literature, the standards of value are established by an official culture and are accepted throughout the country and the world among the higher classes of society. Knowledge of high culture is within reach of all social groups, but not without considerable effort.

Popular culture is the culture of the masses and is a modern phenomenon because its distribution is primarily through the mass media. Songs, clothing styles, commercial jingles, food fads, and other elements of popular culture are available to everyone through radio, television, movies, magazines, and newspapers, and now also through the Internet. Popular culture is important because it is an aesthetic expression of the modern condition. Many Chicano folkloristic expressions have become part of popular culture through a process of adaptation and modernization. For example, *La Bamba* is a folk song and dance from the mid-nineteenth century, but it is now known in popular culture as the name of a catchy tune and a Hollywood movie.

Folklore includes not just old customs and traditions but also modern lore and folk life. Wherever there is a folk, a people, there is the expressive behavior that we call folklore. The process of living creates folklore. Modern folklore is continually being anonymously created in urban centers, college campuses, and business offices. The popular urban tale, new dance steps, joke cycles, dress fads, and traditions for new social situations are constantly being formed in today's society. Practicing old customs and creating current customs for new social situations bind together individuals and groups. In areas where Chicanos live, especially along the United States–Mexico border, the folklore is a combination of traditional and contemporary folklore, some of it even evolving into popular culture. A rich aspect of Chicano oral folklore is that traditional forms, such as belief in the supernatural, can exist side by side with contemporary folklore, such as the many urban legends. So, while traditional Mexican and Chicano folklore continues to endure, newly invented Chicano and American folklore is adopted and incorporated into the corpus of Chicano folklore. As Mark Glazer, another prominent scholar of Mexican American folklore, put it, "This results in a mixture of traditional, updated, and modern folklore which shows every sign of a very strong and vibrant cultural tradition" (1986, 144).

The folklore and culture of Chicanos living in the Southwest, the Northwest, and the Midwest are similar, yet different. Northern New Mexico village folklore, because it has been so widely written about, is assumed to be the norm for all *Mexicanos*, but it is not. Yet, because of the Spanish language, the Catholic religion, and a common history of ethnic discrimination and labor segregation, there are more similarities than differences in the folklore of the *Mexicano* living in the United States. Many Chicanos and *Mexicanos* venerate *La Virgen de Guadalupe*; celebrate *Las Posadas*; narrate *cuentos* of *La Llorona*; dance to *conjunto* music; make *tamales* for the holidays; and still believe in the medicinal powers of *menudo*, in the healing worth of folk remedies, and in tales of spirits, the supernatural, and the devil. People of Mexican ancestry or Chicanos living in the United States have created a rich new cultural life by converting religious, social, artistic, and political traditions inherited from Mexico into customs that are practical and specific to the American experience. Fourth- and fifth-generation Chicanos continue to cultivate and evolve traditions and rituals connected to Spanish Catholicism, and their Mexican heritage, sometimes with little knowledge of the origins or the complex symbolism involved.

An early historical survey by Aurelio Espinosa Jr. on the status of Spanish American folklore research addresses the folklore of the people that are now called Chicano. Even though he is discussing Spanish American folklore at the time of the article's publication in 1947, most of this folklore had been collected and published in English. This prompted Espinosa to state, "With regard to the collecting, it must be stressed that the materials should be recorded as accurately as possible *in Spanish*; the recent tendency to publish Spanish materials in English must be discontinued, since in such form it can not be utilized by the scientific folklorist" (Espinosa, 1947, 377). He goes on to state that while most of the folklore work had been done in New Mexico and Colorado, much work still needed to be done in California, Arizona, and Texas. He also mentions Louisiana and Florida since he is emphasizing the collecting of materials in the Spanish language. This points to a dilemma that is as true today as it was more than fifty years ago when Espinosa wrote this statement. Since the folklorists who first observed, collected, and studied Chicano folklore were Anglo Americans, who even if they knew the Spanish language were not familiar with the Mexican character and culture, they interpreted and wrote about this folklore in the English language and interjected their own values and cultural norms into their writings. Because the Spanish folklore collections of the Espinosas, Sr. and Jr., and of Juan Rael and Arthur Campa were collected and published in Spanish, they have been consigned to the discipline of Spanish literature and have been neglected by Chicano and American folklore scholars. Little analysis or interpretation from a Chicano historical perspective has been published on the early Spanish folklore collections of these folklorists.

For those who want to continue researching Chicano folklore, two excellent bibliographies provide an in-depth and broad introduction to the scholarship and research completed before the late 1980s. One is *An Annotated Bibliography of Chicano Folklore from the Southwestern United States* by Michael Heisley (1977), and the other is "Greater Mexican Folklore in the United States: An Annotated Bibliography," by Olga Najera-Ramirez (1987). The bibliography published in this volume also provides a basic body of literature on Chicano culture, history, literature, and folklore.

References
Alvarez 1995; Espinosa, Jr. 1947; Glazer 1986; Heisley 1977; Herrera-Sobek 1984; Limón 1977; Najera-Ramirez 1987; Paredes 1966b, 1978, 1982; Villarino and Ramirez 1997

Quetzálcoatl.

El Abuelo (Grandfather)

An old-man figure called *el abuelo* (the grandfather) played the role of a bogeyman in Hispano folklore. In literature it is sometimes spelled *aguelo*, and some scholars speculate that it may be a borrowed word from the language of the Pueblo Indians. In Spanish it means "grandfather," and has become synonymous with *coco*, *cucui*, and bogeyman. This folk character is more known in northern New Mexico than in other parts of the Southwest. He appeared at Christmastime to test and discipline children who did not know their catechism or prayers. He was a scary figure, dressed to terrify children with a black cape and a mask with large horns, and always carrying a whip. Children were terribly frightened because of his horrid appearance. Instead of a mask he sometimes had a tortilla plastered on his face, wore buffalo horns and a horsetail, and of course carried the whip. A few days before Christmas, he'd knock on the door of a home, give a bloodcurdling cry, crack his whip, and yell at the children, *"Han sido buenos muchachos estos?"* (Have these children been good?) The children would cringe and hide while the parents defended them. Then *el abuelo* would say, *"Pues que recén y se acuestén"* (Well, let them pray and go to bed). Sometimes he made the children dance *Las Palomitas*, loosely translated as "the little doves." Espinosa describes this experience. "After making them pray, he makes them form a circle, and, taking each other's hands, they dance around the room with him, singing,

> *Baila paloma de Juan turuntún (or durundún) [sic]*
> *'Turun tún tún*
> *Turun tun tún!'*
> (Dance dove of Juan confused or disoriented
> Confused, confused!)
> (1910, 402)

A description of *el abuelo* making children "dance the little dove" is also available in Steele's work (1992, 25). Throughout the year if children misbehaved, parents would threaten them, *"Si no te sosiegas, llamo el abuelo"* (If you don't behave, I'll call the bogeyman).

1

El abuelo is also a prominent figure in the dance of *Los Matachines*, and plays a comical role in which he makes jokes and shouts out instructions to the rest of the dancers. In some performances there is a female character, *la abuela*, who acts as *el abuelo*'s accomplice and plays a similar role. Although he is not heard of often in contemporary times, references to *el abuelo* can be found in the folktales and literature of New Mexico.

See also El Coco; El Cucui; El Kookoóee; Los Matachines
References Brown 1978; Cobos 1983; Espinosa 1910; Steele 1992

La Adelita (Mexican Revolution Woman Soldier)

A feminist symbol of the Mexican Revolution, *La Adelita* was the name of a woman soldier, a *soldadera*, who followed the troops, helped to set up camp, and cooked for the soldiers. Some *soldaderas* were employed to cook and fulfil the needs of a particular soldier, whereas others were relatives or lovers. The legend states that *Adelita* was a woman who fought in the Revolution, but it is not known if she actually existed as an individual; she came to epitomize all *soldaderas* and courageous women of that period. In popular culture, literature, and the cinema, *soldaderas* have been portrayed as self-sacrificing women, usually *mestizas* (mixed-race women) from the lower classes, but *La Adelita* is often seen as a *güera* (light-skinned), "sweetheart of the troops, a woman who is valiant, pretty, and a wonderful helpmate to the soldier" (Salas 121). Several *corridos* (ballads) have been written about her, and she is a powerful symbol for Mexican and Chicana women, representing bravery, self-discipline, and romantic love. In fact, it is primarily through the *corridos* that *Adelita* is known today. Historically, all *soldaderas* became known as *Adelitas*. In performances by *ballet folklórico* groups, the dances and music of the Revolution are often called *Las Adelitas*.

La Adelita is more than a romantic image to modern-day Chicanas. She continues to symbolize feminine independence, integrity, the fight for justice, and a proud heritage. Because the major influx of Mexican immigration into the United States was during the Mexican Revolution, many Chicanos and Chicanas grew up hearing stories about *soldaderas* and *La Adelita* from relatives, parents, and grandparents. In the late 1960s Chicanas who joined the Brown Berets de Aztlán, a political pseudomilitary youth group, often dressed as *Adelitas*, wearing *rebozos* (shawls) and bandoliers crisscrossed over their chests.

One play about *La Adelita*, titled *Soldadera*, written by Josephine Niggli, was produced and performed in the United States in 1936, and is still performed today. Niggli was 25 years old when the play was written. She went on to write *Mexican Village*, a novel that incorporated many of the Mexican people's folk customs and traditions. Born in Monterrey, Mexico, she lived in Mexico City and was taught at home by her mother. Later she moved to San

Antonio, Texas, where she attended high school. She went to the University of North Carolina for playwriting, sometimes acting in her own plays. *Soldadera* is a play about the women in the Revolution, "women who left homes to follow their men, cooking for them, tending their wounds, guarding their ammunition, fighting when necessary," as Niggli put it. The *Adelita* character dies in the play, and Niggli idealizes her bravery.

One variant of the *corrido* "La Adelita" follows:

En lo alto de una abrupta cerrania
acampado se encontraba un regimiento
y una moza que valiente lo seguia
locamente enamorada del sargento.
Popular entre la tropa era Adelita
la mujer que el sargento idolatraba
porque a mas de ser valiente era bonita
y hasta el mismo coronel la respetaba.
Y se oía que decía aquel que tanto la quería. . . .
Y si Adelita fuera mi novia,
y si Adelita fuera mi mujer,
le compraría un vestido de seda
para llevarla a bailar al cuartel.
Y si Adelita se fuera con otro
la seguiría por tierra y por mar
si por mar en un buque de guerra
si por tierra en un tren militar.
(On the loftiest of the sierras
A regiment is camped
And a brave young girl follows
A sergeant that she crazily loves.
Popular among the troops was Adelita
The woman that the sergeant idolized
Because besides being brave she was pretty
And even the colonel respected her.
And one could hear him that loved her so. . . .
If Adelita was my girlfriend,
And if Adelita was my woman,
I'd buy her a silk dress,
To take her dancing at the barracks
If Adelita ever left with another
I would follow her by land and by sea
If by sea, in war ship, and
If by land on a military train.)

References Arrizón 1998; Herrera-Sobek 1990; Niggli 1938; Salas 1990

Adivinanzas (Riddles)

Adivinanzas are riddles. Many Chicano children remember being entertained with riddles narrated by parents and grandparents. A riddle is an intellectual brainteaser, in Spanish called a *quebracabeza*; facts are framed in the form of a question in such a way that the respondent cannot possibly know the answer. An example in Spanish is, *"Qué camina de cuatro patas por la mañana, dos patas en el medio día, y tres patas en la noche?"* (What walks on four legs in the morning, two legs in the afternoon, and three legs at night?) The answer is man, who as a child, in the "morning" of life, crawls on four legs; as an adult walks on two legs; and as an old man uses a cane for support, thus walking on three legs. Another example is a "true riddle," which is a comparison of something to the unknown answer, and that something is described in the question. For example, *"Tengo ojos y no miro; boca pero no hablo; qué soy?"* (I have eyes and cannot see; a mouth, but cannot speak; What am I?) The answer is a photograph. Another type of riddle is the conundrum, where the answer is contained in the riddle itself, such as *"Agua pasa por mi casa cate de mi corazon"* (Water passes by my house pain of my heart). The answer is *"aguacate"* (avocado). Or, *"Lana sube, lana baja"* (Wool goes up and wool goes down). The answer is *"la navaja,"* la-na-baja (the knife). Conundrums contain wordplay and in Chicano culture are sometimes bilingual, playing with words in both the Spanish and the English language. Another type of riddle is the riddling question, such as *"Qué le dijo la luna al sol?"* (What did the moon say to the sun?) The answer is *"Eres tan grande y no te dejan salir de noche"* (You are so big and yet are not allowed to go out at night).

Many Spanish riddles collected in the Southwest reflect in some way the characteristics of the Southwest, both linguistically and environmentally. Since the problem presented in a riddle is linguistically and culturally based on both the teller's and the audience's culture, they must all be members of the same community or group to comprehend the puzzle. Bilingual riddles, those narrated in both English and Spanish, are clearly a Chicano invention growing out of the bicultural experience. Riddles are fun and educational as well. It is usually children who enjoy telling and listening to riddles. Like other folklore genres, riddles serve a function, helping children learn to interpret facts and form an opinion. They use language, humor, and a verbal fun activity to challenge a child's intellect.

References Brown 1978; Campa 1937; Espinosa 1985; Glazer 1994; Lucero-White 1941; McDowell 1979; West 1988

Adobe (Sun-dried Brick)

Adobe is a word with Arabic origins that means "unburnt bricks made from earth." Adobe bricks are made from a mixture of clay and sand, sometimes just called mud-straw, and are slowly dried by the heat of the sun. Various

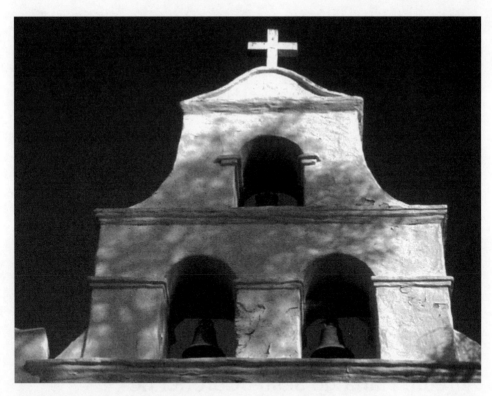

Adobe structures have survived for hundreds of years in the Southwest. This is the San Diego, California, mission belltower. (North Wind Picture Archive)

structures, homes, buildings, and churches are built of adobe bricks and then plastered with more adobe mud. Buildings made of adobe have lasted for centuries when sufficient and constant care is provided to prevent erosion of the mud. Contemporary adobe architecture, as found in what is called the Southwest style, is a fusion of native New Mexican Indian and Spanish forms. The basic structure, adobe walls supporting a flat roof, is an Indian tradition thousands of years old. When the Spanish moved into New Mexico and the Southwest, they adopted this basic structure, but incorporated their technique of forming the mud into bricks. Most of the Catholic missions were built out of adobe. Adobe homes and buildings provide a sense of security and protection from outside noise with their two-to-four-foot thick walls. Often the literature about adobe also mentions the sense of continuity with the earth one feels when living in an adobe home.

Making adobe bricks and adobe *hornos* (outdoor ovens) is still a tradition in New Mexico. Native American and Hispanic women have a long tradition in the construction of adobe structures. The Spaniards noted that it was the Pueblo women who built the adobe walls. Within the Hispanic community it has been the role of women known as *enjarradoras* to plaster the walls of the structures, a task that is done with the bare hands. A saying in Spanish describes this as, *"El hombre las levanta, la mujer las enjarra."* (The man builds the walls and woman plasters them) (Romero and Larkin 1994, 44). In contemporary times, the Museum of International Folk Art in Santa Fe sponsors demonstrations of adobe brick making and *horno* construction, performed by women who are well-known master *adoberas* (makers of adobe) and master *enjaradoras*.

In southern Texas and northern Mexico, small huts called *jacales* were also constructed of mud-straw. Even though this mud was of almost the same composition, it was not called adobe. The mud was not formed into bricks, and the structures were considered temporary, even though many have existed for decades.

References Boyd 1974; Brown 1978; Bunting 1964, 1974; De Leon 1982; Graham 1991; Romero and Larkin 1994; Weigle and White 1988; West 1988

Agavachado
See Agringado

Agreda, María de Jesus Coronel de (The Blue Lady)

A woman dressed in a blue veil or the blue habit of a nun who appeared to help the sick and the afflicted during the seventeenth century. Legends of the appearance of the Blue Lady circulated in New Mexico and Texas during the mid-1600s. There are stories that narrate how she especially liked to help women in need and poor children, although it appears her goal was also to Christianize the Indians of the Southwest, whom she visited often. She was able to speak various Indian languages and would speak to the members of each tribe in their own tongue. Fray Damian Manzanet, while visiting Texas in 1690, reported that the chief of the Tejas Indians spoke of being visited by a beautiful woman dressed in blue garments. The chief was requesting blue fabric that his people wanted to use in the burying of their dead. There is much written evidence of her appearances in Texas, where she was referred to as "The Mysterious Woman in Blue." The Jumano Indians of Texas were reportedly visited by her approximately 500 times between 1621 and 1631.

The first reference to her is in the memoirs of Fray Alonso de Benavides in 1631. Every report we have of her appearances indicates that the Blue Lady was actually María de Jesus Coronel de Agreda. She was born in Spain in 1602 and died May 24, 1665. She never physically visited the Southwest, but she stated that she made "flights" to New Mexico to help the Indians. María de Agredo lived in a convent and wrote several books, including one with the title *The Mystic City of God*.

Adina de Zavala cites a San Antonio legend about a mystifying woman in blue who appears once in a generation, out of the hidden underground passages of the Alamo, bearing a distinctive gift that she bestows on a woman. The woman is always a native Texan; she may be young, old, or middle-aged, but she is always a special woman, "pure and good, well bred, intelligent, spiritual, and patriotic." The gift that is bestowed on her is the ability to see "to the heart of things," and the woman is instructed to use the gift for the good of the people of San Antonio and of Texas.

References Bullock 1972; Castañeda 1936; Colahan 1994; DeBaca 1988; Dobie 1964; Hallenbeck and Williams 1971; Sturmberg 1920; Zavala 1917

Agringado (Anglicized)

An expressive term used among Chicanos to describe other Chicanos who have become very *gringo*-like, very anglicized (*inglesado*), or *americanizado*. Another word used interchangeably is *agavachado*, meaning too much like a *gavacho*, an Anglo. In a bicultural environment, or even in tightly knit Mexican communities, when individuals become thoroughly acculturated to American society and values, the individual may be criticized by close friends and relatives, and be called an *agringado*. *Agringado* is a particularly strong term in comparison to *americanizado*, because the word *gringo* connotes a strong negative image of a North American. All Chicanos are *americanizados* to a certain extent, by learning English and attending public schools. But the behavior of an *agringado* might involve the changing of one's given name, so that Carlos becomes Charlie, Guillermo becomes Will, or Consuelo becomes Connie; or changing a surname, so that Rivera becomes Rivers or Puentes becomes Bridges. In the verbal folklore repertoire of Chicanos, jokes abound about Mexicans who become Anglos and adopt the values, mannerisms, food, clothing styles, and verbal expressions of the dominant society. Besides becoming gringo-like, a Chicano *agringado* may overtly reject Mexican American culture, the music, the values, and even the Spanish language, by pretending not to speak it. Such a person sees the Mexican way of life as inferior to the Anglo, and the *agringado* may marry an Anglo and completely turn his/her back on Chicano culture. An *agringado* will not self-identify because this kind of behavior is perceived as negative or disloyal to his/her cultural group. Rather, identifying or pointing out *agringado* behavior tends to be done by family or peer group members, who use teasing, joking, and narrating exemplary anecdotes characteristic of folkloric behavior. This type of behavior is an outcome of living in a bicultural and bilingual environment and serves to strengthen the in-group's sense of cultural identity.

The *agringado* figure has become a stock character in Chicano culture and is frequently encountered in folklore, literature, and popular culture. The film *Mi Familia*, directed and released in 1995 by Gregory Nava, includes a comical scene depicting the *agringado* son, a UCLA student, bringing his Anglo girlfriend home to meet his Mexican family.

References Limón 1988a; Madsen 1964; Peña 1985b

Aguinaldos (Christmas Gifts)

The translation of this word found in Spanish dictionaries is a "gift given at Christmas." In the folk tradition, it is a small gift given at a Christmas party or celebration, usually in the form of food or candy. During *Las Posadas*, the reenactment of the pilgrimage of Mary and Joseph's search for an inn, when celebrations are held in private homes, the hostess will pass out *aguinaldos* to the children. These can be small bags or baskets filled with candy, nuts, fruits, or toys. It is a gift given as a sharing, a memento, a remembrance, rather than as a Christmas present. Mention of the custom of *aguinaldos* is found in Cabeza de Baca's book, *The Good Life*. Américo Paredes describes a slightly different tradition of *aguinaldos* that he learned in song form from his mother in South Texas. During the days between Christmas and *Día de los Reyes* (the Day of the Kings, or Epiphany), January 6, young boys went from house to house singing carols called *aguinaldos,* and asking for food and gifts. Homes were opened to them and they were offered good things to eat and drink. In this context *aguinaldos* are Christmas songs.

This expression has also been used when describing a children's custom in the Southwest. On Christmas Day children went knocking on doors and visiting homes, asking for and receiving candy or small toys. Sometimes they would sing a song that sounded more like a prayer or a chant, called *Oremos*. Lottie Devine describes a custom in Arizona where the local Indians visited homes on Christmas Day, receiving food and drinks. This was referred to as "calling Christmas."

See also Oremos
References Cabeza de Baca 1982; Devine 1964; Paredes 1976; Sommers 1995

Alabados (Hymns)

Ancient religious hymns that praises the Virgin Mary, Jesus Christ, or a patron saint. The Spanish word *alabar* means to praise, or to glorify, so most *alabados* start with the words "*alabado sea*" (praised be). *Alabados* are usually sung with religious fervor, and many are extremely long with an indefinite number of verses. The *Penitentes* of New Mexico were known to sing *alabados* during Lenten rituals, Holy Week processions, and other religious ceremonies. The songs are mystic in nature; many narrate the story of Christ's life, his anguish, betrayal, his crucifixion and resurrection, and others praise the virtues of suffering and penance. *Alabados* were sung as ritual prayers in homes, at dawn, noon, and at nightfall, and they were almost always sung at funeral processions. Their melodies are fusions of indigenous music and medieval chants. Stories of Mexican California narrate the singing of *alabados* first thing in the morning by a family, each member in his/her own room, but all together at the same time. Like the *décima* (ten-line poetic song) and the *romance* (four-line song), *alabados* were introduced into the New World by the Franciscan *padres*, who taught them to the Indian people as they were teaching them the Bible and converting them to Christianity. In recent times *alabados* have come to mean any religious hymn sung at wakes or religious ceremonies. Many are very old and the authors unknown, although a few collected in southern Colorado were written by a local singer in the 1940s. Folklorists of the 1930s and 1940s were still able to collect some of these ancient hymns from elderly people who learned them from their parents in the nineteenth century. Juan Rael published one of the first essays on the *alabado* in 1950, and a recent researcher, William Gonzalez of the University of Utah, calls them "some of the saddest music" (Ingalls B11).

See also Los Penitentes
References Briggs 1988; Brown 1978; Espinosa 1985; Fisher 1958; Henderson 1937; Ingalls 1996; Rael 1950; Robb 1980

Alambrista (Illegal Border Crosser)

Literally, *alambre* is a wire, and an *alambrista* is a person who uses *alambre*. The term has come to mean a person who crosses a wire fence, regardless of the means or method. In this cultural usage the fence is the wire fence along the Mexican-U.S. border, the term is interchangeable with *mojado* (wetback), which refers to a person who enters the United States illegally by crossing the Rio Grande in Texas. *Alambrista* is not as common an expression as wetback, but it is used frequently by the media. The Mexican cinema has produced many films about illegal entry into the United States with many characters playing roles as *alambristas*. An American film with the title *Alambrista! The Illegal*, written and directed by Robert Young in 1979, deals with the issue of undocumented immigration by portraying the experiences of one man's journey into the United States and back to Mexico. It is considered a landmark film because of the authentic portrayal of a life of fear and alienation experienced by the main character.

Like the term wetback, this is an expression many Chicanos can identify with since many have family members who have entered the United States through nonlegal means. It is part of the folklore repertoire of Chicano culture since the Mexican-U.S. border is politically and culturally a constant element in everyday life.

References Barrera 1992; Madrid-Barela 1975

The U.S.-Mexican border is enticing and challenging to thousands of Mexican immigrants; those who cross illegally are called alambristas. *(Stephanie Maze/Corbis)*

All Souls' Day

See Día de los Muertos

Altars

An altar is a religious shrine (depending on its size, sometimes called an *altarcito*, a little altar) established in the home for the personal worship by the family. Home altars are common in many Mexican and Chicano homes. The word altar is derived from the Latin word *altare*, a combination of *altus*, high, and *ara*, altar, referring to a raised structure for worship, one that goes upward toward the sky or heaven. It provides a space where religious people can communicate with God, the saints, or other spiritual beings. Home altars vary in size, from a small shelf with one votive candle and one saint or statue, to a large table altar, with many religious images, *La Virgen de Guadalupe*, flowers, pictures of saints, candles; a structure that can fill up half a room. Permanent altars can be in a small *nicho* (niche) in the bedroom, the living room, or even the dining room. Daily devout prayer, such as reciting the rosary or praying to a patron or favorite saint, is a normal occurrence in many families, with the prayers often led by the mother or grandmother. A personal home altar may evolve over a period of years, rather than being constructed suddenly in one day. When the creation is such a gradual process, it can reflect and almost chronicle the happy and tragic events that take place in the family. As family

This household shrine to the blessed virgin in a San Antonio home is typical of the tradition of altars, which has been passed down for many generations in Mexican American culture. (Stephanie Maze/Corbis)

members are born, or die, their picture or a favorite personal item of theirs may be placed on the altar, along with their patron saint, a votive candle, or flowers. Eventually, the altar can become so much a meaningful representation of the family that it will be maintained for years and even generations.

The religious observation of All Souls' Day, or *Día de los Muertos*, on November 2, is an occasion for many families to erect altars specifically for a parent or other family member who has recently died. These altars will traditionally have a picture or pictures of the departed with offerings and gifts. Family and friends are invited to visit and add items to the altar, which becomes almost a shrine, and is called an *ofrenda*. In many U.S. cities *Día de los Muertos* ritual celebrations have become community affairs that include more than the Chicano community and may entail a procession through the streets ending at a local school or community center. In the last thirty or so years, the creation and construction of altars have become major art programs for museums, schools, and community centers in the United States. The altars are wonderful artistic creations, a form of folk art, with local artists participating and involving children in the making of *calaveras* (skeletons), *papel picado* (cut tissue paper), paper flowers, and other decorations.

In Chicano and Mexican culture it is usually women who develop home altars, as expressions of devotion, to pay homage to past family members, and to find a space for daily prayer. It is thought that home altars were created as a result of community isolation from a centralized place of worship. After

Mexico gained its independence from Spain, the Spanish friars left Mexico and the Southwest and for many years there weren't enough priests to visit all of Mexico's small villages and rural areas. Isolated communities and individual families created their own places of worship. The wealthy or upper classes were able to build small chapels on their ranches, while the poorer classes built small *nichos* and altars in their homes, in kitchens or other rooms, for private prayer and devotion.

See also Calavera; Día de los Muertos; Folk Art; Nichos; Ofrenda; Papel Picado; La Virgen de Guadalupe

References Carmichael and Sayer 1991; Griffith 1988; Morrison 1992; Sommers 1995; Turner 1981, 1982, 1990, 1999; Viduarri 1991

Americanisms
See Pochismos

Anglicized
See Agringado

Anglo
See Gavacho; Gringo

Arizona Folklore
A large portion of what is now Arizona was once considered part of New Mexican territory. As with Colorado, the folk customs, traditions, and language of Arizona have been closely related to those of New Mexico. The southernmost regions of Arizona, however, have always been more closely related to northern Mexico in customs, language, and folklore. After the U.S.-Mexican War of 1846–1848 and the signing of the Gadsden Treaty in 1854, Arizona experienced the same cultural changes as Texas, New Mexico, and California, although more gradually, since the region was not immediately overwhelmed by an Anglo American invasion as the other areas were. Arizona's oldest and most important Mexican community has been Tucson, founded by Spanish settlers in 1775. Tucson was the frontier fortification of the Mexican state of Sonora until the Gadsden Purchase transferred it to the United States. It functioned as a cavalry outpost established in response to the many Indian raids of the times.

Mexicans were a majority through most of the nineteenth century, and

Tucson had a bicultural spirit that was unique in the Southwest. A Mexican middle class ran some of the largest businesses, held political offices, became artists or intellectuals, funded private and public education, and created a prosperous Mexican society envied by other communities of the Southwest, with elegant theaters like the Teatro Carmen and Spanish-language newspapers. Tucson's proximity to Mexico, especially Sonora, permitted *Tucsonenses* to remain close to their Mexican heritage. According to Thomas Sheridan, "This Mexican elite represented a local florescence of Latin American civilization in Arizona, its society and culture linking Tucson with the finest traditions of both Mexico and Spain" (3). Although there was a strong Mexican middle class, many Chicanos were working class, such as butchers, barbers, and later railroad workers. The railroad arrived in southern Arizona on March 20, 1880, and this changed society in Tucson forever.

There has always been a substantial Chicano and Mexican population in Tucson. The folklore of the region was recognized to be important, and Margarite Collier, an elementary school teacher, organized a Mexican Folklore Club at Carrillo School in Tucson in 1935. An article in the *Arizona Daily Star* of December 19, 1943, states that the club was "to help the children sustain pride and interest in the traditions, customs and folklore of Mexico and to perpetuate these customs among Spanish-speaking people of Tucson." Miss Collier taught the children music, art, and folk dances of Mexico. Every year the school organized a *Las Posadas* procession through the streets of Tucson. The same article in the *Arizona Daily Star* describes this celebration, with the subtitle of the article stating, "Ancient Mexican Custom to be Encouraged in Ceremonial here." The children of Carrillo School carried out this tradition until the late 1970s, and the Mexican Folklore Club continued until well after Miss Collier retired from teaching. Miss Collier worked at collecting songs, games, and other folklore from the children of the school. The Margarite Collier Collection of her private papers is housed at the Southwest Folklore Archives of the University of Arizona library.

James Griffith, a professor at the University of Arizona, is probably the scholar who has published the most on Arizona Hispanic folklore. He has written several works on the traditional folk arts of southern Arizona, a region that also includes the Pimas, Yaquis, and Tohono O'odham Native Americans and borders the Sonora state of Mexico. Griffith writes about the foods of the region, folk art, yard shrines, *cascarones* (decorated eggshells), religious practices, and the various musical traditions. Folklore collected by Griffith's students is also housed at the Southwest Folklore Archives of the University of Arizona library.

Patricia Preciado Martin, born and raised in Arizona, has written extensively about the folklore and traditional past of the Mexican people of Arizona. She has collected oral histories and folktales from elderly Mexican Americans, many of them born in Arizona or Sonora, Mexico. These oral histories nostalgically narrate the lives of men and women born at the turn of the century, describing the rural way of life on cattle ranches and the early city life of Tucson.

Thomas Sheridan has written a social history of the Mexican people of Tucson from 1854 to 1941, thoughtfully showing the social and cultural changes that occurred to the *Tucsonenses* after the coming of the Anglo Americans. The religious and cultural life of the community is carefully researched and impartially presented. A very good description of the foods prepared by Tucson's Mexican restaurants is provided in the work of Suzanne Myal. An early publication of Arizona folklore is a collection of songs published in 1946 titled *Canciones de Mi Padre,* by Luisa Espinel. An exhibit at the University of Arizona Museum of Art reviewed by Amy Kitchener shows the continuity between home and community folk arts. A recent article by Josiah Heyman presents a social history of Douglas, Arizona, presented through the oral histories of residents of that city during the first decades of the twentieth century.

References Campa 1979; Espinel 1946; Griffith 1985, 1988, 1993, 1995; Heyman 1993; Kitchener 1997; Martin 1983, 1988, 1992, 1996; Medina 1975; Myal 1997; Sheridan 1986; Sheridan and Noriega 1987; *Tales Told in Our Barrio* 1984

"Ay Vienen los Yankees!" (Here Come the Yankees!)

This title of a song from early Mexican California vividly expresses fear of the loss of the Mexican culture. The song expresses an aversion to the cultural invasion of the Americans along with a fear that the Mexican women may like the Yankees too much. This song was collected in southern California and according to Hague, the "words date from 1848 or about that time" (109). It is an example of a folk custom the Mexicans used to convey their antipathy toward the Anglo culture. It goes like this:

> *Ay vienen los Yankees,*
> *Ay los tienen ya*
> *Vienen a quitarles, la formalidad.*
> *Ya las señoritas que hablan el ingles,*
> Yankees *dicen* "Kiss me!"
> y *ellas dicen* "Yes"
> Ay here come the Yankees,
> Ay they're coming by
> Now let's all go easy on formality.
> See the *señoritas* who speak English now,
> "Kiss Me!" say the Yankees,
> the ladies answer, "Yes."

References Hague 1917; Schander 1994

Aztlán

According to an Aztec legend, *Aztlán* was the place from which the *Mexica Aztecas* came, known as the place of emergence, in some codices identified as the "seven-cave place." The *Mexica Aztecs* traveled south under the guidance of the god *Huitzilopochtli*, who advised them to look for an eagle perched on a prickly pear cactus, devouring a serpent. This would be their new home, they were told, which they were to call *Tenochtitlán*.

In the late 1960s Chicanos starting calling the southwestern United States, or that portion of Mexico lost to the United States during the U.S.-Mexican War of 1846–1848, *Aztlán*, in reference to the legend of the wandering *Mexica*. The concept of a homeland for Chicanos called *Aztlán* was presented at the First National Chicano Youth Liberation Conference held in Denver, Colorado, in 1969. It was articulated in the manifesto, *El Plan Espiritual de Aztlán*, a document that outlined an ideology meant to unite all Chicanos of the Southwest. The document is accredited to Alurista, a poet who was already presenting *Aztlán* in a Chicano studies class he taught in 1968 at San Diego State University. The manifesto stressed the concept of ethnic nationalism and self-determination, and of the need for Chicanos to control their own communities, schools, and political structures. The document proclaims, "We are a Bronze People with a Bronze Culture. Before the world, before all of North America, before all our brothers in the bronze continent, we are a nation, we are a union of free pueblos, we are *Aztlán. Por La Raza todo, Fuera de La Raza nada.*" *El Plan Espiritual de Aztlán* was published in the journal *El Grito del Norte*, Volume 2, 1969. In 1970, a journal was started at the University of California, Los Angeles, titled *Aztlán: Chicano Journal of the Social Sciences and the Arts*, which is still published today.

The eminent professor Luis Leal states that *Aztlán* has two meanings for Chicanos: the geographic region of the southwestern United States and "the spiritual union of the Chicanos, something that is carried within the heart, no matter where they may live or where they may find themselves" (Leal 1995, 5).

Aztlán takes a prominent place in murals, folk art, and folklore, and it continues to appear in Chicano literature today, as it has for over thirty years, in poetry, short stories, novels, and essay anthologies. The title of one of Rudolfo Anaya's novels is *Heart of Aztlán*, published in 1979; Miguel Mendez wrote *Pilgrims in Aztlán* first in Spanish in 1974, later translated to English in 1992; and Alurista has a poetry collection titled *Floricanto en Aztlán*, published in 1971.

Aztlán is the Chicano homeland, especially for those coming of age during the 1960s and 1970s, who wanted to create a cultural space that they could call their own. For Chicanos born in the United States, Mexico is not home, but neither is the United States, so *Aztlán* is looked upon as the mythical homeland. The affiliation with *Aztlán* also reaffirms the Chicanos' identity as *mestizos* (people of mixed ancestry), as members of the indigenous population of the New World. Chicano writers explore the various meanings of *Aztlán* in an anthology edited by Rudolfo Anaya and Francisco Lomelí titled *Aztlán: Essays on the Chicano Homeland*.

References Anaya and Lomelí 1989; Barrera 1988; Bierhorst 1990; Chavez 1984; Leal 1995; Valdez and Steiner 1972

Quetzalcoatl

Bailando con el Diablo
(Dancing with the Devil)

A popularly narrated legend found throughout the Southwest, south Texas, and even parts of northern Mexico that tells of the appearance of the devil at community dances, dance halls, and discotheques. Called the "devil at the dance" legend or "devil haunts the dance hall" in folklore literature, it is considered to be an urban belief tale that has been adapted to contemporary situations. The devil makes his appearance elegantly dressed, usually in a suit; he is strikingly handsome, *muy suave* (smooth and poised), tall, and refined. Consequently, he stands out from among the rest of the men. Besides his stunning appearance, he is always an amazing dancer, knows the latest dance steps, and selects the prettiest girl to dance.

As the tale is often narrated, a disobedient young girl goes to the dance without her parents' permission, or she goes against her mother's express wishes. While at the dance a handsome beautifully dressed man asks her to dance. They dance all night, until she suddenly notices with a shock that he isn't wearing shoes, and in fact he doesn't even have feet; instead he has chicken feet, goat's hooves, or a pig's foot and a chicken foot. It is usually at this point, after he's discovered, that he disappears into thin air, leaving the odor of sulfur in the air, or, in some versions of the legend, just runs out the door. The girl he was dancing with either faints or burns to death as she goes up in smoke. If the girl doesn't die, as in some stories, she might suffer a burn on the shoulder or a man's handprint might be found on her back. A small circle of people who are present at the dance observe this encounter, and the narrator of the story usually says that she or he heard it from someone who was there.

The lesson learned is that one must not disobey one's parents, for the handsome man is known to be the devil and the personification of evil. It is noted that mostly women narrate these legends, among themselves or from mothers to daughters, in a didactic fashion, to instill fear in young women so that they will not disregard parental authority. In some variants a young girl specifically transgresses religious beliefs by insisting on going to a dance on Good Friday, a religious holy day, and a revered day of prayer in Chicano

Catholic households. The appearance of the devil on this day is an especially ominous sign.

Robe's collection of New Mexico legends contains thirty-four variants of the devil-at-the-dance tale. Although the legends in this collection are from rural northern New Mexico, collected in the 1950s and 1960s, we find contemporary versions of the devil-at-the-dance tales in south Texas and in Baja California from the 1980s. Limón and Herrera-Sobek discuss versions of the tale circulating in nightclubs and discotheques among urbanized young people.

Of course, not everyone believes such stories. Martin's book contains a story by a man born in 1904, who says his friend played a trick on his community in Tucson by coming to a dance dressed in black, with a fake rooster foot. Eventually someone noticed his foot and yelled, "The Devil! The Devil!" The narrator says he was there when his friend played the trick, so he doesn't believe in the legend (50).

References De Leon 1982; Glazer 1984,1994; Herrera-Sobek 1988; Limón 1994; Martin 1983; Robe 1951; Robe ed. 1980; West 1988

Baile (Dance)

El baile is an individual dance step, a party, or a ball. *El baile* is historically one of the most important social traditions among Mexicans and Chicanos throughout Mexico and the United States. Since the Spaniards conquered the Southwest, *bailes* have been important community social and cultural events. In Texas, New Mexico, and California, because of the isolation of the communities, dancing became the principal source of entertainment. The social status of women in Spanish colonial society was limited and cloistered, with their primary social venues consisting of church and home. *El baile* provided entertainment and physical activity. As an early California traveler put it, "I was astonished at the endurance of the California women in holding out, night after night, in dancing, of which they never seemed to weary, but kept on with an appearance of freshness and elasticity that was as charming as surprising" (Shay 100). It was at *el baile* that courtship occurred (since girls, although they may have gone to the dance chaperoned, were allowed to dance with boys); it was at *el baile* that families and relatives interacted, that the week's work was forgotten, and that life's mysteries were discussed. The local dance brought the community together and allowed interaction between the sexes. A girl was never able to reject a request to dance from a boy, because to turn down an invitation exposed the boy to embarrassment and ridicule for his failure in competition, and could be cause for revenge. Countless *corridos* (ballads), *leyendas* (legends), and *chistes* (jokes) narrate events that are supposed to have occurred at *el baile*, from fights to courtships to elopements. Encounters with the legendary weeping woman, *La Llorona*, often occur after a dance when a solitary man is finding his way home. From the devil-at-the-dance narratives to the tragic death of Rosita Alvarez, recounted in the *corrido* of the same name, we learn of the importance of *el baile* in both rural and urban Chicano communities. Major Horace Bell describes the difference between a *baile* and a *fandango* in Mexican California history and Arnoldo De Leon describes the *baile* in eighteenth-century San Antonio.

Most Mexican national holiday celebrations such as *Cinco de Mayo* and *El Diez y Seis de Septiembre* will end with a community dance. Even in modern times, professional Latino and Chicano associations often close their national conferences with a *baile*, bringing in popular Chicano bands. Jose Limón discusses the narratives of *bailando con el diablo* (dancing with the devil), and Manuel Peña shows us the ritualized structure of a Chicano dance.

See also Bailando con el Diablo; Cinco de Mayo; El Diez y Seis de Septiembre; Fandango; La Llorona
References Bell 1927; De Leon 1982; Limón 1983, 1994; Peña 1980, 1985b; Shay 1982

"Ballad of Gregorio Cortez"
See "El Corrido de Gregorio Cortez"

Ballads
See Corridos

Ballet Folklórico
The term refers to folk dance groups, *grupos folklóricos*, that perform traditional Mexican regional dances. The dances are carefully choreographed and well rehearsed; they are representative of the dances from the different regions of Mexico. An important characteristic of the dance performances is the elaborate beautiful costumes, very full and colorful dresses, that are the traditional dress from the various states of Mexico, such as Jalisco, Veracruz, Chihuahua, and Durango. The dances, many of which have been danced for decades, such as *El Jarabe Tapatio* and *La Negra*, are danced to *Mariachi* music, and performed on the Mexican national holidays, *Las Fiestas Patrias*, such as *Cinco de Mayo* and *El Diez y Seis de Septiembre*.

These folk dance groups became popular in Mexico right after the Mexican Revolution, but did not become prevalent in the United States until the 1960s. It was the influence of the Chicano civil rights movement, *el movimiento* Chicano, that launched the institution of *ballets folklóricos* as symbolic of a Mexican American cultural identity. *El Ballet Folklórico de Mexico*, founded and directed by Amalia Hernandez in the early 1950s, became the official cultural representative of the Mexican government and has often

Ballet Folklórico dancers execute perfect twirls at the Fiestas Patrias in San Francisco, California, ca. 1993. (Morton Beebe, S.F./Corbis)

toured the United States. Amalia Hernandez based her folklore costumes and folk dances on the authentic folklore traditions of the Mexican people. This *folklórico* group became the model on which most Chicano *folklórico* groups are based.

Mexican folklore traditions, folk songs, and folk dances had been taught within Mexican *colonias* (neighborhoods), today known as *barrios*, since before the 1930s, usually through the efforts of a single individual in the community, in church halls and mutual aid society halls, but not in the public schools. There was one exception: in Tucson, Arizona, a teacher named Margarite Collier started a Mexican Folklore Club in 1937 in an elementary school, for the specific purpose of maintaining the cultural traditions from Mexico. This club existed until the 1970s, and it established a long tradition of performing *Las Posadas* through the streets of Tucson. Madelyn Loes Soloman documents that in Los Angeles the teaching of folk songs and dances was done by a Mexican-born man in the late 1930s. But it was in the late 1960s and 1970s that there was a revival in the formal organization of elaborate performances by large dance groups, many made up of young children and teenagers. *Folklórico* groups perform for community events, *Cinco de Mayo* festivals, school functions, *Fiestas Guadalupanas* (celebrations of *La Virgen de Guadalupe*, December 12), political events, and other holidays. *Ballet folklórico* dances are now taught in many schools, and students entering college often bring with them a knowledge of the dances and an interest in participating. Several university campuses in California and the Southwest have dance groups totally comprised by and maintained by college students.

See also Las Posadas
References Collier Archives; Griffith 1988; Najera-Ramirez 1989; Soloman 1941

"La Bamba"

The title of a song, as well as the title of a movie directed by Luis Valdez in 1987. The film is about the life of the Chicano singer Ritchie Valens, who recorded the song and made it very popular in 1958. The song actually goes back to early Mexican colonial history; it has been traced to 1790 when it was performed at the Coliseo Theatre in Mexico City. There are printed sources that cite the song being sung and danced in Veracruz during the nineteenth and early twentieth centuries. By the 1830s it was also a popular dance in Mexican California.

"La Bamba" is considered to be a *son jarocho* (country folks' dancing music), an example of the *mestizo* (mixed-race) musical tradition, with strong African influences, from the state of Veracruz. The instrumentation of the traditional *son jarocho* included a small harp, a small eight-string guitar (*jarana*), and a small four-string guitar (*requinto*). The dance that went with *son jarocho* was a *zapateado*, a foot-stomping dance. There are two different accounts about how Ritchie Valens learned the song, since he supposedly

The dance that accompanied the original song "La Bamba" was a foot-stomping step and has been traced to eighteenth-century Mexico City. It is still danced today throughout the Southwest. (Nik Wheeler/Corbis)

never learned Spanish. One source states that he heard the song on a short trip across the border into Mexico, and another states he learned the song from his uncle when he was five years old. His innovative style mixed *jarocho* music with a rock 'n roll beat. His recorded version of "La Bamba" in 1958 is the first known U.S. recording. "La Bamba" has now been recorded more than 150 different times in the United States; for example, in 1966 by Trini Lopez, in 1979 by the Plugz, and in 1980 by Los Lobos. The Rice University Marching Band and the Mormon Tabernacle Choir have also recorded it. The movie, with the soundtrack recorded by Los Lobos, was very successful with mainstream audiences and launched the acting careers of several Latino actors.

References *La Bamba* 1987; Guevara 1985; Holscher, Fernandez, and Cummings 1991; Lipsitz 1990; Loza 1982; Sheehy 1979

Bandidos
See Folk Heroes

Barbacoa de Cabeza
(Barbecued Beef Head)

Barbacoa refers to a method of cooking meat, in a pit of hot wood coals. The English word barbecue comes from *barbacoa*. *Barbacoa de cabeza* is the cooking of a beef head in this manner. It is an old custom and cultural event that in parts of south Texas occurs every weekend, with the *barbacoa* eaten on Sunday mornings. In other parts of the Southwest this style of cooking is reserved for special events such as weddings, funerals, and large family gatherings. According to the *Diccionario de Mejicanismos* (Dictionary of Mexicanisms), *barbacoa* is *"carne asada en un hoyo que se abre en tierra, y se calienta como los hornos"* (grilled meat cooked in a hole in the ground heated like an oven). Cooking the beef head with this method means all the parts can be eaten, such as the brains, eyes, tongue, lips, literally everything. Although originally a discarded part of the cow, now it is considered a delicacy and is prepared and sold in many neighborhood stores and restaurants along the Rio Grande border region. Today the term *barbacoa* is used only to mean the cooking of meat in a pit, also called pit cooking.

References Montano 1992; Peyton 1994

Barrio (Neighborhood)

A *barrio* is a neighborhood, a city district, or a ward in an urban area where Mexicans and Chicanos live. In the early 1900s, Mexican communities were called *colonias*, as they are in Mexico today, but at some point after World War II, Chicano neighborhoods became known as *barrios*. In Chicano culture, *barrios* are identified by given names that in some way describe a characteristic of the neighborhood or reflect its history. Some *barrios* are only a few blocks, whereas others encompass large urban areas. Some of the oldest *barrios* can be found in major cities, like Los Angeles, Chicago, El Paso, and San Antonio. In San Fernando, also known as *San Fer*, two very early *barrios* were *La Rana* and *El Bajillo* (The Frog; The Little Low One). *Hoyo Marvilla*, another well-known *barrio* in East Los Angeles, was famous because it was where farmworkers lived and was extremely poor. *Barrios* are sometimes called ghettos; even though there are very negative and sometimes few positive attributes to living in *barrios*, they can't always be presumed to be ghettos in the sense of places where a group is forced to live against its will. Vigil's work on gang culture explains the allegiance felt by gang members toward their *barrio*. Mary Helen Ponce writes in *Hoyt Street* about the *barrio* where she grew up in Pacoima, California, during the 1940s and 1950s. Many Chicano novelists have set their stories in the *barrios* of the Southwest and Midwest. Raúl Salinas, in his poem "A Trip through the Mind Jail," writes about his *barrio*, and all *barrios*, while he serves time in prison. In one section of his poem he affirms the positive role of the *barrio*:

LA LOMA . . . AUSTIN . . . MI BARRIO . . .
I bear you no grudge
I needed you then . . . identity . . . a sense of belonging.
I need you now.
So essential to adult days of imprisonment,
You keep me away from INSANITY'S hungry jaws;
Smiling/Laughing/Crying.
I respect your having been:
my Loma of Austin
my Rose Hill of Los Angeles
my West Side of San Antonio
my Quinto of Houston
my Jackson of San Jose
my Segundo of El Paso
my Barelas of Albuquerque
my Westside of Denver
Flats, Los Marcos, Maravilla, Calle Guadalupe, Magnolia,
Buena Vista, Mateo, La Seis, Chiquis, El Sur and all
Chicano neighborhoods that now exist and once
existed; somewhere, someone remembers

References Chicano Pinto Research Project 1975; Ponce 1993; Salinas 1970; Vigil 1988, 1996

Barriology

The social science of barriology was conceived of as a discipline of study in the pages of *Con Safos* magazine in 1969. *Con Safos: Reflections of Life in the Barrio* was one of the early Chicano periodicals published by college students; it printed humorous, political, and literary articles. It is an example of a publication where Chicanos could express cultural and political satire. Barriology was created as a spoof on the academic social sciences; it involved testing those Chicanos not so fluent in the traditions and rituals of living in Chicano neighborhoods or *barrios*. *Con Safos* carried monthly examinations developed by Antonio Gómez, "PhD, Barriologist Emeritus." It was also a way of gently poking fun at Chicano culture, reminding the readers of the uniqueness of the Chicano culture. Some of the exam questions consisted of multiple-choice answers; others required the reader to fill in the answer. Some sample questions follow:

Menudo is made from tripe, which is:
a. the cow's stomach, b. the cow's flank, c. horse meat, d. mutton
Someone who is described as a *lechusa* is a:
a. lettuce peddler, b. leach, c. milkman, d. night person
Capirotada is the traditional food during what time of year?

Complete the following children's chant:
Pelon Pelonete, Cabeza de quete, Vendiendo Tamales, (De cinco y de siete.)
Everyone knows that *Juan Charrasquiado's* death was caused by
_____. (title and character from a *corrido* who was killed in
a *cantina*).

Each exam included a rating scale so that those who took the exam could determine their level of knowledge of the Chicano culture. For example a score of 23 to 28 indicated a Chicano Barriologist was *"muy de aquellas"* (very Chicano); 18 to 22 indicated High Potential, *"o ya casi"* (almost a Chicano); 13 to 17 was half Mexican, half American, or "keep trying, you"; 8 to 12 was a *"vendido"* (sellout or culturally deprived); and 0 to 7 was a *"pendejo"* (dummy, jerk).

References Gómez 1970a, 1970b, 1971

Bato (Dude)

Bato is a word centuries old that can be translated as "guy" or "dude." Most recently it has been spelled *vato*, transposing the *v* for the *b*. In Chicano communities, in-group chatter, and published literature one frequently comes across the expression *bato loco*, meaning a "crazy guy," a "cool dude," or a "wise guy." *Bato* was a word incorporated into the *pachuco* jargon of the 1940s, and it is still very much a part of Chicano vocabulary today. The *bato loco*, or *vato loco*, is the descendent of the *pachuco* and a close relation of today's *cholo* (urban youth). The *bato* is often mentioned in connection with his *barrio*, as in *el vato loco del Hoyo Mara*.

The *bato loco* is tantamount to an archetype in Chicano culture; he is that crazy guy who isn't afraid of life. He may be a gang member, a drug user, or just an entertaining street person. He could also be fully immersed in *la vida loca* as described by Luis Rodriguez in his book, *Always Running,* and by Oscar Zeta Acosta in *The Autobiography of a Brown Buffalo.* In the novel *The Road to Tamazunchale,* Ron Arias creates a streetwise character, a *bato* named Mario, who acts as a sidekick to the main character, Fausto. The two wander through a mythical Los Angeles in search of "the song of life." For the contemporary Chicano male, *el bato loco* is not only a symbol of ethnic identity but also an icon of the urban coming-of-age experience itself.

In standard Spanish, *bato* means "simpleton" or "foolish fellow," and it has been in use in rural areas of New Mexico since the seventeenth century. In *Los Pastores,* or the Shepherds' Play, a mystery play performed in Mexico and the Southwest since the sixteenth century, the shepherd who plays the role of a buffoon, a jester, is named *Bato.*

Another good example of the life of a *bato loco* is "La Vida de un Bato Loco," a short memoir written by an informant of Linda Katz, reproduced in her thesis on the *pachuco* language and culture written for a master's degree at the University of California, Los Angeles.

See also Cholos; Pachucos; *Los Pastores*
References Arias 1975; Barker 1950; Cerda and Farias 1953; Katz 1974; Rodriguez 1993;
 Smethurst 1995

Bazaars
See Jamaicas

Beans
See Frijoles

Beliefs
See Creencias

The Black Legend
See La Leyenda Negra

Blankets
See Colchas

The Blue Lady
See Agreda, María de Jesus Coronel de

Bogeyman
See El Coco; El Cucui; El Kookoóoee

Bolillos (Bread Rolls)
A *bolillo* is a small loaf of white bread or a large dinner roll, which in the United States is sometimes called French bread. *Bolillos*, also known as *birotes*, can be found in most Mexican and Mexican American bakeries and are often served in Mexican restaurants. The folkloric use of *bolillo* occurs when it is derogatorily applied to Anglo Americans, supposedly because they are as white as bread, and because the Americans invaded and annexed Mexican territory, the Southwest. Although not as popularly known, it carries the same meaning as *gringo* or *gavacho*. Chicanos also often use the term, as they do *agringado*, to describe an overly acculturated Chicano, one who is trying to be "white."

It is believed the word was originally used to describe French soldiers when they occupied Mexico in the 1860s. Although written references to its use in this way have not been found, there are references to the French eating small loaves of white bread in *corridos*. Américo Paredes cites a stanza from a *corrido* (ballad) the Mexican soldiers sang after the Battle of Puebla (celebrated on *Cinco de Mayo*) that taunts the vanquished French soldiers with the following words:

> *Qu'es de las piezas de pan?*
> *Aguárdenlas que ahi' les van. Pam!*
> (Where are the loaves of bread?
> Get ready, for here they go. Bang!)
> (1993a, 37)

See also Agringado; Cinco de Mayo; Gavacho; Gringo
References Paredes 1961, 1993a

Bone Setter
See Huesero

Bonfires
See Luminarias

Bonus
See Pilón

Bourke, Captain John Gregory (1846–1896)

An early writer of Chicano folk culture and folklore from the Texas-Mexican border. Although Bourke was first and foremost a military man, he became interested in ethnology and anthropology and wrote extensively on these subjects. Born in 1846 to Irish Catholic parents in Pennsylvania, he enlisted in the Fifteenth Pennsylvania Volunteer Cavalry during the Civil War. In 1865 he attended West Point, graduating in 1869 with a commission in the Third Cavalry. He served with General George Crook from 1871 to 1886, and in 1891 wrote a well-received book titled *On the Border with Crook*.

Through his friendship with the director of the Bureau of American Ethnology at the Smithsonian Institution, Bourke studied anthropology and broadened his interests to include ethnology and folklore. At various times he wrote pamphlets for the Bureau of Indian Affairs. He gained fame as an Indian fighter, but was also known as an anthropologist and writer. Although primarily a military man, he managed to conduct fieldwork among several

Indian tribes, and was considered an expert on the Apaches. He was stationed along the Rio Grande for two years, during the era of the Catarino Garza revolt, and his diaries from this period are a valuable resource on the Garza movement. He learned the Spanish language, apparently because of his ethnological interests, and wrote on the *Tejano* and *Mexicano* culture of the border region. During the 1890s he published ethnographic articles about the Texas-Mexican border in the *Journal of American Folklore* and the *American Anthropologist*. Bourke observed, chronicled, and wrote both as a journalist and anthropologist about the folk medicine practices and the folk foodways of the Rio Grande region.

His approach to folklore study was that of the established tradition of the times, which examined current customs, traditions, folkways, and folk narratives as survivals of an earlier civilization. Sometimes this survivalist perspective carried with it an attitude about the prior culture, where the customs originated, as having been a higher civilization. Accordingly, when Bourke became interested in Mexican customs and language, he approached them as the cultural remains of a higher Spanish-Arabic civilization. In spite of the fact that his nineteenth-century biases are very apparent in his writings, the data he collected are valuable for the study of Chicano folklore of the Texas-Mexican border. He was elected president of the American Folklore Society in 1895, and he died in 1896. He is buried at Arlington National Cemetery.

References Limón 1994; *New Handbook of Texas* 1996

Braceros (Laborers)

Mexican workers recruited from Mexico under the Emergency Farm Labor Program known as the *Bracero* Program, which was in effect from 1942 to 1964. The word *bracero* comes from the Spanish word *brazo* (arm), which is used, as English uses "hand," to mean "laborer." In the same way *bracero* commonly means a man who works with his hands, a laborer, and is used when speaking of all farm and agricultural workers. There was a shortage of farm laborers during World War II, and this program offered an answer to that problem, although some *braceros* also worked on the railroad. Until only recently *bracero* was applied to any Mexican farmworker, and is often used interchangeably with words like "wetback" or "greaser." The number of workers brought from Mexico ranged from a low of 4,180 in 1942 to a high of 62,091 in 1944. It is estimated that by 1947 nearly 220,000 *braceros* had worked in the United States under this program. It continued even after the war, and between 1955 and 1959 over 480,000 *braceros* were still working in the United States. Some have compared the *Bracero* Program with legalized slavery, and the impact on the perception of the Mexican farmworker by American agribusiness has been to foster contempt and disdain. Many *braceros* chose not to return to Mexico when their contracts ended and

Many Chicanos are descendants of the braceros, the laborers of agricultural businesses in the United States, who have picked everything from cotton and sugar beets to grapes and strawberries, as in this picture. (Bettmann-Corbis)

instead stayed and hid from *la migra*, the feared Immigration and Naturalization Service (INS).

Many Chicanos of the Southwest and Midwest are descendants of *braceros* who came to the United States and stayed, never returning to Mexico. The *bracero* experience has been written about in novels and depicted in numerous movies, and although the image presented is often a negative one, like other Chicano folk heroes the *bracero* has become an archetype of the culture. He is in the company of the historical *mestizo* character of *Yo soy Joaquín*, the revolutionary figure of Joaquín Murrieta, the mythical *pachuco*, the stately learned persona of Dr. Paredes, the gentle leadership of César Chávez; the *bracero* is the universally exploited farmworker, the *campesino* of the world. Many *corridos* (ballads) describe the experience of coming to work in the agricultural fields of the Midwest and the Southwest. Maria Herrera-Sobek describes the prototype of the *bracero*, as represented in countless *corridos*, in her book *The*

Bracero Experience. In Mexico the experience was written about from the perspective of those who returned, as in such books as *Aventuras de un Bracero*, by Jesus Amaya Topete, published in 1949 and reprinted several times, and in the United States the novel *Macho!* by Edmund Villaseñor, published in 1973.

References Acuña 1988; Galarza 1964; Gutiérrez 1995; Herrera-Sobek 1979, 1993b, 1998; Madrid-Barela 1975; Nelson 1971; Paredes 1993

Bread Rolls
See Bolillos

Brujería (Witchcraft)

Witches and *brujería* (witchcraft) are accepted facts of life in Mexican and Chicano culture. Belief in witches and witchcraft is common in the Southwest, as can be seen by the large number of folk narratives and legends about witches collected in New Mexico and Texas in the last century. This form of occultism is an integral part of the culture of Mexico and the Southwest. The Spanish conquerors and colonists who settled New Mexico in the sixteenth century communicated to the indigenous communities a belief in witchcraft. Beliefs in witchcraft were prevalent in Europe during the fourteenth, fifteenth, and sixteenth centuries, and the missionary friars brought these beliefs to the New World. The Spanish Catholic missionaries worked hard to convert the indigenous populations of New Spain, and any non-Christian belief that was not acceptable to the Spanish friars was often attributed to sin, evil, the devil, or witchcraft. Consequently it was easy to assign unexplainable natural phenomena to the work of witches, and these beliefs have persisted over hundreds of years. Contemporary witches can prepare love potions, lift spells, cure and cause illnesses, and in general cause great harm. They can also take on any form they desire, such as a cat, pig, or owl, and so can make themselves difficult to identify. In folktales from New Mexico, they often appear as balls of fire flying across the sky. *Curanderas* are sometimes mistaken for witches because of their healing power, but they are also often called upon to undo the work of witches.

Many of the folktales, legends, and *cuentos* (stories) collected in New Mexico by Aurelio Espinosa, Juan Bautista Rael, and R. D. Jameson (Robe 1980) are about witches and witchcraft. In the 1930s, writers employed by the Works Progress Administration (WPA) as part of Roosevelt's New Deal collected many *cuentos* and legends about witches from the people of northern New Mexico, and many beliefs expressed then are still held today. For instance, the way to tell if a person is a witch is to stick two needles in the form of a cross into the sill above a door; if the person in the room is a witch, she won't be able to leave the room. Another belief is that only men named Juan or Juan Bautista or women named Juana have the ability to catch or over-power a witch. Conversely the power of a witch cannot be exerted over a per-son named Juan or Juana. A witch cannot sense the presence of a Juan, so he may be able to trap her by drawing a circle on the ground and throwing his shirt, turned inside out, into the circle.

Witches often take the form of an owl, in New Mexican Spanish called a *tecolote*, from the Nahuatl word *teolotl*. The hoot of an owl is an evil omen, so one must be careful to stay away from owls. In other parts of the South-west owls are sometimes known as *lechuzas*. A *lechuza* is a woman who has sold her soul to the devil and becomes an owl by night. Only a woman can become a *lechuza*.

A prayer meant to keep witches away was recited at night in a low voice:

> *Cuatro esquinas tiene me casa*
> *Cuatro ángeles que la adoran*
> *Lucas, Marcos, Juan y Mateo*
> *Ni brujas ni hechiceras*
> *Ni hombre malhechor*
> *En el nombre del Padre,*
> *Y del Hijo y del Espiritu Santo.*
> (My house has four corners
> Four angels adore it
> Luke, Mark, John and Matthew
> Neither witches nor charmers
> Nor evil-doing man
> In the name of the Father,
> and of the Son
> and of the Holy Ghost.)
> (Simmons 1974a, 11)

Besides being present in folktales and legends, the world of *brujas* seeps into discussions of love and lovers, literature, and other forms of Chicano folklore and culture.

See also Curanderismo; Espinosa, Aurelio Macedonio
References Brown 1978; Delgado 1994; Espinosa 1910; García 1992; Jaramillo 1972; Rael 1957; Robe 1980; Simmons 1974a, 1974b; Ulibarri 1977; Weigle and White 1988

Burritos

Literally a little burro or little donkey, a burrito has come to mean a taco made of a wheat flour tortilla instead of a corn tortilla, filled with meat, rice, *frijoles* (beans), and *chile*, then folded and rolled up. There are several theo-ries about the origins of the name burrito, and there may be some truth to all of them. One theory is that when flour tortillas became available in northern Mexico, *tacos de frijoles*, or bean burritos, were easy to carry in the saddlebags of the *vaqueros* (cowboys), so for this reason they came to be called burritos as though they were the sidekicks of the *vaquero's* horse.

Tacos made from corn tortillas are much older; they have been around since the epoch of the Aztecs. Wheat and flour were introduced into New Spain by the Spaniards, and one can see that the flour tortilla is similar to the flat bread found in many Mediterranean countries. Once flour tortillas were discovered, the move to making tacos from flour tortillas was logical. Since corn tortillas are small, and can only bend or fold over once, and flour tortillas are more pliable and can be rolled several times, the flour taco was a natural outcome. A burrito can be made with any type of filling, such as beans, potatoes, *chile con carne, chile colorado, carnitas* (chile with meat, red chile, roasted pork meat), or even peanut butter.

Flour tortillas and burritos are found in northern Mexico and the Southwest, but are not known in other parts of Mexico. Since at least the 1920s, Chicanos from Texas have been making what came to be called burritos. Originally they were called tacos; another story about the origin of the name is that in the 1940s there was an establishment in Juárez, Chihuahua, Mexico, called *Los Burritos* that sold tacos made of *tortillas de harina* (flour tortillas). It became a well-known place to go, and people spoke of going *a los burritos* (to the burritos) when they wanted tacos of that kind. Commercial burritos became available in San Francisco in 1961, according to an article in the *San Francisco Chronicle*, and now there are supposedly over 150 *burrito taquerías* (taco restaurants) in the Mission District of that city. *Burros* is the name reserved for the very large tortilla burritos, in which the tortilla may be a foot and a half to two feet in diameter.

See also Tacos
References Griffith 1988; Roemer 1993

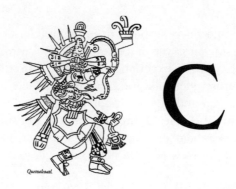

Quetzalcoatl

Cabeza de Baca, Fabiola (1894–1991)

Born in northern New Mexico on May 16, 1894 (although some sources give her birth date as 1898), Fabiola Cabeza de Baca became a famous home economist, teacher, folklorist, and writer. She was one of several New Mexican women, such as Cleofas M. Jaramillo and Nina Otero-Warren, who wrote of the culture and heritage of their Hispano ancestors. Her parents came from long-established Hispano families who had been in New Mexico for over 200 years. Her grandparents raised her from the age of four, after her mother died, leaving Fabiola with one brother and two sisters. She attended the Loretto Academy in Las Vegas and after graduating from high school became a teacher in a rural area six miles from her father's ranch in La Liendre. In 1921 she received a B.A. degree from New Mexico Normal (now New Mexico Highlands University) and in 1929 a B.S. in home economics from New Mexico College of Agriculture and Mechanic Arts (now New Mexico State University). In between she also spent one year studying in Spain.

For over thirty years she worked as an extension agent, teaching the traditional ways of preparing foods and emphasizing the nutritional value in the native diet. Two of her books, *Historic Cookery* and *The Good Life*, depict the way of life of the Hispanos in the late nineteenth and early twentieth centuries. In *We Fed Them Cactus* she presents a biography and ethnography of her family, especially her grandmother, a strong woman and a *curandera*, and retells the stories narrated to her by her father. She depicts the arrival of the Hispano pioneers on the *llano* (plains) of western New Mexico in the 1830s, and also that of the Anglos in the 1880s, the loss of land, the fencing-in of the plains, and the end of the era with the death of her father. The title of the book refers to the custom in New Mexico of feeding cattle cactus to keep them alive during droughts. In *The Good Life*, not a long book, Cabeza de Baca creates a fictional family, the Turrietas, and uses their story to narrate the rituals, customs, food, and culture of New Mexico. The customs of Christmas, Lent, marriage, and a funeral are presented, along with many recipes of the foods prepared for these celebrations. She wrote many articles for various New Mexican publications. In 1959 she retired but continued to work giving lectures, writing, and acting as a consultant to the Peace Corps. She died at the age of ninety-seven on October 14, 1991.

Genaro Padilla refers to her writing as "folkloric autobiography," a significant genre, since it is one of the few kinds of writing by Hispanos that depicts the life they either experienced or learned from their ancestors at the turn of the century. Her folkloric work is extremely important because she wrote about women and how their complicated and elaborate daily work so profoundly maintained the culture and traditions of the Hispanos. Cabeza de Baca was an active member of many community organizations and was president in 1955 of the New Mexico Folklore Society.

References Cabeza de Baca 1954, 1982; Padilla 1991; Perrigo 1985; Ponce 1992; Rebolledo 1989, 1994

Calavera (Skeleton)

A bony skeleton and/or the skull of a skeleton. The *calavera* has become the symbol of the downtrodden, who must laugh at life in order to survive it. It is also used to mean a drunkard or a very stupid person. During the celebrations of the holy day *Día de los Muertos*, candy skulls are made and sold in bakeries throughout Mexico and the United States. These skulls may be placed on home altars or given as gifts to children, family, and friends. The Mexican artist and printmaker Jose Guadalupe Posada started drawing *calaveras* during the late nineteenth century to coincide with this holiday. Their popularity is primarily attributed to him and his work. His images of *calaveras* have been reproduced thousands of times and can be found year-round, but especially during celebrations of *Día de los Muertos*. Posada printed many *calaveras* during the period of the presidency of Porfirio Díaz and during the Mexican Revolution. He introduced the humorous satirical *calavera* that showed the objectionable side of life, that engaged in regular daily activities such as eating, dancing, drinking, fighting, enjoying life, and being a regular Mexican. The Mexican concept of death is exemplified in the satiric antics of the *calavera* and this perspective is also found in the art, literature, and performance arts of Chicanos. *Calaveras* are depicted dancing, drinking in *cantinas* (bars), crowding and falling out of buses, and playing instruments in musical groups. *El Teatro Campesino* in its performances always has a *calavera* character that either represents *La Muerte* (death) or typifies a disturbing alter ego of one of the main characters.

A Mexican tradition of the late nineteenth century was the publication of a poetic broadside that was called a *calavera*. Published before or during the festivities of *Día de los Muertos*, these *calaveras* carried poems that poked fun at socially prominent people such as politicians and the very wealthy. Some *calaveras*, such as the poems, were printed in newspapers, but most were small pamphlets or single sheets that were sold on the street. For a small fee, people could hire a composer to write a *calavera* for them and draw a skeleton to go with it. According to Tinker, "their main functions are to remind

The satiric antics of the calavera *(skeleton) reflect a propensity for laughing at life and at oneself. This perspective can be seen in the art, literature, and performance art of Chicanos. (Charles and Josette Lenars/Corbis)*

us in a good-humored way that we all are mortal, and to poke fun at friends and attack public officials. These last are supposed to take it all in good grace. *Calaveras* are still published every November 1 in many cities of Mexico, and in some cities in Texas, notably San Antonio" (Tinker 1961, 20). The *calavera* is now an integral element of Mexican and Chicano folk art and it adorns murals, stationery, postcards, party invitations and decorations, and even religious art.

See also Día de los Muertos; La Muerte
References Carmichael and Sayer 1991; *Día de los Muertos* 1983; Morrison 1992; Tinker 1961

Califas (California)

An in-group name for California used continuously since at least 1940. It was originally used by the *pachucos* (1940s youths) in the jargon they developed in the 1930s. *Los* referred to Los Angeles, which was also called *Losca*, meaning Los Angeles, California. Barker's glossary of *pachuco* words from Arizona shows that the name *Califa*, without the *s*, was used to mean a boy from California. Today, Chicanos continue to refer to *Califas*, when speaking of California, in an affectionate and proprietary manner. The name can be found in art and literature as well as in academic and official documents. Not infrequently the return address on an envelope will be *Califas, Aztlán*.

See also Pachucos
References Barker 1974; Braddy 1971

California Folklore

The settlement of California by Spanish colonizers happened much later than in New Mexico and Texas. The first Franciscan mission was established in San Diego in 1769, 200 years after the exploration of New Mexico. A second great difference was that many of the Spanish settlers came by way of Mexico, so many of them represented a *mestizo* (mixed-race) culture rather than a purely sixteenth-century Spanish culture, as the earlier explorers had. Many were Mexican Spaniards and of course did not bring the Spanish language and culture of the Golden Age of Spain with them. Their Spanish language and culture had evolved into a slightly New World variant.

The population of California did not grow much during the eighteenth century, and after the independence of Mexico from Spain in 1821, Spanish culture quickly declined in the region. Many Spaniards left the region, and the great migration of thousands of Anglo American gold seekers took place, so the Spanish culture and language could not survive in California as it did in Texas and New Mexico. By 1880 the Mexican, or *Californio*, inhabitants of the state represented 1 percent of the total population. At the turn of the century the Chicano population in Los Angeles was only 5 percent. It wasn't until 1910, with the beginnings of a revolution in Mexico, that the first large wave of Mexican immigration was felt in California.

In discussing Hispano folklore, Aurelio M. Espinosa, the foremost Mexican American folklorist of the early twentieth century, delineated three generations of Hispanics in California. First were the Mexican Spaniards who settled the region in the eighteenth century and their descendents, called *Californios*, who represented the California Spanish traditions that Espinosa most wanted to study. Second were the Mexicans who continued to migrate into California during the nineteenth century, and these people, as Espinosa delicately put it, were "*gente de mas baja condición y cultura*" (people of a lower condition and culture) (1930, 301). And third, as he wrote his study in the 1920s, he found many Spaniards who had recently immigrated to California from Andalucía in Spain and who represented a Spain from a different era, and not that of the Spanish *Californios*. As he states, he collected *romances* from the true *Californios*, mostly from the Monterey region. In addition, he collected folktales, proverbs, ballads, and other lore, which were published in the *California Folklore Quarterly* in the 1940s.

A renowned proponent of Mexican Spanish folklore in the Southwest and California was Charles F. Lummis (1859–1928), a self-taught photographer, ethnologist, musicologist, journalist, and the founder of the Southwest Museum in Los Angeles. Lummis "discovered" the Mexicans in Colorado, New Mexico, and California in the 1880s and 1890s and became enamored of the Mexican way of life, especially of their "hospitality, courtesy, and respect for age" (Heisley 60). He collected oral traditions, specifically Spanish folk songs, from Mexicans in New Mexico and California and felt an urgency to record them before they disappeared. The Southwest Museum holds hundreds of songs he recorded on wax cylinders, songs in Spanish and in twenty-four Indian languages from southern California. He equated Spanish folk songs with the romantic past of the *Californios* and Mexicans and felt almost a nostalgic fascination for early California history and the era of the large *ranchos*. In his own words, "The Romance of California is Spanish Romance. Everybody knows that who knows anything" (1923b, 9).

Although not a trained folklorist, Arnold Rojas writes of the *vaquero* (cowboy) culture of California, especially in the San Joaquin Valley at the turn of the century and into the first third of the 1900s. He describes the life of the Mexican *vaqueros*, how their lives were spent working on large ranches like the Tejon Ranch and the Kern County Land Co. Their lives were very narrowly focused on cattle and ranch life and they all spoke mostly Spanish. In his reminiscences of *vaquero* culture and of the impact Mexican Sonorans had on California, Rojas shows a side of Chicano culture not commonly known. Born in California, where his mother and grandmother were also born, it is clear he loved the life he lived. He writes of *La Llorona* and Joaquín Murrieta, and of Tiburcio Vásquez, who once gave food to his grandmother and mother when they were fleeing from the *gringos* in Los Angeles.

There are no overall written accounts or collections of the oral traditions and folklore of the early *Californios* as we have of the *Hispanos* of New Mexico in Angustias de la Guerra. Ord's *Occurrences in Hispanic California* describes some customs but her work was not intended to preserve for history the way of life of the *Californios*. Glimpses of customs, games, dances, theater, and other traditions can be found in the writings of early western travelers, although these were often depicted prejudicially and with a lack of historical context. Spanish-language newspapers from the late nineteenth century exhibit folk customs and traditions. But the folklore collected from Mexicans and Mexican Americans in the twentieth century, even if it's from a third- or fourth-generation Chicano, generally will be folklore from Mexico transplanted to California since the turn of the century by immigrants fleeing a revolutionary war, or those coming to work in the agriculture fields. Of course it could also originate in New Mexico or Texas, since there has been much migration into California by Chicanos from those states. Folktales, jests, folk songs, *corridos* (ballads), and customs related to religious and secular holidays, foods, and other folk traditions found in contemporary California will have a lot in common with those found in other southwestern states and with Mexico. Chicano students have taken an active interest in folklore in the last twenty years, and archives established at the University of California at Berkeley and Los Angeles hold growing collections of many genres of Mexican American folklore. There are published collections from the 1970s and 1980s of folk medicine rituals and folk narratives collected primarily from Mexican immigrants in the Los Angeles area, but there is still much fieldwork to be done in this area.

See also Espinosa, Aurelio Macedonio
References Espinosa 1925, 1930; Espinosa Jr. 1947; Heisley 1985; Lummis 1923a, 1923b; Miller 1973; Ord 1956; Peña 1989; Robe 1976; Roeder 1988; Rojas 1958, 1979; Sanchez 1993

Caló (Spanish Slang)

Caló comes from the gypsy word *zincaló*, which is one of the idioms of the Spanish gypsies. It is a very old argot influenced by many languages, including French, English, Italian, Greek, and Hebrew, and was spoken by the gypsies of Spain. It was brought to New Spain by the Spanish *conquistadores*, where it continued to be identified as the language of the poor, the uneducated, and also the criminal class. *Caló* became the dialect of the underworld of Mexico City and migrated into the Southwest, as some believe, through the city of El Paso.

Published studies of the speech of the Chicano investigate the diverse communication modes by examining the language that reflects the cultural experiences of the various subcultures of Mexican and Chicano communities. Some of these idioms are the *pachuco* dialect, Chicano Spanish, New Mexico colonial Spanish, south Texas vocabulary, *caló*, and the argot of the *tirilones* of El Paso. The *pachuco* dialect has been especially influenced by *caló*; it was and still is primarily a male speech and if used by women they were considered to be street women or girlfriends of gang members. Today, however, many words from *caló* are fully integrated into the standard vocabulary of Chicano Spanish, and writers incorporate it into poetry, short stories, and novels. What makes *caló* and its appropriation into Chicano Spanish distinct is its use by working-class Chicanos and *Mexicanos*. It is a shared language across the Mexican-U.S. border, equally used on both sides.

The vocabulary of Chicano Spanish is congested with Old World words, words from the *pachuco* era, and consequently heavily influenced by *caló*. Chicanos have a sense of pride in being aware of these words and expressions, and knowing how to use them. There are many studies that examine the Spanish spoken by Chicanos and several published dictionaries of Chicano Spanish and of *caló*. Most of the studies provide examples of the male use of *caló*, but there is recent research that shows that female *cholas* and *pachucas* also have an extensive vocabulary in *caló*. Galindo's studies of Chicana prisoners show the social importance of *caló* in conveying a "sense of intimacy and camaraderie between women who shared similar life experiences and acquaintances" (1993, 34).

One published dictionary of *caló*, by Jay Rosensweig, presents *caló* in a rather harsh manner, referring to it as gutter Spanish, which prompted a reader to take the privilege of writing a comment on the title page of the book. This example of "book graffiti" is presented here because it is an excellent example of the use of Chicano Spanish influenced by *caló* and used at an opportune moment:

> *Este gabacho pendejo y su pinche libro no valen ni un coraje*
> *—que vaya a agarrar las nalgas a la puta que le parió.*
> (This stupid gringo and his f— book aren't worth anger;
> he can go grab the buttocks of the whore that gave him birth.)

"La Vida de un Bato Loco," written by an informant of Linda Katz and reproduced in her work, provides a good example of the literary uses of *caló*. Katz includes a glossary of the *caló* words used in the story.

See also Bato; Cholos; Pachucos
References Barker 1974; Cerda and Farias 1953; Coltharp 1965; Galindo 1992, 1993; Hinojosa 1975; Katz 1974; Ortega 1977, 1991; Rosensweig 1973; Sagel 1992

Campa, Arthur Leon (1905–1978)

One of a handful of Hispanic folklorists who have spent their careers studying the folk songs, folk theater, customs, traditions, and folkways of the Hispanic population of the Southwest. Arthur Leon Campa was a pioneer in his study of the folklore of the Hispanic population primarily of New Mexico and Colorado. His great achievement and comprehensive work, *Hispanic Culture in the Southwest,* was published in 1979, one year after his death. Campa was born on February 20, 1905, in Guaymas, Sonora, Mexico, the third of five children. His early years were spent mostly in Mexico, in Baja California and Sonora. His father, Daniel Campa, was a lieutenant in the Federal Army and was killed in 1914 by Pancho Villa revolutionaries. His mother, Delfia Lopez de la O, American-born, returned with her children to the United States. First they settled in a ranch outside of El Paso, and later she moved to Albuquerque, where she opened a store and restaurant.

Arthur Campa earned a B.A. (1928) and an M.A. (1930) from the University of New Mexico, and a Ph.D. from Columbia University (1940). Campa taught at the University of New Mexico from 1932 to 1942, and again after World War II from 1945 to 1946. In 1946 he became the chair of the Department of Modern Languages and Literature at the University of Denver, and he stayed there until he retired in 1974. Campa wrote nine books, nine bulletins, and forty-nine articles, mostly about folklore, but also on the Spanish language. He considered *Hispanic Culture in the Southwest* his most important achievement. This comprehensive work is a cultural history of the Hispanic population of California, Colorado, Arizona, New Mexico, and the Texas-Mexico border region. Campa presents the salient characteristics of Hispanic culture—customs, language, arts and crafts, and witchcraft—while also discussing distinctive character traits such as individualism, as well as the right to be and the right to do, perspectives on time, and remnants of the medieval honor code. He married Lucille Cushing in 1943 and they had four children. He died of a heart attack on May 13, 1978.

References Arellano and Vigil 1980; Campa 1976, 1979, 1980

Camposanto (Cemetery)

The place where Chicanos and *Mexicanos* bury their dead is called a *camposanto*, a "holy field" or "field of the saints." Although some people use the better-known term *cementerio*, meaning "cemetery," *camposanto* is a word still used in many families. Interestingly, some Spanish dictionaries define the word as a "cemetery for Catholics," whereas they define *cementerio* as an "enclosed place for burying the dead."

Camposantos are important in Chicano families, and the concept of death is always present in personal narratives, songs, and in the religious holy days observed. *El Día de los Muertos*, or All Souls' Day, is a religious and folk holy day that is devoutly celebrated; it usually includes a visit to the cemetery. The family cleans the grave sites of loved ones, sets up flowers and candles, and visits with and prays for the departed. During the rest of the year, attendance to burial sites does not diminish, and graves are kept decorated and colorful.

During the colonial period of New Spain, burials were made within the church itself, as was the tradition in medieval Spain. Spaniards and the clergy were allowed to be buried in the missionary churches, whereas the *mestizos* (people of mixed race) and Indians were buried in the *camposanto* located in front or to the right of the church. By the late eighteenth century, the Catholic Church forbade additional burials inside churches, supposedly for public health reasons, but the *ricos*, the well-to-do, continued to buy their way into the churches. So the *camposantos* were still left for the poor *mestizos*. A recognizable sign of a colonial frontier *camposanto* was a large public, eight-foot wooden cross that stood in the front or center of the cemetery. Some can still be found today in rural parts of northern New Mexico and Texas. Another feature that can also still be found in parts of the Southwest is segregation and isolation from Anglo cemeteries. Many were located side by side but were fenced off and had separate entrances. The sites chosen for rural *camposantos* were often on *tierra muerta*, barren land that was too poor to cultivate.

Cemetery and graveyard decorating traditions have been researched and written about as a means of appreciating and understanding Mexican folk

Two crosses with different designs stand out in this camposanto *(holy ground) in northern New Mexico. (North Wind Picture Archive)*

beliefs about death and grieving. The adornment of grave sites reflects religious folk practices, and ethnic and family attitudes about death and remembrance. Some of the customs include decorating and designing a space that will be revisited by a family for many generations. The intent is to keep the deceased person alive in the family's memory. Some design motifs that are distinctive to Chicano cemeteries are the construction and design of crosses. Terry Jordan's book has an illustration of twelve different "subtypes of wooden Latin crosses found on Mexican graves in Texas" (78). In the nineteenth and even into the twentieth century crosses were built of wood, but these didn't last long, being destroyed either by the elements or by vandalism. More common today are crosses made of molded concrete. Many grave sites have a *cerquito*, a low wood, metal, or concrete fence, an enclosure that surrounds an individual grave. Another common trait is to construct a cement grave marker, with a *nicho* (niche) built into it, so that the statue of a saint, *La Virgen de Guadalupe*, or a photograph of the deceased can be placed in it. Sometimes a concrete cross will have a *nicho* built into its base for the same purpose. Although fresh flowers are often placed at grave sites, paper and plastic flowers are more common. Colorful plastic wreaths are sometimes attached to the wooden or cement cross. Another distinguishing feature in Chicano *camposantos* is the wide range of materials

41

used in decorating a grave. As with home yard shrines and home altars, everyday objects are used as personal and artistic statements. It is often in the performance of highly charged personal rituals that people create folklore, folk art, and folk music.

Many grave markers are brightly painted, and some even have religious scenes painted on them. This tradition has been linked to Mexico's indigenous heritage, for, as Terry Jordan states, "Such use of color in a sacred context has ample pre-Columbian precedent in Mexico, where even the huge pyramids once bore bright paints" (80). He goes on to say, "Hispanic graveyards are places of color, where paints, flowers, and tiles combine to comfort the bereaved and startle the *gringo*" (88).

See also Altars; Folk Art; Nichos
References Barber 1993; Gosnell and Gott 1992; Griffith 1985; Jordan 1982; Sanborn 1989

Canciones (Songs)

A *canción* is a song form that, unlike the *corrido* (ballad), is not a narrative, but presents an introspective state of emotion, such as love, loneliness, sadness, religious feeling, mourning, or gaiety. The form of the *canción* is freer than other song forms. For instance *décimas* (poetic narratives) and *corridos*, because of their narrative function, follow a more structured format. The origins of the *canción* lie in peninsular Spain, but its Mexican development can be traced to Italian opera, which was popular in Mexico during the early nineteenth century. Italian opera was performed in Spanish at the Coliseo Theater in Mexico City beginning in 1799, but by the 1830s it was performed in Italian. This musical tradition, combined with the Romantic poetry of the nineteenth century, shaped the *canción*, which took on its characteristic form by the mid-nineteenth century. Then, as the Mexican folklorist Vicente Mendoza puts it, "The *canción* fulfilled its destiny and gave way to other musical forms. So it is that by 1914, in spite of the Revolution, the aristocracy of the Porfirio Díaz era could be scandalized at the harmonization of popular *Canciones* by Manuel M. Ponce, calling them 'songs of the straw hat, the *huarache* and the *pulque* shop'" (1961a, 53).

John Donald Robb (1954) observes that in many of the *canciones* he has collected, animals are metaphors for human emotions or the human condition, as in one from New Mexico titled "*Palomita que vienes herida*" (Little Dove Who Comes Wounded). Other well-known *canciones* are "Cielito Lindo," "Las Mañanitas," and "Adiós Muchachos." "La Paloma" and "La Golondrina" are two songs typical of the *canción* form that influenced its future growth and development. Campa lists the titles of 228 *canciones* (1930), and in Robb's collection (1980) the *canciones* outnumber all of the other folk songs that he collected in New Mexico. Vicente Mendoza has written a 600-page book on the *canciones* of Mexico (1961b).

See also Corridos; Décimas
References Campa 1930; Mendoza 1961a, 1961b; Robb 1954, 1980

Capirotada (Bread Pudding, Pauper's Grave)

A Spanish dictionary defines *capirotada* as a burial ground for poor people, a common cemetery for the homeless, or a pauper's grave, but it is commonly known in Mexico and the United States as a sweet dish prepared during Lent. Two other dictionaries define it as a food, one as a batter made with herbs and eggs and the other as a Creole dish made of meat that is layered with bread and cheese.

A Catholic religious practice during Lent is to fast and not to eat meat on Fridays. This practice has changed over the years, but it is still adhered to in many Chicano homes, especially during *Semana Santa*, or Holy Week, the week before Easter. Many meatless foods are traditionally prepared for Lent, and *capirotada* is a dish that has come to be associated with this religious season among Chicanos. It is made of layers of toasted sliced bread, cheese, peanuts, and raisins, and drenched with a sauce made of cinnamon and *piloncillo*, or brown sugar. In some families it may also include almonds, bananas, and small brightly colored candies. According to Mario Montano a recipe for *capirotada* appeared in the cookbook of Felipe Martinez Montino, once a chef of King Felipe IV of Spain in 1667, and included different kinds of meats and cheeses. Today it is considered a dessert and in English is often called bread pudding.

References Montano 1992; Verti 1993; Zavala 1990

Carpas (Tent Theaters)

A *carpa* is literally a tent, but it is used to mean the traveling folk theater that became an important institution in Mexico and the Southwest during the nineteenth century. Nicolas Kanellos states that the word *carpa* comes from the Quechua word for "awning." The *Diccionario de Mejicanismos* confims this, spelling it *carppa*. Many *carpa* theater groups traveled throughout the Southwest from the mid-1800s until the early 1900s. *Carpas* were an important popular cultural tradition at the turn of the century. It was the small family-based *carpas* that survived the longest, some performing along the Mexican-U.S. border up until the 1960s. The *carpas* included circus entertainment such as acrobatics, clowns, and vaudeville acts, but they also functioned as "popular tribunals, repositories of folk wisdom, humor, and music, and were incubators of Mexican comic types and stereotypes" (Kanellos 1990, 97).

Many *carpa* companies featured a *pelado* or *peladito*, a lowly clown character who was beloved by Mexican and Chicano audiences. Similar to Charlie

Chaplin, and later developed by the Mexican actor Cantinflas, *el pelado* was a homeless type who could speak out the unthinkable and mock everything and everybody. In *carpa* performances, irreverence and profanity were dispensed equally to all members of society, regardless of stature or class. San Antonio was a thriving city for the performing arts and entertainment, with an eager audience for *carpas*, *teatros* (theater groups), and the kind of circuses called *maromas*. During the Mexican Revolution many actors and performers fled to Texas and continued their involvement in acting and performing in San Antonio. Two well-known *carpas* from San Antonio were *Carpa Garcia* and *Carpa Cubana*.

Chicano theater groups, developing from the mid-1960s to the present, have been greatly influenced by the *carpa* tradition. *El Teatro Campesino*, led by Luis Valdez, is based on the *carpa* tradition of performing, but it takes place on top of flatbed trucks, instead of in tents. One of the *Teatro's* plays from the early 1970s was titled *La Carpa de los Rasquachis*. It told the story, in music, song, action, and comedy, of Jesús Pelado Rasquachi, a *peladito*. This play was successfully performed throughout the United States and Europe.

Recently, the San Antonio Hertzberg Circus Collection and Museum held a *carpa* exhibit. The material was discovered in a barn that was just about to be demolished. Included in the exhibit was "a model of a typical tent, complete with grandstands, a center ring and a stage at one end of the tent. . . . Museum visitors have the feeling of actually entering the tent show." (Swenson, 15).

See also Rascuache; El Teatro Campesino
References Broyles-Gonzalez 1994; Huerta 1982; Kanellos 1990; Swenson 1998

La Carreta de la Muerte (Death Cart)

The cart with a skeleton in it that follows *Los Penitentes* during their Holy Week processions in New Mexico. *La Carreta de la Muerte* is a crude oxcart carrying a skeleton clothed in black with a hood over its head, holding a drawn bow and arrow. This figure of death is called Doña Sebastiana and is affectionately known as *Nuestra Comadre Sebastiana*. One or two of *Los Penitentes* are selected to pull the death cart, a penance that some believe will ensure a longer life for those who suffer through the experience. It is believed that Nazario Lopez of Santa Cruz, New Mexico, was the first person to carve the Death Cart figure, around 1860. His son, Jose Dolores Lopez, born in 1868, also became a wood-carver and *santero* (saint maker), and his two sons also followed in the same tradition. One rendition of *La Carreta de la Muerte* is housed at the Museum of International Folk Art in Santa Fe, created by Jose Benito Ortega sometime before 1907. It is carved from cottonwood, stands a little over three feet, and the figure of *La Muerte* in the cart has glass pane lenses in the eyes. Other depictions of *La Carreta de la Muerte* can be found in religious and folk art books from the Southwest. The northern New Mexicans were conscious that *la muerte* was always present and that one should always be prepared for a good Christian death.

See also Doña Sebastiana; La Muerte; Los Penitentes
References Cruz 1973; Stark 1971; Weigle 1977

Cascarones (Decorated Eggshells)

From the Spanish word *cascara* meaning "shell," *cascarones* are eggshells decorated in bright colors and filled with confetti or other mischievous matter. The egg is very delicately blown out of the shell through a small hole, leaving most of the shell unbroken. The empty eggshell is then painted and decorated, filled with gold, bright confetti, or sometimes with cologne, and cracked over an unsuspecting person's head.

The tradition of making *cascarones* dates back to at least the early nineteenth century in Mexico, and many references to them can be found in early California narratives. At the California wedding of Maria Teresa de la Guerra to William Hartnell in 1826, the *cascarones* were filled with cologne and prepared well in advance of the celebration. Angustias de la Guerra Ord describes the wedding in *Occurrences in Hispanic California*. Bell describes the use of *cascarones* at *fandangos* in 1850s California, when mischievous *señoritas* used them to get the attention of eligible men. Apparently it was a regular custom in Los Angeles to attend *fandangos* with pockets full of *cascarones* filled with flour, ashes, black paint, or cologne as well as the more innocent confetti.

Some early Californian writings, as presented in Genz's work, mention "*Cascarones* Balls," held around Monterey in the 1820s. These balls were held right before the start of Lent, with hundreds of *cascarones* available for playful fighting and teasing. It is probable that *cascarones* were available at all the balls, and consequently one observer came up with the idea of labeling the carnival festivities *Cascarones* Balls.

The tradition of making *cascarones* has been maintained in the Southwest up until the present. James Griffith provides a clear and detailed description of how *cascarones* were made and used in Arizona in the 1990s. *Cascarones* are made for weddings, fiestas, dances, and almost any holiday, but especially in the spring for the Easter holidays.

The fun part of *cascarones* is breaking one over the head of one's rival and laughing as the confetti settles all over the hair and clothing. A new way of making *cascarones* has been developed in Tucson, Arizona, where the decorated egg is mounted on a slim cone made from rolled-up newspaper and decorated with tissue paper. These can resemble puppets and even have faces painted on them, such as *Pancho Villa*, *La Adelita*, or Batman and Bart Simpson.

References Bell 1927; CHICLE 1995; Genz 1970; Griffith 1988, 1993, 1995; Martinez 1996; Ord 1956; Starr 1899

Hundreds of colorful cascarones (decorated eggshells) filled with confetti are sold at the Fiesta Tejana in keeping with a tradition that goes back to the early nineteenth century. (Phil Schermeister/Corbis)

Casos

A *caso* is a folk narrative about a personal experience, or the experience of someone known by the narrator, that involves something natural, supernatural, or miraculous happening. It is usually a brief narrative that describes a single event that happened in the recent past, but that could occur again. The word *caso* can be translated as "case, happening, instance, event, or occurrence," and in Spanish can also be called a *sucedido*, a happening. A *caso* may be narrated to emphasize a point and is often used in a didactic manner to show that "this kind of thing" happens or to illustrate that unusual things do occur. In other words, it is used as evidence, and functions as a testimony to support a folk belief. The majority of *casos* collected in Texas and other parts of the Southwest deal with supernatural or unusual events, or with sickness and healing, *curanderos* (healers), and the use of herbs and prayer for healing. These are the subjects one would expect, since *casos* tend to be personal narratives illustrating a belief, and many shared beliefs deal with illnesses, religion, or mysterious events. A *caso* is different from a *cuento* (story), in that the narrator believes it to be true, whereas a *cuento* is a narrative that may or may not have happened, and the narrator cannot vouch for it. In this sense, the *caso* is related to the belief tale. Folk narratives that describe encounters with witches, or sightings of *La Llorona* late at night when one should already be home, or that describe an unbeliever being cured by a folk remedy, could be classified as *casos*. If the episode reported makes the point that one should believe in witches, or one should not be out late at night, or that folk remedies are reliable, these narratives are *casos*. If such stories don't make a point, they are just called spooky stories, or among folklorists, memorates.

Interspersing conversations with *casos* is important and helps validate the cultural beliefs and social norms of the community. In fact, one reason for narrating *casos* is to control social behavior and to teach children and young adults proper behavior that does not violate social norms. Regarding *casos* that describe folk medicine practices, Américo Paredes states, "This type of *caso* plays an important role among rural and semirural Mexican groups in the United States, who see their folk culture assailed not only by modern science and technology, but by the belief patterns of rural Anglo-American neighbors who may have their own folk beliefs and tend to be contemptuous of those held by foreigners" (1993a, 53). Joe Graham believes that the *caso* is the most important folk narrative found in Mexican American culture.

See also Cuentos; Curanderismo; La Llorona
References Graham 1981; Jordan 1975; Paredes 1993a

Cemetery
See Camposanto

Chanes (Water Spirits)

Mythical water creatures that come out of lakes and rivers and steal little children. Belief tales about *chanes* have been collected in New Mexico and in Los Angeles. They are described as resembling turtles, and as being very ugly with short stubby legs, possibly like mud puppies. If a child crosses a bridge, or walks near a river or arroyo, the *chanes* may touch the child and he or she will become very ill, and sometimes die. Or they may call to the child, saying, "Don't go, stay here, come into the water, come here, let us see you." To avoid this a mother must repeat the child's name three times, saying such things as, "Come on Juan, don't stop . . . come on, keep walking Juan, don't stop, Juan." According to an informant this is a belief of older people, and is used to warn children what will happen if they do not do as they're told. But there is also a related belief that *chanes* are beautiful girls that look like mermaids and want to lure men into the water to drown them.

In order to pacify the *chanes*, mothers would make food and place it on the riverbank, so the *chanes* would not come after the children. An informant's narrative found in the Ernest Baughman Collection at Zimmerman Library at the University of New Mexico states that she heard about *chanes* from her grandmother, who would make "these corn meal cakes and fill them with fruit and cheese," and take them to the river, and "as soon as she left, the *chanes* would eat them." Stanley Robe believes *chanes* are water spirits and the belief in them stems from "pre-conquest native sources" (1971, xii).

References Ernest Baughman Collection 1974; Robe 1971

Charreadas (Rodeos)

A *charreada* is a Mexican rodeo that is performed for an audience, different from rodeos as they used to be, when their function was to round up cattle for counting and branding. A *charreada* is a formal and festive competition where *charros* (rodeo riders) perform and exhibit their mastery of equestrian skills and execute bold feats of horsemanship. During a *charreada* teams of *charros* perform a series of feats that show their skills as riders, and also test precision, style, bravery, and the relationship between the horse and the rider. Unlike the American rodeo, where speed is important, in the *charreada* it is style and horsemanship that are rated. The tradition of the *charreada* goes back to the colonial period of the hacienda and the ranching culture of Mexico and the Southwest. Although the skills of riding and roping were everyday functions, informal competitions developed during the late eighteenth

In a charreada, *a formal and festive competition, the* charros *(horsemen) perform and exhibit their mastery of equestrian skills, as in this rodeo in Gallup, New Mexico, in 1993. (North Wind Picture Archive)*

century. By the early twentieth century, established rules and regulations governed formal riding competitions. It was after the Mexican Revolution of 1910 that *charreadas* became a national urban sport, with the creation of associations to actually monitor and guide the sport. The *charro* is a descendent of the *caballero* (horseman), who had become a symbol of masculinity and patriotism, and an icon of Mexican national culture. When the Spaniards landed in the New World, they brought horses and cattle, but during the sixteenth century they did not allow the Indians or *mestizos* (people of mixed race) to ride the horses. Consequently, only the Spaniards rode, and a *caballero* came to mean a member of the aristocracy and a skilled horseman.

The National Association of *Charros* was formed in 1921, and the *Federación de Charros* was formed in 1933; it now has over 20,000 members and 700 associations. Of these, 80 associations are in the United States, primarily in the Southwest.

A *charreada* always begins with a procession, parading both the American and Mexican flags if it is occurring in the United States. The procession, or *desfile*, exhibits the formality and long historical tradition of the *charreada*, and allows the *charros* to display their dignity, elegance, beautiful horses, and costumes. The first event is the *cala del caballo* (the test of the horse), during which the *charro* spins and slides to show his control over the horse. Next is *piales en el lienzo*, or hind-leg roping, a skill that comes directly from ranching. The next event is called *colas* (literally, tails), during which the *charro* catches a bull by grasping its tail and wrapping it under the right leg, thus throwing it to the ground, all while galloping at full speed. The *charros* perform nine *suertes*, a word that means "luck" but also "feats." The final event is the *paso de la muerte* or the "death pass," when a rider leaps from his galloping horse to the bare back of a mare running around the arena. This final event is a test of courage and skill, and it shows off the *charro's machismo* and masculine adeptness.

Charreadas are held throughout the Southwest, from California to Texas, though only a small segment of Chicanos are actually involved in formal *charreadas*. Young women who like and live around horses may join a kind of horse drill team, called an *escaramuza*. This consists of a team of women who, riding sidesaddle, perform at *charreadas*. Riding with six to twelve riders, they complete different maneuvers and formations. This performance usually closes the *charreada*. *Escaramuza* means "skirmish" and so has a military connotation that brings to mind the role of women during the Mexican Revolution. The costume worn by these women is called the *Adelita* costume, even though it consists of a long dress with long sleeves, a high neck, and many layers of fabric. The *escaramuza* is usually composed of young girls, who are reminiscent of the aristocratic Mexican women who in the nineteenth century were only allowed to ride during special fiestas or in processions. The riding of the *escaramuza* may appear smooth and anxiety-free, but it actually requires much practice, discipline, and courage.

The Mexican singing *charro* and actor Antonio Aguilar regularly brings his touring company, a *charreada* entourage, which performs riding feats and sings *corridos*, to major cities in the United States. Aguilar and his wife of many years, Flor Silvestre, both ride and sing together in these shows. *Charro* Days is an annual festival held in Brownsville, Texas, the week before Ash Wednesday. Started in the 1950s to celebrate the traditions of the *vaqueros* (cowboys), today *Charro* Days attracts hundreds of thousands of visitors and includes concerts, fireworks, folk dances, food, and games. The performers are Mexicans and Mexican Americans.

See also La Adelita; Charros; Corridos; Vaqueros
References Najera-Ramirez 1994, 1996, 1997; Sands 1993, 1994; Simons and Hoyt 1992; Valero Silva 1987

Charros (Horsemen)

A *charro* is a horseman who performs equestrian feats in *charreadas* (rodeos). Through the years the *charro* has come to symbolize masculinity, machismo, and Mexican culture. In Spain, the word *charro* meant a peasant from Salamanca, but it also meant "rustic" or "ill bred." In New Spain *charros* were the *vaqueros* (cowboys) who worked on the ranches in colonial Mexico, but who

In New Spain, charros *were the equivalent of* vaqueros (cowboys) *who worked the ranches in colonial Mexico, but through the years the* charro *has come to symbolize nationalism and Mexican culture. (North Wind Picture Archive)*

during the nineteenth century because of numerous historical processes came to symbolize manhood and power. After Mexico gained its independence in 1821, justice, order, and progress were difficult to maintain. President Benito Juarez established the *rurales*, a national mounted police force that was supposed to establish order and minimize the rise of bandits in the rural areas. The *rurales* were dressed as *charros* and conveyed an image of strong skilled horsemen who were loyal to their government. After the Mexican Revolution the *charro* image became a national symbol reinforced by literature, by becoming the national costume of *mariachi* (singing musicians) groups, and by a nationalism that evoked a romantic regional cultural history of Mexico. Mexican traditions and culture were emphasized through dance, music, and films. During the 1930s, 1940s, and into the 1950s, nationalistic Mexican films featuring the singing *charro* were shown throughout the Southwest. *Ranchera* music, *Mariachis*, and the romantic rural life of the *hacienda* came to represent Mexico to those who lived in the United States. Even though it is a masculine symbol, and a very emotional one, to many Mexican Americans and Chicanos the *charro*, either on horseback or just singing, represents the Motherland and Mexican identity.

See also Charreadas; Mariachi Music; Vaqueros
References Mather 1992; Najera-Ramirez 1994; Sands 1993, 1994; Valero Silva 1987

Chávez, César Estrada (1927–1993)

This man was probably the most famous and loved folk hero of the Chicano people in the twentieth century. When he died, a cardinal and numerous priests presided at his funeral Mass, and over 30,000 people attended, in Delano, California, on April 30, 1993. César Chávez devoted his entire life to organizing farmworkers so they would have the same workers' rights as all laborers in the United States. He reinstituted the use of pilgrimages and marches in his battle against California grape growers in 1966 when he led striking farmworkers on a weeklong march up the San Joaquin Valley, from Delano to Sacramento. For Chicano and *Mexicano* farmworkers he became a

César Chávez, squeezing grapes at a rally in New York, was probably the most famous and beloved folk hero of the Chicano people. He represented hope in the struggle for social justice and a better life for all farmworkers, 1986. (Bettmann/Corbis)

spiritual savior, as well as representing hope in the struggle for social justice and for a better and fairer work life.

Born in Arizona, Chávez grew up working alongside his parents as a migrant farmworker. Because they were constantly moving he didn't receive much of an education and dropped out in junior high school. The family settled in San Jose, California, where Chávez lived until the early 1960s. It was in San Jose that he became involved with the social organizer Fred Ross Sr. and the Community Service Organization (CSO). The CSO worked with the Chicano community, helping it to devise political strategies for the betterment of the community. The organization worked on acquiring city services, paving neighborhood streets, and organizing voter registration drives. Chávez learned labor organizing tactics that he later applied to his union organizing programs. In 1962 he started the National Farm Workers Union (later United Farm Workers of America) in Delano, and by 1966, with 1,700 members in his union, he joined with a Filipino organization to strike grape growers. The strike lasted five years and caught the attention of the entire country.

Chávez was *del pueblo*, one of the people, reminiscent of the traditional peasant leader; he was not an intellectual or a politician. He became almost a divine leader, following the teachings of Mohandas Gandhi and Martin Luther King Jr. in espousing nonviolence. Although gentle and quiet, he was a shrewd statesman and negotiator. During his life he completed three long and serious fasts of twenty-five days or more to reinforce his commitment to nonviolence; these fasts eventually left his body severely weakened. It is believed that it was because of them that he died at the early age of 66 in his sleep. He had a spiritual aura about him, and used religious and cultural symbols, such as the emblem of *La Virgen de Guadalupe*, the crucifix, and a black eagle, to support the sanctity of the just political struggle of Mexican farmworkers.

The farmworkers' strike, *la huelga*, under the leadership of Chávez became *la causa*, a civil rights campaign, and the inspiration for many other Chicano political endeavors of the 1960s and 1970s. The legends and songs about César Chávez boast of his loyalty, dignity, and persona. He emerges as larger than life in the "Corrido de César Chávez," which lifts him from only a "temporal presence" to the "mythical presence" of a folk hero (Griswold del Castillo and García 1995, 15).

References Day 1971; Dunne 1967; Ferriss and Sandoval 1997; García, Richard A. 1994; Griswold del Castillo and García 1995; Griswold del Castillo and Sanchez 1997; Levy 1975; Ross 1989

Chicanismo

The doctrine of *Chicanismo*, from the word *Chicano*, proclaims that Chicanos are a proud *mestizo* (mixed) race with a dual heritage of indigenous and Spanish roots. *Chicanismo* emphasizes ethnic, cultural, and linguistic pride, and a belief in political and economic self-determination. In the 1960s this belief called for a reclaiming of the territory lost by Mexico after the U.S. Mexican War of 1846–1848. *La Raza Unida*, a political party, was founded on the basic beliefs of *Chicanismo*, as was MECHA, *El Movimiento Estudiantil Chicano de Aztlán* (Chicano Student Movement of Aztlán), a national student organization started in the late 1960s. Some early writings on *Chicanismo*, when they focused on the individual, stressed the importance of personal values such as "spiritualism, honest self-examination, complete love of life, and a consciousness of the here and now." The principles of *Chicanismo* proclaim an ideology of acceptance of Chicano culture and describe the experience of being Chicano. The epic poem *I Am Joaquin/Yo Soy Joaquin*, written by Rodolfo Gonzales in 1967, distinctly presents the sentiments embedded in the doctrine of *Chicanismo*. An acceptance and belief in *Chicanismo* underlie Chicano folk art, popular culture, and much of the literature published in the 1960s and 1970s.

See also Chicano; *I Am Joaquin/Yo Soy Joaquin*
References Castillo 1994; Estrada 1971; Jiménez 1992; Martinez 1971

Chicano (-a)

In its most basic definition a *Chicano* is a person of Mexican descent born in the United States. *Chicano* is the masculine form and *Chicana* is the feminine. Historically the term has had a pejorative connotation when applied to lower-class poor Mexicans, although it has always been playfully used in supportive in-group situations. In the late 1960s it was adopted as a self-identifying term by Mexican American youth and college students to emphasize self-determination and self-assertion and to choose one's own identity. It has become an ideologically loaded symbolic code word that expresses cultural pride in a common Mexican heritage. To call oneself a Chicano symbolizes a solidarity with the Spanish language and with a pre-Columbian indigenous past, and an understanding of American racial oppression and discrimination against Mexican Americans.

There are various folk theories regarding the origin of the word. For instance, one theory circulating during the late 1960s was that the word came from the Mexican city of Chihuahua, and that the *chi* from that name was added to the *cano* of *Mexicano*, and this gave birth to *Chicano*. Another theory gives *Chicano* an indigenous base, derived from the *Mexicas* who pronounced the *x* as "sh," so that they were called *Meshicas*, and the word *Mexicano* became *Meshicano*. Eventually the *me* was dropped and the word became *Chicano*. A third theory is that when large numbers of Anglo Americans migrated into northern Mexico and the Southwest, they called all Mexicans "*chico*," equivalent to the designation "boy" for African Americans in the South. This word was eventually lengthened with the *ano* from *Mexicano* to form *Chicano*. Without a doubt the word has been used by Mexicans since at least the early 1900s in Texas and probably in Mexico as well. Ernesto Galarza in his book *Barrio Boy* referred to Mexican residents of Sacramento, California, in 1913 as Chicanos.

Chicano is an old word that symbolizes a complex heritage and identity. Yet only a small percentage of Mexican Americans actually consider themselves Chicanos. These are usually individuals who are politically active or work in academic environments. Several Chicano researchers and professors have written extensively about the origin of the word and specifically about the sociocultural poignancy of its meaning. Throughout different historical periods it has carried many connotations, some pejorative, some affectionately folksy, and it has been analyzed for years. Jose Limón writes of the folk etymology of the term in south Texas during the 1960s, and Tino Villanueva writes an article in Spanish on the history of a negative term and how it came to be used by a group to signify a positive identity.

References Barrera 1988; Gonzales 1972; Gutiérrez 1995; Limón 1981; Macias 1969; Rodriguez 1993; Villanueva 1978

Chicano Park

The site of murals and painted freeway pillars underneath a freeway in the long-established *barrio* of Logan in San Diego, California. In the southeastern part of the city, in an industrial and residential area populated by four generations of Chicanos, freeways and a Bay Bridge that cut across the neighborhood were constructed in the late 1960s. This disruption almost destroyed the community. In 1970, an initial movement to construct a Highway Patrol substation near the Bay Bridge brought the community together to protest the construction and to demand a park under the bridge. Picket lines by students and community people stopped the construction and the community took over the area that became Chicano Park. The concept of making the concrete interchange into a creative park "that looks like a cathedral"

(Cockcroft 1984, 99) when the sun shines right was in the minds of all the people involved in planning Chicano Park. The muralized walls have become a community center where tourists come from many countries to visit and where children play and learn about their heritage. A film titled *Chicano Park* released in 1988 provides a history of the *barrio* (the community), and shows how artists, musicians, and activists came together to create a site for folk art in the community.

A Chicano Park Day celebration was held on April 22 and 23, 2000, to commemorate the thirtieth anniversary of the park. The theme was *Tierra, Liberación y Revolución* (Land, Liberty and Revolution) and the festivities took place in the Barrio Logan community, south of downtown San Diego. Besides food, art, music, and dance, there were poetry readings, a classic low-rider car display presented by Amigos Car Club, and a circus. Chicano Park Day weekend was organized and sponsored by the Chicano Park Steering Committee and cosponsored by the Brown Berets de Aztlán, Amigos Car Club, Calaca Press, Danza Mexícoytl, and Unión del Barrio.

References Cockcroft 1984, 1992; Cockcroft, Weber, and Cockcroft 1977

Chicano Spanish

The Spanish spoken by Chicanos in the United States varies considerably from region to region, reflecting the diversity of the Chicano population. In general, linguistic acculturation has been slow because of the steady influx of Spanish-speaking immigrants due to the nearness of the Mexican border. In addition, labor segmentation of the Mexican population has resulted in less social and linguistic contact between Mexicans and Anglo Americans, another reason for the persistence of Spanish. But the Spanish spoken by millions of Mexican Americans is not considered standard Spanish; it contains a large number of nonstandard lexical items, the majority of which reflect the influence of the English language. Anglicisms or English words, known among Chicanos as *pochismos*, have become a standard component of Chicano Spanish. Some linguistic scholars perceive this influence as a normal consequence of the political and economic dominance that started in the mid-nineteenth century, whereas others just consider it "a barbaric invasion on the Spanish language" (Hernández-Chavez, Cohen, and Beltramo, ix).

Spanish has been spoken continuously in the Southwest since 1598, when Juan de Oñate conquered New Mexico. But the forms of spoken Spanish change from generation to generation and vary from state to state. Complete linguistic assimilation has not been possible but neither has stable bilingualism resulted. The varieties of Spanish spoken in the Southwest reflect the different segments of the Mexican population that have immigrated to the United States in the last 100 years. Spanish from Texas is considered of a high academic standard because of the large number of educated and professional

Mexicans who have entered the state. The Spanish of New Mexico and southern Colorado has been researched heavily through the years and is known for its kinship to sixteenth-century peninsular Spanish. Arizona has had a lot of migration from northern Mexico, specifically the state of Sonora, and consequently the Spanish spoken there is more of a Mexican variety, although it contains some of the archaic features found in New Mexico. California Spanish is similar to Arizona Spanish, again because of the influx of immigrants from northern Mexico and migration from other southwestern states.

Descendants of Mexican immigrants use their ancestors' varieties of Mexican Spanish yet are always absorbing and incorporating new words into a growing dynamic vocabulary. In all languages, variations reflect the individual's education and socioeconomic status. Similarly, all languages are constantly changing and evolving, and what is considered standard at one point in history may be replaced by another form at a later time. Rosaura Sanchez states, "The original forms may continue to exist in the repertoire of the masses even though the elite have discarded them from the standard varieties" (44). What eventually happens is that a language will lose status and thus reflect the status of the speakers. When English became the official language of the Southwest in 1848, the opportunities to maintain formal Spanish declined, since the language was not taught by the educational systems and most Chicanos were forbidden to even speak it in school. Consequently Spanish was relegated to the status of being primarily an oral language spoken in the realm of home, church, and social diversions, as it continues to be used today.

The maintenance of the Spanish language, in all its forms and varieties, has been the primary means of preserving the culture and folklore of Chicanos. Although some scholars look at it from another perspective, according to Arthur Campa, "The most important factor in the preservation of the Spanish language is the rich body of traditional lore which abounds throughout the Southwest in the form of folksongs, proverbs, riddles, games, and folk plays" (1977, 25). In any case, it is clear that language and folklore are intertwined and culturally help to sustain each other and the culture in Chicano communities. For this reason the Spanish language continues to be important to Chicanos today, even to those who do not speak it fluently.

Even those who don't speak Spanish daily still use Spanish words and expressions in connection with the customs and traditions that define the Chicano experience. The use of Spanish helps to maintain the sense of a distinctive shared culture. If the Spanish language had been totally eliminated from Chicano culture, much of the folklore would not be experienced. A *taco* can only be experienced as a *taco*. It is more than just a *tortilla* folded over *chile verde*. It is a binding icon, attached to language and culture, that connotes an invitation to participate; *vamos a comer un taco* (let's eat a taco), to share the communal chile in its hotness, wrapped in a *tortilla* that symbolizes the ancient heritage of *maíz*. Without Spanish one would be eating garlic-flavored green flour pancakes, called "wraps," filled with mushrooms and brie. Words are powerful and important, and the language of every community should be respected.

Caló, a subculture dialect of Spanish, has influenced Chicano Spanish almost as much as English has, and its importance cannot be undervalued. As stated by Hernández-Chavez, "Used by young people throughout the Southwest as an in-group variety, it represents the values of intimacy, comradeship and ethnicity, expressing the *carnalismo* of its users. In modern times it also symbolizes *chicanismo*, the struggle for social justice of the Chicano movement" (Hernández-Chavez, Cohen, and Beltramo, xiv).

See also Caló; Pochismos
References Campa 1977; Cardenas 1975; Espinosa 1911; Hernández-Chavez, Cohen, and Beltramo 1975; Sanchez 1979; Vasquez 1975

Chili Queens

In San Antonio, Texas, in the 1830s the chili stand came into existence. During the evenings in the Military Plaza, Mexican women would arrange their stands, put up huge pots, and cook beans and chili. Tables were set up, and these women, "tastefully-dressed" (Bourke 1895), were called the "chili queens," as they served large bowls of *chile con carne* and beans, with a side helping of *tortillas*. The *chile con carne* dish originated in south Texas, and was made from meat, fat, and dried chilies. The chili stand became a popular place for all to eat, with young roving singers and sometimes dancers providing entertainment. In addition to *chile con carne*, they sold *tamales*, *tortillas*, *chile rellenos* (stuffed chiles), and *huevos revueltos* (scrambled eggs). According to Captain John Bourke, they always had excellent hot coffee and very good chocolate. The chili stands became very famous but were eventually abolished in the late nineteenth century, around the 1890s, by the San Antonio city council. Reference to these stands can be found in various literary and historical works about Texas.

See also Bourke, Captain John Gregory
References Bourke 1895; Cabeza de Baca 1982; De Leon 1982; Montano 1992; Simons and Hoyt 1992

Chiquiao (Poetic Dance Tradition)

A poetic dance tradition attributed to the Hispanos of New Mexico. The poetic form used in the *chiquiao* is a quatrain made up of octosyllabic verses. It was a sort of literary game played out at dances and parties that allowed a man to initiate dialogue with the woman of his choice. The theme of the *chiquiaos* was always love. Cleofas Jaramillo writes of it as a dance that included verses and so was only open to those few young men who had a poetic facility. A young woman would select a young man as a dance partner only if his verse pleased her. Arthur Campa writes of the New Mexico *verso*, which appears to be the same as the *chiquiao*. He provides the titles of seventy-nine *versos* that were actually used in the ballrooms of New Mexico. Rubén Cobos writes of it as a game, but calls it *"Valse chiquiao,"* implying it was also a dance. The New Mexican WPA files also have a reference to it as "Chiquiau—A Spanish Dance." Again, as with Jaramillo's description, the WPA files describe the recitation of romantic verses by young men, performed for the purpose of getting a young woman to dance with them. The reciting of *chiquiaos* was also done by married men and women, sometimes with risqué and insulting messages. A dictionary definition of *chiquear* indicates that it is found in Cuba and Mexico, and means to overindulge, to fondle by word or in writing.

A modern collection of *coplas* (stanzas) from East Los Angeles published in 1981 provides an interesting comparison to the *chiquiao*. These *coplas*, called *versos* by the informants, were collected from *Mexicano* junior high school students, many recent immigrants, who wrote them in school autograph books. The *coplas*, mostly concerning love and courtship, are categorized as nostalgic, positive, painful, practical, aggressive, and picaresque, and are written in Spanish. There appears to be a similarity between the uses of these *coplas* and the *chiquiaos* of late nineteenth-century New Mexico. Two examples follow:

> *En el Océano Pacifico*
> *se me perdió un alfiler*
> *y hasta que lo encuentre*
> *no dejaré de querer.*
> (In the Pacific Ocean,
> I lost a pin,
> and until I find it
> I won't stop loving you.)
> *Para las morenas preciosas*
> *una corona imperial*
> *y para las gueras saladas,*
> *una penca de nopal.*
> (For all the pretty dark girls
> an imperial crown,
> and for the lousy blondes,
> a leaf of a nopal cactus.)

References Aranda 1977; Campa 1930; Cobos 1956; Dominguez 1981; García, 1997; Jaramillo 1972

Chirrionera (Mythical Snake)

The name of a type of snake found in west Texas that in Mexican and Chicano folklore is believed to be attracted to women. The *Diccionario de Mejicanismos* defines *chirrionera* as a very long snake, with a whiplike tail, found in northern Mexico. The snake can give loud wolf whistles when it sees a woman that it wants. A body of folk narratives have been collected that describe instances where this snake has entered a woman's body through the vagina and impregnated her with a litter of snakes. Published sources from the 1890s cite this belief in connection with the *axolotl*, another name for the water dog, which lived near pools of water and would sometimes enter the body of a woman and remain there the same length of time as a human fetus. In other folktales the snake enters the woman's vagina to plant eggs or to strangle an infant in the womb. There are other related tales about snakes that steal a mother's milk, thus depriving a baby of nourishment. In some versions of these tales the *chirrionera* will suck the breasts of a lactating woman and take the milk intended for her infant. The snake hypnotizes a woman to sleep and then suckles at her breast while it plants its tail in the infant's mouth so that the infant will think it's at the breast. Jordan refers to this beast as "the vaginal serpent" and discusses the beliefs that these tales engender among women. It is theorized that these legends indicate a great fear and preoccupation with sex and childbirth and reflect fears of sexual assault and of unwanted pregnancy. The effect of narrating stories of *chirrioneras* to young women is that it frightens them and puts restraints on their behavior. Adults may narrate these tales to young women to discourage them from wandering off alone. Women are often warned about going near rivers or streams.

The root form of *chirrionera* has multiple meanings. In Cerda, Cabaza, and Farias's dictionary of Texan Spanish a *chirriona* refers to a jail or prison and in Mexico it can also mean *marimacho*, a slang word for "homosexual," or *coqueta*, "a flirtatious woman." A *chirrión* is also a whip, braided leather straps attached to a wooden handle, used by wagon drivers or teamsters. This kind of mythical snake is also called *el serpiente diablo* (devil serpent) or in Mexico a *cincuate*, a Nahuatl word for "snake." Legends about snakes near water such as streams and rivers are common in Mexican folklore and culture both in the United States and in Mexico. Along the Arizona-Sonora border a belief is frequently expressed in *la corua*, a very large snake that lives in springs of water. If it is killed the spring will dry up. James Griffith has an essay on the various folk beliefs about water serpents.

See also Chanes
References Cardozo-Freeman 1978; Cerda, Cabaza, and Farias 1953; Griffith 1990; Jordan 1985; Jordan de Caro 1973

Chistes (Jokes)

Humorous tales, *chistes colorados* (sexual jokes), and numskull jokes make up a large portion of the corpus of Chicano folklore. There are several published works of jokes in English and Spanish, collected in the 1950s, 1960s, and 1980s by Jose Reyna and Américo Paredes, mostly from along the Mexican-U.S. border. Chicanos have a propensity for teasing and poking fun at themselves when in alien situations, so a great number of jokes narrate encounters with an unknown language or with unfriendly and unreceptive Anglo Americans. Américo Paredes (1966) wrote about this latter phenomenon, calling it the Stupid American joke. In this type of joke the narrator makes fun of the ignorance of Americans when dealing with Mexican culture and social issues. Often a Chicano will take advantage of an Anglo American, making him the butt of the joke through a misunderstanding of language, or because of superior cultural intellect. Consequently a prominent type of joke narrated by Chicanos deals with misinterpretation of language, both English and Spanish. In addition, the joke collections of Paredes and Reyna contain many jokes about uneducated or unacculturated Mexican immigrants and the cultural mistakes they make upon entering the United States.

Much of Chicano humor is based on the ability to speak and play with two languages, often in midsentence, and to create comical results by making double entendres or incongruous statements. Spanish words are comically interpreted as English words, and English is self-consciously expressed as Spanish. For example, a car becomes a *caro* and a *tortilla* becomes a *tort*. Jokes and jocular expressions involving two languages are a distinct reflection of a bicultural experience. Pleasurable and cathartic sensations are experienced when one is able to make jokes about the anxieties of acquiring a new language and adapting to a new environment. The popularity of these jokes is that they provide a socially acceptable mechanism for releasing anxieties and tensions associated with living in the United States.

An important characteristic of jokes and wit is brevity. An idea expressed in a few words is intellectually more stimulating than the same idea expressed in a fifteen-minute monologue. When an audience laughs at a joke, they are laughing at the technique as well as the text communicated. Sigmund Freud describes the "joke-work" or "technique of the joke" as the formation and structure of the words that convey the message and conclude in producing the laughter. The joke-work of a bilingual joke is linguistically and culturally sophisticated and requires a bilingual and bicultural audience to comprehend and appreciate it. To aesthetically and intellectually understand a joke narrated in two languages means that it must be appreciated on several levels. First, the ingenuity of the use of two languages must be comprehended; second, the cultural values and symbols conveyed in the two languages must be understood; third, the underlying emotive message, anger or hostility, must be accepted; and fourth, the laughter enjoyed and the tension released in comprehending the total complexity must be shared by the group.

In folklore parlance, joking is often labeled expressive performance behavior, jocular behavior, verbal art, or just speech play. The opportunity for creative expression is readily available if a person speaks two languages and finds himself/herself in a situation where that expression is recognized as symbolically meaningful. Several folklorists have understood this aspect of Chicano verbal narratives, prompting one to state, "Much of the expressive culture of urban Mexican-Americans exhibits an evident delight in playing with language" (Jordan 1981, 255) Jose Limón interprets the experiences of Chicano students at the University of Texas during the late 1960s and the way their joking performances "constitute cultural symbolic action, the ultimate significance of which is the expressive rendition and enhancement of a critical ideological perspective on Anglo-Texas society" (Limón 1982, 155). According to Limón, the joking behavior of Chicano students, including the joke text and the joking ritual, contributed to the formation of a social ideology for these first-generation college students.

Very little has been written about *chistes colorados*, or the narration of sexual or "dirty" jokes in Chicano culture. An article from 1983 by Rafaela Castro examined jokes collected from Mexican women who amused themselves by sharing sexual jokes while they worked in a candy factory in California. As Limón mentions, this kind of behavior is a "Mexican working-class tradition left largely unexamined by (his) primary precursors" (1994, 129).

References Castro 1982; Freud 1960; Jordan 1981; Limón 1982, 1994; Paredes 1966, 1993a, 1993b; Reyna 1973, 1980b; Reyna and Herrera-Sobek 1998; Rosaldo 1989; Spielberg 1974

Cholos (-as) (1990s Urban Youth)

Young Chicano males between the ages of eleven or twelve and eighteen or nineteen who are distinguished by the clothes they wear, their speech, gestures, and a defiant street style. Although some may be gang members, some may be low riders (car club members), or just Chicanos influenced by the *cholo* lifestyle. Although the attire of *cholos* varies from *barrio* to *barrio*, many wear baggy khaki pants, white tee shirts, and plaid Pendleton shirts buttoned up to the neck. The khaki pants became popular in Chicano communities after World War II, as a way to identify with family members in the military. Bandanas, sometimes red, are worn around the head as headbands. *Cholos* may be members of gangs and involved in drug use, but not necessarily, since many young Chicanos have adopted the clothing style and behavior of the *cholos* without any gang affiliation. This distinct style of dressing, talking, and behaving has been known since at least the 1940s. Many believe the *cholo* subculture is directly descended from that of the *pachuco* and *pachuca* of the 1940s. Since *cholos* tend to hang out in the streets of urban cities, the subculture and way of life may sometimes involves cars and low riding.

Cholas, in many ways the counterpart to *cholos*, are Chicana girls with a similarly distinct dress style. Unlike *cholos*, *cholas* who adopt the street style usually are members of female gangs. Their long hair may be feathered, with generous use of hair spray, and they tend to wear heavy eye makeup and show visible tattoos, all signs of gang affiliation. Concentrated eyeliner, heavily applied, is considered a sign of power and toughness. A dark liquid foundation and brown lipstick are symbols of power, authority, and competence. The use of a specific application of makeup by *cholas* is an important distinction that sometimes signifies membership in a gang, but also portrays social confidence and gang leadership skills. Every outward physical feature of the *chola* girl appears to be heavily symbolic of a life that is neither Mexican nor American.

Historically, *cholo* has been a pejorative term applied to poor, lower-class, and/or indigenous Mexicans, and *mestizos* (people of mixed race). References to *cholos* are found in Herbert Bancroft's *History of California, 1841–1845*, Volume 4, and *History of California, 1846–1848*, Volume 5; he calls the lower-caste Mexican soldiers "*cholos*" and "thieves and pickpockets." *El Diccionario de Mejicanismos* gives *cholo* a Peruvian indigenous origin, and states that it likely began to be used as soon as the Spaniards mixed with the indigenous people of Peru in the sixteenth century. In present-day La Paz, Bolivia, a *cholo* is a *mestizo* with an improved education, or an Indian who has moved into the city and has a respectable job, such as a butcher or a driver. It appears that from early on, *cholo* has meant a person of mixed blood. After 1848, and the signing of the Treaty of Guadalupe, all working-class Mexicans or Mexican Americans were referred to as *cholos*.

See also Low Rider; Pachucos
References Cordova 1990; Fregoso 1995; Griswold del Castillo 1979; Harris 1994, 1988; Mendoza-Denton 1996, 1997; Moore 1991; Pacheco 1997; Vigil 1988, 1991

Christmas Gifts
See Aguinaldos

Christmas Pageant
See Las Posadas

Cinco de Mayo (Fifth of May)
The Battle of Puebla, when the Mexican troops of General Ignacio Zaragoza crushed invading French troops, occurred in Mexico on May 5, 1862. The French invasion forces were not actually defeated, but rather pushed back, and

Patriotic images of the Battle of Puebla and Cinco de Mayo *are depicted in this mural while young girls jump rope in front. (Philip Gould/Corbis)*

held back for one year. It was a great victory at the time, although France later did send more troops and actually occupied Mexico until 1867. On May 17, 1863, a heavily reinforced French army took Puebla and pushed on and seized Mexico City, and on April 10, 1964, Maximilian von Habsburg was placed on the throne as Emperor of Mexico. But three years later, in June of 1867, Maximilian was executed by a firing squad of Mexican forces loyal to Benito Juarez, and later that year his wife Carlotta returned to Europe with his body.

The triumph of *Cinco de Mayo* showed the world that Mexico could defend itself against foreign intervention. The victorious Battle of Puebla has become a symbol of determined resistance to foreign aggression in Mexico and also among Mexican Americans in the United States. Mexico had gained its independence from Spain in 1821, but lost Texas in 1836, and lost its northern territory to the United States in 1848. When France, with its great military power, invaded its shores, the future of the nation of Mexico appeared in great jeopardy. With the reestablishment of Mexico's independence in 1867, this time from France, the *Cinco de Mayo* battle became a testimonial manifesto of patriotism and pride in Mexican identity and nationhood. *Cinco de Mayo* has been celebrated in the United States since the late 1800s. Throughout the Southwest, celebrations included patriotic speeches from official dignitaries, the crowning of a queen, plenty of food, and such social activities as horse races and rooster games. A buried rooster, with its head sticking out of the sand, was grabbed by riders on horseback. The rider who managed to grab it would chase the other riders and hit them with the rooster, yelling "*Sacó el gallo*" (I pulled out the rooster).

Most recently, in the 1960s Chicano students started organizing celebrations on college campuses, and *Cinco de Mayo* has become a Chicano holiday. The Battle of Puebla symbolizes the triumph of the underdog, the overthrow of tyranny, and for Chicanos a reaffirmation of cultural nationalism. Although *El Diez y Seis de Septiembre* (the sixteenth of September) is Mexico's independence day and a very important holiday for Mexicans in the United States, *Cinco de Mayo* has become an important spring ritual celebration for urban Chicano youth. It is almost a national holiday in the United States, with parades, street fairs, folkloric dance performances, lowrider car shows, music festivals, *tareadas* (afternoon dances), and evening dances in all the major cities of the western United States.

See also Corrida de Gallos; El Diez y Seis de Septiembre; Fiestas Patrias
References Burciaga 1993; Cabello-Argandoña 1993; De Leon 1978; Devine 1964; Melville 1978; Monreal 1993; Muñoz 1991; Najera-Ramirez 1994; Nieto-Gomez 1979; Sommers 1985

Cleansing
See Limpia

Cliques
See Klicas

El Coco (Bogeyman)

Defined by Spanish dictionaries as "the bogeyman," *el coco* is sometimes also called "Coco-man." He is a scary character who comes and snatches naughty children who have misbehaved. *El coco* is historically related to the role played by *el abuelo* in northern New Mexico Christmas traditions, and in the dances of *Los Matachines*. During the Christmas season *el abuelo* came into homes to test children on their catechism and prayers. Parents allowed him to discipline the children because they did do what he asked. *El coco* and *el abuelo* are both used to discipline children. Eventually just uttering the word *coco* was enough to frighten children into obedience. Mothers controlled their children by threatening them with *el coco*. Many variants of the following nursery rhyme sung to children before bed have been collected in Spain and in New Mexico.

A la ruru, mi hijito,
Duérmase ya,
Que viene el coco
Y se lo comera!
(Lullaby, my little son,
Sleep now,
For the bogeyman might come,
To eat you up!)

Another variant is:

Señora Santa Ana, Señor San Joaquin
Arrula este Niño, Se quiere dormir
Duermete Niñito, Duermete nomas
Que hay viene el Coco, Y te comerá.
(Mistress Santa Ana,
Sir San Joaquin
Cradle this child,
That wants to sleep.
Sleep little child,
Sleep now
For here comes *el coco*,
And he will eat you up.)

Coco has other connotations as well. The word has a history of being used in reference to sores and scrapes. For example it is commonly used among Chicanos from Texas to California to describe an injury, such as a cut, sore, knee scrape, or any of the various wounds experienced by children. One would either have a *coco*, *un coquito*, or *un cocote*, depending on the size of the damage. A song from the Mexican Revolution, sung by Cuco Sanchez, mentions *los cocolazos*, meaning the huge hard knocks resulting from hard fighting. *Coco* can also mean "head," such as the brain or skull. An expression used by youth in the San Joaquin Valley during the 1950s was, "*a usted le patina el coco*," meaning "your brain spins" or "you don't know what you're talking about."

References Batchen 1972; Brown 1978; CHICLE 1994; Ebinger 1993; Espinosa 1985; Otero-Warren 1936; Steele 1992

Colchas (Blankets)

In common everyday Spanish a *colcha* is a quilt, a heavy blanket, or a bedspread. During the colonial period in New Mexico the *colcha* embroidery stitch was a type of embroidery for tablecloths and blankets. This embroidery stitch was one of the major handicrafts of that period, used for bedspreads, tablecloths, and altar cloths as well. The embroidery was done on a fabric called *sabanilla*, a homespun wool that was finely woven. Some of the colonial *colchas*

This design is from a colcha *(blanket or quilt).*
(North Wind Picture Archive)

resemble tapestries and have often been referred to as such. The *colcha* embroidery included not only a couching stitch, but also a style of design, an intricate floral design, employing wool-on-wool embroidery. It is a long stitch, laid close and parallel to the previous stitch, and anchored to the cloth by small tied stitches set regularly over the laid thread. While the long wool stitch is creating a design, the small anchoring stitches are also creating a textured visual design that on its own is aesthetically appealing.

Colchas were also made as bedcovers, or quilts, to cover old Rio Grande blankets, or old bedspreads. One of the main purposes of making *colchas* was to reuse pieces of fabric left from old clothing, coats, or older blankets. The cotton cloth from flour and sugar sacks was a good source, but often it was considered too good for this purpose and was instead used to make clothing, kitchen towels, and other useful items. Once these were pretty worn out, then flour-sack material might be used for *colcha* coverings. The covers were tacked or tied to a filling, which could be an old blanket. Sometimes the new cover would be removed and washed and then again retacked to the old filling.

The fabric used in nineteenth-century New Mexico, *sabanilla*, was a white handwoven weave of handspun wool. The embroidery thread was fine wool, dyed with local vegetable and plant dyes. There were two styles of *colcha*, those that were entirely covered with designs, almost solid like a tapestry, and those that had border designs with flower and animal schemes. *Colcha* designs have been found in northern New Mexico and southern Colorado. Although the origin of some of these designs is indigenous, there are also Oriental, Persian, and Moorish motifs brought by the Spaniards. It is thought that during the early sixteenth century the Spaniards traded with China and brought back to Spain embroidered silk shawls, whose designs are the basis of many *colcha* patterns. The geometric and zigzag motifs may be indigenous to the Indians of New Mexico, but the pomegranate, the rose, and the rose-leaf designs are Oriental in origin. Chinese shawls were very popular throughout the Spanish Empire, and the intricate designs were carried into other Spanish textiles. Today the *colcha* stitch, executed with wool yarn, is used to decorate frames, crucifixes, and other religious and household folk arts.

References Fisher 1994; MacAulay 1992; Mather 1992; Museum of International Folk Art 1979; Ortiz y Pino de Dinkel 1988; Spanish Colonial Arts Society 1996; Worth 1985; Zopf 1994

Colorado Folklore

Published research on the Hispano and Chicano folklore of the state of Colorado focuses primarily on that from the San Luis Valley, located in the southern part of the state. This area is geographically an extension of New Mexico and is surrounded by high mountain ranges, which enclose the territory and separate it from other parts of Colorado. The Spaniards and *Mexicanos* who settled the region came from Taos and Arroyo Hondo in northern New Mexico after the U.S. Mexican War of 1848. The governor of New Mexico made land grants to encourage settlement in 1821–1846, while the region was still Mexican, but most of the settlements occurred after 1848. Hispano culture and folklore remained unchanged in this region for decades, as they did for several hundred years in northern New Mexico.

Religious holidays associated with *La Virgen de Guadalupe*, *Las Posadas* (Christmas Pageant), *Los Pastores* (Shepherds' Play), *Los Reyes Magos* (The Three Kings), and *Semana Santa* (Holy Week), along with the many various saint's days, were common celebrations in Colorado. *Moradas* (chapels) of *Los Penitentes* (Penitents) were also active, and along with local *santeros* (saint makers), they kept alive the tradition of religious folk art, as in New Mexico. Family traditions and cultural rituals, such as weddings, dances, folktales, music, and games, were similar to those of New Mexico. Olibama López Tushar has written a history of the San Luis Valley and records the games, rituals, customs, and traditions of the region. She writes in detail of the wedding customs and the leisure activities and provides appendices of proverbs and riddles, as well as of historical personages.

Jose de Onís has compiled a historical anthology of the Hispanic contribution to the state of Colorado. This collection includes two articles by Arthur Campa on the folklore traditions of Colorado. He discusses folk dramas, folk songs, religious celebrations, and various folk narratives. Also included in the collection are an article on *alabados* (traditional hymns) and an essay by Anthony Lozano on the Spanish language of the San Luis Valley.

Aurelio Macedonio Espinosa, Arthur Campa, and Juan Rael collected folklore from this region as they did in New Mexico. In 1980 Jose Reyna collected folklore traditions on the *Fiesta del Día de San Juan* in Center, Colorado, and found that the folktales collected were still akin to those collected by Rael and Campa in the 1930s.

See also Espinosa, Aurelio Macedonio; New Mexico Folklore; *Los Pastores*; Los Penitentes; Las Posadas; La Virgen de Guadalupe
References Campa 1979; de Onís 1976; Echevarria and Otero 1976; Espinosa 1911; Rael and Martinez 1957; Ramos 1950; Reyna 1980a; Stoller 1977; Tushar 1992; Wallrich 1950, 1951

Comadre/Compadre

The system of *compadrazgo* exists within Mexican and Chicano culture when two adults become coparents to a child, to another adult, or to a couple. The usual way two adults become *compadres* is when one is chosen to be the god-parent of the other's child and assists in the baptism or confirmation of that child. The godfather is called a *padrino,* and the godmother a *madrina.* The parents of the child then become *compadres* to the godparents. Another way that two adults become *compadres* is that when two people marry, the parents of the bride become *compadres* to the parents of the groom, since they've all become coparents to the married couple. The best man and maid of honor at a wedding also become *compadres* to the married couple. Godparents are usu-ally chosen from close friends or relatives, and the system of *compadrazgo* re-inforces the closeness of the friendship or the family.

The baptism of a child is usually the most important means of becoming a *compadre/comadre*. It is a spiritual and ceremonial relationship between the child, the parents, and the godparents. The origins of this system go back to medieval Europe and feudal times, when establishing large extended fami-lies was important for social and economic survival. Godparents of a higher economic class ensured material security for the godchild. *Compadres* are considered family, and usually marriage between them is forbidden. The *com-padrazgo* system is an informal, nonlegal system that reinforces neighborhood solidarity and security. If a *compadre* does not live up to his responsibilities, nothing can be done legally, but the person is subject to public scorn from his peers. The *padrinos* are expected to care for the godchild just as the par-ents do, and if the godchild's parents die, the *padrinos* are expected to assume responsibility for the child. The bond between *compadres* is very important, almost sacred, and lasts a lifetime. A godchild shows the same respect to the godparents as he/she would to his/her own parents. The system of *com-padrazgo* creates a larger extended family and helps maintain a respectful society.

Studies of early New World societies indicate that the system was more prevalent in lower economic societies, Indian and *mestizo,* than in the upper classes, primarily because of its mutual aid and extended familial aspects. In the upper classes, in twentieth-century Mexico and Spain, family members were frequently asked to be the *compadres,* thus intensifying the family rela-tionships, but not extending much beyond the immediate family.

At one time the system of *compadrazgo* was very important in Mexican families, and *compadres* and *comadres* became strong friends and helped each other in emergencies and crises. A request from a *compadre* could not be re-fused. Because of the history of strong friendships among *compadres* and *co-madres* there exist scores of jokes and humorous stories about the escapades of *compadres* and *comadres.* Aurelio Espinosa published various folktales about these escapades in his collection *Cuentos Populares Españoles, Recogidos de la Tradición Oral de España.* Jose Reyna collected jokes and anecdotes from Texas for his dissertation, and many deal with *compadres* taking certain liberties with their *comadres,* always with the excuse of misunderstanding directions or information. Américo Paredes states that "*compadrazgo* is a relationship highly charged with tension and suppressed conflict, around which all kinds of jokes, dirty songs, and comic sayings have developed—as one would expect in relationships demanding some degree of ritual avoidance or respect" (1993a, 95–96).

Through the years, the word has become condensed to *compa*, and because *compadrazgo* is still so common in Latino culture, there are consequently many *compas* in every family. The expression is often familiarly used in place of Mac, or Bud, such as "*Oiga compa, muévase*" (Hey Mac, move over).

References Brown 1978; Clark 1959; Espinosa 1923; Foster 1953; Mintz and Wolf 1950; Paredes 1993a; Reyna 1973; Rubel 1966

Los Comanches (The Comanches)

Los Comanches is a heroic folk drama from northern New Mexico performed in the open air and in broad daylight. The drama is based on a battle that occurred in 1774 between the Spanish soldiers and Cuerno Verde, an Indian chief, and his tribe of Comanches. The drama recounts the history of the constant struggles to maintain their independence and resist colonization exhibited by the nomad Apaches and Comanches. The Comanches, coming from Wyoming and Colorado, were first seen in the Taos area of New Mexico around 1705. They were forced southward into New Mexico in search of new hunting areas because of European westward expansion into their territory. In New Mexico they raided Spanish villages and Pueblo settlements, stealing horses and food and kidnapping women and children. There were two memorable battles in New Mexico, in 1774, and in 1779 when Cuerno Verde was eventually defeated. It is believed the drama of *Los Comanches* is based on the battle of 1774 when Cuerno Verde and his people were defeated but he escaped. He was later killed by troops led by Don Juan Bautista de Anza in 1779. The drama of *Los Comanches* can be dated to about 1780.

A second drama by the same title exists, but it is a religious dance that is performed during the Christmas season. It includes the recitation of verses and a great deal of indigenous dancing. In this drama, a group of Comanches attack a small village that is preparing a nativity play and take the Christ child as a hostage. The *Mexicano* people chase after the Comanches and when they catch them, they tell them the story of Jesus Christ, whereupon the Indian chief returns the Christ child, accompanied with various blankets and other gifts. The Spanish friars taught this drama to the indigenous population of New Mexico while converting them to Christianity. For over a century Comanche raids were feared in New Mexico, and their importance is clearly imprinted in these New Mexican folk drama traditions.

References Anderson 1989; Campa 1942; Espinosa ed. 1907; Espinosa, G. 1972; Hurt 1966; Lamadrid 1993; Rivera 1989

Con Safos (Don't Mess with This)

A phrase and a symbol with a long historical tradition that loosely means "whatever touches this returns to you," "the same to you," or more contemporarily, "don't mess with this." Graffiti artists started a tradition of signing off on their work with the symbol "c/s," meaning "this cannot be defaced." Leaving the code "c/s" or "C. S." after a name written on a wall or at the end of an insult or slogan works to reverse its meaning if another party defaces it. In parts of southern California, *con safos* signifies both a hex and a promise of a fight if someone destroys or marks wall writing that was signed with the "c/s" symbol.

It is believed *con safos* is related to the Spanish verb *safar* or *safó*, which means "to slip" or "slipped." Another related word is *safado*, meaning "shameless." Yet *con safos* might also be affiliated with the word *zafar*, a difficult word to translate, which can mean "to loosen" or "to clear." In the 1940s and 1950s there was a custom among Chicano kids playing marbles to yell out "*safis!*" if the marble slipped out of their fingers before it was shot out. By yelling "*safis!*" the marble shooter would get another turn. If he didn't yell the word in time, before another kid grabbed the marbles, he lost his turn.

Con safos is used primarily with names placed on graffiti or as a signing off after a signature. Personal names are very important in Chicano culture, and in fact many Chicanos have nicknames that they bear with pride. Placing a "c/s" after one's name, especially after the name has been elaborately stylized on a wall, is meant to protect that name, and by extension protect a part of that person also. The tradition of signing *con safos* on graffiti has been extended to using the symbol on short essays, letters, and most recently on the Internet. News groups and listserv participants frequently sign off their electronic contribution with the "c/s" symbol.

In the late 1960s a Chicano magazine with the name of *Con Safos: Reflections of Life in the Barrio* was published for several years. In East Los Angeles a rock-soul band of the 1980s was called *Con Safos*, and some Chicanos have even named their sons *Con Safos*.

See also Barrio
References Burciaga 1993; Grider 1975; Rodriguez 1995

Conjunto Music

Sometimes referred to as a *Conjunto Norteño*, a *conjunto* is a group of musicians, a music group, or a small band. *Conjunto* music is a distinct musical form that originated along the Texas-U.S. border and is often identified as *Tejano* music, although it is also popular in northern Mexico. It is also called *Musica Norteña*, and the dominant musical instrument is the accordion. The band is made up of an accordion, a twelve-string guitar called a *bajo sexto*, and a bass.

It is not clear how the accordion came to be introduced into Texas. Manuel Peña, the scholar who has written the most on *conjunto* music, men-

A conjunto *group, Roberto Palido* y *Los Classicos, play music also called* Musica Norteña, *a distinct style that originated along the Texas-Mexico border. (Philip Gould/Corbis)*

tions two theories. One is that the Europeans who settled around San Antonio introduced the instrument to Texas Mexicans. The second idea is that it came from Mexico, specifically Monterrey, where German immigrants settled in the 1860s. Neither idea has been proven, but it is known that by the 1890s the accordion was very popular among the rural poor people along both sides of the border. It was adopted by the folk along with the polka dance, and it has evolved into what is generally referred to as *musica ranchera*, which encompasses *conjunto* music.

Conjunto has been a popular musical style since the turn of the century and continues to be accepted by Chicanos and *Mexicanos* alike. Associated primarily with the working class, *conjunto* music has moved into other parts of the United States and is enjoyed by non-Chicanos as well.

Narciso Martinez is considered the father of *conjunto* music. He was born in Tamaulipas, Mexico, but was raised in Texas. By 1927 he was a professional accordion player and in 1935 recorded his first polka, "La Chicharronera," in San Antonio, Texas. It was so successful that the date of its recording is used as the definitive date of the emergence of *conjunto* music. Martinez became the most popular musician of the 1930s and 1940s, touring throughout the Midwest and Southwest. Another famous accordionist from this same period was Santiago Jimenez, whose primary job was working as a school janitor, but who also became a professional musician and recorded his first songs in 1936. His son later became one of the most popular folk musicians of the 1980s and 1990s.

Since its inception *conjunto* music has represented the music of the working class, whereas *musica orquesta Tejana*, a big band sound, was considered to be the preferred music of the rising Mexican American middle class that evolved after World War II. When dance ballrooms became commercialized during World War II, the *conjunto* music became even more popular, and the many bands that toured the Southwest played at these establishments. Narciso Martinez, Tony de la Rosa, and *El Conjunto Bernal*, another popular group, played all over the country. The musical form and the groups that played it became popular through Spanish-language radio stations located throughout the Southwest and wherever Chicanos worked and lived. By the mid-1950s *conjunto* music was a popular form identified as great Chicano dancing music. One could perform various dances to it, such as the polka, the *huapango*, the *vals bajito*, and the schottische.

Flaco Jimenez, who was born in San Antonio, Texas, in 1939, is one of today's most well-known accordionists, singers, and songwriters. He learned to play the accordion from his father, Santiago Jimenez Sr., and started playing in the early 1950s with a group called *Los Tecolotes*. He won a Grammy Award in 1986 for his album *Ay Te Dejo en San Antonio* (I Leave You in San Antonio). Flaco Jimenez and his band travel and perform on college campuses and at urban theaters throughout the country, and he has often performed with country and western singers and musicians. This type of association has given *conjunto* music a folk and country music identification. *Conjuntos* generally play music of Texan and northern Mexican origin, with themes of love, tragic love affairs, undocumented workers, contraband, and illegal border crossings.

In Texas one can find hundreds of *conjuntos* ready to perform for any function. Since 1982 a *Tejano Conjunto* festival has been held every May, organized by the Guadalupe Cultural Arts Center in San Antonio. The festival includes a *Tejano Conjunto* festival poster competition and recitals by accordion students. A popular film, *Chulas Fronteras* (Beautiful Borders), presents several of the well-known musical groups and musicians from Texas. Other famous *conjunto* bands are: *Los Relámpagos del Norte* (Lightning of the North), *Los Tigres del Norte* (Tigers of the North), and *Los Cadetes de Linares* (The Cadets from the Flax Field).

See also Ranchera

References Arnold 1928; Chabran and Chabran 1996; Graham 1990; *New Handbook of Texas* 1996; Parsons 1990; Peña 1981, 1985a, 1985b; Riedel 1982; Villarino 1992

La Conquistadora (The Conqueress)

The guardian and patron saint of Santa Fe, New Mexico, also known as Our Lady of the Conquest, The Conqueress, *Nuestra Señora del Rosario*, and Our

Lady of Victory. The legend of *Nuestra Señora La Conquistadora* tells of Don Diego de Vargas, who attributed his successful reconquest of New Mexico in 1692 to a statue of the Virgin Mary that he carried with him. De Vargas commemorated his victory with a religious celebration and the construction of a chapel. *La Conquistadora* Chapel was built in Santa Fe in 1717, but De Vargas did not live to see it.

La Conquistadora was crowned by Francis Cardinal Spellman in 1954 and by an apostolic delegate of Pope John XXIII in 1960. It is a statue, twenty-eight inches high, made in the seventeenth century, which possesses a regal air, and which is seen as a symbol of the bloodless reconquest. A thorough study by Fray Angélico Chávez, however, shows that the statue of the Virgin Mary was brought to New Spain by a Fray Benavides in 1625, and was named *La Conquistadora* because it was brought by the Spanish conquerors. During the Pueblo Revolt of 1680 the statue, at this time called *Nuestra Señora del Rosario* because of the founding of a Rosary Confraternity, was rescued and taken to San Lorenzo, Mexico, where it stayed for thirteen years. In the reconquests of 1692 and 1693 De Vargas brought the same statue back to Santa Fe, calling it *La Conquistadora* and placing it again in the "Hermitage of Our Lady," in the tower chapel.

References Boyd 1974; Chávez 1948, 1983, 1985; Grimes 1976; Hallenbeck and Williams 1971; Otero-Warren 1937

Corrida de Gallos (Rooster Game)

A popular sport from the mid- to late nineteenth century in Mexico and the Southwest. Because of its violence it was gradually discontinued, but the sport was played well into the twentieth century. It was a game played on religious and secular holidays, such as *Día de San Juan* on June 24, *Día de Santiago* on July 25, and on *Cinco de Mayo*. Literally, *corrida de gallos* means "running of the roosters," and the games are also known as rooster races, but in actuality the rooster did not run at all. The game entailed burying a rooster in the sand so that only its head was aboveground. Young men on horseback took turns racing toward the rooster, attempting to pull it out of the ground while still on horseback. Sometimes there were two teams and two riders attempted to snatch the bird at the same time. Whoever succeeded in grasping the rooster would race away with the others in pursuit trying to grab the rooster from him. The rider with the rooster would use it to fend off his pursuers. It was obviously a particularly brutal sport. With everyone grabbing at the poor rooster eventually there was not much left of the animal, at which point a new rooster was produced and another round was started. The *corridas de gallos* were meant to test the skill and dexterity of the riders and to show off their bravery. Both in New Mexico and Colorado mention is made that women also played this sport, and Aurora Lucero-White states that they were known as *Las Galleras*.

The tradition of this sport began in the Castile region of Spain, which celebrated a *fiesta del gallo* on February 2 for Candlemas. Aurelio Espinosa believes *corridas de gallos* are related to the Roman Lupercalia tradition brought to Spain in the ninth century.

See also Cinco de Mayo
References Espinosa 1985; Lucero-White 1947; Tushar 1992

"El Corrido de Gregorio Cortez" (Ballad of Gregorio Cortez)

The title of a *corrido* (ballad) sung along the Texas-Mexican border during the early twentieth century, and the subject of the book *With His Pistol in His Hand: A Border Ballad and Its Hero* by the late Chicano folklorist and scholar Américo Paredes. A film based on this book was released in 1982, with Edward James Olmos acting the part of Gregorio Cortez. The *corrido* is based on a real-life incident that included the killing of a sheriff by a *Mexicano*, a long chase by a posse of Texas Rangers, and the capture and conviction of a folk hero.

Gregorio Cortez was born in 1875 on a ranch near the Rio Grande in Mexico, but his family moved to Texas in 1887. Cortez and his brother Romaldo settled in Karnes County, where they rented land to farm for themselves in 1900. The *corrido* opens with the following stanzas:

> In the county of El Carmen
> A great misfortune befell;
> The Major Sheriff is dead;
> Who killed him no one can tell.
> At two in the afternoon
> In half an hour or less,
> They knew that the man who killed him
> Had been Gregorio Cortez.

It was in 1901 that Gregorio Cortez was accused by Sheriff Morris of stealing a horse. The deputy who accompanied Morris to the Cortez farm also served as translator, since the Cortez brothers spoke only Spanish. Cortez was asked if he'd traded a horse, *un caballo*, and Cortez answered no, because he had traded a mare, *una yegua*, not a horse. Based on this exchange Cortez was presumed guilty, and during the confrontation that followed the sheriff pulled his pistol and shot Romaldo, Cortez's brother, which caused Gregorio to react and shoot the sheriff. What followed is well described in the *corrido*, as a posse chased Cortez for ten days, while he rode 400 miles and walked 120. Receiving help from other *Mexicanos* along the way, he fought in other scrimmages and another sheriff was killed. Believing that he would be lynched if caught, Cortez was making his way toward the Mexican border. After learning that his wife and children were imprisoned he turned himself in to the sheriff in Laredo. He was tried and convicted, and sentenced to life in prison, although he was pardoned by an Anglo Texas governor in 1913 after nine and a half years in prison.

Many legends and *corridos* circulated about the heroic exploits of Cortez. As a skilled horseman, he had been able to evade the famous Texas Rangers for days, and his escapade symbolized the resistance to Anglo cultural and political domination by all *Tejanos* (Mexican Texans). The essence of the *corrido* is expressed in these other famous lines from the corrido:

> *Decía Gregorio Cortés*
> *con su pistola en la mano*
> *—No corran, rinches cobardes,*
> *ante un sólo Mexicano!*
> *Decía Gregorio Cortés*
> *—Los gringos no me llevan vivo*
> *porque en Tejas no hay justicia*
> *para un pobre Mexicano.*
> (Gregorio Cortez said,
> With his pistol in his hand,
> "Don't run, cowardly rangers,
> Before just one Mexican."
> Gregorio Cortez said,
> "The *gringos* won't take me alive
> Because in Texas there's no justice
> For a poor Mexican."

See also Corridos; Paredes, Américo; *With His Pistol in His Hand*
References Keller 1985; Limón 1986, 1990, 1992; Paredes 1958

Corridos (Ballads)

A *corrido* is a ballad, a poem that tells a story. It is the New Spain version of an earlier Spanish narrative form known as the *romance*, but one can say that basically the *corrido* is a narrative folk song. The word comes from the verb *correr*, which means "to run," and a *corrido* is an ongoing, or running, account of a story, recited in plain verse. *Corridos* chronicle events, some important, some mundane: love affairs, gun battles, catastrophes, and especially the exploits of male heroes. The *corrido* form consists of a formulaic structure with an *abcb* rhyme scheme and can have any number of stanzas, from four to twenty-four. One Mexican *corrido* about the death of Pancho Villa has forty-eight stanzas. The first stanza usually sets the scene, giving a date, the name of the hero or the event to be narrated, and in the closing stanza the narrator bids farewell, referred to as *la despedida* by the narrator. In between, the story is dramatically narrated. Customarily there is a moral to the story, and the *corrido* acts to instruct its hearers in the social mores of the times. All authorities on the *corrido* agree that the historically crucial element of the *corrido* is that it tells a story. It is a ballad that presents an event from its own time, a narration that is used to exalt the adventures of the masses, the proletariat, the common folk. The stories recited in *corridos* tend to be of the adventures of men—battles, wars, fights over women, heroic deaths—and it is their world that we learn about. Men compose the ballads and sing them, both for themselves and for other men, so the *corrido* is primarily the cultural property of men.

Both in Mexico and in the United States the *corrido* has been viewed as a popular folkloric system that can be analyzed and can assist in understanding a people's assessment of particular events in their lives. Merle Edwin Simmons, in discussing the Mexican *corrido*, states that as an artistic expression the *corrido* accurately reflects public values and the people's interpretation of their own history. The most noted research on the *corrido* in the United States was conducted by the late Américo Paredes of the University of Texas. In his classic study of the heroic *corrido*, *With His Pistol in His Hand*, he analyzes "El Corrido de Gregorio Cortez," the legend of Gregorio Cortez as told in the *corrido* and elsewhere, and the development of the *corrido* along the Texas-Mexican border.

The roots of the *corrido* form lie in the Spanish *romance*, of which hundreds have been collected in New Mexico and other parts of the Southwest. The *romance* was the basic ballad tradition in Mexico until the time of its independence from Spain. Simmons gives the dates for the early development of the Mexican *corrido* from 1820 to 1870. Paredes shows that the *corrido* was also developing during this same period in south Texas. He locates the peak of *corrido* production from 1890 to 1910, which was a period of great social strife along the Texas-Mexican border. There were many clashes with the Texas Rangers, and some *Tejanos*, such as Juan Cortina and Catarino Garza, fought fiercely for social justice. Paredes's thesis is that precisely the cultural conflicts of this period were the primary influence in the development of the border *corrido*. In Mexico the peak development of the *corrido* came later, from 1910 to 1930, during the period of the Revolution.

Because *corridos* so eloquently narrate exploits of valiant and fearless men, the genre attracts many writers, who use it to write about contemporary leaders and folk heroes. After the death of an important or influential personality, *corridos* by the dozens instantly crop up. Some are recorded and heard on the radio, others are circulated by performances at parties and dances, and others are printed in periodicals and broadsides. Dan William Dickey has written of the *corridos* composed after the death of John F. Kennedy and how they reflect the respect and admiration Mexican Americans felt for him. He also shows their connection to the epic-heroic *corridos* of the late nineteenth century. César Chávez, the leader of the United Farm Workers, is another folk hero celebrated in many *corridos*, some written before his death in 1993 and many more written afterwards.

Hundreds of *corridos* have been collected in New Mexico, Texas, and Mexico, and a few in other parts of the southwestern United States. Arthur

Campa published *corridos* collected in New Mexico, dating from 1832 to 1946. One well-known *corrido*, "El Corrido de Kiansis," dates from the 1860s and describes a cattle drive from South Texas to Kansas. "El Corrido de la Pulga," originally from Mexico, is also found in New Mexico and dates back to 1821.

In considering the whole corpus of *corridos*, there are only a few historical ones that narrate the adventures of women. "Rosita Alvarez" is a well-known one, but it is famous primarily because of her death. "La Adelita" and "La Valentina" are two *corridos* frequently cited that proclaim the heroic exploits of *las soldaderas*, the women soldiers of the Mexican Revolution. But the most prevalent female characters found in *corridos* are the marginal ones of *la madre ausente*, the sorrowful absent mother, and *la mala mujer*, the evil woman.

Corridos that narrate the exploits of the heroes of the Mexican-Texas border show that there existed a form of folk resistance against a foreign culture that was taking over the way of life of the region. The "ballad of resistance" that epitomizes this genre is "El Corrido de Gregorio Cortez," as Américo Paredes has shown in his book. The *corrido* tradition is an important cultural symbol to Chicanos, and it is continuously being reinvented and taken into different modern performance forms. For example *El Teatro Campesino* has dramatized many *corridos* with great success and performed them onstage and on television stations such as PBS. "El Corrido de Gregorio Cortez" was made into a film of the same title, with Edward James Olmos playing the part of Cortez.

Maria Herrera-Sobek (1979) has studied the history of the Mexican immigrant in the United States through the *corridos* composed about the lives and tribulations of farmworkers and *braceros*. In a 1998 article Herrera-Sobek shows how *corrido* music has been used to foreshadow events in Mexican immigration films. Interest in the *corrido* continues today, even though some believe the true heroic *corrido* is no longer being composed. The Spring 1997 issue of *Aztlán: A Journal of Chicano Studies* (volume 22, no. 1), published at the University of California, Los Angeles, is entirely devoted to contemporary research on the *corrido*.

See also La Adelita; Campa, Arthur Leon; Chávez, César Estrada; "El Corrido de Gregorio Cortez"; Paredes, Américo; *With His Pistol in His Hand*

References Arteaga 1985; Boatright 1946; Campa 1933, 1976; Campos 1929; Dickey 1978; Espinosa 1985; Foster 1939; Guevara 1985; Hernandez 1978; Herrera-Sobek 1979, 1990, 1993b, 1998; Kanellos 1987; Lea 1953; Limón 1990, 1992; Lucero-White 1941; Robb 1954; Simmons 1969; Tinker 1961

Cortez, Gregorio
See "El Corrido de Gregorio Cortez"

Cowboys
See Vaqueros

Coyote

A coyote is a canine animal indigenous to the New World that is related to the fox or wolf. In some dictionaries it is sometimes translated as prairie wolf. Early Spanish writings describe it as a large dog with a beautiful coat and a bushy long tail. The word coyote comes from the Nahuatl word *coyotl*, or in Spanish *agujerar*, meaning "to make a hole or a dugout," which may refer to the coyote's swiftness and ability to hide in the bush. In folklore this animal figure symbolizes many cultural dimensions and deviations. In Native American folklore the coyote is the trickster figure, the one who outsmarts everyone else. He is found in the oral traditions of the tribes of the coastal Northwest, the West, and the Southwest plains. In colonial New Mexico a person of Spanish and New Mexican Indian ancestry was called a coyote. In this context the coyote was a dark-skinned *mestizo*, a person of mixed race and an outsider. On the other hand, the youngest child in a family is also sometimes affectionately called the coyote.

As a trickster figure the coyote is a cultural hero because he always manages to outwit authority figures, yet he's also portrayed as a loser, thief, cheat, outlaw, and survivor. He is a powerful figure, paradoxically both human and animal, who works both within and outside of the structures of society. He is usually male, although in Mexico a woman who tempts and entices men is known as a *coyota*.

Since at least the 1920s a person who smuggles people across the U.S.-Mexican border into the United States has been called a coyote, and the people being smuggled have been called *pollos*, or "chicks." A love-hate relationship exists between coyotes and illegal immigrants, since it can't be denied that coyotes perform a function that is in high demand, yet they also profit tremendously from poor people's dreams and ambitions. Labor contractors, also known as *enganchistas*, have been called coyotes because they recruit laborers, from both sides of the Mexican-U.S. border, to work in the United States. The word comes from *enganchar*, meaning "to hook," or in this case, to enlist a person for a job. Usually the *enganchista* earns a fee for each laborer recruited, or he may receive a percentage of each worker's wages. Coyotes and their role in arranging illegal crossings into the U.S. are often the subject of *corridos* (ballads), *cuentos* (stories), and other oral folk narratives.

References Bright 1993; Cerda 1953; Herrera-Sobek 1991, 1993b; Meléndez 1982, 1987; Vasquez 1975

The Crazy Life

See La Vida Loca

Creencias (Beliefs)

Folk beliefs that can be traced to religious doctrine or are inspired by a hostile physical environment. *Creencias* often dictate behavior and oral expressions, and they reflect a worldview that is based on spiritual and religious ideas. Having certain folk beliefs could mean believing in witchcraft, superstitions, and folk illnesses that rely on folk remedies for curing. Some beliefs exist as folk knowledge integrated into the behavior of an individual and will be reflected in the way that individual lives his/her life. A familiar expression used in Chicano families, as a way of defending something difficult to explain, is "*Son creencias de la gente*" (they're beliefs of the people). Folk beliefs are found among all peoples, rural and urban, although they're traditionally associated with uneducated and peasant cultures. Folk beliefs reflect a world view based not only on religious training but also on ethnic culture, family culture, and the depth of ethnic and self-identity one has within the culture.

The meaningful passages in the cycle of life, such as birth, marriage, and death, produce cultural and social anxiety, and most peoples not only create rituals and magical ceremonies to help ease these transitions but also hold many folk beliefs concerning these rites of passage. Birth is a traumatic experience for the first-time mother, and an infant child is a miracle to behold. Ceremonies welcoming the newborn include religious rituals such as baptism and selecting godparents. The trauma of pregnancy and childbirth is often looked upon as an illness and when a woman gives birth, in some families, she is described as having recovered. "*Ya se alivió*" (she has gotten well, recovered) is the expression often used. If a woman dies in childhood it is believed that she will automatically go to heaven regardless of whatever sinful transgressions she may have committed in her life. In the same way, many traditions besides the ceremony itself are associated with marriage—traditions that involve extended families, religious observances, the Catholic Church, and *padrinos* (godparents). The parents of the bride and groom become *comadres* and *compadres* and their relationship is believed to be as strong as that of the young married couple. To not be married in the Catholic Church is considered blasphemous, and a couple that only has a civil ceremony is considered to be living in sin. Marriage is considered inevitable, and when one dreams of death it means there will soon be a wedding in the family. Death, *la muerte*, is almost a family member in *Mexicano* and Chicano culture, with countless tales, jokes, and religious interpretations connected to it. *La muerte* is always waiting around the corner and one must be vigilant and prepared for an unexpected visit. Underlying the folklore of *la muerte* are folk beliefs that reflect the anxieties of death and dying.

The extent to which one believes and accepts the folklore of one's cultural group, such as the legends, *cuentos* (stories) of the supernatural, and religious practices, will vary according to an individual's sense of identity with the ethnic group and the religion. Not all Chicanos, especially not all formally educated ones, continue to believe in treasure tales, *susto* (shock), *La Llorona* (The Weeping Woman), or family *remedios* (remedies). But the loyalty that Chicanos feel toward their ethnic group and family may allow them to participate in the folklore and folk customs and accommodate the folk beliefs while adapting them to fit contemporary times and situations. Treasure tales might have originated in the nineteenth century but stories of grandparents burying money in the backyard are still believed; an awareness of the symptoms of the illness *susto* can often bring an understanding to the modern-day malaise of depression; and many contemporary home remedies have their basis in the traditions of mothers, grandparents, and great-grandparents. Folklore and folk beliefs are not static but continually change and adapt as the community changes and adapts to new circumstances.

References Dundes 1975; Espinoza 1985; Glazer 1994; Jordan 1975b

"La Cucaracha" (The Cockroach)

The title of a song popular during the Mexican Revolution that is also associated with *Mexicano* communities in the United States. It translates as "the cockroach," but in slang terms it has meant "dried-up old maid." There are various legends concerning the meaning of the song. One is that *La Cucaracha* was the name of the car Francisco "Pancho" Villa drove during the Mexican Revolution and that the song was written about the car. Another legend is that it was the nickname of Venustiano Carranza, who was president of Mexico right after the Revolution from 1917 to 1920. Apparently the song originated in Spain; some sources date it from the sixteenth century while others put it in the nineteenth century. It was sung in Mexico during the French Intervention, when the French were overcome by the Mexican army in the 1860s.

Anita Brenner refers to "La Cucaracha" as a "jiggling nonsense ballad" (181) that was sung during times of tension and stress in the Mexican Revolution. The *soldaderas*, women soldiers who followed the Mexican army troops during the Revolution, were sometimes called *cucarachas*. The image of these women was that they gave love freely and wanted money for alcohol and marijuana. A film with the title *La Cucaracha* was made in Mexico in 1958 with the beautiful and famous actress Maria Felix. She plays the character of *la cucaracha*, a crude woman who "likes men, wine and fighting," vices attributed to some *soldaderas* (Salas 99). Other famous actors in the film included Antonio Aguilar, Dolores del Rio, and Pedro Armendriz.

The notion of referring to the Mexican and Chicano people as cockroaches was propagated in the 1970s by the late Oscar Zeta Acosta with his book *The Revolt of the Cockroach People*, which described the high school walkouts and a boycott by Chicano students in East Los Angeles in 1968.

There are many variants of the song and stanzas can be created at will, but the main refrain is well known and repeated often. It is an easy stanza to learn, while the others are often silly, nonsensical verses. One can image a marching army singing the song for hours, as a way to quickly pass the time. Following are some stanzas:

> *La cucaracha, la cucaracha*
> *ya no quiere caminar,*
> *porque le falta, porque le falta*
> *marihuana que fumar.*
> *Qué bonitas soldaderas,*
> *cuando bailan el fandango,*
> *Viva Pánfilo Natera*
> *el orgullo de Durango*
> *La cucaracha la cucaracha, ya no quiere caminar . . .*
> *Para sarapes, Saltillo*
> *Chihuahua para soldados,*
> *para mujeres, Jalisco,*
> *para amar, toditos lados*
> *La cucaracha la cucaracha, ya no quiere caminar . . .*
> *Un panadero fue a misa,*
> *no encontrando que rezar,*
> *le pidió a la Virgen*
> *pura marihuana que fumar.*
> *La cucaracha la cucaracha, ya no quiere caminar.*
> (The cockroach, the cockroach
> Does not want to travel.
> because it's missing, because it's lacking
> marijuana to smoke.
> How pretty are women soldiers
> when they dance the *fandango*
> Long live Panfilo Natera
> the pride of Durango.
> The cockroach, the cockroach does not want to travel . . .
> For *sarapes*, it is Saltillo
> Chihuahua is for soldiers
> For women it's Jalisco
> For love, it's found everywhere
> The cockroach, the cockroach does not want to travel . . .
> A baker went to Mass
> Not finding what to pray for
> He asked the Virgin [Mary]
> For marijuana to smoke.
> The cockroach, the cockroach does not want to travel.)

References Brenner 1970; Salas 1990; Sandburg 1955; Valdez and Steiner 1972

El Cucui (Bogeyman)

A scary figure invoked by Chicano mothers of the Southwest to keep their children obedient. His appearance is still used as a threat; if one didn't behave, or do what one was told, "*Hay viene el cucui!*" (Here comes the bogeyman!) was the warning proclaimed, for example, to frighten the child who wouldn't go to bed. *El coco* and *el cucui* are scary villains whose sole purpose for existing is to snatch little children who misbehave. A mother's greatest fear is to have her sons or daughters out late at night, in the unknown, regardless of whether the environment is urban or rural. In Chicano culture, fear of violence after dark is always prevalent. It may be fear of demons, or fear of the weeping woman *La Llorona*, or *el diablo* who is out enticing young girls, but most often it is fear of the unknown that may cause a loss of innocence and fill a mother's heart with dread. Indoctrinating children with fear of *el cucui*, who is out there in the dark, is a way to frighten children about the unknown and save them from it. Folk characters like *el cucui* often appear in Chicano literature, spelled *kukui* or *kookoóee*, and are familiar to many Chicano readers.

See also El Abuelo; El Coco; El Kookoóee
References Anaya 1995b; CHICLE 1994

Cuentos (Stories)

A short story, or a narrative, which, in the terminology of folklore, may be a legend, a folktale, a fable, a children's tale, or a family legend. Hundreds of *cuentos* have been collected in New Mexico and the Southwest, primarily in Spanish, but also in English. Many of the folktales from New Mexico and southern Colorado are European in origin and were brought by the Spaniards in the seventeenth century. Consequently, many tales deal with kings and queens, with variants of the tales of "Cinderella," the "Prince and the Frog," and "Snow White." Many *cuentos* have a religious or moral message about proper behavior, honor, and respect, and often God, the Devil, and Death are the main characters. Other *cuentos* are about bewitchment or enchantment; others yet are animal stories with coyotes or wise animals, which point to traditional values.

In Spanish literature *cuentos* are primarily short stories, and one can find the *cuentos completos* (complete short stories) of major Iberian and Latin American authors in libraries and bookstores. Folktales and other narratives collected from the folk are often called *cuentos populares*. The *cuento chistoso* is a humorous anecdote or a picaresque tale featuring a rogue who learns a social lesson while getting out of a comical situation. Many *cuentos* are narrated as true events that happened to a friend or family member, and are called *casos*, belief tales, or even urban legends. For example, one popular legend is the story of *La Llorona*, the weeping woman who is constantly searching for her lost children. Many narratives describe her appearances to individuals, particularly men, who are out late at night instead of home with their wives. Stories about the Devil at the dance are favorites, and many variants can be found from Texas to Tijuana. The Devil always dances with the prettiest girl, until she sees his goat feet, or chicken feet, and faints or disappears on the spot.

It is thought that contemporary Chicano families no longer narrate *cuentos*, as a sharing family experience, but they still appear in other formats. Collections of *cuentos* are continually being published, so the stories are always available to younger generations. The oral tradition of the *cuento* has influenced the writings of many Chicano authors and is often reflected in novels, short stories, and poetry.

See also Bailando con el Diablo; Casos; La Llorona
References Campa 1963; Espinosa 1985; Espinosa, J. M., 1937; García 1987, 1992; Glazer 1981; Lea 1953; Lucero-White 1941; Rael 1957; Vigil 1994; Weigle 1987

Curanderismo (Healing)

The folk process of healing, similar to much contemporary alternative medicine in its holistic approach, with no recognition of a separation between the mind and the body, as there is in the medicine and psychology of the modern West. The word *curar* means "to heal," and *curanderismo* refers to the process of healing. *Curanderas* and *curanderos* believe that if they are successful in healing a patient, it is God's will, but if they cannot cure a patient, it is also God's will, and that the patient can go elsewhere for care. *Curanderas* have great religious faith and view their ability to heal as a gift given to them by God, calling it *el don* (the gift). *El don* also allows the *curandero/a* to heal through supernatural means, using ritual and ceremonies, and sometimes magic.

Also called folk medicine, the *curanderismo* healing process involves religion, the use of herbs, folk remedies, and a variety of spiritual routines. A male healer is a *curandero*, whereas a female is a *curandera*. There is a long tradition of *curanderismo* associated with Spain and with the indigenous populations of the New World. *Mexicano* and Chicano folk healing beliefs and practices evolved from pre-Columbian civilizations with goals of alleviating not just illnesses not recognized by Western medicine, but also psychological, spiritual, and physical problems. Beliefs in folk healing procedures and folk remedies are not unrelated to the rest of Chicano culture, but make up a complex system of beliefs that includes Catholicism, with its faith in God, as well as faith in family and in the natural world. Most families have an elder who has some knowledge of home remedies, or knows the uses of herbs and teas and is looked to for guidance in curing basic ailments. A *curandero* may only be consulted when all other remedies fail.

There are specialists within *curanderismo* such as *sobadores*, people who massage and relieve illnesses through rubbing and manipulation of the body.

Midwives, called *parteras*, also practice a form of *curanderismo* in their use of postpartum remedies and practices. A *huesero* is a person who understands the human bone structure and can massage and set painful fractures and alleviate soreness. An *arbolario* or a *yerbero* is an herbalist, an authority in the use of herbs. A *curandero* may be consulted for social, psychological, or spiritual problems, along with physical sicknesses, and it is often the case that there is an overlap in the medical diagnosis.

Medical theories and practices introduced in the New World by the Spaniards consisted of a medical system based on Greek and Roman customs combined with Arabic practices learned from the Moors in their 800-year occupation of Spain. These theories and doctrines were shaped gradually by Native American influences and medical beliefs. One basic belief was that good health was based on a balanced state of being that was also in balance with the environment in both spiritual and physical terms. A second belief introduced by the Spaniards was that plants and animals could be the source for medicinal remedies, a belief consistent with indigenous views. "The restoration of health through the restoration of balance to the patient and the experimentation with and use of herbal remedies, have had an enduring influence on the practice of *curanderismo*" (Trotter and Chavira, 30).

Some *Mexicanos* and Chicanos believe in two sources of illnesses, one natural, the other supernatural. An illness from natural sources may be treated by modern Western medicine, or with herbs and other home *remedios*, or by calling in a *curandero*. An illness from a supernatural source cannot be treated by modern medicine but only by a *curandero* or by prayer. Many people use both systems of healing depending on how they interpret their illness. Modern medicine provides surgery, antibiotic drugs, and hospital care, while a *curandero* can provide assistance with herbs, poultices, teas, and spiritual advice. A *curandero* not only knows the use of herbs and home remedies, but through *el don*, the gift of healing from God, can also heal illnesses caused by witchcraft, referred to as *embrujadas*, and use prayer as part of the healing process.

See also Jaramillo, Don Pedrito; Urrea, Teresa

References Applewhite 1995; Foster 1953; Graham 1985; *Homenaje a Nuestras Curanderas* 1996; Macklin 1980; Martinez 1966; Paredes 1993a; Perrone 1989; Roeder 1988; Romano 1965; Sandoval 1998; Torres 1983a, 1983b; Trotter and Chavira 1997; Waterbury 1974

Quetzalcoatl

Dance
See Baile

Dancers
See Los Matachines

Dancing with the Devil
See Bailando con el Diablo

Day of the Dead
See Día de los Muertos

Death
See La Muerte

Death Cart
See La Carreta de la Muerte

Décimas (Poetic Narratives)

Introduced in New Spain by the Spanish, a *décima* is a poetic narrative that may or may not be in song form. With a ten-line stanza, as opposed to the *corrido*, which has a four-line stanza, it has a more inflexible verse form than the *corrido*. The word *décima* refers to the ten verses of the stanza, but each *décima* may consist of several stanzas, so the genre is often referred to in the plural, as *décimas*. Usually a quatrain introduces the *décima*, and a line from this quatrain may be repeated at the end of each stanza and again at the end of the series of strophes. *Décimas* have also been collected in Chile, Argentina, and Puerto Rico. Aurelio Macedonio Espinosa collected *décimas* in New Mexico and shows how they developed almost without change from sixteenth- and seventeenth-century Spanish literature. The subject matter of *décimas* may be religious, political, or philosophical. Espinosa reprints one from the 1860s that describes the political unrest of the people of New Mexico during the American occupation (1985, 156). Arthur Leon Campa provides a list of titles of 137 *décimas* from New Mexico. Stanley Robb states that all the *décimas* he collected in New Mexico were sung to one standard tune, even though the singers lived in different parts of the state. From one informant, Próspero S. Baca, Robb collected "One Hundred Twenty-one *Décimas* and Other Folk Songs."

According to Américo Paredes, singers of the *décima* on the Texas border use an old-fashioned singing style, and the *décima* is sung for informal occasions without musical accompaniment. It is actually chanted rather than sung, with a tendency toward a "parlando-rubato style no matter what the musical background may be" (Paredes and Foss, 95).

References Campa 1930; Espinosa 1985; Herrera-Sobek 1987; Paredes and Foss 1966; Rivera 1989; Robb 1980

Descansos (Resting Places)

The verb *descansar* means "to rest," and *descanso* can mean "a rest" but in religious folk practices refers to "a resting place." A *descanso* often appears as a small pile of stones with a crucifix propped up among the stones, placed at the side of a highway or back road. *Descansos* can be found throughout the Southwest, with some dating back to the eighteenth century. After the 1847 Taos Rebellion, *descansos* were built along the site where many died during the Battle of Embudo. In New Mexico, a *descanso* often marks the spot where a funeral party stopped to recite a prayer for the deceased on the way to the cemetery. *Los Penitentes* (Penitents), during their Holy Week processions and ceremonies, stop to pray at *descansos* located along their routes. *Descansos* also remind travelers to stop and say a *sudario* (prayer for the dead) for the souls in purgatory.

Today, from California to Texas, a *descanso* may mark the spot where a person was killed in a car accident. These *descansos* may be marked by a large cross, or a small tombstone with plastic flowers, or even a photograph stapled to a cross, anything to identify the spot with the image of the person who died there. Some Mexican people believe that a cross must be erected on the spot where a person dies, where the soul left the body, otherwise the soul will not be able to rest and may wander aimlessly, haunting those who didn't put up a cross at the site. *Descansos* are not only religious shrines built to commemorate the life and death of a person, but they are also works of folk art. Although some are merely piles of rocks, others may have intricately carved

Descansos (resting places) often appear as small piles of stones with a crucifix propped up among the stones, along the side of a highway or back road. (Buddy Mays/Corbis)

crosses, "assembled from parts of a wrecked automobile" (Arrellano, 42), and many are continually replenished with fresh plastic flowers. A work on *descansos* by Rudolfo Anaya and Denise Chaves includes text that reads like poetry and beautiful photography by Juan Esteban Arellano.

See also Folk Art; Los Penitentes
References Anaya, Chaves, and Arellano 1995; Arellano 1986; Barrera 1991; Graham 1990; Henderson 1937; Larcombe 1994; Oktavec 1995; Rael 1950; West 1988

The Devil
See El Diablo

Día de la Raza
See La Raza

Día de los Muertos (Day of the Dead)

The Day of the Dead, or All Souls' Day, November 2 in the Catholic calendar, is a holy day of obligation, a time set aside in the year to pray for the souls of the deceased members of one's family. November 1 is All Saints' Day when Catholics pray for the saints of the Church; this has been a custom and ritual for hundreds of years. Halloween, or All-Hallows Day, precedes these more religious holidays. In some parts of Mexico and the United States the celebration of both of these holidays is just referred to as *Todos Santos* (All Saints). All Souls' Day is a reminder to pray for the resurrection of those souls suffering in Purgatory, those who are in a sort of limbo while they are purified of sin on their way to heaven. In Mexico, *Día de los Muertos* is primarily a private family celebration, with all-night vigils held at the *camposanto* (cemetery), whereas in the United States it has become a communal celebration with art exhibits in galleries and shop windows, night processions, celebrations in schools, and public art fairs. One of the main activities in both Mexico and parts of the Southwest is the visit to the cemetery to place offerings on the tombs of the dead. First the graves are cleaned and washed well and the weeds and dead leaves are removed, then flowers, fresh or plastic, and candles are arranged on it. A favorite flower in Mexico for this holy day is the *cempasuchil*, the yellow marigold, also called *flor de muerto* (flower of the dead) because it is so used. Thousands of marigolds can be found in the open markets during this season. This preparation of the grave may occur days before, or the night before, as the family prepares to *amanecer* (awaken in the morning) at the cemetery on the Day of the Dead. Many of the rituals associated with this celebration are indigenous in origin and reveal the syncretism of the European beliefs of the Spanish conquerors and pre-Columbian Indian cultural beliefs. The Indians believe that the soul of a dead person visits its relatives once a year and the family must be ready for this visit by preparing a place with the favorite food and drink, called an *ofrenda*, an offering to the soul.

A primary tradition of this holy day is the assembling of an altar and an *ofrenda* to show the dead that he/she is remembered and revered and the spirit is expected. Many Latino and Chicano families set up altars as shrines and memorials to family and friends that have passed on. The altar is decorated with flowers, *papel picado* (cut tissue paper), portraits or snapshots of the dead, personal items that belonged to the dead, and many fruits and food offerings. These may include *pan de muerto* (bread of the dead), *calaveras* (skeletons), candy, a glass of water, candles, toys, religious pictures, alcoholic drinks if the dead liked them, cigarettes, and food such as *tamales, chiles,* or other special foods that the visiting soul enjoyed during life.

The Mexican perspective on death is reflected in the folk art produced for this holiday. The candied skeletons, skulls, banners, flags, and papier-mâché toys that abound during these celebrations mock death. It isn't a lack of respect, but rather a lack of distinction between the living and the dead. A continued interaction exists between the two worlds, a moving back and forth, as when the *almas*, the souls of the dead, come back for family reunions.

Families visit and sometimes hold all-night vigils at the graveyard on Día de los Muertos. In the United States, the holiday has become a communal celebration with art exhibits in galleries and shop windows and long night processions. (Reuters New Media Inc./Corbis)

This religious holiday emphasizes death as part of the cycle of life and is a celebration that embodies the idea of unity between life and death. The Mexican artist José Guadalupe Posada created hundreds of humorous lithographs of *calaveras*, skeletons that mocked the living, satirizing the lives of the upper classes. To this day, the *calaveras* of Posada are well known and replicated throughout Mexico and the Southwest.

Folk art created in yard shrines or other forms of assemblages is very common in Mexican American communities. Much attention has been paid to this religious holy day in the non-Latino community in the last twenty-five years or so. Magazine and newspapers articles, cultural arts programs, and Internet web sites provide much information about Mexican customs and traditions related to this holy day. Many urban communities organize communal altars in museums and galleries, along with evening processions involving singing, praying, and other types of observances. Suzanne Shumate Morrison has written a detailed description and analysis of the celebration in San Francisco's Mission District. But many families still consider it primarily a religious and private day of prayer.

See also Altars; Calavera; Camposanto; Folk Art
References Carmichael and Sayer 1991; *Día de los Muertos* 1983; Kitchener 1994; Morrison 1992; Paz 1961; Salinas-Norman 1988; Vigil 1998

El Diablo (The Devil)

A prevalent character in the folklore of the Southwest, the devil is more commonly known as *el diablo*. The concept of the devil is of Christian origin and was brought to the New World by the Spanish missionaries. The indigenous peoples of Mexico and the Southwest had no such belief in their religion or traditions. *El diablo* was introduced along with Catholicism to New Spain and soon personified evil, yet he could be defeated by good. Chicanos and *Mexicanos* don't actually fear the devil, because they've learned he can be driven away by making the sign of the cross, and reciting *"Jesús, María y José!"* Although he can tempt people to wickedness, *el diablo* appears in folklore as a proponent of parental obedience and a supporter of Christian traditional values. Belief in *el diablo* is incorporated into a cultural system that maintains close family ties and teaches that wrongdoers should be punished and benevolent acts should be rewarded.

The devil can appear in various forms, but he is most often seen as a well-dressed, *muy guapo* (very suave), handsome man. He can also take the form of a whirlwind, called a dust devil, or he may appear as a crack in the earth that can swallow up an unworthy person. For generations Chicano children have been warned by their mothers that if they don't obey them, or if they're disrespectful, the earth will open up and swallow them. In 1977 Tomas Rivera wrote a very successful novel with the title *Y no se lo Trago la Tierra* (And the Earth Did Not Swallow Him), and Aristeo Brito wrote his *El Diablo en Texas* in 1976. Both authors from Texas use the image of *el diablo* in their writings as an acceptable symbol they grew up with. Both of these novels were reprinted in the 1990s.

In the Rio Grande Folklore Archives of Pan American University, there are over 350 tales about the devil, all collected from south Texas. But in the folklore of New Mexico, collected by Aurelio Espinosa and Arthur Campa, the devil appears very little, and when he does, it is usually in the folktales, not in riddles, nursery rhymes, or folk poems. In Robe's collection of over 700 legends from New Mexico, only 96 are about the devil, and in most of these tales the devil is defeated. Some people believe witches gain their powers and craft by entering into a pact with the devil.

See also Bailando con el Diablo
References Glazer 1984; Herrera-Sobek 1988; Hinckle 1949; Miller 1973; Ramos 1950; Robe 1951; Robe ed. 1980; Wallrich 1950

Dichos (Proverbs)

A *dicho* is a little poetic saying, called a proverb in folklore terminology. Sometimes *dichos* are also called *refranes* (proverbs) and can be a popular saying or a maxim. *Dichos* are commonly used in everyday conversation by Mexican and Chicano elders and will often reflect the philosophy or worldview of the person who uses them. Use of proverbs in daily conversation is probably limited to elders or recent immigrants who speak more Spanish than English and who can incorporate them into their conversations. Proverbs are supposed to express the wisdom of a whole group of people, and usually are passed from one generation to the next.

The verbal art of using the proverb is in the timing, knowing when to insert one in the conversation and in the appropriate situation. It is in the social context that a *dicho* becomes important and meaningful. When introducing a proverb, many speakers will preface it with, "*Como dice el dicho*" (as the saying goes) and then follow with the convenient saying. Hundreds of Spanish proverbs have been collected in New Mexico, Texas, and other southwestern states by folklorists and others interested in the Spanish language, with many collections published in book form.

Properly performed *dichos* in speech and oral presentations convey strong messages about a common culture and heritage. Introduced in a speech, a *dicho* becomes a rhetorical device to establish a bond with the audience. César Chávez, president of the United Farm Workers of America, often used *dichos* to drive home a point about the plight of the farmworker. Mario Obledo, a candidate for the governorship of California in 1982, was a wonderful speaker and very effective in using *dichos* in his speeches. In political speeches the succinct *dicho* can exemplify a human situation that otherwise may not be clearly understood. It is an oratorical device, often a humorous one, that can catch people's attention and make a political point.

Dichos are always in a fixed form. A few examples of *dichos* follow: "*No hay rosa sin espinas*" (there is no rose without thorns). "*Cada oveja con su pareja*" (each sheep with his partner). "*Un gato llorón no caza raton*" (a crying cat cannot hunt the mouse). "*El que nace pa' tamal, del cielo le caen las hojas*" (if you're born to be a tamale, the cornshucks will fall from the sky). "*Panza llena, corazón contento*" (a full belly means a happy, contented heart). If a son or daughter does not complete a family chore correctly and makes excuses for it, a parent might state, "*Un buen gallo en cualquier gallinero canta*" (a good rooster will crow in any chicken coop), meaning a good worker works well in any situation. If an individual relays incorrect information, he may be told, "*El sordo no oye pero compone*" (the deaf person doesn't hear but makes it up), meaning one wasn't listening well to the message being conveyed and consequently relayed it incorrectly. Although *dichos* are not recited as much as they used to be, Chicanos are still very much interested in collecting them, and books of *dichos* can be found in many libraries and bookstores.

References Aranda 1977; Arora 1966, 1982a, 1982b; Campa 1937; Espinosa 1985; Glazer 1987, 1994; Lea 1953; Lucero-White 1941; Paredes 1982

El Diez y Seis de Septiembre (The Sixteenth of September)

The most important Mexican holiday, celebrated throughout the United States by Chicanos and *Mexicanos*, because it commemorates the start of the rebellion against Spain that eventually led to Mexico's independence. Father Miguel Hidalgo y Costilla, triumphantly gave *El Grito de Dolores*, in the town of Dolores, Guanajuato, a cry for independence from Spanish domination. The following year Hidalgo and several of his men were captured and beheaded, and their heads were placed on display. Ten years later, in 1821, Mexico gained its independence from Spain, but *El Diez y Seis de Septiembre* is still considered Mexico's independence day. Chicanos continue to celebrate this holiday in the United States because they feel a part of Mexico, maybe not the political nation, but the Mexican culture. For more than 300 years Spain ruled territories that are now the states of California, New Mexico, Arizona, Colorado, and Texas. After 1821 a Mexican government ruled this territory for twenty-seven years, and the American Occupation, as it is called in the Southwest, began in 1848 after the U.S. Mexican War of 1846–1848. It was possible in one person's lifetime to have been a citizen of Spain, Mexico, and the United States. Yet because of the Spanish language, the Catholic religion, and the culture, many Mexican Americans continued to maintain allegiance to the Mexican nation. Celebrating *El Diez y Seis de Septiembre* is one of the ways this allegiance is expressed.

In many parts of the Southwest, especially Texas, this celebration is referred to as one of *Las Fiestas Patrias* and has been celebrated there since the 1830s. Typically the celebration consists of parades, the election of a queen, fairs, food, lots of music, and an evening dance. It is a tradition that at midnight on the night of September 15, *el grito de independencia* is yelled. In Mexico City the president of the country carries out this custom on the balcony of the presidential palace, but in the United States *el grito* may be shouted throughout the day.

One of the first Chicano journals to be published at the beginning of the Chicano movement was titled *El Grito: A Journal of Contemporary Mexican-American Thought*, published in Berkeley in 1967 by Dr. Octavio Paz. Later there were many other periodicals with similar titles, such as *El Grito del Norte*, *El Grito del Pueblo*, and *El Grito de Aztlán*. All these titles allude to a cry for independence, and for Chicanos in the United States a cry for self-determination.

References De Leon 1982; Melville 1978; Perry 1992; *Señoras of Yesteryear* 1992

Dobie, J. Frank (1888–1964)

James Frank Dobie is well known as the writer and publisher of many ethnographic and folkloric studies of Texas, Texans, *Tejanos*, and Mexicans from Mexico and the Southwest during the first half of the twentieth century. For many years he was the editor of the Publications of the Texas Folklore Society series, which published many volumes of Texas and Mexican folklore. Dobie's ancestors settled in Texas during the 1830s, and his parents became ranchers in south Texas in the 1870s. Three of his uncles served with the Texas Rangers. J. Frank Dobie was born in 1888, and he grew up playing with the Mexican children of his father's *vaqueros* (cowboys). He claimed he could "speak Mexican," but he also once stated that his father disapproved "of our acquiring much Spanish." He was educated at Southwestern University in Georgetown, Texas, and received an M.A. in English from Columbia University. In 1914 he became a professor in the English department of the University of Texas at Austin.

Although Dobie only considered himself an amateur folklorist, he did collect folktales and legends, which he rewrote for publication. His folklore research and his writings are in what is referred to as the romantic regionalist style. That is, Dobie collected stories, legends, and folklore from Texans and Mexicans, and then presented this folklore in literary English, in his own words, in publications meant for an American literary audience. It is assumed that Dobie felt this type of romantic folkloric ethnography would be appreciated more if translated into a literary style far from the actual language of the "folk." He was primarily a writer of stories about the Southwest, and he earned the title of "Mr. Texas" among his peers. A course he taught at the University of Texas, "Life and Literature of the Southwest," was one of the most popular among the students. Jose Limón makes the observation that Dobie made many excursions into Mexico to collect folklore, rather than collect from the south Texas Mexicans readily available on his ranch and in his community. In his *Legends of Texas* Dobie explained that he excluded "all legends not residing among Texans of white skin and English speech" (McNutt, 247).

Dobie considered himself very knowledgeable about Mexicans and used the phrase "talk Mexican" to indicate how well he understood Mexicans and Mexican culture. Yet, he never learned to speak Spanish, and possibly for that reason never actually collected folklore from Mexicans. Dobie romanticized cowboy culture and lore, much of which he learned from the Mexican *vaqueros* of south Texas. What he did in his writings and publications was to take the cowboy out of the *vaquero*, exalting horse culture, cattle, and Anglo ranch life but leaving the Mexican *vaqueros* as the "folk," as the illiterate peons from rural Texas.

Dobie is important in Chicano folklore scholarship because of his connection to Jovita González and their relationship, which took the form of mentor and mentee. He met her when she was a student at the University of Texas and apparently influenced her research and her method of collecting and representing Mexican folklore during the 1920s and 1930s. She became his protégé. He introduced her to the Texas Folklore Society, where she eventually became president of the organization from 1930 to 1932, an unusual feat for a Mexican woman of her time.

See also González, Jovita
References Limón 1994; McNutt 1982; Tinkle 1968, 1978

Las Doce Verdades (The Twelve Truths)

A phrase that refers to *Las Doce Verdades del Mundo*, which translates as "the twelve truths of the world." The story behind this declaration is sometimes narrated as a tale, recited as a prayer, proposed as a riddle, and can also be found in printed versions. This oral tradition has been collected in Mexico, Spain, Portugal, Italy, France, Germany, South America, and in other countries. Various versions exist in the Southwest, and it has been found in New Mexico and Texas. In folktales *Las Doce Verdades* are often recited as answers to a test that will have an effect on the life of an individual. Questions are asked, by either the devil or a judging personage, and the individual must respond. The questions always start with, "Of the twelve truths of the world, tell me one?" The respondent answers, and the second question is "Tell me two?" and so it continues until the twelfth one is reached. The responses are religious answers having to do with the life of Jesus Christ, the Catholic Church, and tales from the Bible. Trotter and Chavira explain that many *curanderos* will recite *Las Doce Verdades* as a prayer while conducting a spiritual cleansing or other curing ritual. The following printed version (Hudson 1957), found in San Antonio, Texas, lists the twelve truths in reverse order as follows: "The twelve apostles, the eleven thousand virgins, the Ten Commandments, the nine months, the eight sorrows, the seven words, the six candlesticks, the five wounds, the four Gospels, the three divine persons, the two tables of Moses, and the Holy House of Jerusalem where Jesus Christ lives and reigns forevermore, Amen."

See also Curanderismo
References Espinosa, A. M., 1985; Espinosa, J. M., 1937; Hudson 1957; Trotter and Chavira 1997

Doctor Loco's Rockin' Jalapeño Band

A band started in the mid-1980s by Dr. Jose Cuellar (Dr. Loco), a professor of anthropology at San Francisco State University in San Francisco. He describes himself: "I'm a vato (guy) with a Ph.D." (Ramirez 1997). At night and during the summers he performs as Doctor Loco with his Rocking Jalapeño Band composed of nine members. All of the musicians have degrees from prestigious universities, but not in music. Cuellar always introduces them by citing their credentials. The band performs all over California, playing Chicano music, a mixture of oldies, rhythm and blues, boogies, shuffles, merengue, *cumbias*, salsa, Tex-Mex, and traditional Mexican music such as *rancheras* (country music) and *corridos* (ballads). Most of the lyrics of the band's songs are in English and Spanish and have been changed to include Chicano culture references. For example "Cherry Pie" becomes "Chile Pie." Other oldies songs pay a tribute to *el movimiento Chicano:* "El Picket Sign," "Las Revolucionarias," and "La Migra" (the immigration). The band's first self-produced recording was titled *Con/Safos*

(Don't Mess with This) and featured "Linda Cholita," "Cumbia del Sol," and "Framed."

See also Bato; Corridos; Ranchera
References Ramirez 1997

Don Cacahuate

A numskull character who appears in jokes, tales, and anecdotes. *Don Cacahuate* and his wife *Doña Cacahuate*, sometimes called *Doña Cebolla*, Mr. Peanut and Mrs. Onion, and their son *Sanmagan* (son-of-a-gun) are favorite folk characters from legends and folktales. In the folk literature he represents the simpleton, the foolish fellow, portrayed as *un tonto* (a dimwit) and described as *"un poco pendijito y muy mentiroso"* (a little stupid and a great liar) (Ornelas 1962). *Don Cacahuate* is always poor and always getting caught in social and technical entanglements that he can't figure out. He interprets everything literally and the joke is always on him. Unlike the picaresque figure who learns that for survival he must outwit everyone, *Don Cacahuate* never rises beyond bare survival, although he is of the same universal tale type as Pedro de Urdemalas (The Numbskull). In Juan B. Rael's collection of folktales from Colorado and New Mexico, tale No. 436, *Don Cacahuate* is told by his wife, *"Don Cacahuate, hágame un bolillo"* (Mr. Peanut, make me a bread roll). He answers, *"Y como quiere que le haga un bolillo, si yo soy mejicano?"* (How do you expect me to make you a *gringo*, when I'm a Mexican). The double entendre here is the word *bolillo*, which means "bread roll" but is also a disparaging word for Anglo, equivalent to *gringo*. The underlying message is that it is not possible for a Mexican to make an Anglo, or to become an Anglo.

It is believed that *Don Cacahuate* is of recent birth in the Southwest, although tales about him have been found as far south as Guanajuato, Mexico. Tales collected in the 1950s by Richard Garnica Ornelas in California were from Mexicans who heard the tales in the United States or from other immigrants. *Don Cacahuate* is a *pocho* (a half Mexican), appearing at the beginning of the twentieth century, and was probably a worker, a section hand on the railroad. Another version of the origins of the *Don Cacahuate* story is that after the Mexican Revolution the government wanted to grow peanuts and put together a pamphlet educating the *campesinos* on how to cultivate the peanut. The peanut was given the name of *Don Cacahuate* and the pamphlet was distributed throughout the school system, titled *La Historia de Don Cacahuate*. Ornelas (1962) remembers him as "a crafty, lean, old man, who made use of his wit and slyness to fool people, or to get out of having to work, or to win money, to make friends."

But according to Gilberto Benito Cordova, *Don Cacahuate* was born of mixed ancestry in the New Mexican village of Santa Rosa de Lima (de Abiquiu) in the mid-eighteenth century. "This community, now a ruin, was situated about three miles east of the *genízaro* Indian pueblo of Santo Tomás Apostel de Abiquiu, which is the present town of Abiquiu. *Don Cacahuate*, according to folk legend, left Santa Rosa at an undetermined date in the late 1700s and with his wife, *Doña Cacahuate* took up residence in the neighboring *genízaro* pueblo."

References Cordova 1973; Lamadrid 1995; Ornelas 1962; Rael 1977; Robe 1971

Doña Marina
See La Malinche

Doña Sebastiana

A nickname for *La Muerte*, Death. The name *Doña Sebastiana* is found and used primarily in New Mexico, often in reference to the figure in *La Carreta de la Muerte*, the Death Cart. *La Carreta de la Muerte* is a crude oxcart carrying a seated figure of a skeleton clothed in black with a hood over its head holding a drawn bow and arrow. This figure is often called *Nuestra Comadre Sebastiana*, or just *Doña Sebastiana*, and her picture can be found in many New Mexico folk art books. There is documentation of an early carved *Doña Sebastiana* in a cart from the 1860s. It is described by Captain John Gregory Bourke in 1881 as "a hideous statue, dressed in black, with pallid face and monkish cowl, which held in its hands a bow and arrow drawn in position" (Weigle 1977, 142). It could be that the drawn bow and arrow, an indication of the unpredictability of death, associate this death angel with the arrows of St. Sebastian and his death as a martyr. *Doña Sebastiana* is feared and respected, but one can find her presence in folk poetry, short stories, and the humorous narratives unique to New Mexican writings.

Much has been written about the Mexican view of death. Octavio Paz's words on death are often quoted, and present-day publicity on *Día de los Muertos* celebrations is a good example of this interest. The continuity of life, the invariable transition from one realm to another, is a commonly held Christian belief, along with the conviction that one should always be prepared for another life. *Doña Sebastiana* represents the uncertainty of life and the abruptness of death; a brush of her arrow could indicate that death is near.

See also La Carreta de la Muerte; Día de los Muertos; La Muerte
References Sagel 1992; Stark 1971; Weigle 1977

Don't Mess with This
See Con Safos

Duendes (Goblins)

In the folk narratives of the Southwest, duendes (goblins) perform mischievous pranks such as throwing stones and dishes. They especially like to frighten the lazy, the wicked, and in particular the filthy. (Burstein Collection/Corbis)

Gnome- or goblin-type characters that figure prominently in the folklore of the Southwest. *Duendes* are believed to be the spirits of dead ancestors who return to invade a house and cannot be removed. They perform mischievous pranks such as throwing stones and dishes, pulling the bedcovers off of those asleep, dumping sleeping individuals out of their beds, eating food off people's plates, and carrying out many other annoying tricks. According to Espinosa, "They frighten the lazy, the wicked, and in particular the filthy" (1910, 397). In some folktales they are helpful and will assist a farmer with his crops, or will aid in household chores, as long as they are taken care of and fed. But if a family wants to get rid of them, even moving out of the house will not help, because the *duendes* will follow along. Usually they are invisible but when seen are described as little childlike creatures. Folktales that narrate the naughty antics of *duendes* have been found in New Mexico and Los Angeles. The collections of Espinosa, Rael, and Miller include several narratives about *duendes*.

References Espinosa, A. M., 1910; Miller 1973; Rael 1977

Quetzalcoatl

Elves
See Pichilingis

Empacho (Indigestion)

Labeled a folk illness, this medical condition is caused when undigested food sticks to part of the gastrointestinal tract, which can result in a hard ball forming in the stomach, sometimes with swelling involved. The condition may cause an internal fever, stomach pains, and possibly great thirst. Children suffer the most from this folk illness because they may not chew their food well, swallow gum, or otherwise not eat well. Some believe it can be caused by forcing children to eat food they don't like. It is not an illness that is caused or can be treated by witchcraft. This condition is not always recognized by Western doctors, and Mexican Americans may seek the help of a *curandero*, or a *sobador*, a person who knows how to massage. A *sobador* may massage the abdomen or the back behind the stomach to dislodge the food that is stuck. Usually, family members know how to treat a condition like *empacho*, by either giving a laxative to clean out the stomach, giving an herb tea such as *yerba buena* (mint) or *manzanilla* (chamomile), or stroking the stomach with olive oil.

See also Curanderismo; Sobador
References Clark 1959; Kay 1977; Roeder 1988; Trotter and Chavira 1997

Espinosa, Aurelio Macedonio (1880–1958)

Professor Luis Leal believed Aurelio M. Espinosa to be the founder of modern Mexican American scholarship because of his research work in linguistics and folklore, two disciplines that form the basis of the study of Chicano culture. Espinosa is thought to be the most important folklorist to do work among Hispanos in the state of New Mexico. A scholar of Spanish and Spanish American language, folklore, and other narrative genres, Espinosa believed in a Hispanist origin of Mexican American culture, and almost completely ignored the *mestizo* and Mexican basis of Mexican American culture. Yet he was the first Hispano to "dedicate himself to the study of popular culture among the Mexican residents of the Southwest" (Leal 1987, 3). He was also extremely influential in training and mentoring future Chicano scholars such as Arthur Campa, Juan Rael, and his own son, Jose Manuel Espinosa.

Aurelio Espinosa was born in El Carnero, Colorado, in 1880. He was educated locally, at the University of New Mexico, graduating in 1902, and received his doctorate from the University of Chicago. After receiving his degree in Romance languages and literature he joined the Romantic Languages Department at Stanford University in 1910. He conducted language-oriented folklore fieldwork in New Mexico for over forty-five years, up until the 1950s. Américo Paredes states that Espinosa's study "New Mexican Spanish Folk-lore" published in the *Journal of American Folklore* in 1910–1911, was the first "scholarly work on Mexican folk-lore."

Espinosa conducted a study of the Spanish language spoken in the United States, *Studies in New Mexico Spanish,* which resulted in his dissertation and was first published in *Revue de Dialectologie Romane.* It was later published by the University of New Mexico in 1909–1910. It was the first real analysis of New Mexican Spanish, which Espinosa identified as an archaic form of sixteenth- and seventeenth-century Castilian Spanish. Between 1910 and 1916 the *Journal of American Folklore* published eleven lengthy articles by Espinosa on the folklore of New Mexico. In introducing the material Espinosa stated, "Folk-lore studies in Spanish North America have been entirely neglected. . . . I do not know of any American publication on Spanish-American folklore" (1910, 25). Twenty years later a student of Espinosa's, Juan Rael, documented more folklore than Espinosa in New Mexico and Colorado. Another of Espinosa's major works was *Cuentos Populares Españoles* (Popular Spanish Folktales), published in Spanish in three volumes between 1923 and 1926. He developed the first and only classification of Spanish folktales, plus an additional comparative study completed in 1940. This was a tremendous amount of work, and placed Espinosa among the prominent scholars and folklorists of his time. He was especially interested in showing the importance of Spain in the dissemination from the Middle East of the European folktale.

Chicano scholars have criticized Espinosa for his emphasis on the origin and influence of sixteenth- and seventeenth-century Spanish culture on the folklore of New Mexico and for omitting the *mestizo* and the Mexican vestiges. Karen M. Duffy, in writing a review of Espinosa's work and research, disagrees with this position and believes Espinosa was not unaware of what he was doing. She states, "His emphasis on sixteenth- and seventeenth-century Spain as the source of his region's tradition had great rhetorical value, which he well recognized and used effectively, for combating American stereotypes of New Mexican Hispanics as ignorant and uncultured" (48). She quotes him as saying, "The Spanish language as spoken to-day by nearly one-quarter of a million people in New Mexico and Colorado is not a vulgar dialect, as many misinformed persons believe, but a rich archaic Spanish dialect" (48).

Espinosa was a dedicated educator and scholar and was a founder of the American Association of Teachers of Spanish and the Linguistic Society of America. He was also active in the American Folklore Society and was elected president in 1923.

References Duffy 1995; Espinosa, A. M., 1923, 1985; Espinosa, A. M. Jr., 1947; Espinosa, J. M., 1978; Leal 1987; Paredes 1970

Evil Eye
See Mal Ojo

Quetzalcoatl.

Fajitas

Literally, a *fajita* is a little belt, or little strip. It is used to mean a cut of beef that in English is called a skirt steak. Since it is a tough cut, the meat is cooked by first broiling it, and then cooking it in a dry pan with lime juice. When ordering *fajitas* in a restaurant, most people don't know that it refers to the cut of the meat and not to the seasonings. The cut was very common in northern Mexico and south Texas before it was found in other parts of the Southwest and in the country as a whole. In Mexico this cut of beef is called *arracheras*, and has always been eaten, whereas in the United States the cut was ground up for hamburger. Today in contemporary restaurants one can find chicken and shrimp dishes that are called *fajitas*; they are served sizzling hot, with *guacamole*, *pico de gallo*, and *tortillas*. But in reality *fajitas* are strictly beef.

References Graham 1991; Montano 1992; Peyton 1994

Fandango (Dance or Party)

Originally the name of a Spanish dance that involved the use of castanets, *fandango* came to be used in Texas and early California to mean a party or a dance. Since at least the early eighteenth century, there have been *fandangos* in the Southwest. The *fandango* in mid-eighteenth-century Texas, as described by Arnoldo De Leon, actually meant a place where festive celebrating occurred, from dancing to gambling. In fact often there were tables for card games that were played continuously. The names of such establishments were just "*fandango* houses," places where revelers could eat, drink, gamble, and dance. In Texas, the *fandango* reached its peak by the 1860s and thereafter declined as ordinances in some cities prohibited this type of entertainment, although they still continued to exist in an illegal manner until the end of the 1800s. This word is now uncommon, but one can still hear it today to describe a party being held in someone's home where there will be lots of food, music, and dancing.

In his book of California life in the mid-1850s, Major Horace Bell describes the difference between a *baile* and a *fandango*. A *baile* is "a select gathering of

Originally the name of a Spanish dance, the fandango *came to mean a party or a dance hall in Texas and California. (North Wind Picture Archive)*

invited guests for dancing and general jollification and amusement," whereas "a *fandango* is open and free for all" (197). Apparently ladies of the upper classes did not attend *fandangos,* and according to Bell the gentlemen only attended in a "half-way clandestine manner" (198). Some of the early literature on the Gold Rush regions of California mentions *fandango* houses, as in Texas, especially in communities that had large Mexican populations. Even the most remote small towns in the foothills of the Sierras had a *fandango* house. In Los Angeles a *fandango* was a public affair that included an assembly of the most disparate and diverse population of all segments of the city. Apparently everybody came extravagantly dressed, the "*señoritas* of the most humble walks in life arrayed in all the costly silks and satins of China and India, resplendent with costly jewelry. . . . Gentlemen attending the *fandango* were always expensively and elegantly dressed, and a *fandango* was a brilliant but overcrowded show" (Bell, 198).

See also Baile; Folk Dances
References Bell 1927; De Leon 1982; Limón 1994; Peña 1980; Shay 1982

Farmworkers' Theater
See El Teatro Campesino

Farolitos, *made out of paper bags filled with two or three inches of sand, with a small candle placed in the center of the sand, decorate homes and streets during Christmastime in Santa Fe, New Mexico. (Danny Lehman/Corbis)*

Farolitos (Little Lights)

Farol is the Spanish word for "lantern," and a *farolito* is a "little lantern." The tradition of lighting *farolitos* during the Christmas season is well established in many parts of the country but especially in Santa Fe, New Mexico. Today, *farolitos* are simply and easily made out of paper bags filled with two or three inches of sand and a small candle placed in the center of the sand. When the candle is lit a mellow light is projected through the bag, creating a festive, glowing, and inviting atmosphere. During holidays and other celebrations, people may place rows and rows of *farolitos* around their homes, walkways, and yards, inviting guests to participate in the festivities of the moment. It is believed the Mexican *farolito* is a descendant of the colorful lanterns from China. The festive Chinese lanterns were introduced into the Spanish Philippine Islands and from there made their way to Spain and Mexico. *Farolitos* made of *papel de China*, Chinese paper, were made into delicate lanterns in Mexico and later in colonial New Mexico. The idea of using paper bags for *farolitos* evolved later, when paper goods were more readily available. The use of *farolitos* has become very popular in general American culture during the holiday seasons, and many media publications such as *Sunset Magazine* carry articles on how to construct them.

See also Luminarias
References Anaya 1995a; Ortega 1973; "Rekindling the Flame" 1986

Festival
See Kermés

Fiestas Guadalupanas

The festive activities and celebrations that take place for the veneration of *La Virgen de Guadalupe* on December 12. In churches throughout the United States, and in Mexican *colonias* (neighborhoods), for months prior to this date much planning takes place to create a memorable celebration. The activities may include a procession to the Catholic church, Aztec dancers, *Matachines* dancers, a High Mass, and a *Mariachi* band or other musicians. Many *fiestas* include a reenactment of the appearance of *La Virgen de Guadalupe* to Juan Diego as an *acto*, a drama that is incorporated into the celebration of the Mass, and is performed somewhere near the altar, or outside the church before the Mass. The drama is based on a dramatic work from Mexico titled *La Aparición de Nuestra Señora de Guadalupe de Mexico*, or *Apparitions of the Virgin of Guadalupe*, published in the mid-1800s.

Many churches schedule a *Las Mañanitas* (morning serenade) Mass at 4:00 or 5:00 a.m. on the actual anniversary of the appearance of *La Virgen de Guadalupe*, December 12, even when it's a weekday and everyone has to go to work afterwards. But the *Fiestas Guadalupanas* are held on the Sunday nearest the actual date for the convenience of the community and for the largest attendance. The altar of the church is transformed, sometimes with hundreds of roses and special altar cloths, and the image of *La Virgen de Guadalupe* is decorated and displayed prominently. The priest may wear vestments with the Mexican national colors, or a *sarape*, or have the image of *Guadalupe* emblazoned on the back of the vestment. *Fiestas Guadalupanas* take place throughout the United States and not just in the Southwest as some might imagine. *La Virgen de Guadalupe* is much more than a religious symbol. She also represents patriotism, love for the Mexican country, and nationalism, the sense of *Mexicanidad*. Her day is the most celebrated holiday in Mexican communities on both sides of the Mexican-U.S. border. See works by Sommers and Valdez for descriptions of the celebrations in the Midwest.

See also Mariachi Music; Los Matachines; La Virgen de Guadalupe
References Dolan and Hinojosa 1994; Sheridan 1986; Sommers 1995; Tijerina 1998; Valdez 1990

Fiestas Patrias (Patriotic Festivals)

Expression used when referring to the celebration of *El Diez y Seis de Septiembre*, and sometimes also *Cinco de Mayo*. The *Fiestas Patrias* are patriotic commemorations connected with the celebration of Mexico's independence from Spain in 1810. Although Mexico did not become free from Spain until 1821, the *Grito de Dolores* (cry of freedom) was cried out by Father Miguel Hidalgo y Costilla on September 16, 1810, in Dolores, Guanajuato. He was executed by a firing squad and did not live to see Mexico's freedom, but he is considered to be the father of his country, and September 16 is celebrated as the date of Mexico's independence. The *Fiestas Patrias* are civic rituals that emphasize and perpetuate Mexican nationalism. Festivals for the *Fiestas Patrias* are held throughout the Southwest and have been held in Texas for over 150 years, with one of the first *Diez y Seis de Septiembre* celebrations held around the 1830s. Even after the signing of the Treaty of Guadalupe in 1848, *Mexicanos* in the Southwest have continued to identify as Mexicans and to participate in patriotic festivals. Celebrations usually include parades, *Mariachi* music, civic speeches by local elected officials, lots of food, and a *grito*. The *grito* is a reenactment of the *Grito de Dolores*, an incendiary sermon given by Father Hidalgo, in which he preached the overthrow of the Spanish colonial government. Supposedly, he ended his speech with the *grito* (outcry), *"Viva America! Muera el mal govierno! Mueran los gachupines!"* (Long live America! Death to bad government! Death to the Spaniards!) This *grito* is still cried out today by Chicanos and *Mexicanos* in remembrance of the history of Mexico, and as a display of ethnic pride and solidarity. By celebrating the *Fiestas Patrias*, Chicanos continue to reinforce a historic and cultural connection to Mexico.

See also Cinco de Mayo; El Diez y Seis de Septiembre
References De Leon 1978, 1982; Melville 1978; *Señoras of Yesteryear* 1992

Fifteenth Birthday

See Quinceañera

Fifth of May

See Cinco de Mayo

Fifth Sun

See Quinto Sol

Filigree

Filigree is an ancient craft, executed by the Greeks and Egyptians, that was introduced into Spain by the Moors. Filigree refers to a type of jewelry, either in gold or silver, that is made of very fine ornamental work. It is a very delicate wire, gold or silver, formed into dainty schemes of scrolls, net-work, and floral designs. Fine threads are twisted, curled, plaited, and united into intricate patterns. Beads of gold or silver are sometimes set at various junctions to offset the work. A framework of a flat thread sometimes surrounds the design and holds it together. The most common work is found in earrings and necklaces, which are made in all sizes, and are often worn as part of the costumes of the Mexican *Ballet Folklórico* dancers of today, and by the *ranchera* singers of Mexico. By the late nineteenth century there were many filigree workers in New Mexico, who were usually called *plateros,* meaning "silver workers," even though they also worked with gold. Filigree jewelry in silver and gold can be found in the Southwest and in Mexico.

In the 1960s, an artist from Texas, Consuelo Gonzalez Amezcua, created filigree drawings by pencil and exhibited her work at the Marion Koogler McNay Art Institute. She called her work "Filigree Art, A New Texas Culture." It was ornamental openwork with very delicate and intricate designs. Filigree is interesting as an ancient craft, but it is also fascinating because of its similarity to the type of patterning found in Chicano wall graffiti. The artwork that goes into Chicano tattooing and customizing of low-rider cars also involves very fine intricate and feathery lines.

See also Ballet Folklórico; Low Rider; Ranchera
Reference Espinosa, C., 1970

Flor y Canto (Flower and Song)

In the Nahuatl language, flowers were the symbol for truth, and song was a symbol for poetry, so *flor y canto* represented a profound truth. Stated in Nahuatl as *"in xochitl in cuicatl,"* flower and song symbolized prayer and poetry. In 1490 a reunion of poets and wise men met in the house of Tecayehuatzin, King of Huejotzingo, to understand the meaning and significance of *in xochitl, in cuicatl,* which metaphorically means poem and symbolic artistic expression. It was thought that poetry, song, and art were able to help man transcend life on earth. Miguel Leon-Portilla states of the Aztecs, *"La verdadera poesía implica un modo peculiar de conocimiento, fruto de auténtica experiencia interior o, se prefiere resultado de una intuición"* (true poetry implies a special knowledge, fruit of authentic personal experience, or results in an intuition).

In the 1970s, Chicano writers, poets, and academics brought the concept of *flor y canto* to the forefront of the Chicano movement. For several years, literary conferences were held throughout the Southwest called *Floricantos,* where writers gathered to read their poetry and literature. The goals of the

The ancient craft of filigree work was introduced by the Moors into Spain; the Spanish conquistadors later introduced it to New Spain. (Jonathan Blair/Corbis)

Floricanto festivals were to provide a forum and promote the creation of Chicano literature for and by the community. These cultural conferences evolved into *Canto al Pueblo* literary festivals; the first one held in the Midwest included East Coast Latino writers as well. Many of the festivals were the source for early publications of Chicano poetry. Numerous literary anthologies resulted from these gatherings, with titles such as *Festival de Flor y Canto: An Anthology of Chicano Literature* (1976) and *Flor y Canto IV and V: An Anthology of Chicano Literature from the Festivals Held in Albuquerque, New Mexico, 1977.*

References Leander 1972; Leon-Portilla 1961; Noriega 1992; Vento 1998

Folk Art

Folk art refers to art objects, also called traditional arts, provided for community consumption and created as an expression of common social and cultural values. Often folk art is created for other than artistic and aesthetic reasons but becomes aesthetically pleasing because of its shared community value. The pleasing arrangement of color and form, the symbolism inherent in the artifact, the display and function of the object, all contribute to a community's acceptance of an art as belonging to the people. Many art objects are created as expressions of religious belief or result from the use of scarce elements available to an economically deprived family that are fashioned together to form an artistic object of love. Home altars, yard shrines, *retablos* (paintings of saints), hand-carved *santos* (saints), embroidery work, paper arts like *piñatas* and *papel picado* (cut tissue paper), weaving, tinsmith work, and straw appliqué are all classified as folk art that fulfills a personal or communal desire and yet also provides aesthetic enjoyment. Many art forms were once crafts created as necessities of daily living, like *colchas* (blankets) and weaving, adobe constructions, *santos* and altars, but these forms have evolved into modest indulgences and powerful affirmations of cultural identity.

The folk art forms of the Hispanic Southwest have been studied extensively by art historians, folklorists, and anthropologists, and what is of special interest is that so many forms survived after the Anglo American invasion in the mid-nineteenth century. The arts and crafts of Mexicans living in Texas, New Mexico, Arizona, and California were considered backward and unsophisticated by Anglo easterners. Yet even though religious folk arts and domestic arts were disdained by the new economic and technological society, they continued to survive in rural and remote towns and villages. In the 1920s, Anglo American interests turned to promoting the traditional arts created by Mexicans in the Southwest. One reason for this was a new fascination with the Spanish colonial history of the region and another reason was pure economics. A revival in the traditions of a romantic Spanish past of California and New Mexico was seen as commercially profitable by eastern entrepreneurs. Charles Briggs points out how elite Anglos assisted in marketing the folk art of New Mexico during the 1920s and 1930s. This renewed interest helped preserve some dying craft traditions and also brought financial resources into communities that desperately needed them. Although many of the arts and crafts promoted were relics of a colonial past, gradually creative artisans refined their work into new forms that reflected the life of a changing contemporary society.

Chicano art, born of the Chicano civil rights movement of the late 1960s, embodied varied social and cultural strategies that connected the strife-ridden reality of daily life to the artistic imagination. An art of and for the Chicano people incorporated ancient indigenous symbols, customs, religious icons, common traditions, and reinterpreted them in new ways that affirmed Chicano culture. The many social movements of the 1960s gave impetus to Chicano artists to create art in the form of murals, sculptures, posters, and gallery displays that aroused political consciousness and achieved ethnic self-determination. The unionization of California farmworkers by César Chávez in 1965, the rise of the black civil rights movement, the Black Panthers, the student and antiwar demonstrations, the rural land-grant rebellions in New Mexico, all contributed to a rise in artistic mediums that would instill Chicano pride and identity. Although not all Chicano art can be called folk art, most Chicano artists have been inspired and influenced by "barrio symbology" (Ybarra-Frausto 1991), Mexican folklore, and pre-Columbian cultural imagery. From murals to low-rider cars, T-shirts, and tattoos, Chicano artists use cultural themes such as *La Virgen de Guadalupe*, indigenous motifs, and gang attire that manifests an ongoing social struggle but also community and ethnic pride.

James Griffith (1995) writes that he sees a connection between Mexican American folk art motifs and what he describes as baroque principles of organization found in Mexican architecture. He points out the dramatic contrasts in color, texture, and design that can be found in the aesthetics of Chicano art, using examples of low-rider cars, a cemetery shrine, and a yard shrine found in Arizona. His analysis provides a principle that can be applied to folk art created by Chicanos that is shared within families, neighborhoods, and regions. Tomás Ybarra-Frausto (1991a) has written extensively on this same aesthetic principle of Chicano culture, calling it *rasquachismo*, a Chicano sensibility that is basically a worldview, "rooted in resourcefulness and adaptability" (134). In creating artistic works, "to be *rasquache* is to be unfettered and unrestrained, to favor the elaborate over the simple, the flamboyant over the severe. Bright colors are preferred to somber, high intensity to low, the shimmering and sparkling over the muted and subdued. The *rasquache* inclination piles pattern on pattern, filling all available space with bold display" (1991a, 135). Although a *rasquache* sensibility may be unconscious in the folk artisan, Chicano artists deliberately experiment with *rasquache* schemes to achieve an aesthetic that speaks to the daily life of the *barrio*.

Amy Kitchener examines a traditional arts display at the University of Arizona Museum of Art, an exhibit that reveals the continuity between home arts and community arts and their interrelationship. The exhibit presented a unique art experience in a new venue by re-creating a complete yard shrine, an altar, and included low-rider bikes and prison (*pinto*) arts. In discussing a similar art exhibit in San Antonio, Texas, Kay Turner and Pat Jasper state, "Many of the objects in this exhibition serve as vital testaments of ethnic identity, as expression of religious belief, as strategies for economic self-sufficiency, and as constant reminders of cultural continuity between Texas and Mexico" (1986, 10).

See also Altars; Colchas; Low Rider; Muralismo; Rascuache; Retablos; Santos; Yardas
References Briggs 1986; Hattersley-Drayton et al. 1989; Gavin 1994; Goldman, D. 1997; Goldman, S. 1990a; Graham 1990; Graham ed. 1991; Griffith 1988, 1995; Kitchener 1997; Lockpez 1986; Mather 1983, 1992; Seriff and Limón 1986; Turner and Jasper 1986; Wroth 1977; Ybarra-Frausto 1991a

Folk Beliefs
See Creencias

Folk Dances

Chicano and *Mexicano* folk dances found in the Southwest are a combination of Spanish, Mexican, and indigenous dance steps. The better-known ones are the foot-stomping dances called *zapateados* that originate from various Spanish traditions. These include such dances as *El Jarabe Tapatio*, *Las Inditas*, and *La Raspa*. Many of the early dances of the Southwest were adopted by the common folk as they learned them from the *ricos*, the wealthy class, who learned them from their travels to Spain or Mexico City. These dances had names like *La Mestiza*, *Los Viejitos*, *La Varsoviana*, *La Vaquerita*, *El Chote*, *La Cuna*. There were also many waltzes with names like *Vals de los Paños* (waltz of the handkerchiefs), *Vals Despacio* (slow waltz), and *Vals de la Silla* (waltz of the chair). *El Vals de Chiquiaos* was a folk dance that incorporated verse, or *coplas*, into selection of a partner for a dance. A young man had to be not only a good dancer but also an articulate poet if he wanted to win over the girl of his choice. Most of these dances required a leader, usually a man called a *bastonero*, who directed the dancers. According to Arthur Campa the custom of using a *bastonero* at community dances in the Southwest existed up until at least World War I.

In California both folk and ballroom dancing were very popular. Campa states that Hubert Howe Bancroft mentions in his work that the *Californios* had many dances and balls, and he proceeds to provide the names of many (Campa 1979, 243–245). The *baile de cascarones* has received some research attention because of the custom of breaking perfume-filled *cascarones* on unsuspecting suitors at the dances. Other dances from California were called *Cuando*, *Queso*, *El Malcriado*, and *La Vaquilla*.

Along the Rio Grande border region since World War II, a type of polka has become the tradition at the dances. Although not called a folk dance, it was introduced into the region by German and Czech immigrants in the nineteenth century. It has become the preferred dance of northern Mexico and is danced to *musica norteña* (northern music) played by a *conjunto norteño* (northern band). In *Ballet Folklórico* performances the *norteño* dances are basically a polka-based dance step always introduced as a typical dance of northern Mexico and the border region. Américo Paredes pointed out this influence in his discussion of the *polca tamaulipeca*, which is a combination of the *huapango* (dance) and the polka. Other dances introduced into the Southwest by European immigrants were the *varsoviana* and the *schottische*, also known as the *chote* or *chotis*.

Since the mid-1940s, after World War II, there has been an interest in Mexican folk dances, such as those performed by the *Ballet Folklórico* of Mexico City. This dance company has performed often in the United States, and many former members have come back to teach the old and new dances of Mexico. Today there are probably hundreds of Mexican folk-dancing groups among elementary-school children and high school and college students. These groups do not call themselves folk-dancing groups, but *Ballet Folklórico* dancers.

See also Baile; Ballet Folklórico; Cascarones; Chiquiao; Conjunto Music; Fandango
References Campa 1979; Huerta 1972; Lucero-White 1940a; Najera-Ramirez 1989; Paredes 1963; Sedillo 1950

Folk Dramas

Open-air performances of plays that in Spanish are known as *actos, autos sacramentales,* and *teatro,* which together constitute what in folklore is called folk drama. The Spaniards introduced many medieval and religious dramas to the indigenous populations, mostly taught orally, since few people could read or write. Eventually someone, such as a friar, would write down the text, and it would be passed on from generation to generation. Often only one text will be found in an entire region of the Southwest. Lucero-White states that in the 1930s she found the only copy of *Los Moros y Cristianos* (The Moors and the Christians) in New Mexico. Most of the plays were didactic in nature and were meant to instruct the natives in religion, with stories from the Old Testament, or about political history by depicting the conquered position that they found themselves in. *Los Moros y Cristianos* is a mock battle between the Moors and Christians from the twelfth century. The final outcome is that the Moors are vanquished, but performed in the New World this drama represents the conquest of the native people. Religious plays, such as *Las Cuatro Apariciones de la Virgen de Guadalupe, Los Pastores, Las Posadas, Los Reyes Magos, El Niño Perdido, Comedia de Adán y Eva,* and the passion plays performed during Lent, are all intended to instruct the new converts in the history of Catholicism. Two native Spanish folk plays have been discovered that were created by New Mexicans and that depict historical events of the New World. *Los Comanches,* dating from the late eighteenth century, presents a battle between the Spaniards and the Comanche Indians. Another play, *Los Tejanos,* discovered by A. M. Espinosa in 1931, dramatizes the defeat of General Hugh McLeod by the New Mexicans in 1841. As a brigadier general McLeod commanded the military component of the Texas–Santa Fe expedition. He and his expedition were captured by General Manuel Armijo and imprisoned in Perote Prison until the summer of 1842.

The tradition of folk theater, part religious ritual and part entertainment, has evolved as an important folk heritage in the Southwest to this day. The *carpas* (tent theaters), comedies, and *maromeros* (trapeze performers) of the nineteenth century that traveled into California and the Southwest from Mexico are examples of this tradition. The work of *El Teatro Campesino* (the Farmworkers' Theater) and other Chicano *teatro* groups has been influenced by the practices of these early folk dramas introduced from Spain. The early dramas were religious in nature, also called *autos de fe,* and were rituals to teach and convert the indigenous populations to Catholicism. In the 1960s, *El Teatro Campesino* performed *actos* and short skits that were meant to politicize California farmworkers and educate them about labor strikes and the importance of union organizing.

See also Carpas; *Los Comanches; Los Moros y Cristianos; Los Pastores;* Las Posadas; El Teatro Campesino

References Anderson 1989; Campa 1934, 1979; Espinosa, A. M., 1941, 1985; Espinosa, A. M., and Espinosa, J. M., 1944; Gutiérrez 1993; Herrera-Sobek 1993a; Huerta 1972, 1982; Lea 1953; Lucero-White 1940a; Robe 1957; Stark 1969

Folk Healing
See Curanderismo

Folk Heroes

Individuals who have gained admiration and respect because they have stood up to defend their rights or avenge an unjust action. Folk heroes and legends about them have always existed in the history, culture, and social experiences of *Mexicanos* and Chicanos. When the life adventures and exploits of a character are sung and narrated by a close-knit group of people, that character has become a folk hero. In Chicano history many men have been called *bandidos,* "bandits," but have been folk heroes to the people. After the signing of the Treaty of Guadalupe in 1848, the Mexican people living in the territory ceded to the United States were terribly discriminated against: they were punished, they lost rights to their lands, and in many cases they were violently assaulted. The treaty "guaranteed Mexicans the enjoyment of all the rights of the citizens of the United States, according to the principles of the Constitution" (Mirandé 1985, 72), and they were guaranteed water rights and the safety of their lands along with linguistic and cultural protection. Yet throughout U.S. history Mexicans have continually been treated as a conquered people.

Even before the U.S. Mexican War of 1846–1848 there were violent clashes between Mexicans and Anglos, along the border region in Texas and in the gold mines of California. These clashes greatly increased after the signing of the Treaty of Guadalupe. Because of the inequities that occurred from the mid-nineteenth century until well into the twentieth century, many Chicanos arose to defend their rights and to fight the military and police agencies established by the new government. In California Tiburcio Vásquez and Joaquín Murrieta became bandits during the latter half of the nineteenth century. They robbed coaches and according to the legends distributed the loot they stole to the poor Mexicans of the countryside. Both were eventually killed, but romantic legends, *corridos* (ballads), poetry, novels, and dramas chronicle their exploits. Folk heroes from Texas include Juan Nepomuceno Cortina, Catarino Garza, and Gregorio Cortez. *Corridos* proclaim the virtues and heroism of these men as they rebelled against the injustices committed against them and their families by the Texas Rangers and other armed forces. In 1859 Juan Cortina (1824–1894) shot the marshal who pistol-whipped his friend, and on the following day, with over forty men, he seized control of Brownsville. The ensuing battle is referred to as the first Cortina war. Catarino Garza (1859–1895) was born in Mexico and lived both in south Texas and Mexico. He was a journalist and publisher of various newspapers during his life, both in Mexico and in the United States, but he is remembered for his run-in with the Texas Rangers. In 1888 he was arrested for criticizing Texas Ranger Victor Sebree and was wounded by him in a shoot-out in Rio Grande City. He was critical of Mexican President Porfirio Díaz and in 1891 plotted to overthrow his government. Struggles with Mexico, the United States, and Texas resulted in the Garza War, which continued even after Garza left Texas in 1892. Gregorio Cortez (1875–1916) killed the sheriff who shot his brother, and fled from a posse of Texas Rangers for three days. The famous *corrido* (ballad) "El Corrido de Gregorio Cortez" chronicles his life and bravery.

Chicanos continue to search for and create heroes and honor those who stand up for dignity and exhibit courageous efforts for their communities. In the late 1960s, Reies Lopez Tijerina became a hero, for his leadership of *La Alianza Federal de Mercedes* (Federal Alliance of Land Grants), an organization that contested the legality of the New Mexico land grants taken over by the invading Americans in the nineteenth century. Rodolfo "Corky" Gonzales is another hero from this period; he established the Crusade for Justice in Colorado and worked for equal educational opportunities for the youth of Colorado. César Chávez, the founder and leader of the United Farm Workers of America, became a respected folk hero among Chicanos during his lifetime, with several *corridos* to his name. He devoted his entire life to improving the lives of farmworkers in the United States. Alongside César Chávez is Dolores Huerta, a tireless folk heroine, who has also devoted her whole life to the farmworker movement. She has been a vice-president of the United Farm Workers since its inception in the early 1960s.

The stereotypical *bandido* image, the violent, mustached, knife-wielding *bandido*, continues to plague the Chicano and is continually shown by the media in films, magazines, and advertising. Most Chicanos reject this image.

See also Chávez, César; "El Corrido de Gregorio Cortez"; Corridos; Murrieta, Joaquín; Vásquez, Tiburcio
References Castillo and Camarillo 1973; Herrera-Sobek 1993b; Mirandé 1985; Pitt 1966

Folk Literature

Folklore genres from the oral tradition, such as folktales, myths, legends, and proverbs, are often referred to as folk literature, oral literature, or folk narratives. These are narratives that are transmitted orally within a culture or a group of people. In fact a basic definition of folk literature is orally transmitted literature in whatever form or whatever society it may be found. In folklore studies it is often the specific genre that is appraised, such as the legend, folktale, proverb, or ballad, and the term folk literature is reserved for the whole body of these genres. The word literature conjures up an image of written works, some derived from folklore, but nevertheless literary works that are consciously crafted and written as art forms. There is a relationship between folklore and literature, but there is also a clear distinction.

Written literature is the result of a creative process that incorporates personal experience, intellectual exploration, and imagination. Folklore is composed of the many elements of culture that are transmitted orally and unconsciously among a common folk, a family, an ethnic group, or a regional group. There has been a great influence of Chicano and Mexican folklore, such as legends, folktales, folk sayings, and other narratives, in the published literature of Chicanos, but little has been written about it. Regional literatures, such as that produced by southern writers, or southwestern writers, are often considered to be more influenced by folklore than literature produced by urban writers. Some literary critics claim that Chicano literature is a folk literature because of the many uses of folkloristic motifs such as legendary figures or witchcraft, or genres, such as *corridos* (ballads). There are Chicano scholars who believe such assertions are made as a way of implying that Chicanos can only produce a type of folk literature, the product of a quaint and less developed culture. Jose Limón argues that previous literary critics saw folklore influence in literature as a lesser element, or a "secondary form of literature," while he believes that "folklore emerges as a dominant influence on written literature and not merely as something that is 'in' the literature" (1990,140).

There are folklorists who have taken the liberty of rewriting folk narratives to make them more literary, or more sophisticated, while still calling them folklore. J. Frank Dobie, a respected writer and folklorist from Texas, rewrote folklore in this manner. Many of his works were published by the Texas Folklore Society. Folklore and literature both blend traditional elements of culture, and many themes found in literature derive from the folklore of a culture. Motifs from folklore found to be literary themes in literature have been indexed by Stith Thompson in the *Motif-Index of Folk Literature*. This "Classification of Narrative Elements in Folktales, Ballads, Myths, Fables, Mediaeval Romances, Exempla, Fabliaux, Jest-Books and Local Legends," as the subtitle states, is an index of literary versions of traditional motifs found in published literature. The use of folkloristic motifs as a way to preserve and maintain a language and a Hispanic way of life is clearly visible in Chicano literature. Maria Herrera-Sobek writes about Chicano writers who incorporate folk narrative motifs into their writings as a means of infusing political and aesthetic forms into a modern literary format. Sandra Cisneros's characterization of *La Llorona* (the weeping woman) in her short story "Woman Hollering Creek" is a good example of this approach to creative writing. *La Malinche* as a character and as a symbol emerges frequently in the poetry of many Chicana writers. In fact it is in poetry that Chicano writers frequently incorporate folkloristic elements from a Hispanic upbringing. Religious beliefs and rituals, Spanish folk sayings, *abuelita* (grandmother) images, *curanderismo* (folk healing) practices, and family values are often woven into the contemporary Chicano condition. The language of the *pachucos* (1940s urban youth), *caló* (argot), and low-rider culture easily adapts to poetic narratives that intensify the literary bicultural state of being Chicano. The connection and identity of folklore and literature are obvious. Archer Taylor, a distinguished American folklorist, states, "The Old Testament can be called a book of traditions, and it can be called the literature of the ancient Hebrews. In some instances, the culture of even a modern people consists largely in folklore" (37).

See also Caló; Corridos; La Llorona; La Malinche; Pachucos
References Herrera-Sobek 1995; Keller 1991; Limón 1990; Taylor 1965; Utley 1965

Folk Medicine
See Curanderismo

Folk Plays
See Folk Dramas

Folk Remedies
See Remedios

Folk Songs
Composing and singing songs are an integral cultural activity in Chicano and *Mexicano* communities. Intrinsic to an oral culture is communication in verse and music and other narrative forms, so the folk song has a long history. All of the songs collected from the early *Mexicanos* and Hispanos by folklorists and musical scholars are considered folk songs because, as songs of the people, their origin is unknown. The earliest folk songs found in the Southwest were the *romances*, the precursors to the *corridos* (ballads), the *décimas* (poetic narratives), and the *alabados* (hymns). Introduced orally by the Spaniards,

these forms were popular in Spain at the time of the conquest of the New World in the sixteenth century. The words were often changed by the singer as the songs were sung because some lines were not remembered and the singer improvised a bit, while still maintaining the essential story line. Consequently, there are many variants of each song. "La Delgadina" and "Bernal Francés," also known as "Elena," are two of the oldest *romances* collected in the New World. *Décimas* and *alabados* are ancient religious ballads that tell the story of religious figures and are sung by *Los Penitentes* and sometimes called "*penitente* songs."

Folk music is usually orally circulated and known by a people who share a language, religion, and nationality. Most early Mexican American folk songs have been collected and recorded orally, although a few folklorists, such as J. D. Robb, were able to find in New Mexico one or two notebooks in which a devoted singer had written down the words to some favorite songs. One singer in the mid-1940s sang 112 songs for Robb, all from memory. The body of Spanish folk songs from New Mexico must have been in the hundreds, because even with the many collected, what has been published appears to be only a handful of what was available. Folk songs collected in California, from the mid-1800s to the turn of the century, are of Spanish origin, but many others appear to be unique to New Spain and California. Charles Lummis collected more than 500 Spanish folk songs from *Californios* between 1884 and 1906. He collected 150 songs from one woman alone, who sang the songs from memory for him as he recorded them on wax cylinders. These wax cylinders were supposed to be housed at the Southwest Museum in Los Angeles, but have actually been lost. A. M. Espinosa collected *romances* and other folk songs from descendents of *Californios* who lived in southern California in the 1920s. He found a variant of the sixteenth-century "Elena" called "La Esposa Infiel" (the unfaithful wife), and also a variant of "La Delgadina" collected from an eighty-nine-year-old man.

Like poetry the folk song is a form of verse, although in musical form, and is perfect for communicating sentiments and feelings. As is common in folklore, Chicanos and *Mexicanos* have also used it for comic expression. A song found in the Hague collection, from early California, expresses the sentiments a young girl has toward marriage. The song is titled "Levántese Niña":

"*Levántese niña,*
Barra la cocina.
Atice la lumbre,
Como es su costumbre."
(Get up child,
Sweep the kitchen.
Stoke the coals,
As is your custom [as a wife].)

In the second verse, she answers,

"*Yo no sé barrer,*

Yo no sé atizar.
Yo no me casé,
Para trabajar."
(I don't know how to sweep,
I don't know how to stoke coals.
I didn't get married,
To be put to work.)

The Hague collection includes songs, transcribed with music, that deal with love, the land, animals, and the sea, and some are still sung today. "El Zapatero" (The Shoemaker), found in the Lummis collection, is a very old song that is still recorded today as a children's song. Another early children's song is "El Piojo y la Liendre" (The Flea and the Louse), also known as "El Piojo y la Pulga," about a flea and a louse that decide to get married. This song has been recorded over and over, even by such popular singers as Pedro Infante. Lummis discusses the onomatopoetic aspect that he found in some early California folk songs, and states that these are songs "in which the rhythm or sound (or both) simulate the subject sung of," as in the swinging of the hammock in "La Hamaca" and the pelt of the falling rain in "Capotin." Other folk songs collected in southern California are "Quieres Que Te Ponga," which is thought to be a political song from around the U.S. Mexican war of 1848, as well as "Ay Vienen los Yankees" (Here Come the Yankees). Songs recorded in northern California during the late 1930s by WPA workers include Puerto Rican children's songs such as "Aguinaldo," a Christmas song from Vieques, Puerto Rico, and "Doña Ana," also known as "Señora Santa Ana," a song sung by Mexican children in New Mexico, Texas, and early California. These songs can be heard on the Library of Congress's American Memory web site.

A collection of songs from Arizona including *romances* and *canciones* was published in 1946 under the title *Canciones de Mi Padre*, by Luisa Ronstadt Espinel. This title was to be used by the popular singer Linda Ronstadt, a niece of Ms. Espinel, forty years later, to commemorate the songs of her ancestry. A 1999 publication titled *Music in the Ruben Cobos Collection of Spanish New Mexican Folklore: A Descriptive Catalogue* lists close to 300 folk songs collected by Cobos. It includes 27 songs on the wedding custom *entrega de novios*, 33 *Inditas*, and 32 songs on the poetic dance custom *Vals Chiquiado*.

See also Alabados; "Ay Vienen los Yankees!"; Canciones; Corridos; Décimas; Los Penitentes; Romance

References Campa 1979; Cobos 1999; Duran 1942; Espinel 1946; Espinosa 1924; Hague 1917; Lummis 1923a; Robb 1954; Schander 1994; Watkins 1942

Foodways

The essential foods of Mexicans and Mexican Americans have evolved from a blend of Spanish foods and native Indian foods found in the New World when the Spaniards arrived in the sixteenth century. There is an old saying whose origins are unknown that states, "The hundred percent Mexican lives on corn, rice, beans, and *chile*." Three of these staples (corn, beans, and chile) were indigenous to the Americas and had never been experienced by the Spaniards, and are still a main staple of the Chicano diet. In fact the cuisine of the many Indian peoples encountered by the Spanish *conquistadores* was very sophisticated. Franciscan Friar Bernardino Sahagún wrote about the foods in his famous work *Historia General de las Cosas de Nueva España*. He described many types of *tamales*, *tortillas*, squashes, *chiles*, and *moles* made with frog, turkey, duck, pigeon, and other fowl. The various drinks, such as *atoles* made from corn and chocolate, flavored with honey and herbs, are also described by him. Spices used for seasoning foods included oregano, coriander, sage, and many varieties of *chiles*.

The Spanish introduced foods that were to have an enormous impact on the diet of the indigenous population. The availability of livestock, such as horses, cattle, sheep, and pigs, changed the cooking and food preparation of the region. The livestock made available not only meat, but also dairy products and lard for frying foods. Fat increased the many varieties of corn-based foods, such as *tostadas*, *enchiladas*, fried beans, and thicker *tamales*. The principal meat in the diet of the native population had been from fowl, fish, and mammals, such as wild turkeys, chickens, rabbits, and a variety of wild game. Wheat, rice, oats, lentils, and peas were introduced by the Spaniards, along with spices such as pepper, cloves, cinnamon, and sugar. The religious evangelists, nuns, and priests greatly influenced the development of Mexican foodways. They trained the Indians how to cook with fat, sugar, and flour. They introduced the making of candies, breads, cakes, and other pastries in the missions, schools, and convents.

Maíz, the Spanish word for "corn," provides the basic food for millions of Mexicans in Mexico and in the United States. Many common Mexican food dishes are made from *maíz*, such as *tortillas*, *gorditas*, *tamales*, *pozole*, *enchiladas*, *elote*, *nixtamal*, *tostadas*, and *chalupas*. Many contemporary cookbooks now have recipes collected from the Lower Rio Grande Valley of Texas, such as *huevos con migas*, flour tortillas, *chile con queso*, *calabaza con puerco*, *chalupas*, *chile relleno*, *menudo*, *fideo*, and desserts like *buñuelos* and *empanadas*.

Mexican foods of today are still based on most of the indigenous foods of the fifteenth century, although with some modifications. Beef and cheese are major components of today's Mexican diet, foods brought in by the Europeans, but the *tortilla* and *frijole* have become fundamental to the American diet.

See also Barbacoa de cabeza; Burritos; Fajitas; Frijoles; Menudo; Tacos; Tamales; Tortillas
References Glazer 1994; Lopez 1976; Montano 1992; *New Handbook of Texas* 1996; Peyton 1994; Quintana 1986; West 1988

Frijoles (Beans)

Frijoles are the mainstay of the Chicano diet. Pinto beans are usually the type preferred by most Mexicans, although black beans are cooked in many homes and in the southern part of Mexico. Plain old beans are what most Chicanos grew up eating, but they can be prepared in many different forms. Freshly cooked beans are called *frijoles de la olla* (beans from the pot); they're usually served in a bowl in their own broth and may be topped with chopped onion, cheese, and chopped fresh *chiles*. Fried *frijoles* (especially tasty when fried in lard, but those alert to health issues now fry them in vegetable oil) are called *refritos*. These are referred to as refried beans but in reality are usually only fried once. *Refritos* can be eaten many ways, on *tortillas*, as a side dish, on *tostadas*, or scrambled and cooked with eggs or with *chorizo* (sausage). Very well-fried beans become dry, but still taste good in a sandwich, or by the handful. *Enfrijoladas* are *tortillas* dipped in soupy *frijoles* and folded or rolled like an *enchilada*. The method of cooking beans is very basic, with water and salt, but the addition of spices, herbs, and sometimes beer requires a new name for the dish. *Frijoles borrachos*, "drunk beans," are cooked with beer, and *frijoles rancheros*, "rural beans," are also cooked with beer, but also with cumin, chopped green *chiles*, *jalapeño* peppers, fresh tomatoes, and bacon.

Beans are an ancient food and have been found in caves of the Peruvian Andes and dated to 8,000 years ago. The seeds appear to have moved northward from South America into Mexico, where bean seeds found in the highland valley of Tehuacán date from 6,000 to 7,000 years ago. In the Southwest beans found in a cave in New Mexico only date from 2,300 years ago, but it is believed that the American Indians grew fifty species of beans.

The consumption of beans has always been associated with lower-income people and with marginal subsistence. Because *frijoles* figure so prominently in the culture of Chicanos and *Mexicanos*, pejorative terms have been applied by the dominant culture to both. Chicanos have been called bean-eaters, beaners, Mexican jumping beans, and still most Chicanos are devotedly attached to beans. Personal anecdotes about eating *frijoles* as children can be found in the CHICLE archives. Chicanos have narrated anecdotes about pretending that cooked dried *frijoles* were fudge or other candy.

References CHICLE 1994; Kaplan and Kaplan 1992; Myal 1997; Peyton 1994

Fritters
See Sopapillas

Quetzalcoatl

Gardens
See Yardas

Gavacho (Anglo)
A derogatory term used to describe Anglo or white Americans. The word was originally used by the Spaniards when referring to the French and comes from the Spanish word *gave*, meaning "a current of water" from a mountain torrent in the Pyrenees. It is an insulting term that can be found in *décimas* (ballads similar to the *corrido*) that expressed extreme hostility against Maximilian's French troops in the 1860s. By the 1930s it was found to be used for Anglo Americans by Mexican Americans in El Paso, San Antonio, and Los Angeles. Américo Paredes stated that it was not until the 1960s that *gavacho* was used in Mexico City. The extension of the word to *agavachado* creates a new word used as a critical expression leveled at a Chicano who is considered to be too anglicized. During the 1970s, Chicano students at the University of Oregon in Eugene used a shortened version, *gava*, to refer to an Anglo student, usually not in a pleasant manner, as in *"todo el* financial aid *es para los gavas"* (all of the financial aid is for the Anglos).

See also Gringo
References *Enciclopedia Universal Sopena* 1972; Paredes 1961, 1993a

Gestures
Any movement of the body, or body parts, either in posture, attitude, or stance. It is not an area of Chicano folklore greatly studied, but there are gestures common to cultural groups as well as to individuals. Gestures are significant when the audience understands them as they are intended. Gestures are an integral part of culture and a form of communication that must be understood within a social context. There are gestures that explicitly signify certain

meanings, such as beating the chest to signify bravery or scratching one's head to indicate an attempt to remember something. A common gesture for having a drink in Chicano and probably other cultures is to form a fist with the right hand, leaving the thumb and little finger extended, and tipping the hand toward one's mouth. This is usually understood to mean, "Let's have a drink," alcoholic or otherwise. There are also unconscious gestures that float within a culture that are so common they are often not even perceived. For instance, Chicanos and *Mexicanos* often use their heads to point in different directions while talking, sometimes to indicate a geographic direction, or just for emphasis in making a statement. Another cultural gesture is to swing the right hand, fingers loose, in front of one's face moving upward over the head. This gesture usually is associated with frustration, anger, or determination to complete an action or event.

There are also conscious gestures agreed upon to show membership in a given social class or group. They may indicate what is appropriate and proper in a social class or culture, or may be contrived to exclude others from an in-group. For example there is a Chicano handshake, with several variations, that was widely used in the late 1960s and can still be seen on college campuses today. The first part of the handshake involves, with the right hand, loosely grasping the front sections of the fingers of the other person, then shaking hands in the traditional manner, then making a slight fist and tapping the knuckles of the other person's hand. A variation of this might involve grasping the thumb of the opposite hand and then shaking hands traditionally. This handshake identified one as a participant in the values and ideology of *Chicanismo* and the Chicano movement. Gang members often have secret codes that are conveyed through hand signs and specific finger movements. These intricate finger positions can sometimes be seen in photographs of members of gangs, who may appear to be simply holding their hands on their laps or over someone's shoulder. Most *Mexicanos* and Chicanos unequivocally recognize the walk and stance of low riders and *cholos* (1990s urban youth). In the film *Born in East L.A.* the main character, played by Cheech Marin, teaches a group of young male Asian immigrants stranded in Tijuana how to walk and stand like *cholos*, and so when they illegally arrive in Los Angeles they are able to blend right into the culture of East L.A.

See also Cholos; Low Rider
References Axtell 1991; Bauml, 1975; Lomas 1974; Meo Zilio 1980–1983; West 1988

Goblins
See Duendes

Gomez-Peña, Guillermo (1955–)

Born in 1955 and raised in Mexico City, Gomez-Peña came to the U.S. in 1978 to pursue an artistic career at the California Institute of the Arts. His experience of crossing the Mexican-U.S. border activated an identity crisis that in turn induced a creative process that has supported him to the present day. He has worked as a journalist, actor, and writer; experimented with radio and video; and has become one of the most prominent Latino performance artists in the United States. Much of his creative work is directed toward exploring border issues and cultural relations. As he sees it, border culture is a hybrid culture, which "expropriates elements from all sides to create more open fluid systems." Living on the border made him an alien in two cultures, the Mexican and the American, a process that he calls "Chicanization," making him an authentic outsider in both cultures. Living between two countries, two languages, two cultural heritages and religious systems, Gomez-Peña contrived the concept of the border as a studio for multicultural performances. Gomez-Peña calls himself a "border artist," a "border *brujo* (witch), El Aztec High Tech," and he often appears dressed as an Aztec priest or in a *Mariachi* suit. In 1991 he was chosen to receive a MacArthur Fellowship.

Gomez-Peña has published several books of poetry, monologues, and performance narratives, in which he postulates cultural concoctions of *cholo* (1990s urban youth) punks, *pachuco* (1940s urban youth) krishnas, Irish *concheros* (indigenous dancers), Buddha rappers, cyber-Aztecs, and Gringofarians. His use of language and creation of cultural characters, such as El Naftazteca, Maori Low-Rider, and Yuppie Bullfighter, are clearly artistic examples of a cultural studies *relajo* (foul-up). Unlike any other Chicano performing artist, Gomez-Peña embodies and represents a whole repertoire of Chicano folk culture. His performances are satirical, humorous, outrageous, yet achieve the effect of raising serious questions about identity, race, and gender. Chicanos understand his artistic performances and identify with the hybrid border culture and folklore enlightenment that he presents.

In an art performance titled "The Temple of Confessions," performed with Roberto Sifuentes of Culture Clash, both act as techno-confessors, sitting in a Plexiglas altar-booth. Sifuentes dresses as a Chicano low rider from East Los Angeles, and is "El Pre-Columbian Vato," while Gomez-Peña is an aboriginal shaman, "San Pocho Aztlaneca." These two act as temple-keepers and encourage visitors to kneel on a prayer bench, place earphones on their heads, and confess their sins, thoughts, or wishes. The fact that people respond is in itself amazing, but what they confess is frighteningly straightforward. Gomez-Peña discusses and publishes some of these revelations (1997). This performance was commissioned by the Three Rivers Arts Festival in Pittsburgh, the Scottsdale Center for the Arts in Arizona, and the Detroit Institute of Art.

References Cummings 1994; Gomez-Peña 1993, 1996, 1997; Gomez-Peña and Sifuentes 1996

González, Jovita (1904–1983)

A Texan folklorist and writer who published articles and books on Texas Mexican folklore during the 1920s and 1930s. Jovita González's work was published in the publications of the Texas Folklore Society, and she became president of that organization in 1930–1932 at a time when white male Texans dominated it. It was an unusual feat during this historical period for a Texas Mexican woman.

She was born in 1904 to an upper-class Mexican American family in Roma, Texas, and was raised on a ranch along the Mexican border. She received a B.A. degree in Texas history from St. Mary's Hall in San Antonio and attended the University of Texas at Austin as a graduate student. It was there that she met J. Frank Dobie and became his protégé. After earning an M.A. degree she taught Spanish at St. Mary's Hall. She married Edmundo E. Mireles in 1935 and her name became Jovita González de Mireles. They both taught Spanish for many years in Corpus Christi high schools. She died in 1983 of natural causes.

Her fieldwork and research in folklore, primarily of the Texas-Mexican border region, were very similar to Dobie's. Her writing has the same romantic regionalist folkloristic style that idealized the *vaquero*'s (cowboy's) Indian ancestry and the laboring peons. Among her publications are her M.A. thesis, "Social Life in Cameron, Starr, and Zapata Counties," and two novels, *Caballero, A Historical Novel*, edited by Jose Limón and Maria Cotera and published in 1996, and *Dew on the Thorn*, published in 1997, also edited by Jose Limón. Both novels were published fifty years after being written and after her death.

González has been chastised by Chicana writers because she never addressed the limited role of women in the folkloric sketches that she wrote. In fact, in most of her short stories and folklore collections there is rarely a female voice. On the other hand, her novel *Caballero* is the story of women and their contact with Anglo Americans after the signing of the Treaty of Guadalupe. Her work is important in the study of Chicano folklore for its literary and historical perspective.

References Garza-Falcon 1938; Limón 1994; Velasquez-Treviño 1985, 1988

Graffiti

Graffiti are illegal writings or drawings displayed on public walls. The word comes from the Italian *graffiare*, meaning "to scratch," and the noun *graffio*, meaning "a scratch." Chicano graffiti are fairly visible in urban cities of the Southwest. Contemporary connotations of the term imply something negative, since it is an illegal activity, yet many look upon it as an art form and also as folklore, since it is a visual expression that communicates values, rituals, and norms of a group of people.

Graffiti art on a wall in Los Angeles is reminiscent of the ancient traditions of pictographs and petroglyphs. (Shelley Gazin/Corbis)

Paintings on walls are an ancient tradition thousands of years old carried out by people creating permanency in their environment. It is a normal instinct to want to re-create on walls, paper, or rocks what one sees in one's surroundings. In Chicano neighborhoods graffiti are primarily names written on local public walls and buildings. Such writing is often considered vandalism and not socially acceptable, but in Chicano communities it has gained particular significance because of its long cultural history connected to identity, names, and naming, and to neighborhood public art. A type of graffiti whose origin is not known is called "barrio calligraphy" and *plaqueasos,* from the Spanish word *placa,* meaning "plaque" or "sign." It has been traced to the 1930s and 1940s. In writing about Los Angeles Mexican Americans, Beatrice Griffith refers to the graffiti in *American Me,* published in 1948. Chicano graffiti are executed in a stylized letter formation that looks like Gothic lettering or Old English lettering. It is interestingly incongruous to find this style in the Chicano *barrios.* The gothic lettering resembles the ceremonial monograms found on official documents. To the casual observer, Chicano graffiti may be difficult to decipher, but to the *barrio* insider, the intricate designs will be recognized as symbols of identity. Other styles of writing found on inner-city walls include block lettering and loop lettering. A depth perspective is created with block lettering, leaving a three-dimensional effect imprinted on the wall. Loop lettering is a style that features an S-loop around every straight line of a letter.

The execution of *plaqueasos* is a process involving identity creation and asserting a place for oneself. The names imprinted are those of individuals, gangs, lovers, and *barrios,* and where they are written defines both social and geographic boundaries.

See also Barrio; Con Safos; Placas
References Cesaretti 1975; Grider 1975; Griffith 1948; Kim 1995; Phillips 1999; Romotsky and Romotsky 1976; Sanchez-Tranquilino 1995

Grandfather
See El Abuelo

Gravemarkers
See Camposanto

Graveyard
See Camposanto

Greaser
Like "wetback," "greaser" is a term with a long history, generally applied pejoratively to Mexicans or Chicanos. It has also been used to describe Italians in California according to H. L. Mencken, who states that the word "greaseball" was used in reference to "any foreigner of dark complexion," but usually to Greeks (Paredes 1961). In this century it has come to be used to describe Mexicans and Puerto Ricans. McWilliams presents the theory that Mexicans greased oxcarts and wagons along the Santa Fe Trail, before they moved on to the New Mexico plateau, and consequently they were called "greasers" (1968, 115). And in the mid-nineteenth century supposedly Indians and Mexicans loaded greasy hides onto clipper ships along the California coast, and they earned the name of "greasers" for this work. It is certain the word was used by 1854 in reference to Mexicans in California. Another belief is that the word is related to the food eaten by Mexican Americans, the food of poor working-class people, and in many cases a diet that others looked upon as inferior. It is thought to come from the Anglos' first encounter with Mex-

ican food in the lower Rio Grande area of Texas. The Mexicans were derogatorily called "pepper bellies," "taco chokers," and "greasers" during the latter part of the nineteenth century. The term has been used for Mexicans in Texas since at least 1836, with northern Mexico referred to as "Greaserdom" (Paredes 1993a, 21).

A newspaper with the title of *Gringo and Greaser* was published in Manzano, Valencia County, New Mexico, in the 1880s. The editor, Charles G. Kusz, was murdered on March 26, 1884, and it is believed he was killed by one of *Los Penitentes* (Penitents) because of the sacrilegious articles published by the paper. About the name of the newspaper, Miguel Antonio Otero, a prominent Hispano, had this to say: "The name given this paper by the editor, *Gringo and Greaser*, were terms used generally in this country at this time. *Gringo* meant 'Greenhorn,' a name given to all Americans by the native citizens in retaliation for the term 'Greaser,' given to all the native New Mexicans by the Americans locating in the territory. Of course, such expressions were not used by the better class of Americans and native New Mexicans" (v. II, 141). During the mid-1800s in California antivagrancy laws were passed that were specifically intended to be used against the Mexican population in the state, and they were commonly called "greaser laws."

"Greaser" films became a genre of movies during the 1940s and 1950s that portrayed Mexicans as lazy and dirty. Titles of some of these films were *Tony the Greaser, Bronco Billy and the Greaser, The Girl and the Greaser,* and *The Greaser's Revenge*.

References Cortes 1983; De Leon 1983; McWilliams 1968; Mencken 1945–1948; Montaño 1992; Otero 1974; Paredes 1961, 1993a; Pitt 1966

Greater Mexico

The late distinguished University of Texas professor Américo Paredes coined the phrase "Greater Mexico" to refer to the "areas inhabited by people of Mexican culture—not only within the present limits of the Republic of Mexico but in the United States as well—in a cultural rather than a political sense" (1976, xiv). Greater Mexico is composed of all parts of North America where people of Mexican descent live and experience their Mexicanness as an identity, from Mexico City to Chicago, from Detroit to Bakersfield, California. There are various popular expressions in the discourse of Chicanos that describe the cultural location of the Mexican American population in the United States. Mexico, the Republic, is seen as the foundation, with its migrating population orbiting about it. The United States is called *el otro lado* (the other side), and the Mexican *pueblo* in the United States is often referred to as *El México de Afuera* (the Mexico of the outside). Another expression that surfaces once in a while is *el otro cachete*, meaning "the other cheek," referring to the other side of the border. Although there is ongoing discussion concerning the ethnic name for the Mexican-descent population in the United States, and regardless of what many call themselves, there is still a preference for considering oneself *Mexicano*. Both Américo Paredes and Arthur Campa emphasize this point.

References Campa 1979; Paredes 1958, 1976; Vasquez 1975

Green Card
See Mica

Gringo (Anglo)

Derived from the word *griego*, meaning "Greek," a *gringo* is an Anglo person. A Spanish dictionary definition is "to talk gibberish." It is also defined as a "foreigner" or "stranger." In sixteenth-century Spain anyone speaking a foreign language was speaking *griego*, so the word was used for either the person or the language. It is believed that in Spain *griego* eventually became *grog* and later *gringo*, probably sometime in the eighteenth century. In referring to an unknown language in *Don Quixote*, Cervantes uses the word *griego*. There is a popular theory that *gringo* originated with the U.S. Mexican War of 1846–1848. Supposedly the American soldiers sang a song with the refrain, "Green grow the lilacs," and as a result the Mexican people then started calling all the *norteamericanos gringo*, from the condensation of "green-grow." In actuality there is no evidence to support this theory.

In his book, *Reminiscences of a Ranger; or Early Times in Southern California*, Major Horace Bell describes the society of Los Angeles during the 1850s. His work is liberally sprinkled with the word *gringo*, and he provides his own witty definition: "*Gringo*, in its literal signification, means *ignoramus*. . . . This meek and humble historian has felt all the mortification, humiliation and disgrace of being a *gringo*. If the reader has been so spared, then the writer congratulates him—because it is an awful calamity to be a *gringo*" (49).

English-speaking Americans are called *gringos* all over Latin America. According to Dr. Américo Paredes, by the 1880s the word *gringo* was used by south Texas Rio Grande Mexicans in reference to all *norteamericanos*. In Mexico during the past century the word *gringo* has been used primarily in reference to Americans because they are the most conspicuous foreigners in Mexico. In the U.S. many Chicanos prefer to use the word "Anglo" when referring to a Caucasian, or a white person, because *gringo* does have a pejorative sound. Among families and close friends, however, *gringo* is used as an adjective to describe a white person.

In 1973 Jose Angel Gutierrez wrote and published *A Gringo Manual on How to Handle Mexicans*, a book meant to teach *gringo* tricks to Chicanos. The book was intended for Chicanos only, because it taught "the devious, treacherous, hypocritical *gringo* machinations used against our *Raza*" (i). The whole manual consists of a list of tricks that Chicanos could expect from *gringos*, and it shows Chicanos how to use those same tricks against the *gringo* first.

Other expressions used to describe Anglos, especially along the Texas-Mexican border, are *gademe* and *sanavabiche*, two expressions used because of the American habit of exclaiming "goddam" and "son of a bitch." Paredes believes that *gademe* is a local Texas invention that goes back to the 1840s. *Sanavabiche* is sometimes expressed to sound like *San Avabiche*, humorously thought to be an American saint, which leads to the follow-up expression, "*hijo de un santo de los americanos*" (son of a saint of the Americans) (Paredes 1993a, 34).

References Bell 1927; Cobos 1983; Fusion 1961; Gutierrez 1973; McWilliams 1948; Paredes 1961, 1993a

Grutas (Grottos)

The word *gruta* actually means "grotto," but it is used to mean a small cave-like structure that houses a saint, either in a yard display or in a cemetery. Almost always *gruta* refers to a shrine of some type, although many times *grutas* are also called *nichos* (niches). Throughout the Southwest, yard shrines will be found as a common religious practice showing a family's faith and devotion. In the center of the shrine will be a *gruta*, or a *nicho*, with a statue of a saint, a madonna, or *La Virgen de Guadalupe* housed inside. Many cemetery gravesites will also be embellished with *grutas*, which may house the patron saint of the person buried there. Families go to great lengths to construct yard shrines that commemorate their faith in a particular saint. *Grutas* that can hold a statue, flowers, or even a photo of a loved one are important symbols of religious conviction.

See also Nichos; Yard Shrines
References Ramos 1991;Vidaurri 1991; West 1991

Guerrero, Eduardo "Lalo" (1916–)

Born in Tucson, Arizona, in 1916, Lalo Guerrero is a living legend among Chicanos in the Southwest, especially in California. A guitar player and singer, Guerrero wrote songs that shaped the music of the 1940s and has continued to be influential well into the 1990s. Considered the father of Chicano music, he learned to play the guitar from his mother, who was also a singer. His career started early as a musician and writer of songs that he tried to record in Mexico during the 1930s, in the big band style of the period. Before the age of twenty he wrote two songs, "*Nunca Jamás*" (Never Again) and

"Canción Mexicana" (Mexican Song) that to this day are standard songs of any *Mariachi* repertoire. During World War II he settled in San Diego, working as an aircraft mechanic and playing with a USO band that traveled the country. During the 1940s he continued to compose songs incorporating a Latin sound like mambo and rumba, and singing mostly in Spanish. He is credited with creating the music of the *pachuco* (1940s urban youth) era with songs like "Marijuana Boogie," "Los Chucos Suave," and "Vamos a Bailar," songs that were featured in the play and film *Zoot Suit*. There were many nightclubs in Los Angeles during the 1940s frequented by Chicanos and *Mexicanos* where the big band swing sound was heard. The songs of Guerrero had a satirical or humorous flair to them, with titles such as "Elvis Perez," "Tacos for Two," "There's No Tortillas," and in the 1980s, a song about undocumented workers called "No Way Jose." In the 1950s he wrote a parody of the television show tune "Davy Crockett," calling it "The Ballad of Pancho Lopez." The song sold hundreds of thousands of records and received so much attention that Walt Disney called to negotiate a deal, since Guerrero had not requested the rights to the tune. With the money made from this record alone he was able to buy and open a club in Los Angeles called Lalo's, which he owned for thirteen years. He has retired and lives in Palm Springs yet continues to play and perform around the country. In 1991 he received a National Heritage Award for his music about Mexican culture, and he is featured in the Tejano Music Hall of Fame.

See also Mariachi Music; Pachucos
References Buckley 1996a, 1996b; Loza 1985, 1993; Sheridan and Noriega 1987; Sonnichsen 1977

Guy
See Bato

Quetzalcoatl.

Hábito (Priest's or Nun's Habit)

A dress or garment worn by religious individuals such as nuns and monks, usually a long-sleeved, simple cotton garment. A lay religious person may also make a promise to wear *un hábito* for certain periods of time or until the garment falls apart. The color of the garment may be that of the saint to whom the vow was made. A *manda* (vow) is made to wear the *hábito* for a week, a year, or just on certain religious holy days, in fulfillment of a vow made to a saint, such as St. Joseph or St. Francis. Although this is a private or personal promise made to the saint, the community of the individual is aware that the person is fulfilling a *manda*, just by the recognition of the color and form of the habit. In parts of the Southwest there is also the practice of making a vow to a saint for the curing of a sick child, and the *manda* may involve a pilgrimage, with the child wearing the garment of the saint invoked. When the child is well he will be taken to a church service with a godparent selected for the occasion, and the godmother will be called *madrina de hábito*. *Hábitos* can still be seen in south Texas, Arizona, and other parts of the Southwest, but rarely in urban areas. It is usually women who make promises to wear *hábitos*, although men may make other types of *promesas* or *mandas*. The wearing of the *hábito* as a sacrifice comes from early Catholic teachings and a strong belief in the religious benefits of penance.

See also Mandas
References Cantú 1991a; Griffith 1992; Kay 1977; Oktavec 1995

Healing

See Curanderismo

Hilitos de Oro (Little Threads of Gold)

The name of a game that is based on an old Spanish ballad from the seventeenth century. In some versions the dialogue is sung or recited in verse. It

The nun in this picture wears an hábito as she walks through a village in Mexico. (Annie Griffiths Belt/Corbis)

was played by little girls in the Southwest and was collected by the Federal Writers' Program in New Mexico during the 1930s. Although played primarily by girls, the game has one role for a boy, that of the King's Messenger (*mensajero*). Another main character role is the Mother, called Nana. As the game is played it appears to be a reenactment of a European folktale. It starts with the King's Messenger going to the Nana with a message from the king asking why she has so many daughters. The Nana and the girls playing her daughters are on her side of the yard or playing area. Her response is that it's none of the king's business. In one variant of the game the messenger is asking for a daughter to do housekeeping for the king. When the messenger threatens to tell the king, the Nana responds that he may select one, to which he responds, "Oh, I will not choose for manners, Nor choose one who does her duty, For I would prefer a beauty, The one who is young and small." He then goes to the last girl and smells her hair, saying "This one smells of wild rose," and continues down the line giving each girl a name of a flower, bird, or animal. Interestingly this is repeated until all of the girls have been named and the last daughter is left, whom he chooses to be the queen's maid. She is called *la hija favorita* (the favorite daughter) or *la hija querida* (the dear daughter) and she stands near a wall with a piece of wood under one foot. The Nana asks her, "Do you have any rice? Do you have *frijoles* [beans]? Do you have bread?" Each time the daughter answers "no." But when the Nana asks, "Do you have meat?" the daughter answers "yes" and the Nana snatches the stick of wood and runs with it, followed by all the girls screaming, and the game ends. The origin of this game and song is unknown, but it appears to be reinforcing social values of beauty and female availability. The last daughter to be chosen has something valuable (represented by the stick of wood), which raises questions about the mentioning of foods. It may reflect the poverty of the area, especially during the Depression, and the lack of food luxuries such as meat. This game is also known as *Hebritas de Oro* (Bits of Gold) and *Ángel de Oro* (Angel of Gold) and is only one of many games found in the Southwest. In Colorado, Olibama López Tushar reports that the game was called *Quiebro Bolitas de Oro* (I Break Little Balls of Gold) and a very similar game was called *Ángel Bueno, Ángel Malo* (Good Angel, Bad Angel). Clearly all of these games derive from the same source, and the varying titles reflect the evolutionary tendency of folklore.

See also La Vieja Inés y los Listones
References Campa 1933, 1979; Ebinger 1993; Espinosa 1985; Gonzáles 1974; Tushar 1992; Writers' Program 1976

Hispanic Culture Foundation

The Hispanic Culture Foundation of New Mexico, established in 1983, is the only public foundation in the country whose sole purpose is to preserve the arts, humanities, and folklore of the Hispano community. The goals of the foundation are to foster traditional Hispanic arts, literature, and humanities and to increase the understanding of the significance and value of the culture. Toward this end it is leading the campaign for the establishment of the National Hispanic Cultural Center in New Mexico. It continuously reiterates its commitment to the preservation of customs and traditions of Hispanic culture as it has developed in New Mexico and in the rest of the nation as well. Its premise is that the history of New Mexico is the beginning of much of Hispanic life in America and that Hispanic culture continues to touch the lives of all Americans. Its publications include a newsletter, pictorial books about the folk art and folklore of New Mexico, and an exciting new web site. Every year during Hispanic Heritage Month, major events are scheduled that include art exhibitions, music and dance festivals, and various receptions and awards banquets.

Hispanic Heritage Month was established and signed into law by President Ronald Reagan in the early 1980s. Lasting from September 16 through October 15, this month is meant to recognize the contributions of Hispanics to the United States, and to assist in creating understanding of the nation's growing Latino community. The Hispanic Culture Festival, organized by the Hispanic Culture Foundation, is a festival of art, music, dance, theater, and literature, which fosters a recognition of the Hispanic community and Hispanic leadership.

References Hispanic Culture Foundation 1991, http:\\www.hcfoundation.org

Hispano Culture

The people of New Mexico have historically been called Hispanos, or Spanish Americans, and the culture from this region has been distinct from other Spanish heritage people of the United States because there was less migration to this territory than to other parts of the Southwest. The Hispanos of New Mexico are descendents of the Spaniards who settled there during the seventeenth and eighteenth centuries, and the culture was preserved, sheltered, and isolated for many years. Located primarily in northern New Mexico, the region was pastoral and agricultural, and very Catholic. Franciscan friars taught the Indians and *mestizos* (mixed-race people) the language, folk narratives, folk dramas, Catholic traditions, and the civilization they had known in Spain. The region had ties to Spain through Mexico, but it was an isolated area, and it became more so after Mexico became free from Spain and the Spaniards withdrew. After Mexico's independence from Spain, its northernmost lands, what is now the Southwest, were neglected by Mexico City, the center of the nation. Mexico ruled the area for only twenty-seven years, from 1821 to 1848, at which point New Mexico became part of the United States, after the U.S. Mexican War of 1846–1848. The culture, language, and folklore of New Mexico are still referred to as Hispano culture, rather than Mexican American or Chicano. The Spanish language spoken by the Hispanos maintained an antiquated quality for hundreds of years because of the isolation of the region. One can still find older Hispanos who narrate wonderful *cuentos* in an archaic form of Spanish. Some contemporary Chicano writers from New Mexico are endeavoring to duplicate this Spanish in short stories and novels.

The culture and way of life have been well represented in literature and folklore collections by scholars and folklorists. Excellent descriptions of late nineteenth-century culture in Rio Hondo, New Mexico, are found in *Shadows of the Past* (1941) by Cleofas Jaramillo, a descendent of one of the early families of northern New Mexico. She describes weddings, *Los Penitentes* (Penitents), holiday celebrations, games, and other traditional customs. Nina Otero-Warren's *Old Spain in Our Southwest* (1937) is another work that describes the culture, traditions, foods, and customs of the upper class of Spanish Americans. Aurora Lucero-White also wrote of the folkways of the Hispanos in her work, *Los Hispanos: Five Essays on the Folkways of the Hispanos as Seen Through the Eyes of One of Them* (1947). More recent descriptions of the lives of women in New Mexico can be found in *Las Mujeres* by Nan Kyle Elsasser.

Many published collections of New Mexican folklore include *cuentos* (tales), *dichos* (proverbs), *corridos* (ballads), songs, games, descriptions of *fiestas*, medieval dramas, and religious celebrations. The notoriety of *Los Penitentes* has been well researched and documented by religious scholars, anthropologists, folklorists, and curious freelance journalists. Aurelio M. Espinosa, Juan Rael, and Arthur Campa were early collectors of folk narratives, *corridos*, *décimas* (poetic songs), *cuentos*, *dichos*, and other folk traditions and customs from New Mexico that date from the eighteenth and nineteenth centuries. Writers such as Fray Angelico Chavez, Sabine Ulibarri, and Rudolfo Anaya have published great collections of stories and *cuentos* that realistically and humorously depict the lives of New Mexicans.

Charles Briggs has studied *la plática de los viejitos* (the conversation of the elders) and shows us how the elders continue to narrate tales, stories, and proverbs and carry on other oral traditions from their past. Life in colonial New Mexico is described and discussed by Marc Simmons, and the lives of two women born in the mid-nineteenth century and living well into the twentieth are presented in Marta Weigle's *Two Guadalupes*. Life as it was lived in the early twentieth century is narrated in the creative works of Nasario García. In his 1997 publication, *Comadres*, women born in the early twentieth century narrate in their own words how life was on the ranch, the cooking, bearing children, and making their clothes from flour sacks.

The *santero* (saint maker) art tradition that we praise and appreciate today so unique to New Mexico has evolved from the Hispano religious culture of the seventeenth century. Introduced by the Spanish friars, the creation of *santos* (saints) as a distinct art form has flourished for over a hundred years, from the late eighteenth century to the late nineteenth. It was resurrected in the twentieth century over the last fifty years.

Contemporary Chicano researchers who are descendents of the Hispanos continue to be fascinated with the history and culture and persist in revisiting the work of the early scholars. The literary tradition is presented in a collection of essays titled *Paso por Aqui: Critical Essays on the New Mexican Literary Tradition, 1542–1988* (1989) edited by Erlinda Gonzales-Berry. Enrique Lamadrid brings together many of the oral traditions related to the rituals of everyday life in one volume, *Tesoros del Espíritu: A Portrait in Sound of Hispanic New Mexico* (1994) and even includes sound recordings.

References Batchen 1972; Briggs 1988; Brown 1978; Campa 1979; Chavez 1974; Elsasser 1980; Espinosa 1985; Frank 1992; Garcia, N. 1987, 1992, 1994, 1997b; Jaramillo 1972; Lamadrid 1994; Lea 1953; Lucero-White 1941, 1947; Mills 1967; Otero-Warren 1936; Simmons 1991; Ulibarri 1977; Weigle 1987

Hoodlums
See Tirilones

Horsemen
See Charros

Huelga (Strike)

Huelga (labor strike) is a charged symbol in Chicano culture. The expression *"Viva la huelga!"* is historically very close to the heart of the Chicano experience. The majority of Chicanos in the United States come from a working-class background, farmworking for many, and during the twentieth century countless labor strikes were either initiated by Chicanos or unenthusiastically involved them.

The most commonly known recent *huelga* is that of the farmworkers in California, organized by the National (later United) Farm Workers led by César Chávez in 1965. The grape workers' strike lasted over five years. There is a whole subculture surrounding the *huelga* experience that includes songs about picket lines, *huelga* chants, *teatros* (theater groups), and legendary heroes. *"Viva la huelga!"* is an expression that is often ceremoniously bellowed out at the opening or closing of meetings and gatherings of Chicanos. For many years it was meant to show support for the farmworkers' strike, but it eventually became a generic chant that promotes cultural and ethnic solidarity. The speech is meant to rile people up and incite them to work as a group, and it implies that "regardless what happens, we can always go on strike and don't forget it."

Organized strikes as strategies of resistance and as ways to demand labor, social, and educational equality have always been prevalent in the lives of Chicanos in the Southwest. Labor organizing and striking have been a way

"Viva la Huelga!" is an expression close to the heart of the Chicano experience. It is particularly well known in California, where the National Farm Workers Union led by César Chávez staged a walkout of the grape fields in 1965. (Ted Streshinsky/Corbis)

of life for farmworkers in California. Throughout the 1920s and 1930s, Chicanos in California were involved in countless farmworking strikes, from the Imperial Valley to the great San Joaquin Valley of cotton and grape fields. In 1903 over 1,000 Mexican and Japanese sugar beet workers went on strike in Oxnard. To name a few other strikes, there was a strike of cantaloupe workers in the Imperial Valley in 1928; the pecan shellers' strike of San Antonio, Texas, that involved over 10,000 workers in 1938; the DiGiorgio Fruit Corporation strike of 1945 that Ernesto Galarza wrote about in *Spiders in the House and Workers in the Field*; the Los Angeles Chicano high school students' strike of 1968; the Farah pants strike in El Paso in the early 1970s; the Third World strike at UC Berkeley in 1969; and innumerable hunger strikes.

The film *Salt of the Earth*, produced in 1953, tells the true story of a year-long strike of Mexican American zinc miners in New Mexico. The miners went on strike after learning that they were paid a lower wage rate than the Anglo miners. In an effort to break the union the New Mexican mining company made it illegal for the men to picket, so instead their wives took over the picket line. Some of the actual strikers acted in the movie, which was filmed near Silver City, New Mexico. The film was directed by Herbert J. Biberman. It has become a classic cult film and is shown often in college classes.

In Texas, the phrase *"hacer huelga"* means to have a good time, or to get crazy. *Huelga* is a culturally loaded expression not only in a labor sense but also as a symbol of ethnicity because it implies, "once a striker, always a striker." Through the performances of *El Teatro Campesino* (Farmworkers' Theater) songs and stories about the farmworkers' strike spread in Chicano culture and raise awareness for support of all strikers. "Huelga en General" and "El Picket Sign" are *huelga* songs recorded by *El Teatro* well known to 1960s Chicanos, who still dance to these tunes as played by Dr. Loco's Rockin' Jalapeño Band.

See also Chávez, César Estrada; Doctor Loco's Rockin' Jalapeño Band; El Teatro Campesino
References Jiménez 1992; Paredes 1976

Huesero (Bone Setter)

The Spanish word for bone is *hueso*, and a *huesero* is a person who knows the bones of the body and how to set them when broken. A *huesero* is a type of *curandero*, but one who specializes in the problems of bones, such as fractures and breaks. When doctors were scarce, a *huesero* was indispensable to a community, treating children with broken limbs and men who fell off horses or tractors. Robert Trotter maintains that medical clinics and osteologists have displaced *hueseros*, and that individuals now may seek out the services of a *sobador*, a person who massages sore muscles and treats muscles detached from bones, and performs a similar community function as a *huesero*.

See also Curanderismo; Sobador
Reference Trotter and Chavira 1997

Hut
See Jacal

Hymns
See Alabados

Quetzalcoatl.

I

I Am Joaquin/Yo Soy Joaquin

The title of an epic poem written by Rodolfo "Corky" Gonzales in 1967, which has been republished many times since and is now available on the Internet. It became a personal manifesto of many young Chicanos when it was first published with the following opening lines:

> I am Joaquin, lost in a world of confusion,
> caught up in the whirl of a gringo society,
> confused by the rules, scorned by attitudes,
> suppressed by manipulation, and destroyed by modern society.
> My fathers have lost the economic battle
> and won the struggle of cultural survival.
> And now! I must choose between the paradox of
> victory of the spirit, despite physical hunger,
> or to exist in the grasp of American social neurosis,
> sterilization of the soul and a full stomach.

The poem goes on to describe a journey of a young Chicano as he goes into the historical past of Mexicans in the United States. It angrily expresses commentary on the difficult lives of all Chicanos in the Southwest and declares a rallying cry to all Chicanos to unite. It has been reproduced hundreds of times and performed by *teatro* groups in the United States and Mexico, including *El Teatro Campesino* (Farmworkers' Theater). It was adapted into film and has been required reading in many Chicano Studies courses during the past thirty years. It has been quoted over and over by professors, students, organizers, and many other speakers. A beloved quote of many students is:

> *La Raza!*
> *Mejicano!*
> *Español!*
> *Latino!*
> *Hispano!*
> *Chicano!*
> Or whatever I call myself,

I look the same
I feel the same
I cry and sing the same. (98)

See also El Teatro Campesino
References Gonzales 1972; Keller 1985; Limón 1992

Immigration Officials
See La Migra

Indigestion
See Empacho

Indita (Indian Chant)

A song form related to the ballad, the *indita* is found in New Mexico and Mexico, and probably dates from the late eighteenth century. It is written in octosyllabic verse that is often sung like an Indian chant. A variety of songs may be called *inditas*, and in many the word *indita* appears in the title, but at times it is difficult to interpret why a song is considered an *indita*. It has Indian influence either in subject matter or musical rhythm, and is the result of the Indian contact that most Spanish and *Mexicano* people experienced in the Southwest. *Inditas* often narrate in the first person a significant event that occurred between the communities of Hispanos and Indians. There are performances of these ballads that include drums, and the performers may dance between reciting the verses. Several hundred *inditas* have been collected in New Mexico by Arthur Campa, Rubén Cobos, and J. D. Robb. *Inditas* collected from a later period have also been called *cautivas*, because they describe the recurrent hardships of women captured by Indians on the frontier.

References Campa 1930; Campos 1929; Cobos 1999; Lamadrid 1993, 1994; Rivera 1989; Robb 1954, 1980

Insignias
See Placas

Quetzalcoatl

J

Jacal (Hut)

A *jacal* is a hut or shack, but in south and west Texas it refers to a specific type of structure that was home to the *Tejano* of the eighteenth and nineteenth centuries. *Jacales* were the first houses built by the Spanish settlers in 1749 and became the houses of the *mestizo* (mixed-race) population of Texas. Constructed from posts and mud, with the vertical posts embedded in the ground, tied together with rawhide, and covered with a mixture of mud or clay, it is similar to the adobe house of New Mexico, except that the mud was not formed into bricks. The roofs were made of dried weeds, cane thatched with tule, straw, or coarse grass. Some of the straw roofs lasted for thirty or more years. Usually *jacales* were only one room, measuring twelve by twelve feet, and blankets covered the door and window, but they were well insulated, keeping out heat and cold, and lasting for many years. Construction of

Constructed of posts and mud, jacales (huts) were the first houses built by the Spanish settlers in 1749 and often became the homes of the mestizo *population of Texas. (North Wind Picture Archive)*

jacales started in the eighteenth century and persisted into the early twentieth century; it is identified with the *Tejano* way of life. When the Anglo Americans moved into Texas they too lived in *jacales* until their "big houses" were built, but their *vaqueros* (cowboys) continued to live in *jacales* in clusters surrounding the ranches. To this day many people on the Mexican side of the border still live in *jacales*. The grandparents and parents of many Chicano baby boomers were born and raised in *Tejano jacales*, and the expression *"nací en un jacal"* (I was born in a hut) has often been heard as the beginning line of a *cuento* (story).

References De Leon 1982; Graham 1991, 1993; Robinson 1979

Jamaicas (Bazaars)

A term used in Chicano and Mexican communities for a bazaar when its purpose is connected to raising funds for church activities or a church building. The *Diccionario de Mejicanismos* states that *jamaicas* were organized to sell objects for charity, as a means of raising money for *algún propósito piadoso* (for a pious cause). *Jamaicas* were held in the 1920s, 1930s, and 1940s from the Midwest to the San Joaquin Valley of California, to raise money for the building of churches, usually in the name of *La Virgen de Guadalupe*. *Jamaicas* are popular folk fairs held in the afternoons or evenings, and consist of food stands, games for kids, and music for dancing. It is likely that millions of *tamales* have been made and sold at *jamaicas* for the holy purpose of raising capital to construct a church in a Mexican or Chicano *barrio*. In his poem "A Trip Through the Mind Jail," Raúl Salinas has a delightful stanza where he reminisces about the *jamaicas* of his youth:

> Neighborhood of Sunday night *jamaicas*
> at *Guadalupe* Church.
> Fiestas for any occasion
> holidays, holy days, happy days,
> 'round and 'round the promenade
> eating snow-cones . . . *raspas* . . . and *tamales*
> the games . . . bingo, cake walk, spin the wheel,
> making eyes at girls from cleaner neighborhoods
> the unobtainables
> who responded all giggles and excitement.

See also Kermése
References Lane and Escobar 1987; Salinas 1970

Jaramillo, Cleofas Martinez (1878–1956)

One of a handful of New Mexican women writers and folklorists of the late nineteenth and early twentieth centuries, Cleofas Martinez was from an early New Mexican family and one of seven children. Born in Arroyo Hondo in 1878, she was educated in New Mexico in Taos and Santa Fe and in 1898 married her cousin, Venceslao Jaramillo. Unfortunately, by 1920 she was a widow, and in 1931 the last of her three children also died. It was at this time in her life that she turned to folklore and to writing as a career. She translated twenty-five of her mother's stories and wrote a cookbook of New Mexico recipes published in 1939. In 1941 she published *Shadows of the Past*, a folkloric work that describes many of the traditions and customs that she learned as a child. In 1955 she published *Romance of a Little Village Girl*, an autobiographical work. She was a founder of *La Sociedad Folklórica*, the New Mexico Folklore Society, in 1935, an organization meant to keep Hispano folklore alive in New Mexico. Rules established by the group were meant to keep control of the organization in the hands of the New Mexicans. Spanish descent was a required criterion for membership and all the meetings were conducted in Spanish. Like Nina Otero-Warren and Fabiola Cabeza de Baca, other pioneer Hispanic family descendents, Jaramillo felt a need to preserve the customs, traditions, and folktales of her culture by writing them down. Although Genaro Padilla refers to these works as folkloric autobiographies, they were also ethnographic studies of Hispano culture. Much of the writing was a direct response to the influx of Anglo writers and artists whom the Hispanos saw as appropriating their customs, local color, and folklore. Padilla calls Jaramillo's cookbook "a gesture of cultural assertion" (54). In organizing *La Sociedad Folklórica*, Jaramillo states about her work, "These rules were that the society should be composed of only thirty members, all of whom must be of Spanish descent, and that the meetings must be conducted in the Spanish language, with the aim of preserving our language, customs and traditions" (1955, 176). "And still these smart Americans make money with their writing, and we who know the correct way, sit back and listen" (173). She died in El Paso in 1956 at the age of 79.

References Jaramillo 1955, 1972, 1981; Padilla 1991; Ponce 1992; Rebolledo 1989

Jaramillo, Don Pedrito (18??–1907)

A famous *curandero* known only as Don Pedrito, or the Healer of Los Olmos, he went to Texas from Mexico around 1881 and settled in Los Olmos. He claimed he was a *curandero* and proceeded to heal people. For at least twenty-five years he cured the people of Texas and Mexico, traveling on horseback throughout the countryside. As a traveling *curandero* in Texas he went to Corpus Christi, San Antonio, and Laredo, and in this way he saw many people. He believed that God had given him the power to heal and that it was his mission to help the sick. Thousands of people were healed by him, yet he believed it was their faith in the power of God that assisted in their healing. He never charged for his services and was a very generous man, feeding whoever came to see him. Many times there would be 500 people camped out on his property, and he would find food to feed them all. A friend gave him 100 acres of land, where he built himself a small hut and developed the rest into a farm, growing corn, squash, peppers, and other vegetables. This food was prepared and given to the people. Although he was not formally educated he did have a power to cure that was recognized by local doctors and priests. Many of his cures did not involve medication or herbs but instead consisted of baths, being thrown in a creek, or drinking glasses of water for six or nine consecutive days. He died on July 3, 1907, and his burial place near Falfurrias, Texas, has become a shrine that is visited and venerated by hundreds of *Tejanos* yearly.

References De Leon 1982; Hudson 1951; Romano 1964

Jokes
See Chistes

Joking Behavior
See Relajo

Quetzalcoatl.

Kermés (Festival)

From the word *kermis*, which meant an "outdoor fair or festival" in the Low Countries, usually an event organized to raise money for charitable purposes. In the sixteenth century the word was spelled *kermiss* and referred to the dedication of a church. Pronounced by Spanish speakers as *kermés*, and sometimes found in literature as *quermes*, these outdoor fundraisers were often held in association with school and church activities. References to *kerméses* can be found in the social histories of Chicano communities throughout the Southwest. After Mexico gained its independence from Spain in 1821, the Spanish missionaries left and were replaced by other religious friars. It is possible that this expression was introduced by the many European, and particularly Irish, priests that could be found throughout many Chicano communities. Another expression used by Chicanos to designate this same type of event is *jamaica*, also a type of bazaar organized to raise money for the building of churches in Mexican communities. The *Diccionario de Mejicanismos* states that the word *kermés* was most often used by *gente de postín* (people who put on airs).

See also Jamaicas
Reference Sommers 1995

Klicas (Cliques)

Within structural organizations of Chicano gangs in California, a *klica* is a subgroup, a division of a larger gang. The word is a Spanish version of the English word "clique." Members of a *klica* may be the younger-age boys, or a *klica* may be the female division of a larger gang. Many southern California gangs have been in existence for fifty to sixty years and have developed a complex organizational structure. Age-graded divisions may include from two to five age sets within the larger gang, and all are called *klicas*. Gangs usually originate within a *barrio* (neighborhood), a street, or a housing project, and the name of the gang comes from the street or neighborhood. "*SanFer*" is from San Fernando, "*Sepas*" from Sepulveda, and "*Pacas Flats*" from Pacoima. A gang could be composed of two, five, or even ten *klicas*, each being different and distinct for specific reasons, and each with its own name. Yet all of the *klicas* will identify with the overall gang and its *barrio*. "Tiny Locas" (small crazies) is a name given to the young female *klicas*, made up of young girls ages thirteen to sixteen, and they can be found in many of the larger Chicano gangs of the San Fernando Valley.

Klicas are also found in Chicano prison gangs as subdivisions of larger gangs from the whole prison system. Chicano culture has a strong penchant for descriptive naming, giving nicknames to individuals and to groups. In fact there are many words used to define and identify groups or gangs, such as *palomilla*, *pleva*, *ganga*, *klica*, *masa*. Some groups may even be erroneously identified as *cholos* (1990s urban youth) or low riders or *chicanos*. The term *klica* has been used in some communities, such as Tucson and Los Angeles, for at least forty years.

See also Cholos; Low Rider
References Harris, Mary G., 1988, 1994; Moore 1991; Moore, Vigil, and Levy 1995; Vigil 1983, 1988

El Kookoóee (Bogeyman)

A *cucui* was a bogeyman sometimes known as "cocoman" that Chicano children were warned about when they misbehaved. Kookoóee has come to be the name of a realistic giant puppet for the *Festival de Otoño* (Autumn Festival) held in the South Valley in Albuquerque, New Mexico. Rudolfo Anaya named and described *El Kookoóee* as a masculine ghost who played the role of a father figure in warning young men of the dangers of sexual experimentation. In order to not lose this important archetype of Chicano culture, Anaya proposed to a group of Chicano artists to create an effigy of *El Kookoóee* and burn it at a public *fiesta* in 1990. This *Kookoóee* was sixteen feet tall; made of wood, paper, and metal; had roosters' feet, large hands with long arms, a big head, and a green *chile* for a nose. His long, matted, shoulder-length hair was full of weeds like those found along the river's banks. He carried a big bag that children and adults were encouraged to fill with pieces of paper that listed worries and fears. Each year he is burned at the festival, and the worries and fears are burned away, leaving a cleansing effect on the hearts and minds of the participants, who look forward to the arrival of fall. Each year the number of people who attend the festival grows and new locations to burn the monster have had to be found. *El Kookoóee* is different each year. He has grown in stature (sixteen feet in 1990, thirty feet tall in 1994) and in importance. Anaya believes that this burning ritual provides the same kind of cathartic effect on young people as listening to scary stories narrated by one's parents.

See also El Cucui
References Anaya 1995b; CHICLE 1994; Montoya 1994

Quetzalcoatl.

Legends
See Leyendas

La Leyenda Negra (The Black Legend)

La Leyenda Negra is the term used for a myth and it describes a very negative attitude that many believe pervades the historical perspective regarding Hispanics and Mexicans. The Black Legend embodies a belief that Spaniards are basically a cruel, evil, lazy, greedy, treacherous, and fanatical people. It originated in the era of Inquisitorial Spain and has misrepresented the history of Spain since the 1500s. The printed history of the conquest of the New World depicts a violent and corrupt invasion, but there is a belief that the Black Legend has influenced the way this history has been written.

The Black Legend originated in the sixteenth century during the Protestant Reformation, with the beginnings of a rejection of Catholicism and abhorrence of the political and military power of Spain. When Spain and Portugal remained loyal to Catholicism, and expanded their empires by settling in South America, Central America, the Caribbean Islands, and parts of North America, the rest of Europe looked on very disapprovingly. This viewpoint has continued to color everything about Spain since then, including the grim legacy left by Spain in the New World. It has justified the dictatorial treatment of Latin America and Mexico by the United States since the early nineteenth century. Biased attitudes toward Catholic Spain were inherited by Anglo Americans and brought to the New World colonies by Protestant English settlers.

The term *Leyenda Negra* was assigned to this belief by Julian Juderias, a Spanish intellectual, in 1914. He stated that anti-Spanish propaganda and misconceptions had continued to develop since the sixteenth century, and historical distortions in both Europe and America constituted a *Leyenda Negra*. It is thought that the Black Legend is actually the basis for the discriminatory treatment of Mexicans by Anglo Americans during the conquest of the frontier in the 1800s, and even for the current treatment of Chicanos in the United States in the twentieth century. The cause for derogatory stereotyping of Mexicans, and other Latin Americans, is difficult to understand, and the negative stereotype seems to have no historical basis, until one understands the history of the Black Legend. Publications by early American travelers to the Southwest and Mexico depict the Spanish Mexicans in not only horrendous terms, but with extreme passion. Thomas Jefferson Farnham, a New England attorney, wrote in the 1840s, "In a word, the Californians are an imbecile, pusillanimous, race of men, and unfit to control the destinies of that beautiful country" (Weber, 295). Stephen Austin, in 1822–1823, after a trip to Mexico City wrote, "To be candid the majority of the people of the whole nation as far as I have seen them want nothing but tails to be more brutes than the apes" (Weber, 298).

During the U.S. Mexican war of 1846–1848 the uncivil treatment of Mexicans and *Californios* and the public conviction in the righteousness of the war are cited as examples of how Mexico was disrespected by Americans. Historically powerful stereotypes of inferior Mexicans and Mexican Americans, perpetuated by arrogant Americans such as Austin, led to the acceptance of Manifest Destiny as America's right. "The result of such efforts to discredit Mexico and justify war was a widespread belief that the God-forsaken Mexicans were unworthy to keep the valuable resources and land they had inherited from Spain" (Sanchez 1990, 9).

The popular image of a Mexican with a large *sombrero* sleeping under a cactus very likely originated from these early writings of traveling Americans, with the result that the icon has become imprinted forever upon the collective character of Chicanos and Mexicans. The common reference to "finally the sleeping giant awakens" when conferring on Mexican American social-political issues is made often by educated and acculturated Chicanos, manifesting an internalization of an image imposed from outside the Mexican culture. Although no one actually mentions the Black Legend belief, its legacy permeates a lot of Chicano oral folklore.

References Powell 1971; Sanchez 1990; Weber 1979

Leyendas (Legends)

A *leyenda*, a legend, is an oral narrative different from a folktale in that it is narrated as if the event described occurred in the recent past and the story is believed by the narrator to be true. There is often a supernatural element to the narrative, such as a person's disappearance into thin air, yet it will be recited as having occurred in a specified locale. Often the narrator states where the story originated and explains that the events were observed by a grandmother, cousin, father, or friend. The names of persons and places in the narrative will be familiar to the audience. In Chicano oral tradition, stories about *La Llorona*, the Blue Lady, or Joaquín Murrieta can properly be called legends and almost always tell a story the audience wants to believe. The Chicano community's cultural belief system is inherent in the narrative, otherwise the legend would not be recited and retold, again and again. There are hundreds of variants of the *La Llorona* legend, all narrated about known encounters with her, during the past 200 years. Her tragic story is believable, and one can say she is probably the quintessential legendary figure of the Chicano folk belief system.

The urban belief tale, sometimes just called an urban legend, is a subtype of the legend and is called such because it circulates among all classes and ages and reflects modern stresses and anxieties. It is not only found in urban centers but in rural regions as well. In addition to the legend of *La Llorona* (Weeping Woman), another widespread legend in Chicano folklore is the Vanishing Hitchhiker, although not always known by this name. A California folklore journal first carried an article about it in 1942, and a Chicano version appears in Miller's narrative collection from Los Angeles with a date of 1939. The story usually involves a driver who picks up a hitchhiker, often late at night and often a young girl, and he drops her off at or near her home. She leaves something in his car, or he lends her a jacket or sweater, and the next day he returns to retrieve it and learns that she was a ghost, and has been dead for several years. Sometimes she is met at a dance, and asks a boy to drive her home, or she might be a nun, but the ghost is rarely a male. Brunvand calls it a classic automobile legend, and its prevalence has increased since cars became affordable to all social classes. Interestingly, the Vanishing Hitchhiker legend is one of the few narratives shared by both Anglo American and Chicano folklore. Mark Glazer discusses a collection of 152 variants from the Rio Grande Folklore Archive at Pan American University in Texas and states that the legend is "part of a culture which believes in miracles, mystery, and romance" (1987, 35).

See also Agreda, María de Jesus Coronel de; La Llorona; Murrieta, Joaquín
References Brunvand 1981; Glazer 1986, 1987b; Miller 1973; Robe 1980

Limpia (Cleansing)

A folk medicine ritual also called a *barrida*, from the Spanish verb *barrer*, meaning a "sweeping," as in housecleaning. *Limpiar* means to clean and a *limpia* is similar to a *barrida*. Both words mean a cleansing, in a medical and in a spiritual sense. Some people use the word *limpieza* instead of *limpia*, but the significance is the same. An individual may seek a *limpia* from a healer if the person is not feeling well with no specific cause or feels that bad luck or misfortune is prevalent in his or her life. A *limpieza* can expel the hostile forces and also provide spiritual strength so that the person can effectively fight off negative energy. Spiritual healers who are not *curanderos* perform *limpias*, although mostly it is *curanderos* who perform this ritual. The patient may be standing, sitting in a chair, or lying down while the ritual is performed. The healer will sweep the patient with a little broom made of herbs, such as sage, rosemary, and rue, believed to be effective in eliminating evil influences. Herbal water, holy water, or alcohol is sprinkled over the person in the form of a cross, and the healer's hands are used to sweep along the whole body, pushing away the evil spirits. While this is being done prayers are recited. The prayers may be the Lord's Prayer or *Las Doce Verdades del Mundo* (The Twelve Truths of the World). Instead of herbs some *curanderos* use an object for the sweeping, such as an egg or a lemon, believing that it will absorb the harm or illness affecting the patient. These objects are burned after the ritual, ensuring the recovery of the person. The person is swept on all sides, front and back, and if there is pain in a particular spot, special attention will be given to that area. Trotter states that "the presence of the *curandero*, the soothing effect of the sweepings (touching), and the low-key monotone chant of the prayers produces in the patient a light trance state that is comforting and reassuring" (Trotter and Chavira 1997, 82).

See also Curanderismo; Las Doce Verdades
References Roeder 1988; Trotter and Chavira 1997

La Llorona (The Weeping Woman)

This is the name of probably the most famous legendary woman found in Greater Mexico. The ancient legend of *La Llorona* has been traced to pre-Columbian times in Mexico, and there is continuing discussion whether it may also have medieval European origins. Most Chicanos heard of her as children, read about her in literature, or learned of her from friends. *La Llorona*, meaning "the weeping woman" or "the howling woman," may be represented as an Indian woman, an ugly old witch, or a beautiful woman in white with long flowing hair. She always appears late at night, and her crying and weeping can be vividly heard as she shrieks, "*Ayyy, mis hijos!*" (Oh, my children!).

According to the tragic legend, there once was a woman who was abandoned by her husband, or lover, and left with two or three children. Angry and seeking revenge, she kills her children by throwing them into a river, or sometimes by other means. When she realizes what she's done, she goes insane. She is condemned to spend eternity searching for her lost and dead children. Consequently she is often heard in the night calling her children. She frequents rivers and other bodies of water, and is sometimes seen floating above the water looking, searching for her children. Her legend has been recited for over 300 years, and in contemporary times she is still believed to be wandering the streets in large cities, as well as in the small towns of the Southwest where numerous people report encounters with her. At times she is seen as a beautiful woman, wearing a white dress, roaming back streets and country roads, crying and weeping. Sometimes she becomes visible to the wayward husband who is out late, drinking, and when he approaches her, she turns into an ugly horse-faced hag, scaring him into swearing abstinence forever. Parents use her name to scare little children into obedience: "*Hay viene La Llorona . . . portaté bien*" (The *Llorona* is coming, behave yourself). Even adults who've heard the story many times and do not want to admit belief still fear a late-night encounter with *La Llorona*.

There are ancient texts of indigenous mythology narrated by the Aztecs and recorded by the Spaniards that very closely resemble the *La Llorona* legend. In some tales she is believed to be *Cihuacoatl*, the patron goddess of women who die in childbirth. It is said that *Cihuacoatl* carried a little baby cradle on her back, or a dead baby in her arms, as she roamed the country crying through the nights. Those who saw her considered it an ill omen. Sahagún mentions in *The Conquest of Mexico* that "a woman was often heard [as] she went weeping and crying out. Loudly did she call out at night. She walked about saying: 'O my beloved sons, now we are about to go!'" (Horcasitas and Butterworth, 208). Horcasitas and Butterworth reprint several texts of these early chronicles. Diego Muñoz Camargo (ca. 1529–1599) also reported that before the Spaniards arrived, "many times and many nights was heard the voice of a woman who cried out in a loud voice, drowning herself with her tears, and with great sobs and sighs, wailing" (Horcasitas and Butterworth, 209).

Contemporary texts of *La Llorona* collected in Mexico assert that the original *Llorona* was *La Malinche*, the mistress of Cortés. Cortés abandoned her to return to Spain, and according to the legend *Malinche* killed their son with a knife. This could be the source of another characteristic of the *La Llorona* legend. In many variants the reason for her abandonment by her lover is their class differences. He leaves her for someone of his own class, or she is an Indian woman or a *mestiza* (mixed-race woman) and he is of pure blood. In other variants, she is a woman of the streets, who doesn't want her illegitimate children, so she throws them into the river. She is always described as having long hair, down below her waist, and is seen wearing a white gown. Sometimes men see her as a temptress and a siren; she entices them to follow her, and then she frightens them with her horrible looks. They are usually found dead the next day. What appears to be an unjust punishment is that *La Llorona* is condemned to wander for eternity, crying and repenting, searching for her lost children. All mothers who have lost children identify with her, and feel her pain.

The prodigious amount of published literature about *La Llorona*, by folklorists, literary critics, anthropologists, and feminist writers, attests to the complexity of the legend. Children's books, short stories, novels, and films have been created based on this basic story of infanticide and repentance. We find narratives in rural and urban areas of the Southwest, on college campuses, in juvenile halls, in large cities of the Midwest such as Chicago, and among the native populations of Mexico.

Many Chicanos see themselves as orphans of *La Llorona*, as the lost children of the marriage between the Aztecs and the Spanish Conquerors. She is a beloved female archetype among contemporary Chicanas, who write poems, short stories, and academic research articles about her. As one writer put it, "It is finally time to let go of a single, narrow understanding of the tale and to see *La Llorona* instead as an always evolving emblem of gender, sexuality, and power—and, too, as another female victim of history's tender mercies" (Candelaria, 115).

Cesar Rosas, one of the founders and original members of Los Lobos, plays guitar during the filming of the music video La Bamba, *for the movie of the same name. (Henry Diltz/Corbis)*

See also Leyendas; La Malinche; La Muerte
References Anaya 1984, 1995; Arora 1981; Barakat 1965; Candelaria 1993; García 1992; Gonzalez Obregon 1947; Horcasitas and Butterworth 1963; Limón 1988b; Paz 1961; Rebolledo and Rivero 1993; Simmons 1974; Vigil 1994; Zinam and Molina 1991

Los Lobos (The Wolves)

The name of a musical group formed in 1973 in East Los Angeles, with the full name of *Los Lobos del Este de Los Angeles*. The group has been together ever since, with four of the same musicians, all raised in East Los Angeles. Starting out playing Top 40 band music, they eventually decided to play traditional Mexican folk music, using traditional Mexican instruments. They've incorporated into their music the instruments, such the *bajo sexto* (a twelve-string guitar), *el guitarrón* (a bass guitar), and *el quinto* (a five-string guitar).

Their repertoire reflects the variety of Mexican and Chicano music, such as Tex-Mex, *Música Norteña*, rock and roll, blues, salsa, rhythm and blues, and other Latino styles. The group plays *norteño* music interspersed with rock and roll. They played and recorded the music for *La Bamba, Zoot Suit,* and other films and have toured worldwide. *Rolling Stone Magazine* named the group Band of the Year in 1985. They received a Grammy Award for "Anselma" in 1984, a 75-year-old Mexican song.

In 1988 they produced an album, *La Pistola y el Corazon* (The Pistol and the Heart), of acoustic Mexican folk songs, which is considered a great collection of Mexican folk music.

References Freedman 1987; Guevara 1985; Loza 1985; Monsalvo 1989

Low Rider

The expression "low rider" is used to describe the car, the subculture, and the person who drives a vehicle that has been lowered, rides very low, and has been customized. A car, truck, bicycle, van, or motorcycle that has been lowered, and this can be achieved by various methods—means that it sits very close to the ground and has a sleek streamlined appearance. The driver and/or owner is called a low rider and the act of low riding refers to all the activities associated with driving the car: cruising, caravanning, and hopping. Low riders have commonly been associated with *cholos* (1990s urban youth) and gangs, but traditionally Chicanos seriously involved in low riding and customizing low-rider cars are not involved in gangs, and low-rider clubs actually present an alternative to gang involvement. Low-rider car clubs communicate a message of cultural pride and unity. Although different, the *cholo* subculture can be closely linked to the low-rider subculture.

It is not clear when low riding started, but it was already a custom by the 1930s in Los Angeles and Sacramento, although the name "low rider" did not come into usage until the 1960s. After World War II, because of the growth in the economy, many Chicanos could afford to buy cars, old and new, and the practice of customizing cars and cruising became very popular throughout the Southwest and California during the 1950s. The most popular cars to lower are long ones, such as Fords, Buicks, and Chevrolets. Hydraulic lifts are used to lower and raise both the front and rear ends of a car. Before it was discovered that a hydraulic lift could be used with the batteries stored in the trunk of the car, different methods were used to lower the chassis of the car. Early crude methods were to place heavy bricks and cement bags in the trunk, or to cut the spring's coils, or lower the car's blocks. To give the car that lowered look the top might be cut back to lower the roof. In recent times, once a car is "lifted" or "all juiced up," the driver controls the lift with a hand control.

The painting and decorating of the exterior and interior of the car are very important for appearances, personal identity, and also for belonging to a car club and participating in car shows. The interior may be upholstered in crushed velvet, red or black, have wall-to-wall carpeting, a bar, a chandelier, a TV, and a stereo tape deck. The exterior may be painted in two tones, a lacquer mixed with iridescent flakes, or have a pearl finish. Sometimes the undercarriage is chromed and gold-plated. Painting low-rider cars

Lolo Medina and his brother drive a customized low-rider Cadillac through the desert in New Mexico. (Macduff Everton/Corbis)

is a specialty only available at certain paint and body shops, so low riders must be aware of such businesses. Besides the painting of the car, other decorative designs or motifs may also be applied, such as pinstriping, fancy lace (a fire design), and murals. Murals of an Aztec or Mayan scene or *La Virgen de Guadalupe* are popular icons painted on the trunk, hood, or roof of the car. Even though there is similarity in the styles, each car is very different in the final production. There are many techniques employed to arrive at a unique personal style. For instance accessories from different-year models are interchanged, such as side panels from a 1957 model may be cut and welded to a 1952 car, or "'57 Cadillac tail lamps on a '62 Chevy Impala" (Bright, 196).

Low riders are usually young urban Chicanos, between the ages of eighteen and thirty, and there can be two and three generations of low riders in one family. The cost of fixing and maintaining a low-rider car is fairly high, so the owner typically is a working person. Since finding older cars, say from the 1950s, is becoming difficult, some low riders now customize small trucks, motorcycles, and bicycles as well. The movie *Mi Vida Loca* (My Crazy Life) depicts the work that goes into customizing a pickup truck.

Cruising involves driving very slowly up and down city streets, such as Mission Street in San Francisco, Whittier Boulevard in Los Angeles, and King and Story Roads in San Jose, California. The objective of cruising is to socialize, to see and be seen, to give others the opportunity to admire one's car and to admire the other cars; consequently the driving must be very slow, *muy despacito*. Driving a great customized car, beautifully painted, is a unique experience for the low rider. Cruising slowly and smoothly, sitting low in the driver's seat, glancing out at the street, nodding the head slightly when being recognized, all these make up an experience only a Chicano low rider who has invested lots of time and money in his car can appreciate. Cruising is often compared to the custom of promenading around a plaza, referred to as *el paseo* in many Latin American and Mexican cities. In this sense, the low-rider car becomes a cultural vehicle, as represented by the artist Gilbert Lujan in his series titled "Cultural Vehicles."

A low-rider 1969 Ford LTD called "Dave's Dream" is on display at the Smithsonian National Museum of American History in Washington D.C., the first and only low-rider car in the museum. From Chimayo, New Mexico, Dennis Martinez, Richard Martinez, and David Jaramillo worked on customizing the car, starting in 1975. It has two hydraulic pumps, with the batteries stored in the truck, that lift and lower the car and can make it rock from side to side and give it an appearance of dancing. Actually "car dancing" is an event held at low-rider car shows.

Within the low-rider subculture there exist several divisions of traditions. For instance, car clubs are an important aspect of the culture and a way to showcase cars in competitions. One of the oldest ongoing car clubs in Los Angeles is named the Dukes. Members of car clubs are referred to as "clubbers," and they compete for trophies, ride in car caravans, and often participate in fund-raising events. "*Cholos*" are considered another group, less financially stable with more modern cars, less ornate, and likely more *Mexicano* in orientation. A third group, the "*cha chas*," are Mexican immigrants, who drive the Toyotas and Volkswagens, and are a smaller group.

Low Rider Magazine was founded during the 1970s to provide a forum for low riders and the culture that surrounds low riding. *Low Rider* has been very instrumental in the widespread growth of low-rider car clubs, and "Low Rider Happenings," throughout the Southwest. Low riding is looked upon as a very Chicano cultural phenomenon, yet it has spread to other ethnic communities. There are many non-Chicano car clubs, and the Japanese have also adopted it. *Low Rider* has been publishing a Japanese edition for the past four years and has organized low-rider car shows in Tokyo and Osaka. As a form of artistic expression and folk art, the customizing of low-rider cars by Chicanos is an expression of tradition and cultural pride.

References Bright 1994, 1995; Chabran and Chabran 1996; Gradante 1985; Griffith 1988; Marks 1980; Parsons 1999; Plascencia 1983; Stone 1990; Thomas 1994; Vigil 1991

Luminarias (Bonfires)

Not to be confused with *farolitos*, *luminarias* are small bonfires, and the custom of lighting them dates back to the Roman history of Spain. These small fires are built in New Mexico to celebrate *La Noche Buena*, Christmas Eve, and to light the way for the announcement of the birth of the Christ child. One family may light three *luminarias* in front of their home, one each for Jesus, Mary, and Joseph, while another may light twelve, one for each of the twelve apostles. It is believed *luminarias* originate from the huge bonfires built in pre-Christian times to celebrate rituals to the gods and goddesses. Also in ancient times shepherds built fires to keep themselves warm and to scare off the wolves. This tradition continued in New Mexico with the shepherds' fires to illuminate the way for the coming of Jesus Christ. They are not as well known as *farolitos* in contemporary American popular culture, and one often finds *farolitos* mistakenly called *luminarias*, and magazine articles describe how to make them, especially during the Christmas holidays.

References Anaya 1995a; Brown 1978; Ortega 1973

Quetzalcoatl.

M

Machismo

Machismo describes a stereotypic image of a Chicano/Latino man who is extraordinarily aggressive, stresses dominance over his wife and family, exhibits physical and sexual prowess, and places strong emphasis on masculine rigidity. Chicano social scientists have authored studies about *machismo,* noting that it is a stereotype often used against Chicanos to blame them for their underclass social position in American society. *Macho* literally means "male," and *machismo* is the concept of "maleness," but in American culture it has come to mean an exaggerated masculinity. A masculinity associated with violence, self-centeredness, chauvinism, or alcoholism is not a *macho* concept recognized by most Chicanos. For Chicanos, *un hombre macho* is a man who symbolizes dignity, takes care of his family, has respect for all women, especially his mother, and possesses a strong sense of self-identity and character. Many Chicanos grew up influenced by Mexican movies, with characters like Pedro Infante, Cantinflas, Antonio Aguilar, and Jorge Negrete, as men who sang to the beautiful girls and defended the poor by fighting for justice and social equality. These were positive images of *machos.*

The famous Mexican folklorist Vicente Mendoza has stated that the concept of *machismo,* and the word *macho,* were not prevalent in Mexican *corridos* (ballads) and popular culture until the 1940s. Supposedly the word gained popularity after Avila Camacho became president of Mexico because in ballads *macho* easily rhymed with Camacho.

In an article published in 1975, José Armas describes *machismo* as a mode of behavior necessary for an individual to live life with integrity, self-reliance, and dignity. He states, "*Machismo* is a personal code of honor that is self imposed in a world devoid of universal moral law or justice. It is maintained and sustained by individual pride and dignity" (56).

A Latino men's group calling themselves *Hombres Latinos* was formed in California with the purpose of redefining the image and concept of *machismo*. This was reported in a *Los Angeles Times* article in 1992 written by Christopher Heredia. The group is organized on the "the *compadrazco* system," meeting regularly and holding yearly retreats.

Their definition of the Macho is:

1. He who is dignified
2. He who is a protector
3. He who is responsible
4. He who is nurturing
5. He who is spiritual
6. He who is faithful
7. He who is respectful
8. He who is friendly
9. He who is caring
10. He who is sensitive
11. He who is trustful
12. He who provides
(Tello, ca. 1988)

For some Chicanos *machismo* is an emblem that symbolizes resistance to social and historical control. Excessive masculinity is seen by some as adaptive behavior in situations where Chicano men feel racial oppression and discrimination. The idea of exaggerated masculinity has crept into American popular culture and language, so most Americans have an idea of the meaning of *machismo* and we find it regularly used by the media. For instance the Marlboro Man is viewed as a *macho* man, strong and independent as he rides his horse herding cattle. This was a model that many young men grew up trying to emulate, but this symbol is no longer acceptable to modern American society.

See also Pintos
References Andrade 1992; Armas 1975; Baca Zinn 1982; Castillo 1994; Davidson 1974; Heredia 1992; Limón 1978; Mirandé 1985, 1986, 1997; Najera-Ramirez 1994; Paredes 1993a; Peña 1991

Mal Ojo (Evil Eye)

Mal ojo, or "bad eye," is commonly known as "the evil eye." It may also be called *mal de ojo*, or just *ojo*. It is a syndrome, a folk illness, believed to be transmitted by certain individuals, witches, some think, who have a special power. *Mal ojo* may be transferred by a peculiar person who gazes at a weaker person, a woman or a child, and the ill effects are felt immediately. Socially, it can indicate that a person has been more familiar with another person than social and cultural manners permit. The glance or power of a stronger person causes an adverse consequence on the weaker person, who is often a baby or a child. The fear of *mal ojo* also indicates that mothers and other adults are distrusting of a person who acts in a more familiar way than is culturally appropriate. It is thought that people with "weak blood," *sangre liviana*, are more susceptible to receiving *mal ojo*. The symptoms of *mal ojo* are vomiting, diarrhea, loss of weight, and sometimes even death. Witches can deliberately give someone the evil eye; other times it is done unintentionally by persons who just happen to have a powerful gleam. A person may give another the evil eye because of a feeling of jealousy or covetousness. If a person covets or is envious of a child he or she may give that child the evil eye. Preventive measures that may diminish the possibility of a child getting *mal ojo* are to touch the child's cheek, or make the sign of the cross on the child's forehead. Sometimes the evil eye may be undone and the illness avoided if the person who cast the glance pats the person's head or temples, immediately relieving him or her of the curse. If the illness is induced by a witch another type of remedy must be sought.

Belief in the evil eye or that someone can harm another by looking at him or her in a certain way is found all over the world. It has been documented in Mediterranean countries, eastern Europe, North Africa, Central America, Mexico, and in the southwestern United States In many of these countries the evil eye is associated with envy and malice.

Various cures for *mal ojo* exist; one well-documented method is to *barrer con un blanquillo* (sweep with an egg) the ill person with an uncooked unbroken egg. The egg is swept over the body of the person without touching them, while prayers are recited, such as the Hail Mary and the Our Father. The egg serves to extract the fever from the ill person, and is then broken into a bowl of water and placed under the bed of the person. During the night the egg is believed to still be extracting fever from the patient, and in the morning if the egg is found to be cooked, it is a sign that the patient had *mal ojo*. The egg is then thrown over the shoulder of the mother, in the direction of the sun.

References Baer and Bustillo 1993; Dundes 1992; Hand 1981; Jaramillo 1972; Kearney 1976; Martinez and Martin 1966; Roeder 1988; Rubel 1966; Simmons 1974; Spicer 1977; Torres 1983a

La Malinche (c. 1502–c. 1528)

This is the common name given to the Aztec princess Malintzin Tenépal, also known as Doña Marina. Although of noble birth, she was sold as a child into slavery to Mayan merchants, supposedly by her own mother. In 1519 she was one of the women given to Hernán Cortés when he landed in Mexico. She spoke both Nahuatl and Maya, among other Indian languages, and quickly learned Spanish, becoming Cortés's translator and also his mistress. Upon learning her name, Cortés had her christened as Doña Marina, and she became known to everyone by that name, although her Aztec name was Malintzin, which possibly the Spaniards pronounced *Malinche*, so she was also called by this name. She bore one son by Cortés. During the whole Spanish Conquest period she spoke for the Indians to Cortés and translated Montezuma's dialogue to him. According to Mexican and Chicano folklore she metaphorically represents the raped Indian woman that produced the *mestizo* (mixed Spanish and Indian) race, the Mexican, but she is also considered a double-crosser. She informed Cortés about a planned ambush at Cholula, which saved his life and caused the massacre of thousands of Indians. She became known as *La Lengua*, meaning "the tongue," because of her work as a translator for Cortés. Del Castillo believes that Doña Marina was following her religious faith and belief in a godly force, the prophecies of Quetzalcoatl, and did not think she was betraying her people. Cortés is supposed to have stated, "After God we owe this conquest of New Spain to Doña Marina." Because she gave birth to the first *mestizo*, the first *Mexicano*, she is considered the mother of *la raza cósmica* (the cosmic race).

In Chicano culture a person who turns his back on his people is call a *malinchero* or, if it's a woman who has betrayed her community, a *malinche*. Contemporary Chicanas have taken *La Malinche* as a positive role model to illustrate and explain the survivalist psyche of the Chicana in modern society. Her influence in the conquest of Mexico may be debatable, but there is no doubt that she is considered a heroine, almost on the same plane as *La Virgen de Guadalupe*. Octavio Paz writes of *La Malinche* as the "violated woman," *La Chingada*, and his writings have influenced several generations of Mexicanos and Chicanos in seeing the Mexican people as *"hijos de la chingada,"* that is, "sons of a conquest by rape."

Cortés married Doña Marina off to one of his lieutenants, Juan Jaramillo, and they had one daughter. She went with them to Central America and there died of an illness when she was approximately twenty-three years of age. Some scholars regard *La Malinche* as the archetype of *La Llorona* and others think of her as the original *Llorona* (weeping woman), while some consider her to be the source of *La Llorona* legend.

To many Chicanas *Malinche* has become a symbol for the socioeconomic and educational limitations of contemporary life. They feel the defamation of her character is equal to the denigration of Chicanas. The victimization and criminalization of *Malinche*, a double oppression, is parallel to the experiences of young Chicanas and Mexicanas. *Malinche* and *La Virgen de Guadalupe* are two archetypes of womanhood in Mexico and in the Southwest, the whore and the virgin, who symbolize the precarious dilemma of being female. *Malinche* has played an enormous role in the literary production of Chicana writing, in essays and short stories, but especially in poetry.

See also La Llorona

References Alarcon 1989; Candelaria 1993; Del Castillo 1977; Glantz 1994; Harris 1996; Paz 1961; Rebolledo and Rivero 1993; Soto 1986; Zinam and Molina 1991

Mandas (Promises)

The Spanish dictionary definition of *manda* is a "proposal" or an "offer." It comes from the verb *mandar*, meaning "to order" or "to command," and the phrase *mandar hacer* means "to have made" or "to command to be made." In folk religious practices a *manda* is interpreted as a promise or contract made with a saint, the Virgin Mary, or God. The contract is not a legal commitment nor made with the approval of a priest or the Catholic Church. It is purely a personal promise made to fulfill or complete a journey, a devotional act, or to recite a certain number of prayers. This promise is in exchange for the curing of an illness or for a solution to a problem. The *manda* may involve the placing of a *milagro* (symbol of a miracle) at the shrine of a saint, *La Virgen de Guadalupe* cathedral in Mexico City for example, or the lighting of candles at the local church. Although the fulfillment of the *manda* in itself may not be difficult, its completion often involves some sacrifice, and this aspect is also considered part of the *manda*. Lighting daily candles could be a financial strain, and a pilgrimage may take several years to complete, yet neither is ever forgotten, and a *manda* is taken more seriously than a legal written contract. There may be fear of retribution from a saint if the *manda* is not fulfilled, and sometimes individuals actually suffer this retribution. If a woman makes a *manda* asking for a cure to her child's illness and the child is cured but she does not complete the *manda*, the child may become ill again. The woman will believe the second illness was caused because she did not complete her *manda*. A *manda* may be completed after the request is fulfilled in thanksgiving, or it may be fulfilled before the petition is answered, with the assumption that it will be answered. *Mandas* are very private and often only very close family members are aware that a person has made one.

References Cantú 1991a; Durand and Massey 1995; Egan 1991; Oktavec 1995

La Mano Negra (The Black Hand)

In parts of the Southwest, children were disciplined by parents with scary stories of The Black Hand. If they didn't behave or do as they were told, *La Mano Negra* would take them away. In the Ernest Baughman Collection at the University of New Mexico Library, an informant narrates being told by her grandfather in Tesuque, New Mexico, about *La Mano Negra*. A young woman remembers, "My grandfather used to tell us when we were little, about *La Mano Negra*, that appeared every time little kids were bad and that if we weren't good and helped him carry in wood and water and feed the animals 'la mano negra' would come for us at night. It would get really big, take us from our beds and never bring us back home" (November 1974). Members of the academic electronic listserv CHICLE have held discussions and reminisced about *La Mano Negra*. One member remembered it by the name of *La Mano Pachona* without knowing its origin, but the fear of it was well remembered by all.

Marc Simmons writes about a legend of *La Mano Negra* from the town of Bernalillo, New Mexico. An old priest dies, but the villagers believe he was unable to complete all his work because his spirit frequently returns. When the bell of the church is heard ringing late at night, the local Indians come to listen, and they see the spirit of the priest going into the church and praying. They call the Hispanos to come and see, and when the priest is seen in the church one of the observers cries out. At this point the priest places his hand on the missal and vanishes. "Burned through several pages was the scorched imprint of the padre's hand, *La Mano Negro.*" Simmons states that he recalls a similar legend from Ireland (2).

References CHICLE 1995; Ernest Baughman Collection; Simmons 1989

Mariachi Music

Mariachi music is the most traditional music associated with Mexico. This type of musical group has become a national symbol of Mexico and of most *Mexicanos* living in Greater Mexico. They are contracted to play at traditional ritual celebrations, such as baptisms, weddings, *quinceañeras* (fifteenth birthday parties), *fiestas patrias* (patriotic festivals), most festivals, and sometimes funerals.

A traditional *Mariachi* group can consist of anywhere between five and thirteen musicians. The uniqueness of the group is that it is composed of brass and string instruments only: trumpets, violins, and guitars. Some groups may also include a harp, a *guitarrón* (bass guitar), or a string bass. *Mariachis* have traditionally been male musicians, but since the 1980s female musicians have been accepted into many groups, and there are now complete groups composed of only females.

The attire of the *Mariachis* is a *charro* (horseman) suit that incorporates elements of the Spaniards' dress of the eighteenth century: boots, tight-fitting pants, short waist-length jackets, all embroidered with braid or silver ornaments. White shirts with ribbon ties made into bows, and the traditional wide-brimmed *sombrero* complete the ensemble. Some outfits are all white, black, dark blue, or even red, and can be very striking when twelve or more musicians, all standing, start playing a typical Mexican song, such as "La Negra" or "Las Mañanitas." According to Najera-Ramirez the early *Mariachi* groups dressed like peons with white muslin shirt and pants. It was not until 1901 that they started wearing *charro* costumes, following the example established by Miguel Lerdo de Tejada and his *orquesta típica*, the national folkloric orchestra. "By the 1930s the *charro* costume became an institutionalized part of the *Mariachi* tradition when the government required *Mariachis* performing for official functions to wear *charro* outfits" (1993, 17).

Mariachi groups have been very popular in southern California since the 1930s, and currently hundreds of groups have been formed in the Los Angeles area. Even students at the University of California at Los Angeles formed a group in 1970 called *Mariachi Uclatlán.* One famous group from Los Angeles is *Los Camperos de Nati Cano* (The Horsemen of Nati Cano), organized in 1961, who perform at their restaurant La Fonda, owned by Nati Cano. This *Mariachi* performs at many *Mariachi* festivals and is also on a university

Mariachi *music is traditional music associated with Mexico. It has become the national symbol of Mexico for most* Mexicanos *living in the United States. (Sergio Dorantes/ Corbis)*

campus circuit and can often be seen in theaters throughout California. Nati Cano recorded with Linda Ronstadt on her famous *Canciones de Mi Padre* album, and received a lot of fame from this exposure. He is also an adjunct lecturer at the University of California, Los Angeles.

In the last thirty years *Mariachi* festivals have become very popular throughout the Southwest. They have been held in San Antonio, Texas; Tucson, Arizona; San Jose, California; and even Universal Studios in Hollywood originated a festival in 1985. Los Angeles is home to the largest assemblage of *Mariachi* musicians in the United States.

Theories about the origin of the word *Mariachi* are interesting. There is the idea that it evolved from *María*, the name of the mother of Jesus Christ. Another idea is that it comes from the French word for marriage. But it is likely that the etymology of the word is of an indigenous nature. *Mariachi* groups originated in the region of Jalisco, even before it was named as a state, a region greatly influenced by the Coca people, and in fact the *Nahuatl* word for contemporary indigenous performers is *mariachitos*.

References Harpole 1990; Loza 1985, 1993; Najera-Ramirez 1994; Narváez 1978; Pearlman 1988; Rafael 1983

Masseuse
See Sobador

Los Matachines (Dancers)

The name of the dancers and the dance they perform on Christmas Eve in many parts of the Southwest. In New Mexico the dance is performed by the Pueblo Indians in honor of the Madonna. The dance is also performed in Mexico, Texas, and Arizona during other holidays and saints' days. Controversy over the origin of this ritual dance-drama has not been resolved, and the literature and research produced keep growing. It is based on a medieval Spanish mystery play, but in the New World version, influenced by Aztec culture and customs, it portrays the betrayal of Montezuma by the Spaniards, and the acceptance of Christianity by Montezuma. Its Iberian origins lie in the conflict between the Christians and Moors. The *Danza de los Matachines* is probably the only ritual dance that is danced by both Hispanic and Native American communities in New Mexico.

The word *matachines* can translate to mean "clowning" or "trickery," but can also mean "puppet player," "jester," and "buffoon." *Matachines* refers to the men who dance as a group; the group is composed usually of twelve men, but can have from ten to fourteen. In sixteenth-century Europe a *matachin* was a masked dancer, an entertainer who danced with a sword. It is likely that the Moors transplanted the dance to Europe and that *matachin* may come from the Arabic word *mutawajjihin*, meaning "to assume a mask." There are many eighteenth- and nineteenth-century literary references to a *matachine* sword dance, indicating that such a dance was performed in Europe.

Similar to the dance-drama of *Los Moros y Cristianos*, the dance of *Los Matachines* was taught to the subjugated Indians by the Spanish missionaries as a custom to celebrate on Christian feast days but also as a means of converting them to Catholicism. Flavia Waters Champe's interpretation is that the dance was brought to New Mexico by Spanish and Mexican settlers who came with De Vargas at the time of the second conquest in 1692.

In New Mexico the dance group is open only to men and it is considered an honor to be a part of it. The masked men, with decorated headdresses, dance in two parallel rows, in bright costumes decorated with long ribbons that appear to be a combination of Aztec and southwest Indian in origin. The main characters in the drama are *El Monarca*, the King, who represents Montezuma, and four *Capitanes*. The swords referred to earlier have become three-pronged *palmas* (palms) in the New World. In the performances of some groups there is a queen, *La Reina*, but in others she might be called *La Malinche*, the Indian woman who became the mistress of Cortés, who represents innocence or the Church. *La Reina* is often a little girl dressed in a white dress. In some locations it is believed the dancers represent the Twelve Apostles, but in others they are just ordinary men. They carry an image of the

For centuries the Matachines dance has been a part of New Mexico history. The roots of this beautiful performance extend from Mexico and the conquistadors of Spain to the Spanish Moors. (Danny Lehman/Corbis)

Madonna and move along in a candle-lit procession. One and sometimes two prominent performers are *El Abuelo* (the grandfather) and *La Abuela* (the grandmother), who act as leaders and also as clowns throughout the dance. *El Abuelo* wears a rubber mask, and is dressed somewhat like a white man, sometimes carrying a whip, and directing the rest of the dancers. He calls out songs and dance instructions and cracks his whip against the ground. Another dancer, sometimes a small boy, will represent *El Toro* (the bull), who initiates a bullfight with *El Abuelo* and is slain. This side battle symbolizes the battle between good and evil. The music is usually played with nonindigenous instruments like the violin and guitar. The costumes and masks of the dance are very important and are usually made by the dancers themselves or their families.

In some towns *Los Matachines* perform their dance on Christmas, New Year's Day, or the town's patron saint's day. There is documentation of the *Matachines* dance performed during church fiestas and funerals by the Tarahumara Indians of northern Mexico. In Laredo, Texas, the *Matachines* from the Ladrillera *barrio* venerate the Holy Cross and *La Virgen de Guadalupe* as their patron saint. In this instance the tradition here is closely related to the Yaqui and Mayo *matachines*.

Interestingly both Native Americans in the United States and Mexicans in Mexico are still performing a dance introduced into the New World over

400 years ago. This tradition performed today in the United States reinforces a heritage with roots in the culture from the eighth century. Because Indians, Mexicans, and *mestizos* (mixed-race people) perform it, the dance has evolved with different interpretations and has different meanings for each group. The experience of having a religion imposed on a culture is very different for the people it was imposed on, than for the people who imposed it.

References Ancona 1995; Bennett 1935; Cantú 1991b, 1995; Champe 1983; Harris 1996, 1997; Kent 1986; Ortega 1973; Robb 1961, 1980; Rodríguez, S., 1994, 1996; Romero 1993

Menudo (Tripe Stew)

A soup-type dish made with tripe, the stomach lining of a cow, pig's or calf feet, and maize, such as *posole* (corn) or hominy. The tripe with onions and garlic is cooked for several hours, *posole* or hominy is added, along with red *chile*. Sometimes it is made without *chile* and may be called *menudo blanco*. In parts of Mexico some people may call it *panza*, which is a slang word for "stomach."

In South Texas during the early 1900s, *menudo* was called *café de hueso* by street vendors and local people, literally, "bone coffee" or "coffee from bone." This name may refer to its understood medicinal value, which is to cure a hangover, known as *la cruda*. It is typically eaten early in the morning, anytime after midnight, and on such holidays as New Year's Day, or other big celebrations. It is served in deep bowls and topped with chopped onions, lemon juice, crushed oregano, and more *chile*. Spicy hot, with lots of *chile* along with hot tortillas, it is a delicious dish that somehow does cure many ailments. A body feels fortified and strong after such a meal. One can find Chicanos proudly wearing T-shirts with the slogan "Menudo, Breakfast of Champions" boldly printed on the front.

In the novel *Fabricated Mexican*, the author Rick Rivera describes how he and his stepfather cut and cook *menudo* in their garage, since his mother refuses to let them cook it in the kitchen, because of the awful smell. There is a very distinct odor to tripe as it cooks.

Everyone has their own way of cooking *menudo*, and recipes can be found throughout the literature and folklore of Chicanos. In many southwestern cities, *menudo* cook-offs are held as fund-raisers and social events. Keith Cunningham discusses the difference between the *menudo* from northern Arizona and that found in the southern part of the state and even compares the Tucson *menudo* to French cuisine.

References Cunningham 1980; Montaño 1992; Rivera 1995

Mermaid
See Sirena del Mar

Lo Mexicano

An expression and concept that came into usage in Mexico around 1900, but was not completely culturally defined until after the Mexican Revolution in the late 1920s. The concept had to do with Mexican nationalism and a sense of self-identity with a Mexican consciousness. The term conceptualized a new identity and an awareness of Mexicanness that was native, drawing on the indigenous and the *mestizaje* (mixed-race nature) of the country. It was in the 1920s when the term *lo Mexicano* became more known in association with nationalism and could be seen in the life of Mexico and in the art and literature produced after the Revolution. Even in the United States, the art of Mexican painters, such as Diego Rivera and José Clemente Orozco, was admired and well received because of its Mexican character. The writings and research of the Mexican philosopher Samuel Ramos brought attention to the national character of the *Mexicano*, and to a definition of Mexican identity. *Lo Mexicano* referred to the *Mexicanidad*, the national character of the Mexican, which was *mestizo* (mixed-race) and not European.

This essence called *lo Mexicano* can be found in art, literature, music, and folklore, for it encompasses the whole experience of being culturally Mexican. The lore of *Mexicanidad* has migrated to the United States from Mexico with the waves of immigration in the last 100 years, and *lo Mexicano* forms part of the identity of all Chicanos. Américo Paredes's life work was an attempt to understand *lo Mexicano* of the Chicano experience through folklore, in the text of narratives and in the context of folk performances.

References Nájera-Ramírez 1989, 1994; Paredes 1982; Peña 1983; Schmidt 1978

Mexico Lindo (Beautiful Mexico)

A nationalistic sentiment among Chicanos of the United States or *el Mexico de afuera* (Mexico from the outside) shown by patriotic activities such as parades, *fiestas patrias* (patriotic festivals), and celebrations of Mexican holidays. The expression was used to reflect a nationalistic ideology during the 1920s and 1930s in the United States that in effect reduced regional differences among the various Mexican communities throughout the United States The *Mexico Lindo* sentiment expressed a nationalism and a love of homeland and anything Mexican. It made the difficult life experiences of immigrants in the United States more acceptable. The concept was popularized by a song with the same title sung to *Mariachi* music by the famous singer and actor Jorge Negrete. The last stanza of the song states:

México lindo y querido
Si muero lejos de ti
Que digan que estoy dormido
Y que me traigan aquí.
(Mexico, beautiful and dear,
If I die far from thee
They should say that I am asleep
And bring me back here.)

These words have brought tears to the eyes of Mexicans born in the United States, including many who have never traveled to Mexico.

Reference Rosales 1996, 1999

Mica (Green Card)

This is the Mexican people's slang term for the government card issued to legal immigrant residents, also known as the "green card," in the United States. The legal name of the card is Alien Registration Receipt Card (Form I-151 or I-551). The card is no longer a green color, but it has continued to be called this since at least the 1970s. Illegal trafficking in the *mica* is very common, and there have always been forgeries of the green card and social security cards as well. Undocumented immigrants manage to learn where to purchase such forgeries. In the streets of southern California a person who sells *micas* is referred to as a *miquero*. It is unknown how the word *mica* originated as a name for the green card. In Spanish a *mica* is a female monkey, but it is used for a woman who flirts with men or a coquette. The *mica* is definitely an enticement that lures men to the United States.

Illegal immigrants come from Mexico in search of work in California and other states of the Southwest, and most are willing to do anything for employment. The folklore generated from this experience has been frozen into legends and family oral histories. The *mica* is a coveted trophy that opens doors to employment. Sometimes it can be gotten illegally by purchase or legally by marrying an American and becoming a legal resident. These experiences are dramatized in *corridos* (ballads). One *corrido*, "Mi Micaela," hides the word *mica* in a woman's name *Micaela*, but the first line gives it away: "Tú eres mi Mica, Mica, mi Micaela, Tú representas todo lo que mi alma anhela" (You are my Mica, Mica, my Micaela, You represent all that my soul desires). Later in the song there is the following line: "Tienes que ser mi Mica, mi Micaela, Verde como los pastos de las praderas" (You have to be my Mica, my Micaela, Green like the pastures in the fields) (Herrera-Sobek 1993b). The play on words, unknown to the average observer, refers to the acquiring of the green card, the *mica*.

Reference Herrera-Sobek 1993b

La Migra (Immigration Officials)

La migra is an abbreviated and slang term for the Immigration and Naturalization Service (INS) and the Border Patrol. The phrase *"hay viene la migra!"* has been cried out in fear for many generations in *Mexicano* and Chicano communities and in the workplaces where they are employed. Raids by *la migra* are commonplace and have been depicted in films, novels, jokes, and verbal narratives for many years. *Migra* is short for the Spanish word *immigración*, and has become an important and viable character in the vocabulary and culture of Chicanos and *Mexicanos* alike. Cartoons and jokes often depict *la migra* officials as overweight policemen who chase down innocent women and children. In the folk dramas of *El Teatro Campesino* (the Farmworkers' Theater), *la migra* was often characterized as an unscrupulous arrogant patrol officer who accepted bribes from the growers and ordered raids in the agricultural fields to arrest undocumented immigrants the day before payday. Starting in the late 1940s and into the present, *la migra* made raids in the San Joaquin Valley of California, rounding up *braceros* who had overstayed their contract time allocation. In recent years *la migra* has acquired a much more sinister image as individual abuses are shown on television evening news programs. Still, many Chicanos grew up being threatened by their parents that if they didn't behave, *"te vay llevar la migra,"* *la migra* would come and take them away, presumably to Mexico. Native-born Chicano children have played a game of *"la migra* chasing the Mexican," similar to the "cowboys and Indians" games of earlier generations.

See also El Teatro Campesino
References Calvillo 1981; Herrera-Sobek 1991, 1993b; *El Teatro Campesino* 1985

Milagros (Miracles)

A *milagro* is literally a miracle, but in folk religious practices *milagros* are tiny objects presented to a saint at a shrine or church, as a token or offering intended to fulfill a vow made to that saint. Sometimes these objects are called *ex-votos*, meaning "from a vow," and are in the shape of the object that symbolizes what the vow was about. For example the *milagro* could be in the shape of an arm, heart, leg, or baby. In Mexico and the Southwest such vows may be called *promesas* or *mandas* and can be fulfilled by prayers, pilgrimages, and promised visits to a saint's shrine if the wish or favor is granted. This is an important folk religious tradition common among Latinos and Chicanos in the Southwest, Mexico, and throughout Latin America. A mother may make a *promesa* to *La Virgen de Guadalupe*, to visit her shrine in Guadalajara, if her daughter is cured of breast cancer. When the *promesa* is fulfilled this mother may leave a tiny silver breast, a *milagro*, to symbolize the realization of the *promesa*.

Milagros are made out of wood, wax, or bone, but the most common material is silver or a silverlike metal, and they are usually very tiny objects, about one inch in diameter. The custom of offerings to saints goes back hundreds of years and can be traced to the Mediterranean among pre-Christian Greeks, Romans, and Iberians. The tradition as it has evolved in the New World is an amalgamation of African, Native American, and Spanish beliefs. Saints are very important among Chicano Catholics, influencing every aspect of daily life and acting as mediators between man and God. *Promesas* made to saints and the *milagros* presented are a reflection of their strong predominance in daily life. In the Southwest, this custom has been documented since the colonial period and was undoubtedly introduced by the Spanish missionaries.

It is known that Hernán Cortés, the conqueror of Mexico, had a *milagro* made in the shape of a gold scorpion, which he offered to the patroness of his home, Our Lady of Guadalupe, in Guadalupe, Spain. This was in thanks for surviving the bite of a scorpion that he received in Yautepec, Mexico, in 1528. In the past most *milagros* were commissioned, and the local silversmith made them out of silver or sometimes gold. Today they are mass-produced and can be bought at religious stores. Thousands may be found in various shrines, cathedrals, and on saints' clothing throughout the Southwest and of course in Mexico. The *milagros* are pinned to the clothing of the saint and left there until collected by the priest or caretaker of the church.

See also Mandas; Retablos
References Durand and Massey 1995; Egan 1991; Oktavec 1995; Toor 1973

Mojado (Wetback)

A translation of the word "wetback," sometimes spelled *moja'o*, which literally simply means "wet." It is a pejorative expression, although it is sometimes used by Mexican people to describe themselves and their experience of illegally crossing the Rio Grande to come to the United States. Also it is a designation used against all Chicanos, with the same prejudicial meaning as "greaser" or "spic." Some Chicanos use the term to refer to recent Mexican immigrants and also to differentiate themselves from undocumented immigrants. Among teenage Chicanos the word *mojado* is translated to English and illegal Mexicans are often just called "wets."

Descriptions of the wetback experience have been chronicled and narrated in *corridos* (ballads) and novels. In Mexico, the term sometimes used is *espaldas mojadas*, a literal translation for the word wetback. In 1955 a well-established Mexican director released a film titled *Espaldas Mojadas*, which intended to persuade Mexicans not to go to the United States. It was a political film that incorporated all of the standard characters that would appear in countless other films and novels of the Chicano experience: the wetback, the *pocho* (half Mexican), the *coyote* (smuggler) who smuggles people into the United States, and the grower Mister Sterling. An ironic, yet justified ending shows Mister Sterling dumped into the Rio Grande by Mexicans, and as he swims to the U.S. side of the border he is shot by the Border Patrol. In a 1998 article Herrera-Sobek discusses the use of *corridos* in several Mexican films that depict the plight of the illegal immigrant, or *el mojado*.

References Cordova 1990; Herrera-Sobek 1993b, 1998; Madrid-Barela 1975; Mora 1982

Mollera, Caída de (Fallen Fontanelle)

Caída de mollera (literally, the fall of the fontanelle) is a medical condition that can occur in infants, is often classified as a folk illness, but has obvious medical symptoms. The fontanelle, on the top of an infant's head, is a membrane-covered opening between two incompletely grown bones, a soft spot that will disappear when the bones grow together as the child grows. Mexican children are greatly guarded so *la mollera* will not fall and cause grave illness to the child. The soft spot on the top of the head may fall if a child falls or is knocked around, shaken too hard, or suffers a trauma or an accident. It is believed that *la mollera* has fallen when a baby becomes ill with ceaseless crying, fever, diarrhea, and possibly vomiting. Remedies for *caída de mollera* involve trying to return the fontanelle to its proper position. This can be done by sucking on the soft spot, by pushing upward on the roof of the infant's mouth, by holding the child upside down and patting the feet, or by using a warm compress. If the *mollera* is not repositioned death can occur.

There is considerable evidence to support the idea that the concept of *caída de mollera* is of Aztec origin. It is not a health concept found in Europe or even in other countries of Latin America. The Aztecs believed in an inner force that provided warmth, courage, vitality, and in children, growth. This force was known as *tonalli*, and was found throughout the body, but resided primarily in the head. If this force was lost through violence or a trauma, death could occur. Children were especially at risk, because this force could be lost through the fontanelle, which was not yet fully closed. By not cutting a child's hair and by watching the *mollera* and the head, mothers took care to not lose the *tonalli*. Some of the remedies for *caída de mollera* reportedly performed by the Aztecs are similar to those still used by Chicano families and *curanderos*. Many of a child's symptoms, as described by mothers, can be linked to medical conditions such as dehydration, which can occur from diarrhea.

La mollera is also considered important as the child grows older. Before entering a pool of water, or getting wet at the beach, many mothers insist that their children first wet the top of their heads, so as not to catch a cold or another illness. "*Mójese la mollera antes de entrar al agua*," children are instructed. Some Mexican Americans refer to this condition as a Mexican folk disease because American doctors may not recognize the medical conditions. Often the only person who can cure *caída de mollera* is a *curandera*.

See also Curanderismo
References Clark 1959; Kay 1977; Martinez and Martin 1966; Ortiz de Montellano 1987; Roeder 1988; Trotter, Ortiz de Montellano, and Logan 1989

A relic of the past in Penitente history, this morada constructed of adobe is located near the outskirts of Mora, New Mexico. (Buddy Maze/Corbis)

Moradas (Penitente Chapels)

A *morada* is a meetinghouse and chapel of *Los Penitentes*, The Brotherhood of Our Father Jesus of New Mexico. Each chapter of the *Penitentes* has its own *morada*, which functions as a community center for the members as well as a prayer house and center for religious rituals. Some *moradas* consist of one room whereas others have two or three rooms, sometimes lined up in a row. *Moradas* were usually constructed of adobe and were set apart from the rest of the village or the town center. They were located on the outskirts of the town. One of the rooms was always a chapel with an altar. One *morada* in Abiquiu, a three-room adobe structure built between 1820 and 1850, is considered the oldest surviving *morada* in the state of New Mexico. See Wallis and Varjabedian for contemporary photographs of ancient *moradas* still found in northern New Mexico.

References Ahlborn 1986; Boyd 1974; Bunting 1964; Romero and Larkin 1994; Wallis and Varjabedian 1994; Weigle 1976

Los Moros y Cristianos
(The Moors and the Christians)

A folk dance and drama first performed in Mexico in the year 1531, according to Bernal Diaz del Castillo. There is documentation indicating it was staged by Juan de Oñate in New Mexico in 1598. The drama originates in Aragón, Spain, during the twelfth century, when Jaime I reconquered a region in southern Spain that was controlled by the Moors. It used to be performed completely on horseback and seems to have traveled the world, following the Spanish army into Mexico, Cuba, the Philippines, British Guiana, and California. In Mexico it became a warlike spectacle, involving many soldiers riding the best horses and wearing extravagant clothing. Unlike the religious plays performed in New Mexico, this one is secular. Although it was traditionally performed on horseback, since the Indians of New Mexico were not allowed to use horses, they performed it as a dance. The objective of the drama is to have the *Moros* steal the Holy Cross that sits in the center of a plaza and the *Cristianos* win it back by staging a sword battle between the two battalions of soldiers, the Moors and the Christians. Once the cross is returned to the Spaniards (Christians) the Moors (infidels) pledge obedience to the Spanish king. The defeated Moors are forgiven and become Christians in the last scene. In New Mexico the drama was staged to show the Indians that their subjection was already complete, just as it happened to the Aztecs. The ideological message is that enemies of the Spanish are not annihilated but rather absorbed as fellow subjects of the empire. In New Mexico, the famous Chimayo *Moros y Cristianos* continue to perform this drama up to the present day. Lea's book reproduces the dialogue of the drama, and she states that no other complete copy exists "of this, . . . the first play to be presented on the American continent" (23).

In contemporary Spain, the province of Alicante continues to have a major festival known as *Las Fiestas de Moros y Cristianos* that is a combination of religious and secular processions, with up to 5,000 lavishly costumed participants. The festival is celebrated from three to four days, with several battles taking place to win back the Holy Cross. For a day or two the Moors are in the lead, but eventually they lose to the Christians.

References Aceves 1988; Gutiérrez 1993; Harris 1994; Lamadrid 1993; Lea 1953

La Muerte (Death)

Death, personified as a woman and dressed in white clothing, is a well-known character in Chicano and *Mexicano* folklore. Commonly accepted as just *La Muerte*, she is a frequent personality in legends, urban belief tales, and is integrated into many family folk belief systems. Death is sometimes feared, but it is also accepted as the transition to another stage of the life cycle. A common saying is *"De la muerte y la suerte nadie se escapa"* (No one escapes from death or luck) (Espinosa, A. M., 1910, 404). She habitually appears late at night, to men who are out alone, some intentionally, others innocently on their way home from work. In tales collected in the Southwest, *La Muerte* is seen standing at streetlights, or waiting by a bridge or the side of the road. She appears to be a beautiful, young voluptuous woman, wearing a long flowing white dress, with her face covered or averted. Once she is picked up and seated in the car, or on the horse, she shows her face to her victim. She has no face; what the men see is a skull. In South Texas she is called *La Vieja Blanca*, the old lady in white, and she acts as a siren, enticing men, but when they get a look at her face, they see her hideous white skull instead. The men faint, run away, or become deathly ill of *susto* (fright). In most tales of *La Muerte* her appearances occur after midnight to men who have nonmoral or immoral schemes. The basic structure of the legend of *La Muerte* will involve a man alone at night, in his car, buggy, or he may be on a horse, and he sees a woman in white, often with blond hair, standing by the side of the road or near a river. The man is immediately attracted and wants the woman, but when he gets near her and sees the skull face, he faints and hours later awakens in the hospital with his wife and family surrounding him. Tales of *La Muerte* are narrated by relatives, parents, grandparents, and friends to reinforce an adherence to social cultural norms and marital fidelity. The legend of the appearance of another woman, *La Llorona*, is structurally similar to stories of *La Muerte*, and sometimes the same story will use both characters interchangeably.

La Muerte is also known as *Doña Sebastiana* in New Mexico. She is found in the death cart of the *Penitentes*, in the form of a skeleton sitting and carrying a bow and arrow. During Holy Week ceremonies *Los Penitentes* pull the death cart along in their processions.

See also La Carreta de la Muerte; Doña Sebastiana; La Llorona; Los Penitentes
References Espinosa 1910; Flores-Turney 1996; Glazer 1980, 1984; Miller 1973; Vigil 1994

Muralismo (Mural Art)

The artistic movement of painting murals in Chicano barrios. The development of Chicano *Muralismo* grew out of the political context of the Chicano civil rights movement, a nationalistic political struggle waged by Chicanos during the 1960s. It imitated the Mexican mural art that was created during the postrevolutionary period of Mexico's history, and was intended to promote political action and raise consciousness. In California the mural movement started about 1970. It involved a variety of interested individuals; as described by Alicia Gonzales, "The emergent Chicano Mural Movement brought together the self-taught artist, the sign-painter, the house painter, the mass-production painter from the billboard companies, the college art student, and the graffiti artist" (155). A statewide meeting of Chicano mural artists was held in September of 1974 as a means of developing cooperation and communication

A mural in the background depicts a pre-Columbian scene while in the foreground the spectators watch Cinco de Mayo *festivities in St. Paul, Minnesota. (Richard Hamilton Smith/Corbis)*

for the artists working throughout California. The early murals were considered public folk art because of the common themes of community and civil rights and because most of the murals were located in working-class neighborhoods and urban *barrios*. Often, these early murals were referred to as a people's art. This concept was well expressed by a group of women artists in San Francisco who called themselves *Mujeres Muralistas* (women muralists). "Our interest as artists is to put art close to where it needs to be. Close to the children; close to the old people; close to everyone who has to walk or ride the buses to get places. We want our art either out in the streets or in places where a lot of people go each day, the hospitals, health centers, clinics, restaurants, and other public places" (Cockcroft, Weber, and Cockcroft, 107).

The scenes of many early Chicano murals consisted of pre-Columbian indigenous themes and motifs that reflected a *mestizo* (mixed-race) heritage and a Mexican cultural nationalism. Images of Aztlán, a concept from the pre-Conquest, and other Aztec symbols represented cultural pride and national loyalty. Chicano and Chicana artists turned to symbols that portrayed the traditions of Chicanos, traditions that distinguished them from mainstream American culture. These images can still be found in murals located in Chicano communities across the United States. Chicano muralists followed the tradition of the Mexican muralists Diego Rivera, David Alfaro

Siqueiros, and José Clemente Orozco, and used murals to rewrite the history of the Chicano experience. Murals were also intended to educate the community on the antiquity and ancestry of the *Mexicano*. What was not provided in textbooks and the classroom was flashed across walls in Chicano neighborhoods. The Chicano muralists sought to paint the history they knew, a history often based on "oral traditions, legends and myths" (Romo, 136).

Finally, as Tomás Ybarra-Frausto explains, Chicano/a art reflects a "continual effort toward developing an enhanced art of resistance—an art which is not a resistance to the materials and forms of art, but rather a resistance to entrenched social systems of power, exclusion and negation" (1990, 67).

See also Aztlán; Chicanismo

References Cockcroft, Weber, and Cockcroft 1977; Drescher 1994; Dunitz 1993; Goldman 1982, 1990a; Gonzales 1982; LaWare 1998; Romo 1992–1996; Ybarra-Frausto 1990, 1992

Murrieta, Joaquín (18??–1853)

The legend of Joaquín Murrieta is the romantic story of a handsome Mexican highwayman, considered a bandit by history but a great folk hero by Chicanos. At a time when the Mexican people were terribly mistreated in California, it is believed that Murrieta was falsely accused of crimes he did not commit and this prompted him to fight for his rights and those of his people. Joaquín Murrieta, whose name is also spelled Murieta and Murietta, roamed the back roads and hills of northern and southern California from Mount Shasta to the Mexican border in the mid-1850s, stealing horses and robbing Yankees and Chinese alike. There have been countless books, chapters, and articles written about Murrieta or about the legend of this famous Mexican *bandito*. According to the legend, Joaquín Murrieta was born in Sonora, Mexico, and migrated to California with his new bride in search of gold. He became a bandit and robber after many wrongs were committed against him by Americans. There are several variants of his story, but all have a similar general theme as to why and how he became a bandit.

During the mid-1850s there were at least five men named Joaquín, all of whom are credited with committing robberies and banditry. There was Joaquín Murrieta, Joaquín Valenzuela, Joaquín Carrillo, Joaquín Ocomorena, and Joaquín Botilleras. Some say that Valenzuela and Ocomorena were one and the same, and when he was hanged, two Joaquíns were eliminated. Although it is possible that Murrieta used all of these names as aliases, it is likely that there were at least two Joaquíns at the time. Murrieta started his life of banditry and crime after his home was invaded by white miners, who raped his wife Rosa and beat up Joaquín. Later he and his brother Carlos were accused of stealing a horse, a crime for which Carlos was lynched and Joaquín flogged.

There have been over twenty-one published versions of the Joaquín Murrieta legend. The first and for many years the one considered most authentic was by John Rollin Ridge, serialized in the *California Police Gazette* and eventually published under the title of *The Life and Adventures of Joaquín Murrieta, the Celebrated California Bandit* in 1854. John Rollin Ridge, a Cherokee also known as Yellow Bird, wrote his story one year after the death of Murrieta. This is the basic story of Joaquín that all subsequent histories are based on. In 1859 the *California Police Gazette* printed Ridge's story in ten installments and this publicity helped to further disseminate the story. The book was translated into French and Spanish and for many years it was better known abroad than in this country. In doubting the details of the Murrieta legend, researchers go back to Ridge's version, which some say was based on newspaper stories about the various bandits named Joaquín. It is believed by some researchers that Ridge just applied the name Murrieta to the Joaquín that was finally captured and decapitated. As a Native American, Ridge identified with the discriminatory treatment of California Mexicans, and he stated that he wanted to do justice to the Mexicans.

Joaquín Murrieta's life has been depicted in novels, stories, newspaper serials, and movies. Charles E. B. Howe wrote a play about Joaquín in 1859 that covers his escapades from the spring of 1851 to July 24, 1853, the day he was captured and killed by Captain Harry Love. It is not known if the play was ever performed, but the portrayal of Murrieta is moving and especially interesting because of all the negative publicity following his capture and death. Howe portrays him as an aristocratic intelligent leader and a man who commits crimes to avenge the wrongs committed against himself and his countrymen.

Joseph Henry Jackson's work traces the history of the legend, claiming all the information came from the John Rollin Ridge version and that he should be credited with starting the "fictitious" legend. Although Jackson does quote from the *San Francisco Alta* newspaper demonstrating that many people suspected it was not Joaquín Murrieta who was killed and decapitated by Captain Harry Love, but quite possibly another Joaquín, "every murder and robbery in the country has been attributed to 'Joaquín.' Sometimes it is Joaquín Carrillo that has committed all these crimes; then it is Joaquín Murrieta, then Joaquín something else, but always Joaquín!" (Jackson, 13).

Marcus Stewart wrote a long epic poem in 1882 titled *Rosita, A California Tale*, in which he speculates on the life of Murrieta. In this poem, Joaquín lives and flees in a ship to Mexico or South America, and the body that is decapitated is actually that of his good friend Ramón. Ramón's girlfriend, Rosita, also disappears at the time of his death, and only after her death, thirty years later, is it revealed that she had been living the life of a man. This story is commingled with the story of Charlotte (Charlie) Parkhurst who lived as a man in California during the latter half of the nineteenth century. The Murrieta legend has also been written by Latinos and Europeans, and Pablo Neruda, the Nobel Prize winner, wrote an opera about Murrieta entitled *Splendor and Death of Joaquín Murrieta*, insisting that Joaquín was actually Chileno and not Mexican.

Arnold Rojas, a Californian *vaquero*, writer, and memoirist, writes that Joaquín Murrieta was from the city of Alamos, Sonora, Mexico, where church records show that he and Rosita were married. When his wife was raped and he was beaten, Murrieta saw the faces of his murderers. According to Rojas, Joaquín lived for revenge, and he searched every mining camp in California until he found all thirteen men who committed the crime and killed them. After this he returned to Sonora to live out his life. Supposedly he is buried in Cucurpe, Sonora.

Major Horace Bell (1927) states: "In any country in America except the United States, the bold defiance of the power of the government, a half year's successful resistance, a continuous conflict with the military and civil authorities and the armed populace—the writer repeats that in any other country in America other than the United States—the operations of Joaquín Murrieta would have been dignified by the title of revolution, and the leader with that of rebel chief. For there is little doubt in the writer's mind that Joaquín's aims were higher than that of mere revenge and pillage. . . . it is easy to perceive that Joaquín felt himself to be more the champion of his countrymen than an outlaw and an enemy to the human race" (100).

Chicanos have taken the legend of Joaquín Murrieta seriously and identify with his heroic exploits of stealing from the rich and giving to the poor. He is viewed as a social bandit and a cultural leader, and several *corridos* (ballads) describe his life and death. At the University of California in Berkeley, a Chicano cooperative student house first established in 1970 is named Casa Joaquín Murrieta after this famous folk hero.

References Bell 1927; Castillo and Camarillo 1973; Herrera-Sobek 1993b; Howe 1983; Jackson 1949; Klette 1928; Leal 1997; MacLean 1977; Neruda 1966; Pitt 1966; Ridge 1927; Rojas 1979; Stewart 1882

Quetzalcoatl

N

Nacimiento (Nativity Scene)

From the Spanish word *nacer*, *nacimiento* is the name for a Christmas nativity scene. In the Southwest the creation of *nacimientos* has been a tradition since the seventeenth century. A *nacimiento* may resemble a religious altar in that it is an assemblage of many articles and objects, all depicting the recent birth of Jesus Christ in the manger, but a *nacimiento* can also include other Christmas-related images, biblical scenes, and possibly artifacts relating to the life experiences of the creator. The set of the *nacimiento* can vary in size from a small table to half a room, or to the whole front yard of a home. Outdoor *nacimientos* will have life-size figures of Mary and Joseph and various other biblical characters and animals. This custom is not particular to the Chicano community, and nativity scenes can be found throughout the country during the Christmas season. It is thought that Saint Francis of Assisi is the saint responsible for much of the veneration of the infant Jesus, and the custom of creating nativity scenes or monuments to the birth of Christ has been going on for hundreds of years.

In private homes *nacimientos* are usually set up for the first night of *Las Posadas*, which start on December 16 and continue until December 24. A *nacimiento* is left in place until *El Día de los Reyes*, Epiphany, on January 6, when the three kings arrive to visit the Christ child.

See also Las Posadas
References Griffith 1988; Heisley and MacGregor-Villarreal 1991; Kitchener 1994; Sommers 1995

Naranja Dulce (Sweet Orange)

A very popular old children's game and song frequently recited in novels and poems. Children form a circle with one child in the center and they sing this song:

> *Naranja dulce*
> *Limón partido*

> *Dáme un abrazo*
> *Que yo te pido.*
> *Si fueran falsos*
> *Mis juramentos,*
> *En algun día se olvidaran.*
> (Sweet orange
> Sliced lemon
> Give me a hug
> That I ask of you.
> If my promises were false
> Someday they will be forgotten.)

After this verse is sung, the child in the center of the circle chooses one from the group that is forming the circle and embraces that child. The child picked enters the center and the other child moves out. While this is going on they keep the circle moving around, and clapping hands, they sing the following verse to a fast beat:

> *Toca la Marcha*
> *Mi pecho llora*
> *y adiós Señora*
> *Yo ya me voy.*
> (Play the march
> My breast [heart] cries
> Good-bye my Lady
> I am leaving.)

For many generations mothers have sung this little verse to their babies as they lull them to sleep. Girls play this game in Mexico also, with a boy as the center player, which Inez Cardozo-Freeman interprets as a portrayal of betrayal and abandonment preparing little girls for marriage.

References Cardozo-Freeman 1975; Gonzáles 1974; Writers' Program 1976

Nativity Scene
See Nacimiento

Neighborhood
See Barrio

New Mexico Folklore

Of all the areas of the Southwest where Chicanos have settled and lived, it is New Mexico's culture and folklore that has been historically studied the most. Aurelio M. Espinosa was the first Hispano (a person of Spanish heritage born in New Mexico) to conduct research into the culture and language of New Mexicans. His most important work was published during the early part of the nineteenth century, 1910–1916, with a series of publications in the *Journal of American Folklore*. He collected folktales, folk songs, proverbs, superstitions, riddles, children's games, and much more. Students who were trained by Espinosa and who later continued folkloric work in New Mexico were Arthur Campa, Juan B. Rael, and Espinosa's son, Jose Manuel Espinosa, who published *Spanish Folk-tales from New Mexico* in 1937. Rael published *Cuentos Españoles de Colorado y Nuevo Mejico* in 1957, which is considered by Américo Paredes to be one of the best collections of Mexican folk narrative. Campa's work includes collections of folk poetry, riddles, folk songs, and folk drama from the late nineteenth and early twentieth centuries, published mostly in the 1940s and 1950s.

John Donald Robb (1892–1989) collected folk songs throughout New Mexico in the 1940s and 1950s using wire recorders. He came to the University of New Mexico as chair of the music department in 1941. He was a composer and educator but always had an interest in folk music. The John Donald Robb Archive of Southwestern Music is located at the university's library. His two books on New Mexico are *Hispanic Folk Songs of New Mexico* (1954) and *Hispanic Folk Music of New Mexico and the Southwest: A Self Portrait of a People* (1980).

Hispanic women have always been involved in creative and artistic work in New Mexico even up until contemporary times. Although there have been many publications about the *santeros* (saint makers), wood-carvers, tinsmiths, and other male artists, very little has been written about the work accomplished by women. Women have created religious folk art, such as *santos* (saints), *retablos* (religious paintings), straw appliqué crosses, and tinwork. Women wove blankets and embroidered *colchas* (blankets). Whitewashing and plastering of homes have always been women's work. Those who do it are called *enjarradoras*, and today they continue this work, also making adobe *hornos* (ovens) and fireplaces for the International Museum of Folk Art located in Santa Fe. Marianne Stoller writes of the work of New Mexican women artists and why they have been left out of history.

Several New Mexican women who descended from the early Spanish settlers of the region wrote personal life histories that incorporated the traditional way of life of the Hispano community of the late nineteenth and early twentieth centuries. Fabiola Cabeza de Baca, Nina Otero-Warren, and Cleofas Jaramillo each produced several books that present the folklore, rituals, and customs of the New Mexicans. Rebolledo discusses how these women used their writings as "narrative strategies of resistance" because they saw their culture and way of life slowly eroding away and being assimilated by a dominant and foreign culture. Because they all came from upper-class families, they were educated in Spanish traditions and language and consequently ignored the *mestizo* (mixed-race) and indigenous aspects of the culture, often depicting their past in romantic pastoral terms. Nevertheless, they all wrote of the loss of land and loss of culture, and sought to preserve the folklore, customs, and stories of their grandparents, close friends, and those who worked for them.

The *Penitentes*, the ancient religious brotherhood, have attracted much research and been scrutinized by many writers and journalists. De Cordova, Henderson, Sprott, and Weigle have conducted the most perceptive and sensitive writing on the *Penitentes*. The popular arts of colonial New Mexico, particularly the *santos* and *santeros*, have received a lot of attention by such researchers as E. Boyd, Marta Weigle, and William Wroth.

In recent years Chicano writers from New Mexico have collected folklore from their ancestors and friends. Nasario Garcia has published several collections depicting the way of life of the elders of the Rio Puerco Valley, and Rudolfo Anaya has written several children's books that bring forth the folklore of the region. Because of its long history New Mexico will always be a bountiful reservoir for the serious folklorist.

See also Adobe; Hispano Culture; Los Penitentes
References De Cordova 1972; Espinosa, A.M. Jr., 1947; Henderson 1937; Rebolledo 1993, 1994; Sprott 1984; Stoller 1986; Weigle 1976; Weigle and White 1988

Nichos (Niches)

A *nicho* is a nook or niche built into a wall that is similar to a shelf inside of a home. It can be as small as six inches or as high as one foot or even three feet. Anything can be placed in a *nicho*, from books to knickknacks, but the usual purpose is to house a holy picture or statue of a saint. Consequently in some Chicano homes the word carries almost the same meaning as altar or shrine. A *nicho* decorated with votive candles and saints becomes the site for daily devotional prayers. *Nichos* are also constructed as part of yard shrines to house a favorite saint or *La Virgen de Guadalupe* or another Madonna. Yard shrines that incorporate a *nicho* are set up as a place of worship in the yard to commemorate a deceased relative or as a fulfillment of a vow. In some parts of the Southwest these outdoor shrines are also called *grutas*, "grottos," and the two words are often used interchangeably. A cemetery shrine may also incorporate a *nicho* or a *gruta*. Since a *gruta* is primarily outdoors it can be constructed as a yard or cemetery shrine. *Nichos* that are found in front yards may be constructed of cement or wood, and may appear as a small house, chapel-shaped, or as a small cave. A wrought-iron door may be installed for privacy or to prevent vandalism. Yard *nichos* can vary in size from one foot to six or eight feet high. Invariably they are decorated with plastic flowers and plants, and are often painted in pastel colors.

See also Altars; Grutas; Yard Shrines
References Cash 1998; Griffith 1992; Ramos 1991; Vidaurri 1991; West 1991

Nun's Habit
See Hábito

Quetzalcoatl.

Ofrenda (Offering)

Sometimes used interchangeably with altar, *ofrenda* means "an offering" and is set up as a component of an altar. On *Día de los Muertos*, the Day of the Dead or All Souls' Day, an offering is made for a particular individual who has died, or for several members of a family who have died, such as parents and grandparents. An *ofrenda* may be set up in a home and personalized for a particular person. In some homes an altar is permanently set up for general and daily prayer, but an *ofrenda* is specifically for *Día de los Muertos*. An *ofrenda* will have lit votive candles that are meant to help guide the soul to the *ofrenda*. It will also have bread and a glass of water, because these elements are considered to be the main supports of life. In addition the personal favorite items of the deceased will be placed out for him or her, such as sweets, beer, beans, photographs, and even an especially liked shirt or dress. During *Día de los Muertos*, altars are set up in galleries and exhibit halls as artistic and cultural expressions, with *ofrendas* created for particularly known individuals.

See also Altars; Día de los Muertos
References Cash 1998; Morrison 1992; Portillo 1989; Sommers 1995

The Old Mother Game

See La Vieja Inés y los Listones

La Onda Chicana (Chicano Wave of Music)

A phrase used to describe Chicano music, especially that of the late 1960s, which is a combination of Mexican and American music styles. In musical terms, *La Onda Chicana* was created by the Texas *orquesta*, which synthesized the elements from different music styles, such as *ranchera* and big band swing, to create a blend of music that characterized Chicano music of the 1960s and

This ofrenda is "offering" fruits, flowers, breads, and personal items for a special soul on Día de los Muertos (Day of the Dead or All Souls' Day). (Sergio Dorantes/Corbis)

1970s. *La Onda Chicana* also reflected a cultural and political sentiment, an ethnic pride in being Chicano and working class, and it also embodied a recognition of being American and accepting American popular culture. The lyrics of the songs may be in English or in Spanish, and sometimes both languages are used in the same song. Although the *conjuntos* of *norteño* music and the *orquestas* of Texas were all accepted as *Mexicano* and Chicano, the music of *La Onda Chicana* was purely Chicano music.

One band that typified this sound was Little Joe y La Familia (Little Joe and the family). Little Joe Hernandez was born into a migrant farmworker family in Texas and started his musical career as a teenager. He sang with his cousin's group, David Corona y Los Latinaires, for two years before taking it over and calling it Little Joe and the Latinaires. When that group split up he reorganized it as Little Joe y La Familia. He recorded many successful albums in the 1960s, and has been called the "King of Brown Sound."

Peña describes *La Onda Chicana* well: "It synthesized all the musical elements. . . . to achieve a highly innovative bimusical sound that combined a *ranchera* (country music) and *jaitón* (high class music) within the same piece." Other bands that fit into this genre were Sunny Ozuna and the Sunliners, Los Lobos, Los Alacranes Mojados, Ray Camacho and the Tear Drops, and La Rondalla Amerindia.

See also Conjunto Music; Los Lobos; Ranchera
References Loza 1993; Peña 1985; Villarino 1992

Oremos (Christmas House Visits)

A custom from New Mexico and parts of Texas, at least El Paso, where on Christmas Day children go from house to house asking for treats, much like on Halloween. This custom was sometimes just called *Oremos* (literally, "we pray"). Children would knock on the doors of their neighbors and chant:

> *Oremos, Oremos*
> *Angelitos somos*
> *D'el cielo venimos*
> *A pedir Oremos*
> *Si no nos dan,*
> *Puertas y ventanas quebrarémos.*
> (We pray, we pray
> Little angels we are
> From heaven we come
> To ask we pray
> If we don't receive
> Doors and windows we will break.)

The chant states that they're angels from heaven and are asking for gifts, although if they receive none, they may break doors and windows. The origin of this custom is not known, but some believe it is to remind society that the stranger at the door should not be forgotten. Lorin Brown reports that in northern New Mexico the children went out on Christmas Eve, but in Canutillo, Texas, around the 1920s, it was the custom for children to go door to door on Christmas Day, although they didn't recite the above chant. The neighbors expected them and were ready with gifts of fruits and candies.

Lottie C. Devine makes reference to the Papago Indians in Arizona, saying that on "Christmas Day most of them came to town, all dressed in party clothes, and went from house to house 'calling Christmas.' Everyone gave them candies and apples and many of them in turn gave baskets or pottery" (29). Cabeza de Baca refers to this custom as *aguinaldos,* and the chant she records is similar to the one above, except that the last line is "A *pedir Aguinaldos y Oremos."* Aguinaldos are gifts given during the Christmas season.

See also Aguinaldos
References Brown 1978; Cabeza de Baca 1982; Devine 1964

Oso, Juan

The name of a folk character found in tales collected in Spain and New Mexico by Aurelio Espinosa and his son, Jose Manuel Espinosa. In some tales Juan Oso (John Bear) is the son of a princess and a bear. The princess is kidnapped by a bear when she is out of the palace and is taken to a cave where she eventually has a son who is half bear and half human. Finally she and Juan Osito, her son, are able to run away from the bear and go live in the palace with her father. After Juan grows up he leaves his mother to wander the land, and from this point on, various tales describe the different adventures of Juan Oso. In a variant of the tale, a young woman and her baby son are captured by a bear and taken to live in a cave where the son grows up learning the ways of the bear. They also escape and return to live with the woman's uncle, and Juan Oso wanders off to explore the world. Even though he is half wild, Juan Oso develops into a strong, smart, and sensitive man who will not be outwitted. In variants collected by Elaine Miller in Los Angeles, where he is called Juan del Oso, he has magical abilities. After he saves three princesses he is usually allowed to marry one of them.

References Espinosa, A. M., 1985; Espinosa, J. M., 1937; Miller 1973

Otero-Warren, Nina (Adelina) (1881–1965)

Nina Otero-Warren is known primarily as the writer of the book *Old Spain in Our Southwest* (1936), a memoir of life in early New Mexico. It is more than an autobiography, since it is interspersed with folklore narratives, Hispano traditions, and early southwest history. Nina Otero was born in Los Lunas, New Mexico, a town named after her grandfather's family, a descendent of an early influential Hispanic family. They were fairly wealthy and the marriage of her mother and father in 1880 was lavish and elaborate. The details of the wedding are well described by Charlotte Whaley in her biography of Nina. Her father, a member of the famous Otero family, was killed in a shoot-out when Nina was still a baby, and her mother later married A. M. Bergere. They had a large family together, all of whom are well-known citizens of New Mexico. Nina attended school on the East Coast, married and divorced, and eventually settled into New Mexican politics. She was appointed superintendent of schools in the Santa Fe area and was active in the Congressional Union and the Republican Party and lobbied for the vote for women in 1920. In 1922 she ran for the U.S. House of Representatives but was defeated. She continued working for government agencies as an educator and supporter of Indian education. In the early 1960s she worked as a consultant for the Peace Corps, which had a training program at the University of New Mexico in Albuquerque. Like her contemporaries Cleofas Jaramillo and Aurora Lucero-White, she had an interest in folklore, and her book *Old Spain in Our Southwest* was one of the first private ethnographies to be published by a woman of her era. In it she describes the early Spanish settlers, life on the *hacienda*, the religious *fiestas*, the *santos* (saints), foods, folk songs, folktales, and the customs of the region. In her later years, up until her death in 1965, she was a businesswoman in Santa Fe.

References Otero-Warren 1936; Ponce 1992; Rebolledo 1989; Whaley 1994

The Outcast
See El Tiradito

Quetzalcoatl.

Pachuco Cross

A design in the form of a small cross that is tattooed on the left hand, between the thumb and forefinger, with lines, or dashes, radiating out from it. George Carpenter Barker states that it must be seven rays, or lines, that radiate from the cross. It is a well-known symbol among Chicanos and has been traced to the era of the *pachucos* (1940s urban youth), hence its name. It is also known as the *cruz del barrio* (cross from the neighborhood) and has been found throughout major cities of the Southwest. Tattoos of Christian images have always been popular among Chicanos, and the custom of tattooing images of Jesus Christ, crucifixes, *La Virgen de Guadalupe*, and other Madonnas has a long history. In the Middle Ages the Crusaders cut a cross into Christian converts on the hand a little above the wrist. Some social scientists believe that the *pachuco* cross was meant to symbolize violence and membership in a gang. But it is known that it was used as an initiation ritual among friends and peers, to show solidarity and allegiance to a particular *barrio*. In describing the tattooed cross Haldeen Braddy is of the opinion that each ray jetting out from the cross represented a six-month stay in jail. In his view, *pachucos* liked to stay in the *jaula* (cage, jail) so that they could "accumulate these 'rays' as souvenirs of their imprisonment" (1971, 142). There is no evidence to support this speculation.

References Barker 1974; Braddy 1960; Chicano Pinto Research Project 1975; Coltharp 1965; Demello 1993; Govenar 1988

Pachucos (-as) (1940s Urban Youth)

A name adopted by Mexican Americans and Mexican nationals to designate those who make up a fascinating urban subculture, detached from U.S. culture and from Mexican American urban life also. The first appearance of *pachucos* was in the El Paso–Juárez area during the 1920s and early 1930s. It is thought the word *pachuco* was a colloquial way of referring to El Paso. A person from El Paso was referred to as *del pachuco*. Sometimes a person considered a *pachuco* was called a *chuco*. Haldeen Braddy discusses the origin of the word *pachuco*, providing several theories. One is that the *pachucos* of the 1930s came from the city of Pachuca in the state of Hidalgo, Mexico. He also presents the definition from the *Diccionario General de Americanismos*, stating that *pachuca* is a five-card poker hand in which all the cards are of different suits, or in other words, a poker hand with no value, a losing hand. Braddy believes this well describes the *pachucos* of El Paso (1971). The other theory is that *pachuco* comes from the Nahuatl word *pachtli*, which refers to a grass like hay that grows parasitically on trees.

Pachucos were identifiable by their clothing, hairstyles, and a distinct language with its own vocabulary. The men wore "zoot suits," that is, pegged pants, long coats with padded shoulders, and pancake hats. Their hair was worn long and slicked back with a ducktail effect. Some also wore a long chain hanging from their pants, well displayed and connected to a belt. *Pachucas* were the girlfriends of the *pachucos*, but they also had a dress style all their own. They wore short, very tight skirts, with their hair high and long. Makeup was heavy, especially around the eyes. Supposedly they were very streetwise and liked to hang out with their *pachuco* boyfriends.

Large numbers of young men from El Paso, speaking the *pachuco* argot, settled in Los Angeles during the early 1940s, and it was there that they became recognized as an identifiable group, and considered to be gang members. Young men who relocated and settled in Los Angeles, even for short periods of time, upon returning home to the small towns of the Southwest, would spread the *pachuco* beliefs and jargon to their communities. In this way *pachuquesmo*, a Mexican subculture, became known throughout the Southwest.

The *pachuco* speech, a combination of English and Spanish, also called *caló*, was a fascinating fusion drawing from many linguistic sources. *Caló* was originally the language of the Spanish gypsies, or a dialect of Spanish showing traces of many languages acquired by the gypsies throughout their world wanderings. The *pachuco* argot utilized several linguistic sources in developing a vocabulary or jargon. These sources were southwestern Spanish, the older archaic Spanish from New Mexico, Mexican slang, standard Spanish from Mexico City, and also words invented by the *pachucos* themselves. The *pachuco* dialect was the product of an urban environment, and it is believed the language may have originated in the underworld and drug scene of El Paso. George Carpenter Barker pinpoints almost exactly where the *pachuco* jargon originated, from the 7-X gang who first met in the neighborhood of Florence and Eighth Streets in El Paso. Arthur Campa believes that *pachucos* originated as a linguistic group first and had no distinctive dress style. That came later as they moved into a more stable economic environment and had some financial resources.

Expressions and vocabulary used by Chicanos today come from the *pachuco* argot of the 1940s. For example, such words as *órale* (what's happening, or O.K.), *bato* (guy, as in *bato loco*), *califas* (California), *hay te wuacho* (I'll be seeing you), and *la pinta* (jail/prison) have been used for generations. The film *Zoot Suit*, written and directed by Luis Valdez in 1981, depicts the dress, language, and problems of Mexican American youth and especially *pachucos* in Los Angeles in the 1940s.

During the 1940s a caricature of the *pachuco* was created for the Mexican media in the person of Tin Tan, whose real name was Germán Valdéz (1919–1973). He was an actor and performer who dressed as a stereotypical *pachuco* and zoot-suiter. Tin Tan made several Mexican films portraying the Mexican American *pocho* who code-switches between English and Spanish, and speaks *caló*.

The *pachuco* was disdained in the U.S. by both the Mexican American and Anglo communities, and likewise in Mexico by the media and the intellectuals. Octavio Paz, much quoted, disparagingly discusses the phenomenon of the *pachuco* in his book *The Labyrinth of Solitude*, published in English in 1961. Although almost any urban Chicano who was young in the 1940s was affected by the style and language of the *pachuco*, the stereotypic *pachuco* was often associated with violence and deviancy. The zoot-suit riots of 1943 are held up as the epitome of the *pachuco* experience, totally disregarding previous and later experiences. According to Alfredo Mirandé, "The *pachuco* has been an especially visible symbol of cultural autonomy and resistance. His distinctive dress, demeanor, mannerism, and language not only express his manhood but set him off culturally from the dominant society. To be a *chuco* is to be proud, dignified, and to uphold one's personal integrity as well as the honor and integrity of the group. It is at once an affirmation of one's manhood and one's culture" (1985, 179–180). The *pachuco* is the precursor to the *bato loco*, the *cholo*, and the low rider of more contemporary times.

The *pachuca* was the counterpart of the *pachuco* of the 1940s but also the home-girl archetype that comes together in the young Chicana growing up in an urban ghettoized environment. During the 1940s, *pachucas* were the girlfriends of or those who hung around with *pachucos*. They developed their own style of dress, wearing very tight short skirts and sweaters and doing their hair in a pompadour style. Their behavior was loud and brash: they smoked cigarettes in public, wore lots of eye makeup, and supposedly were quick to fight. *Pachucas* knew the vernacular of the times, speaking *pachuco* and scandalizing their families. They were not necessarily gang members, but they can be considered the precursors of present-day *cholas*.

See also Caló; Cholos; Low Rider; Pocho; Tin Tan; Zoot Suit

References Barker 1974; Braddy 1960, 1971; Campa 1979; Cerda and Farias 1953; Coltharp 1965; Cosgrove 1989; Fregoso 1995; Griffith 1948; Hinojosa 1975; Katz 1974; Keller 1985; Luckenbill 1990; Madrid-Barela 1973; Mazon 1984; Mirandé 1985; Montoya 1977; Orona-Cordova 1992; Paz 1961; Plascencia 1983; Valdez 1992

Paintings (Religious)
See Retablos

Palomilla (Group of Friends)

A term used primarily in south Texas during the 1940s and 1950s to describe an informal group of guys that hung around together. *Paloma* means "dove," so a *palomilla* is a flock of doves. One rarely hears the expression today, but it is occasionally used in literature, such as the short stories of Mario Suarez. A *palomilla* would be one's peer group, or a very close group of friends, but not a gang. Consisting of a core of three or four males, with a few fringe members, a *palomilla* was an important socialization unit that provided a safe space for young men to joke and express themselves. Arthur Rubel writes about the supportive social environment provided by the *palomilla* of young coming-of-age Chicanos in the *barrio* of New Lots in south Texas. Joseph Spielberg describes the quick wit and aggressive bilingual humor found among the members of his *palomilla* during the early 1960s, and how their jostling and jesting allowed for the full bloom of each person's personality.

References Cerda and Farias 1953; Limón 1994; Rubel 1965; Spielberg 1974

Papel Picado (Cut Tissue Paper)

The craft and final product of cutting out intricate designs and patterns on sheets of tissue paper. In Mexico the artists who do this work have been doing it for several generations and can cut through fifty or more sheets at a time. A pattern is made and used as the top sheet while the outline design is cut out with different-sized chisels. Most often the small banner-sized sheets are made to decorate altars and *nacimientos* (nativity scenes), or for such celebrations as *Cinco de Mayo* (the Fifth of May) and *El Diez y Seis de Septiembre* (the Sixteenth of September). Mexican restaurants are often decorated with streams of colorful *papel picado*. Some of the cutout designs are scenes related to specific holidays, such as skeletons for *Día de los Muertos* (the Day of the Dead), dancers, floral patterns, the Mexican flag, and other patriotic scenes. In Mexico experienced paper cutters can make large wall hangings and tablecloths out of *papel picado*. *Papel picado* is often taught in public schools, although on the small eight-by-eleven-inch paper.

See also Cinco de Mayo; Día de los Muertos; El Diez y Seis de Septiembre
References Carmichael and Sayer 1991; Lomas Garza 1999; Trenchard 1998; Vigil 1998

Paredes, Américo (1915–1999)

Considered the foremost scholar of Chicano folklore, Américo Paredes was a professor emeritus of English and anthropology at the University of Texas, Austin. His classic work, *With His Pistol in His Hand: A Border Ballad and Its Hero*, first published in 1958, has become a standard work in Chicano studies and American folklore. A whole generation of Chicano scholars regard Paredes as their intellectual role model and mentor, and his original research on Chicano folklore engendered a new wave of scholarship and academic achievements.

As a young man, Paredes was always interested in music, *corridos* (ballads), and singing. His early published scholarship focused on ballads and ballad heroes of the Texas-Mexican border, and through this research he developed a theory about the formation of Chicano folklore. The resistance to an encroaching foreign culture, the loss of political and economic power, feelings of social marginality, and the resulting conflict of cultures all contributed to the creation of folklore in the form of legends, jokes, and songs by the Chicano people. His research and publications encompass various disciplines from anthropology to literature to social history.

Américo Paredes was born in Brownsville, Texas, on September 3, 1915. He attended Brownsville Junior College in the early 1930s, earning an A.A. degree in 1936. In 1944 he joined the army, wrote for the military newspaper *Stars and Stripes*, and worked in Japan for a couple of years. Returning to Texas in 1950, he earned a B.A. degree from the University of Texas in 1951, an M.A. in 1953, and a Ph.D. in 1956.

The distinguishing feature of Paredes's scholarship has been his humanistic approach to conducting research. Besides knowing and studying his own culture and ethnic community, he was able to bring another consciousness to the study of folklore in general and to Texas-Mexican folklore in particular. He taught that the examination of a cultural or folkloric phenomenon cannot be divorced from the social context in which it is performed or expressed. Before the publication of Paredes's work, most of the Hispanic and Chicano folklore collected was classified, published, and placed on a library shelf. Paredes's research emphasized the importance of the informant's culture, and the social setting and history of the community of the informant. It was in his book, *With His Pistol in His Hand: A Border Ballad and Its Hero*, that Paredes proposed his theory of the development of Chicano folklore through a process of cultural conflict generated by the invasion of Anglo culture and values into south Texas in the 1800s. Many writers have dedicated their books to him, and the journal *Aztlán* devoted a double-issue volume to him in 1982. Besides publishing over sixty articles in academic journals, he was editor of the *Journal of American Folklore* from 1968 to 1973 and published *Folktales of Mexico* in 1970 and *A Texas-Mexican Cancionero: Folksongs of the Lower Border* in 1976.

Besides his scholarly writings, Paredes was a poet and novelist. His first publication was a collection of poetry titled *Cantos de Adolescencia* in 1937. Most recently he has published *George Washington Gomez: A Mexico Texan*

Novel in 1990, *Between Two Worlds* in 1991, and *The Shadow* in 1998. Don Américo died unexpectedly in April of 1999.

References Leal 1987; Limón 1980a, 1986, 1992, 1994; Paredes 1958, 1976, 1978

Los Pastores (Shepherds' Play)

A religious medieval nativity folk play. Also known as *La Pastorela*, the complete title of this folk drama is *El Coloquio de los Pastores*, and it is written in verse and performed on Christmas Eve. It is an ancient mystery play, brought to the New World by the Spanish Franciscan priests, and is performed throughout the Southwest. As a folk production, it is performed for entertainment, but it is also a religious presentation that is maintaining a long tradition. The full title means "the dialogue of the shepherds," and it is an interpretation of the dialogue and reaction the shepherds may have had when they learned of the birth of Jesus Christ. It narrates the story of the shepherds who are visited by Michael the Archangel who informs them of the birth of the infant Jesus and urges them to go to Belén (Bethlehem). Before the shepherds decide what to do, they are visited by Lucifer, who is angry about the birth of the Christ child to the Virgin Mary. Lucifer tries to challenge the shepherds but Michael the Archangel returns just in time to defeat him. The shepherds then continue on their journey to Bethlehem bringing gifts for the infant Jesus. The structure of the play is formulaic, and so the sequence of acts can be rearranged into many different patterns, with jokes, songs, speeches, and other events added at different points. The underlying story of the drama is the universal battle between good and evil. It has evolved from the literature of sixteenth-century Spain and the indigenous traditions of Mexico, and for this reason the play has provided a political format for the poor masses throughout the last 400 years.

Because of its ancient history there are many variants of *Los Pastores*, and several versions have developed a comic dialogue between Lucifer and Cucharón, Bartolo, and the other characters. One character is named Bato, as in *bato loco* (crazy guy), a phrase of contemporary usage among Chicanos today. Variants of this play have been collected in Texas, New Mexico, and California, and it has been performed in Mexico since the sixteenth century. In San Antonio the performance of *Los Pastores* at Our Lady of Guadalupe Church as been ongoing since 1913. Richard Flores, both as an ethnographer and as a performer, presents a thorough analysis of the historical conditions that continue to provide an environment for the performance of *Los Pastores* as both ritual and drama. In 1991 *El Teatro Campesino* produced a video film of their production of *Los Pastores* titled *La Pastorela—The Shepherds' Tale*.

References Bandini 1958; Cole 1907; Espinosa 1985; Flores 1995; Herrera-Sobek 1995a; Igo 1985; Lea 1953; Lucero-White 1940; Ortega 1973; Pearce 1957; Rael 1965; Robb 1954; Robe 1957; Romero 1984; Silverthorne 1990; Wright 1920

Pedro de Urdemalas

Also known as Pedro di Urdemales or Pedro Ordimales, meaning "Peter of the holy water font," he is a rogue folk hero with hundreds of tales to his name. This trickster character is known throughout the Spanish-speaking world and the Southwest of the United States. He is the classic Spanish *pícaro* (rogue), who incorporates "three ancient literary types, the wanderer, the fool, and the have-not," according to Claudio Guillen. He is the trickster figure who is constantly dissatisfied, always wanting more, yet is always outwitting everyone and acting as the social critic along the way. Pedro de Urdemalas lives by his wit, has no shame, and at different times makes a pact with the devil, God, the Virgin Mary, and St. Peter. Tales of Pedro de Urdemalas collected by Aurelio M. Espinosa in Spain and in New Mexico were published in the *Journal of American Folklore* in 1914. Ramón Laval gives a brief literary history of de Urdemalas and publishes a small series of tales collected in Chile in the late nineteenth century. Cervantes wrote a play about him in 1615, *Comedia Famosa de Pedro de Urdemalas*, so we know Pedro de Urdemalas was already a folkloric character in the seventeenth century. Wardropper states, "Pedro de Urdemalas is a shadowy, even elusive, figure in the oral tradition of Spanish folktales. Because these tales were not—as far as we know—collected in the Renaissance and because, like ballads and songs, they must have been subject to endless variation and mutual interference, we cannot now know the Pedro de Urdemalas who endeared himself to the folk" (218). But it is clear that Pedro de Urdemalas is a Hispano precursor to *Don Cacahuate, el pelado,* Tin Tan, Cantinflas, and an antecedent of Chicano joking behavior.

See also Don Cacahuate; El Pelado; Tin Tan
References Guillen 1971; Lamadrid 1995; Laval 1943; Wardropper 1982

El Pelado (The Plucked One)

Literally, "plucked," or "bald," *el pelado* was a designation used for a clownish performer, an improvised character type developed by performing theater groups in the 1920s, in Mexico and in the Southwest. Also known as *peladito,* this comic hobo is the underdog, a nobody who is criticized and made fun of by the whole world. The *pelado* was a verbal artist who, according to Samuel Ramos, "has created a dialect of his own, a diction which abounds in ordinary words, but he gives these words a new meaning. . . . His terminology abounds in sexual allusion" (1962, 59). Many *carpas* (tent theaters) featured *pelado* or *peladito* characters, and the *agringado* (anglicized) and the *pocho* (half Mexican) were special targets of his comic wit and satire. Beloved by working-class audiences, the *peladito,* using *caló* (Spanish slang) and *pochismos* (Americanisms), particularly poked fun at the acculturation of Mexicans who couldn't speak Spanish and pointed out to them American discrimination against

Mexicans. Similar to Charlie Chaplin, and later developed by the Mexican actor Cantinflas, *el pelado* was a homeless type who in dialogue could state the unthinkable and mock everything and everybody. Many Chicanos, who may not have known the appellation *pelado*, nonetheless became familiar with the comic vagabond through Mexican films. *El Teatro Campesino* (the Farmworkers' Theater) effectively used this character type in skits and *actos* (dramas) and succeeded in intensifying, with humor, the serious social issues presented in their performances.

See also Agringado; Carpas; Pocho; El Teatro Campesino
References Broyles-Gonzalez 1994; Kanellos 1990; Limón 1998; Ramos 1962; Spielberg 1974

Penitente Chapels
See Moradas

Los Penitentes (The Penitents)

A Catholic fraternal order of men, formally known as *La Fraternidad Piadosa de Nuestro Padre de Jesus Nazareño*, or informally as *Los Penitentes*. This lay religious society related to the Roman Catholic Church is still found in rural northern New Mexico and southern Colorado. Originally it was organized for religious observances and practices, including pious prayer and bodily penance, but the society eventually became very important in providing mutual aid to the local communities. *Los Penitentes* cared for the sick, arranged funerals, and conducted the religious rituals associated with wakes. Their social role in contemporary New Mexico is not as pronounced but some *moradas* still remain active.

Their primary religious ceremonies commemorated the passion and death of Jesus Christ, during the celebrations of *Semana Santa*, "Holy Week." It is speculated that the starting date of the brotherhood is somewhere between 1790 and 1810. The origins of *Los Penitentes* have been debated for years, but it is likely they were heavily influenced by the Franciscan Third Order, who were the friars in New Mexico until Mexico separated from Spain in 1821. *Los Penitentes* became a strong institution in rural New Mexico because there were too few Catholic priests to oversee the religious life of the people during the early nineteenth century. The village chapters governed themselves without benefit of the few priests in the colony. Consequently *Los Penitentes* had strong influences in conserving the language and culture of the Spanish Americans of New Mexico. Membership consisted of between thirty and fifty adult men per chapter (called *moradas*) and were divided into two groups: common members, called *hermanos disciplantes* (brothers who discipline), and officers, called *hermanos de luz* (brothers of light). By the early twentieth century the various chapters had become secret societies with restricted membership.

Journalism about *Los Hermanos Penitentes* has been sensationalistic, with lengthy descriptions of their *Semana Santa* rituals, especially when Anglo Americans migrated to New Mexico during the late nineteenth century. Their custom of self-punishment, in the form of flagellation during the Holy Week ceremonies, aroused much interest and was reported widely in many East Coast publications. The most sensitive and nonjudgmental writing and research have been conducted by de Cordova, Henderson, Sprott, and Weigle. A worthy, contemporary (1970–1986), descriptive account of the ritual ceremonies associated with Holy Week in Cordova can be found in Charles Briggs (1988).

References Boyd 1974; Briggs 1988; Brown 1978; Darley 1968; De Cordova 1972; Espinosa, G., 1972; Henderson 1937; Horka-Follick 1969; Rael 1951; Sprott 1984; Steele and Rivera 1985; Weigle 1970, 1976; Woodward 1935

The People
See La Raza

Pichilingis (Elves)

Elves or leprechauns that Anthony John Campos refers to as little people, *pichilingis* are goblins who perform mischievous pranks. Santamaria's *Diccionario de Mejicanismos'* definition for *pichilingo* is *chiquito, muchachito,* and *niño pequeño,* meaning "very small" and "little child." The word *piciligue,* which comes from the Aztec, has the meaning of "to become small that which was thick or large." Another closely related word also found in Santamaria is *pichilingui,* which is a common word for *pato silvestre* (wild duck), which is found in lakes in the interior of Mexico. *Pichilingis* are similar to *duendes* (goblins) and are possibly the indigenous version of a *duende,* and have only been found in the folklore literature of New Mexico. *Duendes* are very common in Chicano folktales, and many people still believe in them. They are often invisible yet their presence is felt because of the annoying tricks and antics they concoct.

See also Chanes; Duendes
Reference Campos 1977; Santamaria 1978

Pilón (Bonus)

A custom, often expressed only after it occurs, of giving a little extra when making a transaction or closing a bargain. For instance, when buying candy, the vendor may add one extra piece, *de pilón*, to surprise and make a child happy. John Bourke writes about an ancient custom in Mexico still used in the late nineteenth century: a merchant kept a tin cylinder for each customer, and after each purchase he'd drop a bean into it. After the total number of beans reached sixteen or eighteen, the customer was given six cents in money or goods. This was the *pilón*, a type of dividend given to the client for purchasing from the same merchant.

The phrase *de pilón* is used when referring to the occurrence of an unplanned episode or accident. In narrating a personal story with an unhappy ending, an individual might add, "*Y de pilón me caí*" (and to top it off, I fell down). Although it is not found in common usage among contemporary Chicanos, many will remember how their parents used this expression. The word has several meanings, including "a heap of stuff," such as a heap of grapes, a heap of mortar, a heap of something, but it also means a lump of sugar. In her personal memoir *A Place in El Paso*, Gloria Lopez-Stoppard has a delightful description of the use of *pilón* during her childhood. Thus *de pilón* may express something positive, or something unexpectedly negative.

References Bourke 1895; De Leon 1982; Lopez-Stoppard 1996

Piñatas

A colorfully decorated clay pot or papier-mâché figure filled with toys and candies, confetti, or party favors that is brought to celebrations such as birthdays, Christmas festivities, and other parties. Often it is decorated as a star or an animal, such as a burro or elephant, but it can also be a fruit or a puppet. The size varies from small to very large. *Piñatas* have traditionally been a part of birthday and Christmas celebrations, but are now also brought out for other holidays. In Mexico a *piñata* was always broken on Christmas Eve, especially among the poorer classes, so that children would receive small inexpensive gifts from the *piñata*. The real Christmas gifts were not presented until *Día de los Reyes* on January 6, also known as Epiphany in the Catholic calendar.

A game is made of breaking the *piñata*, and a song accompanies the game. The *piñata* is hung from a tree, with a long rope that is manipulated by an adult, who is able to move the *piñata* up and down, so it won't be broken too quickly. A child is blindfolded, twirled around three times, handed a bat, and led to the *piñata*. Everyone will usually have a turn or two, and finally the manipulator allows someone to break it. The candy and prizes fall to the ground and everyone jumps to grab some.

The custom of breaking a *piñata* during the Christmas Mass celebrations was introduced by the Augustine priests in the seventeenth century. Later

Children all over the United States love to break piñatas at birthday parties. (Tony Arruza/Corbis)

the custom of celebrating many Christmas Masses evolved into *Las Posadas* (Christmas pageant). The *piñata* was considered to be a symbol of evil, with the clay pot representing Satan or his spirit and the colorful decorations serving to tempt humanity. The candies and goodies inside the *piñata* were the unknown pleasures that Satan held out to attract man. The blindfolded child was supposed to represent innocence and faith, which must be blind to combat the evil spirit. The breaking of the *piñata* symbolized the struggle that man must sustain to destroy evil and receive the gifts and pleasures of God (the candy).

The word *piñata* derives from the verb *apiñar*, which means to cram, tie, or join together. In Italy *pignattas* were hung from the ceilings during masquerade balls. It is accepted that there is an oriental influence, since *piñatas* are always decorated with colorful crepe paper. It is thought *piñatas* originated in China and were brought to Sicily and Spain by the Arabs and to New Spain by the Spaniards.

See also Las Posadas
References Burciaga 1993; Gallegos 1991; Griffith 1988; Ortega 1973; Perl 1983; Silverthorne 1990; Verti 1993

Pintos (-as) (Prisoners)

Pinto is a term used for prison and also for a Chicano prison inmate. A *pinto* is a male prisoner, a *pinta* a female prisoner. *La Pinta*, referring to prison, is believed to come from the word *penitenciaria*, or "penitentiary." Other common words for prison are *bote*, meaning "can," and *corre*, which is short for "correctional institution," referring specifically to one in Texas. "Joint" is another word frequently used to mean prison.

There has been a lot of sociological literature written about the formation of gangs in prisons as a means of surviving incarceration in the United States. The media, including *60 Minutes*, has done stories about the activities of the Mexican mafia and *La Familia*. Often ignored is the subculture of the *pinto* experience that is exhibited in behavior, art expression, and published poetry. In the early 1970s several Chicano magazines devoted whole issues to literature and art by *pintos*, always referring to it as *pinto* art and *pinto* poetry. A combination of Mexican and prison cultural values dictates the behavior of *pintos* inside prison and out on the street. Chicano prisoners have a strong sense of family and community and feel they are constantly being watched by their *barrio*, family, women, and their home-boys peer group. Most Chicano convicts have little education, speak primarily in Spanish, and have a strong sense of Mexican nationalism. Regardless of place of birth, *mexicanismo* and *machismo* are a very important part of being a *pinto*. Ex-*pintos* are often identifiable by their mannerisms, gestures, language, haircuts, and dress. They are usually extremely clean and well groomed, have very short hair, wear well-pressed pants, and are in excellent physical shape.

Within the prison world *pintos* have established a well-defined and -structured social environment, which they carry to the outside world when released. In discussing the film *American Me*, Rosa Linda Fregoso states that Edward James Olmos depicts extremely well the expressive behavior of *pintos* both in prison and outside. In her words, "Besides rendering a Chicano *pinto* presence in the rhythms of speech, Santana [the movie character] represents it in the stylized walk and prose of a *pinto*, a stance honed in the corridors behind prison walls or in the barrios of East L.A." (1993, 130).

The *pinto* experience is a subculture of the Chicano experience. Because of the low socioeconomic status of a large percentage of Chicanos in the United States and the lack of equal opportunities in education and employment, many Chicano families have been inadvertently introduced to this subculture. A special issue of the Chicano magazine *De Colores*, vol. 3, no. 1, was devoted to "Los Pintos de America," and the issue was published as a separate monograph in 1976 by Pajarito Publications. Female Chicana prisoners also undergo the *pinta* experience, and one scholar, Letticia Galindo, has written about the specialized language use and street experiences of *pachucas*, *cholas*, gang members, and female prison inmates.

See also Cholos; Pachucos
References Chicano Pinto Research Project 1975; Coltharp 1965; Davidson 1974; Estrada 1971; Fregoso 1993; Galindo 1992, 1993

Placas (Insignias)

The word *placa* means "an insignia of an order," and in the United States it also means the license plates of a car. But within *cholo* and youth gang culture it refers to the sign and name of a gang or club as it appears on the walls of buildings in the *barrios* of Chicano communities. What may appear as graffiti is actually the *placa* of a person, or of a gang. Where the *placa* appears signifies that territory as belonging to that gang, and it may also serve as a challenge to other gangs. The use of public walls for asserting a fraternal identity is really an ancient tradition, and within Chicano culture it can be traced back to at least the 1930s. Chicano street culture uses *plaqueasos* as a system for conveying information about territory and youth socialization customs. If one *placa* is written over by the *placa* of another gang, it is accepted as a challenge to a confrontation.

A *placa* also refers to the individual name of a gang member. Nicknames are very common among Chicanos, but a *placa* is specifically a gang-related name and often very well describes the person as perceived by friends or other gang members. Names, such as "Sad Girl," "*Diablo*" (devil), "Joker," and "*Malo*" (bad) could be names used within a gang, and may signify sadness, wildness, or craziness. Sometimes the writing of names on walls is referred to as *plaqueasos*, or in contemporary terms, "barrio calligraphy." In more recent times the individual who writes on walls has been called a tagger, and the art

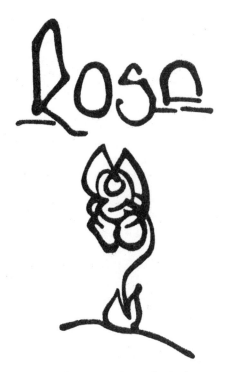

of writing is tagging. Many Chicano taggers use a stylized medieval writing, such as Old English and German Gothic forms.

Sanchez-Tranquilino has analyzed the displacement of graffiti by murals in Chicano communities and finds that murals can be an extension of the barrio calligraphy rather than an attempt to control gang vandalism, as is sometimes assumed.

See also Cholos; Con Safos; Graffiti
References Chabran and Chabran 1996; Cockcroft 1992; Cockcroft, Weber, and Cockcroft 1977; Harris, M., 1988, 1994; Kim 1995; Sanchez-Tranquilino 1995

The personal insignia of an individual carries great importance. (North Wind Picture Archive)

Pochismos (Americanisms)

A term that describes the use of English expressions in Spanish, or Americanisms interjected into conversations when speaking Spanish. Sometimes this kind of speech is called Spanglish, or Chicano Spanish, or just *pocho* talk. Examples of some *pochismos* are words such as *parkear*, meaning to park (the car), and *wachar*, meaning to watch (*hay te wacho*, "I'll see you"), also spelled *guachate*, meaning "watch out." Other simpler examples are *dona* for doughnut, *el dompe* for the dump, *troque* for truck, and *yarda* for yard. According to Manuel Peña the word *jaitón*, meaning "snobbish," evolved from the words "high tone" when one was discussing music. It came to be used to mean pretentious high class, as in *"se crea muy jaitona"* (she thinks she's real high-class), but at the same time it can mean that one has elegance or style.

Various dictionaries of Chicano Spanish and Chicano slang have been compiled that list many other *pochismos*. Chicano novelists and poets have consciously incorporated the use of *pochismos* in literary works to reinforce the precarious cultural and linguistic status of Chicanos in American society.

See also Caló; Pachucos; Pocho
References Campa 1977; Galvan 1985; Hernández-Chavez, Cohen, and Beltramo 1975; Peña 1985b; Vasquez 1975

Pocho (Half Mexican)

A *pocho* is a term used in Mexico to describe a person of Mexican heritage born and raised in the United States. It is meant to describe a person who may not be fully fluent in Spanish, or "Mexican enough," culturally and linguistically. The word can also mean "discolored," "truncated," or "small." It has been adopted by some Chicanos to describe and ridicule themselves as they survive within an antagonistic and discriminatory environment. The word became more nationally known in 1959 with the publication of the novel *Pocho* by Jose Antonio Villarreal, which depicted the coming-of-age of a Chicano growing up in the Santa Clara Valley of California during the 1940s.

Mexicans like to call Chicanos *pocho*, ridiculing their sometimes poor Spanish and their lack of knowledge about Mexico and Mexican customs. Mexicans who have spent time in the United States and have acquired the mannerisms, values, and the English language may be considered *pochos* because they've become *agringados* (anglicized). In the 1950s and 1960s the Mexican cinema produced several films depicting the lives of *pochos*, from both sides of the border, but emphasizing the importance of maintaining *mexicanidad*. Titles of some of these films are *Soy Mexicano de Acá de Este Lado* (I Am a Mexican from This Side) (1951), *Los Desarraigados* (The Uprooted) (1958), *México de Mi Corazón* (Mexico of My Heart) (1963), and *El Pocho* (The Half Mexican) (1964).

As with the word *cholo*, individuals have attempted to find the origin of the use of the word *pocho* in reference to Chicanos. In his autobiography, *Barrio Boy*, Ernesto Galarza writes about the *pochos* he found in Sacramento, California, in the second decade of the twentieth century: "They had learned to speak English of sorts and could still speak Spanish, also of sorts. . . . Concerning the *pochos*, the *chicanos* suspected that they considered themselves too good for the *barrio* but were not, for some reason, good enough for the Americans" (1971, 203).

In Los Angeles, the writer Lalo Lopez has created a comic industry based on *pocho* caricatures that includes a comic strip, political cartoons, *Pocho* Productions, an Internet web page, *Pocho Magazine*, a political satire zine, and a calendar. He refers to a modern Aztec calendar as a *Pochteca* calendar, which features wisdom from the "wise guy ancestors of the modern day *Pocha* and *Pocho*." The whole Southwest is referred to as *Pocholandia*. A Chicano who does not speak fluent Spanish may be said to speak *pocho* Spanish, but the reverse is never stated about a Mexican who cannot speak fluent English. Many English and Spanish words that have become altered by the opposite language, through cultural contact, are called *pochismos*. Some examples of *pochismos* are *yonque* for "junk," *tichar* for "to teach," and *carro* for "car."

See also Agringado; Caló; Pochismos
References CHICLE 1995; Galarza 1971; Maciel 1992; Madrid-Barela 1976; Paredes 1993a; Vasquez 1975; Villanueva 1978; Villarreal 1959

Las Posadas (Christmas Pageant)

A tradition marking the beginning of the Christmas season with the dramatization of the search for lodging in Bethlehem by Joseph and Mary. It always includes a procession with singing and music and starts nine days before Christmas. The story, in the form of a novena (Catholic nine-days devotion), is based on the gospel of St. Luke. For nine consecutive nights before Christmas Eve, *la Noche Buena* (the good night), *los peregrinos* (the pilgrims) representing Joseph and Mary visit a different home each night, reenacting the search for an inn by Joseph and Mary. *Los mesoneros*, those who portray the innkeepers, keep refusing them lodging. *Los peregrinos* form a procession, and children and angels hand-carry the small figures of the Holy Family. When they arrive at a home they ask for shelter and sing carols. *Las Posadas* occurs from December 16 through December 24. Nine different homes are opened to the pilgrims and food and drink are offered after the *peregrinos* have been denied lodging. Most homes will have a nativity scene, a *nacimiento*, set up for the prayers and singers. An important tradition of these festivities is the *piñata* that is brought out and broken by the children. There is evidence that *piñatas* originated from this Christmas celebration.

Posadas are still held today in many Mexican communities in the United States. Some are organized by church groups, but recently others have been organized for commercial purposes by city entities. The reenactment of *Las Posadas* is an ancient tradition that can be traced back to the early conquest in Mexico and to the christianization of the Aztecs by the Augustine priests. They originated in the small village of San Augustin Acolman located near the pyramids in Teotihuacán. The Aztecs celebrated the birth of their god Huitzilopochtli for one night, and celebrations were held all of the following day in every home. This occurred about the same time of the year that the Catholic Church celebrated the birth of Christ. The Augustine priests saw the similarity between these Aztec celebrations and the Christmas festivities and chose this opportunity to teach the new religion to the Aztecs. While the Aztecs were celebrating the birth of Huitzilopochtli, the priests reenacted the pilgrimage of Mary and Joseph. The nine nightly journeys symbolize the nine months of pregnancy for Mary. These Christmas Masses, as they were called, were celebrated in the convents and churches, but eventually were moved to the *haciendas*, farms, and ranches, and finally to the neighborhoods. The celebrations ended with firecrackers and the breaking of a *piñata*. Today many cities in the Southwest reenact this pilgrimage for one night with a procession winding through city streets. In Monterey, California, the whole city comes out for *Las Posadas*, and in San Antonio, Texas, a *posada* is held during the *Fiesta de las Luminarias* (Festival of the Bonfires) that includes a procession on the *Paso del Rio* (river pass).

See also Nacimiento; Piñata

References Campa 1934; Chabran and Chabran 1996; Espinosa 1985; Heisley and MacGregor-Villarreal 1991; Ortega 1973; Silverthorne 1990; Sommers 1995; Steele 1992; Verti 1993; Vigil 1998; Waugh 1955

Prisoners
See Pintos

Promises
See Mandas

Proverbs
See Dichos

Quetzalcoatl.

Q

Quermes

See Kermés

Quetzalcoatl

A god, one of the major deities of the Aztecs. *Quetzal* is a Nahuatl word referring to a bird found in Central America, and *coatl* means "snake," so *Quetzalcoatl* means a "feathered serpent," and this god is often called the Plumed Serpent. Stories about him indicate that he was an earthly hero, a lightskinned man, who acted as the ruler of the Toltecs for some time. In one legend Quetzalcoatl is sent to the underground to get the bones of the ancients. After the end of the Fourth Sun (an Aztec era), when the ancient people have been drowned or changed into fish, the spirits decide he should go seek the bones in order to start a new race. He must try three times, overcoming many obstacles, before he succeeds in bringing the bones to the sky. They are ground to a powder and placed in a bowl by the goddess Cihuacoatl. The other gods shed blood into the bowl and humans are born. Quetzalcoatl discovered corn, which he brought for the new humans to eat. He saw an ant bringing a kernel of corn from inside a mountain, and he changed himself into an ant and followed it. Lightning was used to split open the mountain to bring the corn to the people. He left the Toltecs to return to his home. It just happened that Quetzalcoatl promised to return in the same year that Hernán Cortés landed in Veracruz. It was to the Spaniards' advantage to use the Indians' belief in Quetzalcoatl's return. Cortés was well received because he was thought to be Quetzalcoatl and the conquest of the Aztecs by the Spaniards was legitimized.

Quetzalcoatl is one of the better-known Aztec gods and has been greatly idealized by the moderns, including Chicanos. His image has influenced artists, writers, philosophers, and painters for hundreds of years. As the celestial dragon, he is patterned after the rattlesnake, a common mythical creature in Mesoamerica. This dragon has come to symbolize the Chicanos' early heritage and has been embraced by Chicanos, especially those coming of age

A major deity of the Aztecs, Quetzalcoatl, a feathered serpent, is depicted in this relief sculpture on the outside walls of the Pyramid of Quetzalcoatl in Xochicalco, Mexico. (Charles and Josette Lenars/Corbis)

in the 1970s. Quetzalcoatl can be found in the literature, murals, and graphic art reflecting Chicano culture and the Chicano movement of the 1960s and 1970s. In 1970 an American Indian and Chicano college was started in northern California with the name Deganawidah-Quetzalcoatl College. This college was still in existence in the year 2000 and has struggled to maintain a curriculum that meets the needs of both Indian and Chicano students. Deganawidah was the name of the chief of the Iroquois Federation, and after the college was given his name, it was learned there was a common belief that the name could not be mentioned publicly. Since that time the college has become known as D-Q University.

References Bierhorst 1990; Brundage 1979; Carrasco 1992; Lafaye 1983

Quinceañera (Fifteenth Birthday Party)

A coming-of-age celebration and ceremony for a young girl on her fifteenth birthday. The word *Quinceañera* comes from the Spanish word *quince*, meaning "fifteen" and *añera*, which together mean "the fifteen-year-old." This celebration marks the beginning of adulthood for a young woman. It is a custom throughout Latin America, Mexico, the Caribbean, and in many areas of the United States to distinguish this birthday with a special observance. It is

A quinceañera, or fifteenth birthday party, is a very important coming-of-age ritual in Chicano culture. (Courtesy of Gilbert L. Tapia)

assumed the custom has origins in pre-Columbian cultures, as a coming-of-age ritual for young women. In his *Historia de Nueva España*, Bernardino de Sahagún narrates that it was traditional for the parents of a young Aztec maiden to formally acknowledge her passage into womanhood. "Advice of an Aztec Mother to Her Daughter" is reprinted in William H. Prescott's *The Conquest of Mexico*.

Communities in Texas have formally observed *Quinceañera* birthdays for many generations, whereas such celebrations are not as common in California and other parts of the Southwest. Traditionally this ceremony serves as a coming-out party to indicate that a girl has reached womanhood and is ready for marriage. In the United States this is no longer the case, but the celebration does symbolize the transition from childhood to womanhood. In some celebrations a doll called *la muñeca de los recuerdos* (the doll of memories) or *la última muñeca* (the last doll) is given to the celebrant as a symbol of the childhood she is leaving behind. Some people see it as the last vestiges of childhood and *la última muñeca* as the last doll she will ever receive.

Although not a religious sacrament, the celebrations of *Quinceañeras* take on a strong religious undertone. The ceremony usually includes a special Mass, where the parents give thanks for having a wonderful daughter, and she gives thanks for having a wonderful family, and the young woman may receive a formal blessing from the priest. The Mass is very similar to a wedding Mass, with the celebrant and her entourage slowly marching down the center aisle of the church. A ceremonial dinner and a dance with live band music usually follow. The celebrant wears a long white gown, similar to a wedding dress; has fifteen maids, *damas*, with their escorts, *chambelanes*; and sometimes performs a choreographed dance or waltz. *Quinceañera* celebrations are held in major cities with large Latino populations, such as Miami, San Antonio, Chicago, Los Angeles, and El Paso. These cities now offer many businesses that cater to Latino families planning *Quinceañera* celebrations. Although this is a family tradition and ritual, some families use the occasion to lavish on their daughters an extravagant day, never to be forgotten.

Besides the traditional doll, other folkloric elements continue to be incorporated into *Quinceañera* ceremonies. In Idaho and Oregon, Eva Castellano has continued a tradition she learned from Mexico of making *coronas* (crowns) made of waxed and paper flowers to be worn by the young girl. Only unmarried girls wear the *coronas*, which symbolize innocence and purity. Much of the research on *Quinceañeras* shows that families want to maintain a cultural historical tradition, and the celebration of a daughter's fifteenth birthday is a means of continuing cultural ties to a Latino heritage.

A booklet by Angela Erevia provides an outline of the Catholic Mass including biblical readings and a schedule of the types of classes required of a young lady. Michele Salcedo's book is a planning guide that discusses everything from the dress to the invitations, the music, the limousine, and the food, including the recipes. Internet sites are now available to guide a parent in planning every aspect of this ritual.

References Chavéz 1983; Davalos 1996; Erevia 1980; Horowitz 1993; Martinez-Chavez 1989; Ortiz 1992; Salcedo 1997; Siporin 1984; Vigil 1998

Quinto Sol (Fifth Sun)

The narrative of the Fifth Sun is based on an Aztec myth that has become an important cultural expression commonly incorporated into Chicano cultural events. The first publisher of contemporary Chicano literature in the 1960s, based in Berkeley, California, was named Quinto Sol Publications. Worship of the sun was an integral part of Aztec culture. The sun was viewed as a warrior with the solar rays as his darts. Time consisted of a fifty-two-year calendar that was divided into five ages, or series of ages, called Suns. The first age was the Age of the Earth Sun, and the god was Tezcatlipoca, whose familiar animal was the jaguar. The second age was the Age of Great Winds, the sun was Quetzalcoatl, and the age ended with great hurricanes. Then came the Age of Fire with the sun Tlaloc, and it ended with volcanic eruptions. Next was the Age of Floods with the goddess of waters, Chalchiuhtlicue, as the fourth sun. This age ended when the sky fell upon the earth and the waters gushed up, turning men into fish. The present and fifth age, *El Quinto Sol*, has Nanahuatl, also known as Tonatiuh, as the god, and it is the Age of Earthquakes. With *El Quinto Sol* a full culture was created, with maize grown for the first time, fire domesticated, and the creation of the Toltecs. This age is supposed to end with earthquakes. Each age came about when the god of an aeon died or sacrificed himself to be reborn as the sun of the next aeon.

References Bierhorst 1990; Brundage 1979; Florescano 1999; Griffith 1990

Quetzalcoatl.

R

Ranchera (Country Song)

It is accepted that the word *ranchera* refers to a type of Mexican song, although sometimes it is an adjective that describes a character or a type of person. *Ranchera* comes from the word *rancho*, meaning a "cattle ranch, farm, or rural settlement." A poor unsophisticated person may be called a *ranchero or ranchera,* implying he or she is from the countryside, the sticks, and a hick. In the context of Mexican folk music *la canción ranchera* is a love song, sung by the common folk, the peasants of the rural countryside. After the Mexican Revolution *rancheras* became more agreeable to the upper classes because of the movement toward a Mexican identity and nationalism and a rejection of European cultural values. The modern *canción ranchera* was made popular in Mexico City in the early 1950s by the songwriter José Alfredo Jimenez. The poetic structure of the *ranchera* is brief and simple, yet emotionally it is very intense. According to Rubén Campos as quoted by Gradante, "it is a moan and a sigh . . . , the briefest form of composition and, as such, requires a greater intensity of expression than any other compositional form. It must say precisely what it means" (1983, 105). The themes of *rancheras* are love and unrequited love, but from the point of view of the ordinary common man. *Rancheras* express the poetry of the masses. The famous *ranchera* singer Amalia Mendoza states, "the *canción ranchera* expresses the sensibility of the masses and reaches them: thus, its popularity. . . . One might say that the *canción ranchera* reflects the personality of the masses because it expresses something vital that we all have in common" (Gradante 1983, 105).

The *ranchera* originated in Mexico but is very popular in the United States among Mexicans and Chicanos. José Alfredo Jimenez wrote over 500 songs, many becoming classics that continue to be sung today by younger artists, that have a universal sentiment that speaks to the hearts of Chicanos. Because of the style of these romantic songs, sung to *Mariachi* music and sung in Spanish, untranslatable *rancheras* express the epitome of Mexicanness. The musical poetics arouse emotional sentiments about lost loves, nostalgia, and by extension about being Mexican. Songs such as "Ella" (Her), "Camino de Guanajuato" (Road to Guanajuato), "La Vida no Vale Nada" (Life Has No Value), and "Llego Borracho el Borracho" (The Drunk Arrived Drunk) all elicit memories of fathers, grandfathers, and stories of Mexico. Many are drinking songs, frequently shown in movies being sung in *cantinas* (bars), but they are also dancing songs, so they are played at celebrations and family gatherings. Although *rancheras* are intensely male centered, there are several female singers who became famous singing *rancheras*, such as Lola Beltran, Lucha Villa, and Amalia Mendoza. The performance of *rancheras* is always dramatic and emotional, whether performed by men or women, and the audience can always empathize with the situations depicted in the verses. The life experiences portrayed in the songs of José Alfredo Jimenez, who came from a poverty-stricken background himself, are about the struggles of Everyman, the need for social acceptance, personal happiness, and some type of financial security. These are concerns that the average *Mexicano* and Chicano can identify with. Although most *rancheras* speak of love, other life situations found in the songs deal with fortune, destiny, and life's choices. In "Camino de Guanajuato," these existential words open the song:

> No vale nada la vida,
> La vida no vale nada,
> Comienza siempre llorando,
> Y así llorando se acaba.
> (Of no value is life
> Life is worth nothing
> It always begins with weeping
> And with weeping it ends.)

References Gradante 1983; Peña 1985a, 1985b

Rascuache (Downtrodden Folk)

Also spelled *rascuachi, rasquache, rasquachi,* and *rasquachismo,* this Mexican word characterizes a poor people's and working-class people's worldview and defines how engaging and cultural beauty is created by them. It means that in spite of poverty, a pleasurable outlook on life inculcates a perspective that results in the creation of a pleasing cultural environment, composed of whatever elements are available. These elements may be art, home decorating, entertainment, language, the creation of religious objects, altars, anything connected to the creation of a special and spiritual life. For an individual it defines an attitude, a sensibility, or a social condition. It can describe the car, the house, clothes, a whole way of life. The *Diccionario de Mejicanismos* defines *rascuache* as *pobre,* "a miserable person," poor, lowly, wretched. The *rascuaches* are the downtrodden, the lowly people, *persona que no vale nada* (person that is worth nothing). In English it could be interpreted as "funky," humble, unsophisticated. What is most important about the concept of *rascuache* is that it captures a propensity or an aesthetic, according to Ybarra-

Frausto, to persevere and make whatever one possesses, or has at hand, work well together. All resources are considered riches, and an inventiveness in the use of available resources results in a *rascuache* lifestyle. Whether one is cooking a meal, dressing for a party, assembling a garden, or decorating a Christmas tree and nativity scene, a *rascuache* sensibility will ensure that the final outcome will be elaborate, colorful, an unrestrained aggregate of rich resources. This aesthetic can be observed in the creation of yard shrines, graveyard sites, and in home decorating. Ybarra-Frausto has written a wonderful essay about *rasquachismo* that shows how Chicanos incorporate this spirit in the cultural life of the community. In his words, "*Rasquachismo* is brash and hybrid, sending shudders through the ranks of the elite who seek solace in less exuberant, more muted, and purer traditions. . . . To be *rasquache* is to be down, but not out" (1991b, 156).

This underclass aesthetic was vigorously exhibited by *El Teatro Campesino* (the Farmworkers' Theater) in the creation of the stock characters that constituted the core of the *Teatro's actos* (dramas). In the 1970s the group created and successfully performed a play called *La Carpa de los Rasquachis* (The Tent of the Rasquachis) about a family named Rasquachi. The figure of *el pelado* (the clown) distinctly exemplifies the *rascuache* outlook, the underdog figure, who is both victim and hero at the same time, a Cantinflas archetype. The prototype of the *rascuache* character was Pito Perez, the protagonist of the novel *La Vida Inútil de Perez* (The Futile Life of Pito Perez) by Jose Ruben Romero, first published in 1938 and reprinted many times, most recently in 1993; and also Don Chipote of *Las Aventuras de Don Chipote* written by Daniel Venegas in 1928, a journalist who lived in Los Angeles.

See also Carpas; El Pelado; El Teatro Campesino
References Broyles-Gonzalez 1994; Mesa-Bains 1999; Ybarra-Frausto 1991b

La Raza (The People)

The literal translation of this term is "the race," but it has come to be used as an in-group name for Mexican and Chicano people. Translated as "the people," it is recognized as meaning all mixed-race Spanish and Indian people, known as *mestizos*. The term encompasses all Latinos (Latin Americans) who are descendents of the Spanish and Indian encounter. The Mexican intellectual José Vasconcelos wrote a book in 1925 titled *La Raza Cósmica: Misión de la Raza Iberoamericana*. Publishing after the Mexican Revolution, Vasconcelos envisioned the successful future of Mexico to lie in the strong bonds of its mixed-race population. Before the Revolution, in the nineteenth century, Mexicans looked toward a European identity, and most of the upper classes considered themselves white Europeans. The indigenous population of Mexico was segregated and not racially mixed, and the *mestizos* were more closely aligned with the Indians than with the upper classes. Vasconcelos wrote his slim volume in his search for a Mexican identity for himself and for Mexico's population. *La Raza* is used by Chicanos because they identify as *mestizo* people and see themselves as members of a special race, a group of people with a distinct heritage and destiny. Chicano writers, artists, professionals, musicians, and students are invigorated by the proclamation of *"La Raza!"* and inspired to work toward a creative and political unity. In the words of Jose Angel Gutiérrez, as quoted by Arnoldo Vento, *"La Raza* is the affirmation of the most basic ingredient of our personality, the brownhood of our Indian ancestors wedded to all the other skin colors of mankind. . . . As children of *La Raza*, we are heirs of a spiritual and biological miracle" (225). The *"Viva la Raza!"* chant is a frequent opening and closing statement at festivities, concerts, political meetings, anywhere Chicanos might come together. In the 1970s, the first political party to be formed by Chicanos in the U.S. was called *La Raza Unida* Party. October 12, known in the United States as Columbus Day, is celebrated throughout Latin America as *Día de la Raza*, or Day of the People. It is celebrated by New York Puerto Ricans and Cubans and Chicanos throughout the country. It marks the birth of Hispanic heritage and the beginning of Hispanic culture because it is the day Columbus landed in the New World. It is unclear if President Ronald Reagan was aware of this when he declared Hispanic Heritage Month to be celebrated September 16 through October 15.

References Schmidt 1978; Vento 1998

Relajo (Joking Behavior)

A form of joking behavior visible among Mexicans and Chicanos, with close friends and family, that creates solidarity within the group, but that also allows humorous or satirical discussion of taboo topics that are of importance to the group. Jorge Portilla's essay on *relajo* is often cited as the fundamental study of this comic conduct found among the Mexican working class. His analysis focuses on the dynamics of this joking behavior, *relajando*, and how the working poor utilize it to disrupt values imposed on them by the social classes in power or the dominant culture. *Mexicanos* living in urban poor communities experience almost daily a breakdown in social relations. In brief, Portilla's definition states, "In summary, *relajo* can be defined as the suspension of seriousness that rejects a value maintained by a group of people" (25). This suspension of seriousness in the face of officially serious issues, such as life and death, permits an individual to feel free and detached. Through verbal performances, joking, and narrating humorous anecdotes, an individual can suspend elements of gravity, snobbery, or socially imposed acceptable conduct.

In Mexican social thought the role of *relajo* behavior is shown to be a criticism of the political corruption of the government, but also a burlesque of the divisions of the social classes. Cantinflas, the Mexican actor, was the great *relajero* of all time. As a comic actor, he was the premier artist of the *relajo*, whereby in a single ludicrous, narrative monologue he could inadvertently chastise the urban poor, and champion the social needs of the upper classes, thus highlighting the obvious disparities. But his *relajando* behavior, the social situations and entanglements he got into, were also subversively configured to emphasize the extreme illegitimacy of the social structure. His personality not only entertained but also fulfilled a seditious function, taunting the excesses of the wealthy and the absurdities of a structured social system.

Relajo can also describe a joking relationship, a bantering back and forth, which through the laughter relieves tension and disintegrates the cause of the tension of the moment. But it is the breakdown of decorum, the rejection of a social value that everyone knows is necessary, yet proscribed, that the *relajo* subverts. The cultural consequence is that through this type of behavior one can become temporarily free from social constraints that in daily life cannot be rejected. If one could find a phrase in English that encompasses the *relajo* concept, it would be "to put one over on" a system or a situation. *Relajando*, or *echando relajo* (joking), can be lighthearted joking around or can be heavy in a serious way about a grave topic.

Farr has studied the joking behavior of Mexican women in Chicago and found that through *echando relajo*, married and young single women find relief from their gender roles and the social propriety imposed by their husbands, parents, and the Mexican culture. Laughter created by farcical comportment, or by satire, creates an opposition to the prescribed value and to the seriousness of it. Portilla calls the shared laughing *una burla colectiva* (a collective joke), and states that collective laughter facilitates the collective "*negación a la conducta requerida*" (negation of required conduct). *Relajo* can overturn values or what is assumed to be valued. *El Teatro Campesino* (the Farmworkers' Theater) practiced the art of *el relajo* in the execution of its *actos* (dramas) and in the social protest messages propagated through satire and laughter.

See also El Teatro Campesino
References Barriga 1997; Broyles-Gonzalez 1994; Farr 1994; Fregoso 1993; Portilla 1966

Religious Folk Art

The creation of folk art is an unconscious aesthetic expression of community social and cultural values, and religious folk art is the aesthetic reproduction of images and symbols for a religious or spiritual purpose. The most obvious examples of religious folk art in Chicano culture are religious statues, the *santos* (*saints*), *retablos* (religious paintings), *ex-votos*, and paintings of *La Virgen de Guadalupe*. But there are many other shared religious experiences among Chicanos that result in the creation of religious folk art objects. The *descansos*, erected alongside rural roads where someone has died, become works of art that convey spiritual sentiments. Yard shrines that gradually swell with

This retablo *of Jesus Christ is typical of the folk art of New Mexico. (Craig Aurness/Corbis)*

multicolored paper or plastic flowers, plants, statues of saints, and rosaries are also religious art when lovingly tended by family members. The same can be said for altars, *nacimientos* (nativity scenes), and *camposanto* (cemetery) graves, which are assembled with artistic care, while always communicating a devout religious sentiment. Bright *coronas* (wreaths) for cemetery grave markers with built-in *nichos* (niches) for saints and photos result in glorious displays of decorative art. During the celebrations of *Día de los Muertos* (Day of the Dead), galleries exhibit beautiful altars and *ofrendas* (offerings) assembled by artists for community viewing but also for the spiritual sharing that results. Religious icons carry great meaning in Chicano culture and always find their way into many folk art displays. *La Virgen de Guadalupe* is tattooed on the backs or chests of hundreds of Chicanos, and this too can be considered religious folk art.

See also Altars; Camposanto; Descansos; Día de los Muertos; Nacimiento; Retablos; Santos
References Awalt 1998; Boyd 1974; Espinosa 1967; Griffith 1985, 1988; Vidaurri 1991; Wilder 1943

Religious Folk Practices

Folk rituals, customs, and traditions based on religious or spiritual beliefs and on the ceremonial disciplines of the Catholic Church. In Mexico and in small southwestern communities the church was often located in the center of town, and the soul and rhythm of the people were synchronized with the liturgical seasons of the Church. Processions, *fiestas*, blessings, home prayers, *velorios* (wakes), and religious societies were integrated into daily life. The rural nature of many *Mexicano* communities meant that often a priest or official church clergy was absent, so popular religiosity or folk religious practices developed among the strong spiritual people. Some neighborhoods had *rezadores* or *rezadoras*, spiritual leaders who led the community in prayer for funerals, saints' day celebrations and whenever the priest was unavailable. The home shrine or *altarcito* (little altar) in many homes took the place of a house of worship. Margaret Clark's study of the Mexican community in San Jose, California, in the 1950s found that over 50 percent of the homes had *altarcitos*.

The American Roman Catholic Church was not always receptive to Mexican or Hispanic Catholicism. In many communities the church clergy openly discriminated against Mexicans. In Emporia, Kansas, "the basement of the Sacred Heart Church was renovated and Mass was said for Mexicans two Sundays of each month" (Beeson, Adams, and King, xix). The lack of hospitality and the shortage of priests who spoke Spanish kept many *Mexicanos* from participating in the American Catholic Church.

This situation served to reinforce religious folk practices and rituals brought from Mexico, many based on a syncretism of Indian religious beliefs and medieval Catholicism from the sixteenth century. The strong spiritual faith in the power of particular saints was frowned upon by the American church and considered to be an "exaggerated superstitious" belief (Dolan and Hinojosa, 57). Recent histories of Chicanos and the Catholic Church suggest that Mexicans were not dependent on a priest-centered religion and developed their own popular devotions performed without a priest. "Mexican American spirituality developed both private and public expressions. Private spirituality, which was practiced individually or within the family, stressed sacramental and personal devotions, while the public religious stressed processions, *fiestas*, symbols, and symbolic action that displayed the beliefs of the Mexican Catholic to the rest of the community" (Dolan and Hinojosa, 177).

Eventually every Chicano community had its own parish, due usually to the commitment and work of one individual priest in the diocese. There is probably a *Virgen de Guadalupe* parish in every single Mexican community in the United States. In spite of the fact that in some regions there was hostility by church officials, the importance of the Catholic Church in creating Chicano communities cannot be overemphasized. It was the church that created an environment where people could speak Spanish; celebrate religious, social, and political ceremonies; cook the special foods of the holy days and holidays; and of course pray together. The experience of Chicanos in Kansas, as described by Beeson, Adams, and King, was repeated throughout the

Southwest and Midwest. "The church remained the most powerful center and cohesive force in the Mexican American colony. It was a religious and social haven in an alien, often hostile, environment. In the church the immigrant could use his Spanish language, wear traditional costume, celebrate Mexican Independence Day with a *fiesta*, and eat traditional food. The church also perpetuated the separateness of the Mexican-American and their Anglo neighbors" (Beeson, Adams, and King, xx).

Religious celebrations for a saint's day brought a community together and reinforced religious conviction and ethnic solidarity. Throughout the Southwest, *fiestas* for *San Juan, San Isidro, San Francisco, La Virgen de Guadalupe*, and many other favorite saints incorporated religious rituals and secular revelry. When paying homage to a saint, the church held Masses and processions early in the day; picnics, horse races, *corridas de gallos* (rooster games), and dances were held later in the day and evening. A community's social calendar was based on the Catholic liturgical calendar, which provided frequent occasions for religious and cultural celebrations. Lent started with Ash Wednesday, and the belief was that, if one received ashes, one would live to see the end of the year. *La Cuaresma*, Lent, was and still is a time of sacrifice, prayers, *Vía Cruces* (stations of the cross) every Friday, special meatless foods, and spiritual preparation for *Semana Santa* (Holy Week). Palm Sunday with the distribution of holy palms resulted in the palms being made into crosses and tacked over doorways to protect the family from illness or harm. Good Friday included processions and in some communities the burning of Judas. *Sábado de Gloria* (Holy Saturday) and the end of Lent was often celebrated with jubilation and a dance. Easter Sunday celebrations and the customs of new clothes and Easter egg hunts were adopted by Mexican American communities later, probably after World War II.

One of the most important religious celebrations is the *fiesta* for *La Virgen de Guadalupe*, held on December 12. It often includes a *Mañanitas* (dawn) Mass and serenade with *Mariachi* music, a procession through the streets, and a dinner and dance. During the Christmas season there are usually *Las Posadas* for nine nights and performances of *Los Pastores* (Shepherds' Play).

Many religious practices and beliefs have survived in some families without anyone knowing the source of the custom. For example, there is a custom of kissing a parent's hand after receiving Holy Communion. Before this act is performed the communicant drinks exactly three swallows of water. There are many beliefs, *creencias*, connected to Holy Week observances, such as not working on Holy Thursday and not taking baths on Good Friday. On *el Día de San Juan*, St. John's Day, on June 24, there are also traditions about swimming and taking baths. In some regions this day is referred to as *el día de bañar*, meaning the day to take a bath of some kind. It could be jumping in a river, lake, or waterway, or just being splashed with water. The tradition is connected to the baptism of St. John, and throughout Mexico, it is common to see water fights on this day, with buckets of water thrown on friends and family. The maintenance of a family altar and reciting the rosary every day, lighting votive candles, blessing the children every night, the blessing of homes and yards, and making promises, *mandas,* to particular saints are all folk practices passed on from generation to generation. Believing in the benevolent power of the saints and developing a special relationship with one particular saint is still a common habit. Mary Helen Ponce, in her book *Hoyt Street,* has some wonderful descriptions about the religious practices in her family, from First Communion celebrations to Holy Week rituals.

See also Altars; Camposanto; Descansos; Hábito; Mandas; Religious Folk Art; Santos
References Arnold 1928; Beeson, Adams, and King 1983; Clark 1959; Dolan and Deck 1994; Dolan and Hinojosa 1994; Griffith 1985, 1988, 1992; Ponce 1993

Remedios (Remedies)

Folk remedies often involving the use of homeopathic methods, herbs, and medicinal plants. *Remedios* are also known as *remedios caseros* (home remedies). Herbal remedies have been used for generations by the people living in Mexico and the Southwest, and many of these are now of interest to general health care practitioners. *Curanderas* (healers) use herbs to heal, but many families rely on their own traditional *remedios* passed down from generation to generation. Family knowledge and use of *remedios* may involve the preparation of teas, salves, ointments, and the use of herbs for basic health maintenance. A person who specializes in the application of herbs for healing purposes is called a *yerbero,* and a person considered to be a healer is called a *curandera* or *curandero.* Some *remedios* are simple and basic, such as drinking *yerba buena* (mint) tea for an upset stomach, to very complicated ritual procedures only known to a trained *curandera.* Many of the herbal remedies used in Chicano and Mexican homes today were introduced to New Spain by the Europeans, and were ancient herbs used by the Greeks, Egyptians, and Arabs. They brought many herbs not native to Mexico and the Southwest, such as chamomile, anise, cinnamon, coriander, mint, oregano, rosemary, garlic, and orange blossoms.

There are literally hundreds of medicinal herbs used by the people of northern Mexico and the U.S. Southwest. Several collections of herbs have been catalogued and are located at the University of Michigan's Ethnobotanical Laboratory. These have been described by Karen Cowlan Ford and are listed by both the Spanish name and the botanical name. In addition many Internet web sites have been established by health organizations, individual folklorists, and other entities for the purpose of collecting and disseminating information about homeopathic and herbal healing.

See also Curanderismo
References Ford 1975; Kay 1977; Moore 1990; Roeder 1988; Sandoval 1998; Spicer 1977; Torres 1983a, 1983b

Resting Places
See Descansos

Retablos (Religious Paintings)

A *retablo* is a painting of a religious scene with a saint, *santo*, in a two-dimensional format. Found throughout Mexico, *retablos* date from the middle of the eighteenth century in New Mexico. The *retablo* paintings were painted on either hide or wooden boards, sometimes also on tin, but usually pine wood smoothed over on one side. The surface of the board was covered with gesso before the design was painted on it. Most were painted with tempera, using a gesso ground with bright colors, but contemporary *retablos* are often painted on tin. Some dyes and pigments were made from plants and earth, whereas others were probably imported from Mexico. Since the early twentieth century, *retablos* have been produced in the same form as they are to the present day.

These *retablos* may be painted for a specific saint in gratitude for a favor granted, or in praise of the powers of the saint. For example, Durand and Massey have compiled and written about the many *retablos* to the *Virgen de San Juan de los Lagos* in Mexico. The paintings usually depict an event survived or celebrated, an illness, an operation, imprisonment, or having received a passport to the United States, or they may depict a person praying to the saint. A few sentences written on the *retablo* express the favor granted, starting with the words "*Doy gracias*" or "*Doy infinitas gracias a la Santisima Virgen de San Juan de los Lagos*" (I give thanks, I give infinite thanks to the most holy Virgin of San Juan of the Lakes) and the reason for the *retablo* is written out, with the location and date added at the end.

Another expression for this religious art is *retablo ex-voto*, a votive painting created in payment to a saint according to a vow. The Latin term *ex voto* means "from a vow," so the *ex-voto* is specifically created to complete a vow made to a particular saint. Other *retablos* may be painted in gratitude for something gained or accomplished but not because a vow was made. A *retablo ex-voto* is a work of art, a religious painting, and also a historical document. The painting depicts the favor or miracle that occurred, the holy image or saint responsible for the miracle, and a short text that describes what occurred, including the location and date of the event. The text describing the event may begin with "*Doy Gracias*" (I give thanks) and express a need to state the miraculous event and tell how at the moment of crisis "*me encomendó a la Virgen*" (I entrusted myself to the Virgin). The text usually ends "*por eso dedico este retablo*" (this is why I dedicate this *retablo*). The *retablo* is then placed in a church or a shrine devoted to that particular saint. The tradition of creating votive paintings goes back hundreds of years in Mexico, and can be found along the U.S.-Mexican border region and in the cities of the Southwest. Many people immigrating from Mexico, for instance, have painted or commissioned a *retablo* in gratitude for surviving a disaster or an illness. Art exhibits in the United States have shown *retablos ex-votos* that depict the treacherous experience of immigrating to the United States.

See also Mandas
References Awalt 1998; Boyd 1959, 1974; Durand and Massey 1990, 1995; Mills 1967; Toor 1973

Riddles
See Adivinanzas

Los Rinches (The Texas Rangers)

The Texas Rangers, known by *Tejanos* as *Los Rinches,* probably a Spanish pronunciation of "ranger," became notorious within Chicano communities because of their brutality. Established in 1835, right before Texas's independence from Mexico in 1836, the Texas Rangers were viewed as a state militia. They were actually organized by Stephen F. Austin, who hired the first ten in 1823 to wage war against Indians. Often portrayed as heroic figures, protectors of law and order, by Hollywood and in literature, *Los Rinches* were greatly feared and hated by Texas Mexicans. During the U.S. Mexican War they led the way for General Zachary Taylor's march to Monterrey, Mexico.

Texas Ranger Colonel Homer Garrison, director of the Department of Public Safety in Texas, does not look typical of the notorious Los Rinches of the early twentieth century. (Bettmann/Corbis)

The Rangers have evolved over the years and have had periods of low activity and other periods of important law enforcement work. Today they are under the Texas Department of Public Safety and have become a kind of detective agency. As they have become better trained, better educated, with high-tech equipment and higher salaries, they are looked upon as the elite law enforcement of Texas.

But there were many bloody periods when the Rangers were extremely violent and cruel along the

Texas-Mexican border. Between 1914 and 1919 they killed about 5,000 Mexicans. It is believed that many of the folklore and superhero legends known about the Texas Rangers were created at the expense of the Mexican population. Among the *Mexicanos* of the border they were known as *Los Diablos Tejanos*, "the Texas devils." The Rangers' battles with Texas border Mexicans helped create the image of the fearless fighters. The word *rinches* as used in the border area is almost equivalent to the word pig, when used in relation to their law enforcement responsibilities. According to Richard Flores, "The term *'rinche'* not only signifies mistrust or deceit, but also the violence and exploitation inflicted upon the *Mexicano* community by the Texas Rangers" (1992,171). *Corridos* (ballads) from the Texas-Mexican border originating from the late 1800s until the turn of the century narrate episodes of border conflict in which the antagonist is often a member of the dreaded *rinches*. Several *Tejano* folk heroes, such as Gregorio Cortez, Juan Cortina, and Catarino Garza became memorialized because of their confrontations with the Texas Rangers.

See also "El Corrido de Gregorio Cortez"
References Flores 1992; Meed 1992; *New Handbook of Texas* 1996; Paredes 1958; Samora 1979

Rio Grande Blankets

A Rio Grande blanket was a blanket woven in New Mexico during the nineteenth century that was meant to be worn during the day and used as bedding at night. Blankets were woven before this period, actually since the seventeenth century, but not many survived from the period of 1600 to 1800. The Rio Grande blanket has particular characteristics, with designs that include wide bands and various zones of narrow stripes. During the early 1800s the wool was not dyed and was left in colors of brown and white. It was called *churro* (a kind of sheep) wool, because it came from the common sheep introduced by the Spaniards. Later, the wool was combined with natural dyed yarns of indigo. This wool was woven on a narrow treadle loom. The designs for the Rio Grande blankets are very distinct, with indigo-dyed stripes, and later were influenced by Saltillo *sarape* motifs that were introduced in the late 1800s. There was much borrowing and exchange of materials, fibers, and dyes between the Pueblo Indians and the Spanish in the textile weaves of New Mexico. The Saltillo *sarape* motif has a large complex diamond in the central layout of the blanket, and sometimes is surrounded by a scalloped border. Rio Grande blankets from the late nineteenth century incorporated many of the Saltillo *sarape* motifs. Today, reproductions of the Rio Grande blankets can be found on stationery, cards, and other types of artwork.

See also Sarape
References Fisher 1994; Museum of International Folk Art 1979; Siporin 1992; Spanish Colonial Arts Society 1996

Rodeos
See Charreadas

Romance (Sixteenth-Century Spanish Ballad)

The *romance* is a very old ballad form introduced by the Spaniards to the New World. It was the main ballad tradition in New Spain until the *corrido* evolved from it, around the period of Mexico's independence. Research into the literary folklore of New Mexico reveals a great love of traditional poetry, and the *romance* is a form that flourished for over 300 years. Written in a sixteen-syllable verse, it is usually printed in eight-syllable lines. Lea classifies the *romance* into three types: those of a religious nature, those that were sung to children or are of a nursery rhyme nature, and those about universal and emotional adult topics. The subjects of the *romance* were not the doings of the common folk, but rather of those in the higher classes or in military office. Two very old *romances* still sung in the Southwest are "La Delgadina," which deals with incest, and "La Aparición," which dates from the fifteenth century in Spain. J. D. Robb lists eleven variants of "La Delgadina" in his 1980 collection. Espinosa collected many *romances* from *Californios* in the 1920s. The *romance* is actually an old form of lyrical poetry that dates from medieval Spain.

See also Corridos; Folk Songs
References Campa 1930; Espinosa, A. M. 1924; Lea 1953; Rivera 1989; Robb 1954, 1980

Rooster Game
See Corrida de Gallos

Quetzalcoatl

Santa Fe Fiesta

This major fiesta held in Santa Fe every year during the first weekend of October was first started in 1625. It is believed that the first fiesta was held in honor of the Virgin Mary, called Our Lady of the Rosary. The more formal and structured celebrations actually began after the second conquest of New Mexico, when Don Diego de Vargas led an expedition in 1692–1693 and reconquered the territory. On this trip de Vargas brought with him a statue of *La Conquistadora*, as the Virgin Mary was called, and built a throne for her, from which she could reign over the kingdom of New Mexico. The celebrations were to venerate *Nuestra Señora de la Conquesta*, in conjunction with the *Cofradía del Rosario*, the Confraternity of the Rosary, which is celebrated on the first Sunday of October as decreed by Pope Pius V in 1571. The fiesta always includes a procession that carries the statue of *La Conquistadora*, and a reenactment of the triumphant reconquest by Vargas.

The fiesta is very popular and receives a lot of publicity in the media of New Mexico, especially in journals such as *El Palacio*.

References Mather 1992; Pierce 1985

Santeros (Saint Makers)

According to Jose E. Espinosa the word *santero* has several meanings, and one special meaning is "caretaker of a sanctuary," or the person involved in the care of sacred images. In recent years it has come to refer to a person who creates or repairs *santos* (saints). *Santeros* create *santos* out of stone, plaster, or any other material. During the seventeenth and eighteenth centuries, oil paintings of saints on skins were found in the churches of New Mexico; most likely these were brought from Mexico. During the eighteenth century, *santeros* imitated and developed their own styles of painting on skins. When Archbishop Lamy arrived in the newly created New Mexico diocese in 1851, he ordered that all the *santos* be discarded and replaced with plaster statues from France. Not all of the *santos* were destroyed, but it took many years before local artists starting creating their own images of *santos* again. These artists have become known as *santeros* and *santeras* and comprise an important heritage of New Mexico Spanish colonial art. One of the earliest known *santeros* is the "*Laguna santero*," who painted the altar screen in the church of *San José de Gracia* at the Pueblo of Laguna. Another well-known *santero* was Jose Aragón who signed and dated a few of his *retablos*; one is dated 1827 and two others are dated 1830.

Renewed interest in *santos* as art objects was initiated in the 1920s by Anglo artists in Santa Fe and Taos. Tourists and collectors became interested in buying *santos* at fairs, festivals, and curio shops. This tradition continues today, carried on by both men and women artists of New Mexico who see the tradition as a symbol of their Hispanic heritage.

See also Folk Art; Santos

References Awalt 1998; Awalt and Rhetts 1995; Berkenfield 1994; Boyd 1946, 1959, 1974; Briggs 1980; Espinosa 1967; Frank 1992; Kalb 1994; Spanish Colonial Arts Society 1996; Steele 1974; Wroth 1982

Santos (Saints)

A figure or image of a saint, but it can also mean a holy person. A popular compliment for a mother is "¡*Es una santa!*" (She is a saint!). *Santos* in the sense of images are found in most Chicano homes, the most well known being *La Virgen de Guadalupe*. *Santos* as religious artworks or as folk art can be found in two forms, either as *bultos*, figures in the round, or as *retablos*, flat paintings on pine panels or any other flat material. Such an image is then called *un santo de retablo*. The image can be made of any material: stone, wood, plaster, or paper. The artist who makes *santos* is called a *santero*, with the tradition and skill passed on from generation to generation within a single family. Traditionally the creation of *santos* as an art form originated in New Mexico when the craft was introduced by the Spanish friars. For a period of almost 100 years, from the late eighteenth century to the late nineteenth century, this distinctive art form flourished in New Mexico. According to William Wroth, this Christian folk art survived for such a long period because of four major factors. These were the isolation of New Mexico from New Spain, the influence of the Franciscan friars, the traditions of the rural people, and the influence of Mexican and New Mexican indigenous cultures upon Spanish American cultural expressions. For glossaries of well-known New Mexican *santos*, with color plates, see both Steele and Wroth. Beautiful color photographs of contemporary *santo* artwork can be found in both Awalt and Kalb. Some popular saints known among Chicanos are *La Virgen de Guadalupe, San Antonio de Padúa, San José, Santo Niño de Atocha,* and *Santiago*. Catholic Chicanos believe that *santos* intercede with God on behalf of the supplicant. They are considered to be alive and are talked to and treated as real people.

Traditions mentioned in the literature of New Mexico but also found in other parts of the Southwest and Mexico reveal that visible responses are expected from *santos*. If a *santo* does not accede to a request made by a supplicant, the saint is punished by being turned against a wall, placed in a dresser drawer, or even buried under a house until the request is granted. Frances Toor, in her major work on Mexican folklore, mentions that in a village near Cuernavaca the people would pray to their saints for rain, and when their prayers and offerings were not answered they undressed the saints and placed them in the fields to experience the heat from the sun. And when it rained too much, they put the saints in the streams so they'd also suffer from too much water. Currently there is a folk practice among American home sellers in California that, if a home does not sell quickly enough, a statue of St. Joseph is buried upside down in the yard facing the house. Supposedly, this ensures that the seller will soon receive a respectable offer.

See also Folk Art; Retablos; Santeros; Yard Shrines
References Awalt 1998; Bacigalupa 1972; Boyd 1946, 1959, 1974; Cash 1999; Espinosa, G., 1935; Espinosa, J. M., 1967; Frank 1992; Kalb 1994; Mills 1967; Oktavec 1995; Spanish Colonial Arts Society 1996; Steele 1974; Toor 1947; Wilder and Breitenback 1943; Wroth 1982

Sarape (Shawl)

A blanket worn primarily as a covering and outer garment, with a very long and ancient tradition. The use of the *sarape* was common among the Indians and some *mestizos* (mixed-race people) of central Mexico. After Mexico became independent from Spain in 1821, as a result of and an effort toward nationalism, the *sarape* was adopted by all *mestizos* and by all Mexicans. Eventually, the upper-class horseman, *el caballero* (gentleman), and the *charro* (horseman) added the *sarape* to the ensemble of the horse's gear. It wasn't until the mid-nineteenth century that the *sarape* became the common costume of most people of Mexico. The Saltillo *sarape* was a finely woven textile, very expensive, and widely admired throughout Mexico. The weavers of the Rio Grande blanket adopted many of the motifs of the Saltillo *sarape* when it was introduced into the northern territories of Mexico. The Saltillo *sarape* originated in the state of Coahuila, and was originally woven by Tlaxcalan Indians. The origins of the design are unclear; some think the motifs are Moorish, others claim Chinese. The serrate diamonds and figures are probably of Tlaxcalan origin. During the late 1960s many Chicano students took to wearing *sarapes* on college campuses as a visible symbol of their Mexican heritage. In the 1990s this custom is not noticed as frequently, but the designs and motifs of the Saltillo *sarape* have influenced the artwork of many Chicano artists.

See also Rio Grande Blankets
Reference Museum of International Folk Art 1979

Shepherds' Play
See Los Pastores

Shock
See Susto

Sirena del Mar (Mermaid)

A *cuento* narrated in south Texas that tells the story of a young girl being transformed into a mermaid. It is a moral tale passed from mother to daughter in situations where a daughter is supposed to follow structured family disciplines. The tale is associated with Catholic folk beliefs because it is often narrated in connection with Good Friday religious observances. Basic elements of the tale are that on Good Friday, the day Jesus Christ was crucified, a girl is told by her mother that she cannot bathe in the river. Usually no work, especially housework or cooking, is done on Good Friday, and the day is spent in prayer or at the church, and the daughter is told it is a sin to go into the water. The girl badly wants to either bathe or play in the water, and she goes in spite of her mother's warning. Gradually she sees her lower body turning into a fish, and she's doomed to stay in the water forever. Sometimes she is seen by friends and relatives, but in some variants she disappears into the river or ocean forever. The connection to Good Friday religious practices is ambiguous, as is its relationship to water. In one variant daughters are told by their mother that they cannot take a shower or they will turn into fish. There are many prohibitions on Good Friday, and in strictly observant Catholic families the day is usually a day of prayer, with no television, radio music, or dancing allowed. Mark Glazer's analysis of the legend is that a girl who disobeys her parents, and becomes a mermaid, is showing "the individual in a completely inferior non-human position" (1981b, 62). The girl's sexuality is insinuated by the bathing. Breaking away from her mother's rules and the water are supposed to represent destruction. On the other hand, the Spanish word for mermaid is *sirena*, related to the word siren, meaning "enchantress," so one could surmise that the transformation into a mermaid symbolizes sexual maturity, a human stage that mothers try to postpone as long as possible.

Reference Glazer 1981b

The Sixteenth of September
See El Diez y Seis de Septiembre

Skeleton
See Calavera

Sobador (Masseuse)

A person who massages and knows how to knead sore muscles and sprains. *Sobar* means "to massage" and as a practice and branch of folk healing, *sobadores* (men and women) work quietly within communities, providing a service that people can afford. Some individuals believe that an imbalance in the body may result in pain, headaches, and nervous tension. They may seek assistance from a *sobador* who will treat them with a general massage that is meant to right the imbalance. Others may seek help for a particular sprain or cramp. A *sobador* can also take care of *empacho* (indigestion) and *descomposturas* (dislocations). This branch of folk healing is the counterpart to the work of chiropractors and is usually a skill passed down, learned from a relative such as a parent or grandparent. In some communities a folk healer who takes care of sprained bones is called a *huesero*, but in other communities a *sobador* may perform all chiropractic functions. Sometimes a good *sobada* may include a *limpieza*, a ritualized cleansing that may include spiritual elements and prayer. Many *curanderos/as* are also *sobadores*, but not all *sobadores* are *curanderos/as*.

See also Curanderismo; Empacho; Huesero
References Kay 1977; Trotter II and Chavira 1997

Songs
See Canciones

Sopapillas (Fritters)

A semisweet bread, sometimes eaten as a dessert, made from flour *tortilla* dough. It has been referred to as puffed bread because it is deep-fried and puffs up into a fluffy pastry. *Sopapillas* are traditionally from New Mexico, and are served in many restaurants as bread with a meal, but are not often found outside the state. The dough is rolled out and usually cut into triangular shapes. When fried and puffed up, the pieces are covered with a sugar-cinnamon mixture, or sometimes drizzled with honey. All references to *sopapillas* mention that it is unique to New Mexico. A Spanish dictionary defines *sopapa* as a "fritter drizzled with honey." Frying was unknown in the New World because there was no lard. Animal fat was introduced by the Spaniards, along with wheat, later in the eighteenth century. *Buñuelos* are another pastry similar to *sopapillas* made in Mexico and the Southwest. These are made from flour, eggs, butter, and milk. They are rolled out like a *tortilla* and also fried in hot oil. They come out very crispy and are then covered with cinnamon-sugar. *Buñuelos* are often made for the Christmas holidays.

References Lopez 1976; Ortiz y Pino 1993; Peyton 1994; Pilcher 1998; Zelayeta 1958

Spanish Colonial Arts Society

An organization founded in New Mexico by Mary Austin and artist Frank Applegate in 1925 as a means of reviving the historic craft traditions of the region. The society established the Spanish Market, still operating today, which sells crafts and artwork during the Santa Fe Fiesta. It became inactive for many years, especially during World War II and with the death of Mary Austin, but it was revived again in 1951. Throughout the years it has worked closely with the Spanish Colonial Arts Department established at the Museum of New Mexico, and this relationship has helped to revive the society. Together they work to keep traditional arts and artifacts in New Mexico, instead of allowing them to be taken out of state by other museums. The work of these agencies has been very important for the history of folk art in the country and in New Mexico.

See also Folk Art; Santa Fe Fiesta
Reference Weigle and Larcombe 1983

Spanish Market

A folk arts and crafts market in Santa Fe, New Mexico, held in July or August of every year since 1951. It was sponsored by the Spanish Colonial Arts Society to "preserve and perpetuate Spanish Colonial art forms." A fundamental regulation of the traditional market is that all participating artists must be from either New Mexico or Colorado and of Hispanic heritage. The market is held in the Santa Fe Plaza, and in 1998 it exhibited the work of 300 native New Mexican artists. In order to preserve and perpetuate colonial art forms it is stipulated that in the production of their crafts the artists must use the skills, materials, and techniques that would have been used in New Mexico during the Spanish colonial period. This has encouraged the continuation of the creation of *santos* (saints), *retablos* (religious paintings), *colchas* (blankets), the weaving of blankets, and many other folk arts. Other categories of Spanish colonial art are straw appliqué crosses and chests, textiles such as handwoven blankets and wall hangings, furniture, tinwork and ironwork, jewelry, and pottery. In the mid-1980s a group of Hispanic artists started a Contemporary Hispanic Market, held during the Santa Fe Fiesta, but just a few blocks away from the colonial market. This market allows the Hispanic artists to use contemporary techniques in the creation of their work. For example, photography is an art form that was not available during the Spanish colonial period but is used by contemporary artists. This market has exhibited the work of sixty-five to seventy artists. Both markets have demonstrations by the artists that allow them to display their abilities and expertise while they create their handicrafts and art. Each year the market distributes awards, such as the Spanish Market Master's Award and the Spanish Market Master's Award for Lifetime Achievement. The recipients of these awards are individuals who have worked for many years in creating and sustaining the folk art traditions of New Mexico.

See also Colchas; Folk Art; Hispano Culture; Retablos; Santos
References CHICLE 1994, 1998

Spanish Slang
See Caló

Stories
See Cuentos

Straw Appliqué
A decorative art related to the marquetry work that was found in Europe in the seventeenth century. Marquetry involves inlay, where small pieces of wood are inlaid in a carved hollow area. Another marquetry skill is to create a design on a thin sheet, then lay this sheet on an object such as a table or box, and veneer it. Straw appliqué work found in New Mexico was introduced by the Spaniards in the eighteenth century. Marquetry work was done in Mexico in Pueblo, Tlaxcala, Oaxaca, San Luis Potosí, and various other states, but the use of cornhusks and straw was not found in New Mexico until the eighteenth century. The appliqué of straw on crosses, picture frames, small boxes, and the interior of *nichos* (niches) has evolved into a distinct style in New Mexico. Geometric patterns may be the influence of Native American motifs from northern New Mexico. During the 1930s the Federal Arts Projects hired local craftspeople to teach some of the vanishing skills and crafts of regional communities. In New Mexico a man named Eliseo Rodriguez was hired as a painter, but later he revived the art of straw appliqué,

making mosaics that reflected religious scenes and saints. The Spanish Market, held in Santa Fe every year, shows the work of New Mexican artists, several of whom do straw appliqué work.

See also Folk Art; Nichos; Spanish Market
References Siporin 1992; Spanish Colonial Arts Society 1996

Strike
See Huelga

Susto (Shock)

The word literally means "fright" but in Chicano and many other cultures it is a folk illness, sometimes a very serious condition, brought about by a shock. A person who suffers a *susto* may develop the following symptoms: inability to sleep or restlessness during sleep, depression, weakness, chills, a lack of appetite, listlessness, and a lack of interest in their body and in cleanliness. Usually *susto* occurs when a person has experienced an emotional shock, an accident, or a great fear. This can occur in children if they witness a car accident or a violent event. Adults can likewise experience *susto* if they suffer a great emotional trauma, like learning of the death of a loved one, living through a natural catastrophe such as an earthquake or flood, or being in an accident themselves. This illness has not only been documented among Chicanos in the United States, but it has also been found in South America, Mexico, Guatemala, the Philippines, India, the People's Republic of China, and Taiwan. A person may feel a loss of spirit or loss of soul, and it is perceived as a tribulation to the spiritual makeup of the individual. Some early anthropologists believed that the concept that emotions can cause illnesses is indigenous in origin and was not transmitted by the Spaniards to the New World. The folk concept that fright, or a shock, may be the cause of illness is actually Aztec in origin. Illness due to fear was also an Inca medical concept in the Andes. There are many home remedies for curing *susto*, some involving making a tea from lemon or vinegar, or visiting a *curandera* as a last resort.

See also Curanderismo; Remedios
References Clark 1959; Foster 1953; Kay 1977; Martinez and Martin 1966; Perez 1954; Roeder 1988; Rubel 1966; Rubel, O'Neill, and Collado-Ardón 1984; Spicer 1977; Torres 1983

Quetzalcoatl

Tacos

This word actually means "a bite," a snack or even a light meal. When unexpected company arrives at a Chicano home, they are often invited to *"comer un taco,"* to have a snack. This can mean to have a cup of coffee and *pan dulce* (sweet bread), or a cup of soup, or beans and *tortillas*. If one is eating with a *tortilla*, flour or corn, the custom is to break off a small piece; use it to scoop up a piece of meat, beans, *chile*, or whatever one has on one's plate; and pop the whole thing into the mouth. Some people call these small pieces *bocaditos*, or "eating your spoon," but it is basically eating a lot of small *tacos*. But if the whole *tortilla* is filled with meat, *chile con carne*, or whatever, and rolled up, it is called a *taco*. The *tortilla* may be fried crispy, which also adds flavor, or may be left soft, and the filling mixture may be chicken, beans, beef, fish, vegetables, or cheese. Consequently, a *tortilla* rolled up and filled with anything is considered a *taco*. The contemporary American *taco* is filled with ground beef, cheese, lettuce, tomato, and chile salsa and thanks to many fast food restaurants has become part of the American diet. A corn *tortilla* rolled up tightly around chicken or cheese, fried crispy, and topped with guacamole, chile, and sour cream, is not a *taco* but a *taquito* or a *flauta*, depending on what state or country you're in at the moment.

See also Tortillas
References Kennedy 1975; Peyton 1994; Sewell Linck and Roach 1989

Tale of the Lost Mine

A well-known treasure tale from Cordova, New Mexico. This legend belongs to the narrative body of "treasure tales" and was first published in 1932. It is the story of a gold mine first discovered by Spanish conquerors or colonists near the town of Cordova. It was mined by members of a Sanchez family from Mora, and also by three German immigrants who settled in a village near Mora. In some variants of the legend the foreigners are three Frenchmen or three *Americanos*. Eventually the Germans die and the secret of the location of the mine dies with them. The granddaughter of one of the Germans verifies that the mine exists, because she has read a memoir written by a judge who was taken blindfolded to the mine by one of the Germans. Years later the mine is accidentally found by a sheepherder from Santa Fe, who is convinced by two Anglo American U.S. Forest Service employees to work the mine and split the profits with them. On the way to the mine the sheepherder realizes he'll be killed by the *Americanos* once he shows them the mine so he pretends he can't find it. He dies with the secret of the location of the mine. The mine is again found accidentally by a Cordovan sheepherder, Juan Mondragon, who tries to share the wealth with his rich boss. The boss does not believe the poor shepherd and refuses to see the mine. Mondragon promises to show the mine to a man named Romero, but he dies unexpectedly before their trip to the mine takes place, and the secret of the mine is again lost. The unbelieving boss changes his mind and tries to find the mine, but he never does. Descendants of Romero, especially his grandson, have been looking for the gold mine ever since. Briggs and Vigil recorded the most recent narration of the tale from Romero's grandson.

Of folktales and legends collected in the Southwest a large percentage deal with lost treasures. Almost any book of western folklore will contain several tales of haunted mines and searches for buried treasures. For Texas tales of lost treasures and mines see J. Frank Dobie's *Legends of Texas*.

References Applegate 1932; Briggs 1988; Briggs and Vigil 1990; Brown 1978; Campa 1963; Carson 1974; Dobie 1964; Robe 1980

Tamales

Like the *tortilla, tamales* are an ancient food prepared by the Aztecs and encountered by the Spaniards when they arrived in the New World in the sixteenth century. In the Nahuatl language the original word is *tamalli*. The Spanish priest Bernardino de Sahagún documented the many types of *tamales* made by the Indians: honey *tamales*, bean *tamales*, fruit *tamales*, turkey egg *tamales*, *tamales* of green corn. They were made in various shapes, pointed, flat, and square. More than any other food, *tamales* carry a strong social and cultural significance for Chicanos because they are often made in a family setting. It is a food and a custom that invoke sensitive feelings, savory sensations, family memories, and a heritage that many Chicanos do not want to give up or lose.

Making *tamales* is very labor-intensive work and is usually performed by women. The *masa*, or dough, for *tamales* is made from dried corn soaked and boiled in lime, so that it loses its tough hulls and pops open. When it is ground up it is called *nixtamal* and becomes the *masa* for *tortillas* and *tamales*. Coarse *masa* mixed with lard is used for *tamales*, and finer *masa* is used for *tortillas*. Mixing the *masa* thoroughly with lard, or vegetable oil, is hard labor and is still done by hand by many women, although prepared *masa* can be purchased at most Mexican stores. The best *tamales*, according to some Chicanos, are made with *chile colorado* (red chile) and the well-cooked meat from a hog's head. Since hog heads are sometimes difficult to find these days, various cuts of pork meat are used instead. But *tamales* are also made with chicken, *chile verde* (green chile), cheese, potatoes, beans, and other fillings.

The *tamale* is cooked in dried cornhusks, which must first be soaked in water to cleanse them and to make them pliable. The *masa* is spread on the cornhusks, the filling of *chile colorado* is placed in the center of the spread *masa*, and the cornhusk is folded inward on three sides. Sometimes the *tamale* is tied at each end, but some people just fold them over. These are then steamed for thirty to forty-five minutes, depending on the size of the container. Most Mexican cookbooks include recipes for *tamales*, with variations on the meat filling, and advice on how to cook them if cornhusks cannot be found (using parchment paper instead). Since making them is a laborious activity, *tamales* are usually made only for special occasions or holidays. Christmas and New Year's are two holidays when families come together to make their *tamales* for sharing and celebrating. When many people come together to make *tamales* and share the labor and the feasting, it is called a *tamalada*.

In many families making *tamales* is a folkloric performance, particularly when it occurs within a family where traditional roles are assigned and annual social rituals have been instituted. In one second-generation Chicano family, an anonymous informant narrates the importance that making *tamales* has taken on in her family. Everyone plays a significant role that through the years has been adopted gracefully by some members and humorously by others. For over twenty-five years the mother and her three daughters have been making *tamales*, an all-day affair on a Saturday, one week before Christmas. At one time they made them on Christmas Eve, just as it was done during the mother's childhood in El Paso, but once it became too big a chore, they switched to a Saturday. The mother is the undisputed leader, who gives the orders and distributes the jobs. Only she can make the *chile colorado* from the dried red *chile* pods, combining just the right amounts of New Mexico and California *chiles*, the night before the *tamales* are to be made. As the expert, only she can fill each *tamale* with just the right amount of *chile con carne*, place each individual *tamale* in the cooking pot, and oversee the cooking. One daughter is assigned the early-morning task of picking up the prepared *masa* from a local Mexican delicatessen, along with freshly made *tortillas*, the *hojas* or cornhusks, and warm-from-the-oven *pan dulce* (sweet bread). There is a rotational system, and the one whose home it is cooks the meat, washes the pots, and prepares the kitchen. The job of washing the cornhusks falls to one daughter, who always jokes about how much she hates to wash the *hojas*, but she manages to get assigned the task every year. As the grandchildren have grown up, the females have joined in and they have also been assigned various tasks. Close family friends have joined them throughout the years as the tradition has grown and everyone has learned of the annual ritual. Refreshments and snacks are plentiful, and the custom of having champagne and orange juice, mimosas, somehow developed. Through the years the event always involves ten to fifteen women, and the most enjoyable aspect of the tradition has been the communion and conversation. When the *masa* is ready, the *chile* is ready, and the *hojas* are ready, everyone sits around the kitchen table and spreads the *hojas* with *masa*, and a festive, joking atmosphere envelops everyone. Former errors in making *tamales* are humorously remembered, reminiscences of the flavor of past *tamales* are brought up, and reverence for the mother who knows best is always emphasized. Family stories, love affairs, and family secrets are repeated and passed from one generation to the next as the younger ones sit wide-eyed. The cooking affair takes all day until all the *tamales* are cooked, from fifteen to twenty dozen, all the pots are washed and dried, all the champagne is finished, and the kitchen is cleaned up. In this informant's family it is a tradition that the *tamales* are saved for the holidays, and nobody can sneak one until Christmas Eve.

The Texas writer of an autobiography remembers the tradition this way: "Since the making of the *tamales,* like the American quilting bee or barnraising, was a social event, there was always a lot of conversation, and much of what I learned about individual family members and the genealogy and history of the family came about while helping out in the making of the *tamales*" (Cardenas 1997, 66).

References Brown 1981; Cardenas, J. A. 1997; Robertiello 1996; Sewell Linck and Roach 1989; Williams 1984

Tattoo
See Tatuaje

Tatuaje (Tattoo)

Tattooing is found among a good number of Chicano young people and is especially common among *pintos* (prisoners) and gang members. Many tattoos are self-applied and are called *dibujos de mano*, or hand-made drawings. It may only be a small symbol, such as the initials of a girlfriend or boyfriend or gang affiliation, although a large percentage of Chicano tattoos are Christian symbols. Some researchers believe the motive for tattooing is not simply exhibitionist but that in reality it is a much more complex phenomenon. Tattooing is an ancient custom and was a feature of Aztec, Inca, and Mayan culture. Mummified remains with definite tattoo marks have been found in Peruvian excavations that date from the first century A.D. It is known that Captain James Cook coined the word tattoo from the Tahitian word *ta-tu*, which means "to strike" or "to mark." He found that in Tahiti both men and women painted their bodies, and our present use of the word stems from Cook's writings.

Alan Govenar's research shows that among Chicanos, religious images

This young man shows off his tattoo of La Virgen de San Juan de los Lagos. *Tattooing has become a custom clearly expressing pride and identity. (Danny Lehman/Corbis)*

and symbols are the most frequent tattoo designs. Images of *La Virgen de Guadalupe*, Jesus Christ, and the Crucifix, often in the form of a small cross on the hand, are very common. A popular symbol, the *"pachuco* cross," printed between the thumb and forefinger on the left hand with four dashes jetting out from it like flashes, is a common tattoo among Chicanos that dates back to at least the 1930s. Govenar states, "The devotional impulse expressed in Christian tattoos among Chicanos echoes the tradition of Coptic and Abyssinian Christians living in villages surrounding Jerusalem and in upper Egypt" (209). A small cross incised a little above the wrist of converts was a practice proudly adopted by the Crusaders.

The custom of tattooing is clearly an expression of Chicano pride and identity. When questioned about their tattoos, Chicano youth state that they felt "tough" when a tattoo was done. Among gangs tattooing may be an initiation ritual or something done to feel a closeness and commitment to *barrio* friends. For Chicano prisoners tattoos of either Christian or ethnic symbols are important, since they connect them to their previous lives and families or allow them to maintain some control over their own bodies. Tattoos are illegal in prison and must be performed in hiding from the guards. Institutional control over the body and mind is subverted by creating an imposing body art that sets the individual apart, yet brings him closer to those who are like him.

Sociologically, tattooing is considered deviant behavior, and society immediately places the tattooed individual into a designated socioeconomic class. Deciding to become tattooed is a highly social act. According to John Burma, "The decision to acquire a tattoo is motivated by how the recipient defines him or herself. The tattoo becomes an item in the tattooee's personal identity-kit and, in turn, it is used by those with whom the individual interacts to place him or her into a particular, interaction-shaping social category" (41).

See also Pachuco Cross; Pintos
References Burma 1965; Demello 1993; Govenar 1988; Sanders 1989

El Teatro Campesino (Farmworkers' Theater)

The name of a folk theater group started by Luis Miguel Valdez in 1965 to publicize the cause of the United Farm Workers and to assist the union in organizing farmworkers in the San Joaquin Valley of California. The *Teatro* was conceived during the grape strike of the United Farm Workers of America, and its objective was to perform for the striking grape farmworkers (*huelguistas*) so as to inform them of the issues involved in the strike. The headquarters of the UFWA was in Delano, California, and this is where *El Teatro Campesino* was started. Most of the actors were farmworkers, and they wrote and developed *actos*, fifteen-minute skits, each meant to convey a specific message about the strike. They used no scenery and no scripts, and the only costumes were props like a mask, dark glasses, or a hat. A sign hanging around the neck of the actor identified his character, such as *Esquirole* (scab), *Contratista* (contractor), *Patroncito* (grape-grower boss). Some of the *actos* included music and singing, some were full of burlesque comedy, but all had the goal of social propaganda and education. The group performed nightly throughout the San Joaquin Valley, from Delano to Sacramento, educating farmworkers on the issues of the "strike" movement.

The *acto*, the short, one-act dramatic sketch, was a form perfected by *El Teatro Campesino* and was usually performed bilingually in English and Spanish, incorporating *caló* (Spanish slang) into the dialogue. The comedy was somewhat slapstick, and the "opposition" masterfully satirized. This technique was particularly effective during the days of the farmworkers' strike, since the *acto* was meant to inspire social action. Songs, music, and folk narratives integrated the language and communication symbols of the people into the *actos* and expressed what the people were feeling. Another technique developed by the group was the dramatization of myths, *mitos*, using allegorical figures, such as Superstition, *La Muerte* (Death), and *El Sol* (the Sun). Valdez especially liked to incorporate indigenous beliefs and Aztec gods into the performances, always keeping in mind how to connect contemporary Chicano life to the pre-Columbian history of Mexico. The *carpas*, vaudeville tent shows of the early nineteenth century, greatly influenced the work of *El Teatro*. Other *teatro* groups later adopted this same form of performance.

In the fall of 1967 the *Teatro Campesino* left the United Farm Workers and ventured out on its own, starting a farmworkers' cultural center, *El Teatro Campesino Cultural*, in Del Rey, California. The group continued to perform *actos* that politicized the issues of the grape strike, but started to incorporate broader issues dealing with social injustices and discrimination experienced in Chicano communities throughout the state of California. From Del Rey the *Teatro* moved to Fresno in 1969 and performed *actos* about Mexican culture and history for college students, professors, union organizers, and community activists, becoming an inspirational voice of the Chicano movement. In 1971 *El Teatro* moved to San Juan Bautista, California, to establish a home base and to explore other forms of theater art.

During the 1970s Luis Valdez experimented with various dramatic forms and took his *Teatro* to Europe and Mexico. His name became well known throughout the Southwest, as *El Teatro* performed such plays as *La Carpa de los Rasquachis* (The Tent of the Rasquachis), *El Fin del Mundo* (The End of the World), *El Corrido* (The Ballad), *Rose of the Rancho*, and *Bandido!* (Bandit). During this period Valdez created a series of plays based on ancient Spanish religious folk drama depicting miraculous events, such as the appearance of *La Virgen de Guadalupe*, and a medieval shepherds' play. *La Virgen de Tepeyac* and *La Pastorela* are performed annually during the Christmas season in San Juan Bautista. In 1978 Luis Valdez was commissioned by the Mark Taper Forum in Los Angeles to write *Zoot Suit*, a play about the Sleepy Lagoon murder trial, which occurred in Los Angeles during the 1940s. It was a successful play, running for forty-six weeks and receiving many awards. Valdez directed the movie version, released in 1981 with Daniel Valdez in the leading role and Edward James Olmos playing *El Pachuco*.

The dramatization of *corridos* (ballads) also originated with *El Teatro Campesino*. *Corridos* especially lend themselves to performance, since the song itself chronicles an event or a history of an individual. Audiences of the *Teatro* were usually familiar with most *corridos* and would many times sing along with the performers. The cultural values and folk beliefs vocalized through song and performed by the *Teatro* reinforced the values to the audience and the community. In the early 1980s the *Teatro* revived the early 1970s version of *El Corrido* and adapted it to *Los Corridos*, a dramatization of old Mexican ballads dealing with tragicomic-musical episodes of love, incest, and death. This show was successfully performed in the Marines Theater in San Francisco in 1983, and has been shown on PBS several times.

In its twenty-year anniversary publication from 1985, *El Teatro Campesino* states its aesthetic: "*El Teatro Campesino* is thus a professional multidisciplinary theater company dedicated to the growth of popular theater, by reaching beyond the confines of traditional drama to include the images and audiences of communities normally ignored by the theatrical mainstream: notably, the indo-hispanic people of America. Our work springs from its own aesthetic approach, which we call 'Theater of the Sphere,' a belief in the cyclical nature of history, the unity of the universe, the oneness of actors and audience in performance. Basically inspired by ancient American (Mayan) concepts of dynamic form and movement, our approach finds universal application in other techniques and traditions, including but not limited to commedia dell'arte, music theater, dance theater, magic realism and sociopolitical theater. Our aim is to create stimulating, holistic images of humankind" (*El Teatro Campesino*, 39).

El Teatro Campesino continues to grow and evolve, aesthetically and commercially. In 1987 Valdez directed the film *La Bamba*, the life story of the Chicano singer Ritchie Valens, which received many good reviews. *El Teatro* planned a move into new and expanded performance and theater space in San Jose, California, sometime in the 1990s, although their permanent home is still in San Juan Bautista. Although the group is sometimes under heavy scrutiny and criticism, its dramatic performances continue to touch the souls and embody the folk traditions of the Chicano people.

See also La Bamba; Caló; Carpas; Corridos; Folk Dramas
References *El Teatro Campesino* 1985; Broyles-Gonzalez 1994; Cavillo 1981; Chabran and Chabran 1996; Diamond 1977; Flores 1986; Kanellos 1983; Orono-Cordova 1992

El Tejano (The Texan)

The legend of *El Tejano* is narrated in southern Arizona, by both Mexicans and Anglo Americans, yet the historical basis for the legend is not fully known. According to a Mexican informant whose narrative is found in the University of Arizona Folklore Archives, *El Tejano* robbed stagecoaches on the way to Yuma and Prescott. It is believed he stole from the rich and took the money to Texas to distribute among the poor. The informant, Mrs. Alexandra De Grazia, states that she heard of the legend from her grandmother who came to Arizona from Hermosillo, Sonora, in 1888. It was around the 1870s that *El Tejano*, a Mexican from Texas, became a defender of the underdog, a "*cristiano y caballero*" (a Christian and a gentleman) and not an "*asesino*" (assassin) because he never killed anyone. He always wore a mask; some say it was black, and some say it had the face of a cat on it. But his main trademark, a feature that appears in several versions of the legend, was his ingenious getaway technique. Supposedly, after a robbery, he would stop and turn the horse shoes on his horse around, facing backwards, so the hoofprints would go in the opposite direction than the horse had actually gone. Because of this trick he would never get caught. Unfortunately he was betrayed by a friend, who gave the customary whistle to show all was clear but had a posse waiting for *El Tejano*. The legend states a hidden treasure was left by *El Tejano* near *El Cerro del Gato*, Cat's Mountain, in southern Arizona. Some versions of the legend include tales of people finding the treasure but being frightened off by his ghost. Other variants of the legend narrate that one can hear the thundering hooves of his beautiful black horse riding after dark and stopping at a favorite watering hole for the horse to drink. It is believed that if anyone sees the ghost and gets to see his face, he or she will go crazy. Roach writes that there is too much similarity between the *El Tejano* legend and the real life of William Bazelton, a bandit in Arizona, who was killed by a posse in 1878 and placed in "state at the courthouse for all the world to see." They are thought to be one and the same. Bazelton also reversed the shoes of his horse to get away, but it is not known why he was referred to as *El Tejano*, since Bazelton was thought to be from California and had never been to Texas.

References Martin 1983; Roach 1968

Tent Theaters
See Carpas

Texas Folklore

The area that is now south Texas in the United States and Tamaulipas in Mexico was established as a province of New Spain in 1742 and named Nuevo Santander. José de Escandón, with 3,000 soldiers and colonizers, settled various communities, and by 1755 there were twenty-three settlements and fifteen Franciscan missions in the province. The settlers were Spanish Mexicans who set up ranching communities with thousands of cattle and other livestock. After Mexico gained independence from Spain in 1821, Anglo American settlers moved into parts of Texas and in 1836 revolted against the Mexican government, declaring themselves a free territory. This change did not affect south Texas very much, until after the war of 1846–1848, when U.S. military presence was clearly visible. The immigration of Americans increased, and landownership shifted from the *Tejanos* to the Anglos. According to Joe Graham landownership among Anglo Americans increased by 67 percent between 1860 and 1870 and decreased by 76 percent among the Mexican population during this same period. By the early 1900s, Texas society and culture had changed considerably, but there still remained a distinct *Tejano* culture in south Texas, distinct in language, religion, family relations, and folk traditions. Many of the folk traditions, folk arts and crafts, and music are still associated with a rural and ranching life.

The Texas Folklore Society played a very active role in publishing the folklore of the *Tejano* and *Mexicano* experience in Texas. The society has regularly published folklore collected by Anglos and *Tejanos* alike throughout the early twentieth century and into contemporary times. Although most of the folklore collected was by non-*Tejanos* and was published in English, many small collections of legends, folktales, customs, folk beliefs, and music were first published by the TFS in its monograph series.

Early published folklore from the Rio Grande border region was collected by Captain John Bourke and appeared in the *Journal of American Folklore* in the 1890s. After the turn of the century, in the 1920s, a student studying at the University of Texas, Jovita González, collected *Tejano* folklore. She wrote an M.A. thesis in 1930 titled "Social Life in Cameron, Starr, and Zapata Counties." Fermina Guerra, another student at the University of Texas, wrote her thesis on "Mexican and Spanish Folklore and Incidents in Southwest Texas" in 1941. Both of these women studied with the famous professor J. Frank Dobie, who was teaching at the university during this period. Guerra was born in 1897 and died in 1988. She was a teacher for over fifty years, teaching at Texas A&I University and at various elementary schools throughout Texas. Some of her folklore work was published by the Texas Folklore Society. Another University of Texas student was Maria del Refugio Gonzalez, who wrote a thesis in 1952 titled "The Spanish Folklore of Webb and Zapata Counties." Soledad Perez also had some folklore material published in the monograph series of the TFS. It is interesting that from the late 1920s to the early 1950s it was women who were researching and exploring the traditions and culture of their *Tejano* communities.

The most illustrious researcher of *Tejano* folklore was Dr. Américo Paredes, who was conducting research on the Texas-Mexican border from the 1950s to 1970s. His most celebrated work is *With His Pistol in His Hand: A Border Ballad and Its Hero*, published in 1958. This work spawned a whole generation of Chicano scholars, many trained under Dr. Paredes, and many others across the country were influenced by his groundbreaking research. Jose E. Limón, a protégé of Dr. Paredes, has written extensively on many cultural traditions of south Texas, from joking behavior to popular dancing, children's games, *corridos* (ballads), and the infamous *La Llorona*. His work often falls into the growing interdisciplinary zone of cultural studies. Joe S. Graham is another scholar who has written and published about Texas-Mexican folk art and material culture. Another *Tejano*, Manuel Peña, is the foremost authority on *conjunto* music of south Texas, with several publications about the appeal of this border music.

Arnoldo De Leon has written about the *Tejano* communities of the late nineteenth century, discussing the importance of folklore in the daily lives of the people. He expounds on the use of oral narratives, such as legends and *cuentos* (stories), to understand the complexities and phenomena of a changing society. Andres Tijerina, in a recent publication, provides a historical account of rural *Tejano* culture from 1836 to 1886, basing much of his research on the early folklore collections of Guerra and González, along with other unpublished histories.

Many early works of Chicano folklore written by Anglo Americans were clearly biased. The folk materials collected were sifted by the eyes of an alien and unfriendly people. A good example of this type of work is a short cursory thesis by Charles August Arnold on the folklore of San Antonians collected in 1928. This could be a very useful historical work if it weren't for the many errors in it. The author either didn't know Spanish or he just inadvertently misspelled names. For instance the name of the saint *Santo Niño de Atocha* is referred to as *Santo Niño Apocha*. Arnold also chose to write a whole chapter on the character traits of the *Mexicano* of San Antonio, which he titled "Procrastination." Clearly this chapter was not written from a sympathetic and amenable perspective.

See also Bourke, Captain John Gregory; Conjunto Music; Corridos; Cuentos; Dobie, J. Frank; González, Jovita; Paredes, Américo
References Arnold 1928; De Leon 1982; González, J., 1930a, 1930b; Gonzalez, M., 1952; Graham 1989, 1990, 1991; Guerra 1941; Limón 1978, 1983, 1988, 1992, 1994; Paredes 1958; Peña 1985a; Perez 1954; Perry 1992; Reyna 1980b; Riedel 1982; Tijerina 1998

The Texas Rangers
See Los Rinches

Tin Tan
The artistic name of Germán Valdéz, born in Mexico City in 1915. Tin Tan moved to Juárez in 1931 and lived there until adulthood. He developed the character of *el pachuco* (1940s urban youth), wearing *pachuco* garments, and speaking Spanish and English with plenty of *pachuquismos*. In the mid-1940s he moved to Mexico City to work in vaudeville. Frequently compared to the actor Cantinflas, Tin Tan was actually a different type of character. Not a comic, he portrayed an *agringado* (anglicized) Mexican who symbolized the complex linguistic and cultural identity of the Mexican American. As such, he was the first media character representative of border culture. He appeared in films, such as *Hotel de Verano* (Summer Hotel) and *El Hijo Desobediente* (The Disobedient Son). But to be successful in Mexico City, far from the border, he had to cast off his *pachuco* caricature and his bilingualism. His later films, as a regular comic from the lower class of Mexico City, were *El Rey del Barrio* (King of the Neighborhood) and *Calabacitas Tiernas* (Tender Squash), and one American movie, *Song of Mexico*, in 1945. Tin Tan was a character very much in the media and typified the Chicano experience for Mexicans on both sides of the border.

See also Pachucos
References Fregoso 1993; Monsiváis 1978; Mora 1982

Tinwork
The term tinwork refers to the craft of creating decorated tin folk art articles, such as religious frames, *nichos* (niches), crucifixes, jewelry boxes, and mirrors.

The tinwork tradition in colonial New Mexico was most likely introduced from Mexico. Known as the poor man's silver, tinwork increased significantly in New Mexico after the great influx of American soldiers. The army sold its five-gallon tin cans to the local community, who in turn recycled them into art objects. Beautiful photographs of tin frames can be found in the publications of the Spanish Colonial Arts Society. It is a skill that has been passed from father to son. One New Mexican family named Delgado has maintained the tin tradition since the nineteenth century. Francisco Delgado, born in 1858, had a tinwork shop for many years in Santa Fe. His son, Ildeberto Delgado, also had a shop called Delgado's Curio Shop, and he worked for forty years as a master tinworker. Much of the tin used by the Delgados was taken from tin cans. The daughter of Ildeberto, Angelina Delgado Martinez, now over seventy-five years old, is also a tinworker who has worked at this craft for over sixty years. Her work has been displayed at the International Folk Art Museum. Her daughter, Rita Younis, is now learning the craft from her mother and wants to continue the family tradition into the fourth generation. Another family from New Mexico, Emilio and Senaida Romero, received a National Heritage Fellowship for their artistic work as tinsmiths. They work together, combining two folk traditions of tinwork and *colcha* (blanket) stitching. They make tin crosses, *nichos*, wall socket plates, mirrors, and frames, decorating them with *colcha* embroidery (Siporin 1992, 152).

See also Colchas; Folk Art; Nichos
References Coulter 1990; Goldberg 1994; Siporin 1992; Spanish Colonial Arts Society 1996

Tío Taco (A Traitor)

An expression used among Chicanos to describe a person who has "turned traitor" to Chicano culture and is considered a *vendido*, or sellout. The expression dates from the 1960s. Literally, it means "Uncle Taco," and it is equivalent to the Uncle Tom of African American culture. Sometimes a *Tío Taco* finds ways to profit at the expense of his own people or family. To some people the expression is based on the Anglo stereotype of the Mexican as a submissive, lazy person who accepts being in a subservient position. In an article from 1970 Arnoldo De Leon defines *Tío Taco* as the media caricature of the "Mexican or Mexican American *hombre* taking the endless *siesta* under a big *sahuaro* cactus." He says of him, "He is the God fearing, ignorant, uninspiring individual who in broken English, meekly obeys, '*si señor*'" (1970). De Leon believes in the demise of *Tío Taco* because politically he was awakening in 1970. A creative drawing in the innovative *Con Safos* magazine of the late 1960s shows the evolution of a typical Mexican to a full-fledged *Tío Taco* through the satirical eyes of the artist.

Reference De Leon 1970

El Tiradito (The Outcast)

A historical site, the *El Tiradito* wishing shrine is located in downtown Tucson. It is on Main Street, south of the corner of Main and Cushing. The legend behind the shrine is that of a young man involved in a love triangle who was killed and buried on the spot. *El Tiradito*, meaning "the outcast," refers to this person, but there is also a water spring there and the site has become a religious as well as a wishing shrine. The shrine is half-surrounded by a scalloped adobe wall, with a small *nicho* in the wall that sometimes holds a statue.

The story of *El Tiradito* is the story of Juan Oliveros, a married man who lived on Dr. F. H. Goodwin's ranch around the 1870s or 1880s. He fell in love with his mother-in-law and one day was with her when her husband came home and found them together. In his anger the father-in-law physically forced Juan out of the house and took an axe and killed him, then fled to Mexico. Juan was buried exactly where he was killed, and thus the site of his burial became a shrine.

This version of the legend was adopted by the Tucson City Council in 1927. People from Tucson have heard the story for generations. But, as James Griffith states, there are actually many different legends regarding *El Tiradito*. Regardless, the shrine has evolved into a site for petitioners to pray, light candles, and make wishes.

See also Nichos
References Griffith 1992, 1995; Martin 1983

Tirili (Language of Hoodlums)

The word *tirili* is a slang expression from the *caló* dialect that refers to the talk of hoodlums or gang members. To *tirili* meant to "to talk nonsense." In a study of the special language of this Mexican American subculture, this jargon was referred to as the "tongue of the *tirilones*." The *tirilones* were the "hoodlums," who were at times also called *pachucos*. The dialect and vocabulary of these individuals were called *tirili* in a south El Paso neighborhood. As the dialect was studied the words *caló* and *tirili* were used interchangeably. It is difficult to find an exact etymology of the word, but some references indicate that it has to do with the lower classes and the jargon of thieves and rogues. This speech from the El Paso of the 1950s, according to Coltharp's study, established a social class. It was only spoken within a certain group and was kept secret from other segments of the community, and was understood as *"tirili contra tirili"* (hoodlum to hoodlum). It provided a sense of identity and also a means of protection against other groups or gangs. Many of the words came from either English or Spanish, and sometimes were a mixture of both. In California these words would be dubbed *pochismos*: words such as *daime* meaning "dime"; *lechuga*, "lettuce" in Spanish, but meaning "paper money"; *swingear* for "to swing" (as in dancing); *chantarse* for "to get married"; and *sainar*, meaning "to sign" (one's name). It seems apparent that *caló* is the basis of several argots and regional vocabularies of the border area and southwestern United States. Wherever *Mexicanos* have come in contact with the English language, and existed as a marginalized social group, a specialized language has developed. The languages of the *tirilones*, the *pachucos*, the *bato locos*, the Chicanos, and the contemporary *cholos* have all evolved from the basic *caló*.

See also Bato; Caló; Chicano Spanish; Cholos; Pachucos
References Barker 1974; Braddy 1960; Cerda 1953; Coltharp 1965; Katz 1974; Rosensweig 1973; Sagel 1992

Tonantzin (Aztec Goddess)

The name of an Aztec goddess representing female power. *Tonan* was the Nahuatl name given to several mountains, so *Tonan* was the Earth. *Tonantzin* of *Tepeyac* was known as *Teteo Innan*, Mother of the Gods, the patroness of midwives and healers. The Aztecs traveled to visit her shrine to pray for cures. The shrine where she was venerated was *Tepeyac*, the hill where *La Virgen de Guadalupe* appeared to Juan Diego in 1531. The acceptance of *La Virgen de Guadalupe* was not difficult for the Aztecs because to them she was *Tonantzin* dressed in Spanish clothing. After the temple was built for *La Virgen de Guadalupe* at *Tepeyac*, the Aztec people continued to visit the shrine seeking cures from *Tonantzin*. Even though the miracles and cures were attributed to *La Virgen de Guadalupe* the Indians called her *Tonantzin*. She is also a beloved icon of Chicanos, and her name and image are frequently invoked in poetry and art. In San Antonio, Texas, the Guadalupe Cultural Arts Center's quarterly publication is named *Tonantzin*.

See also La Virgen de Guadalupe
References Alarcon 1989; Bierhorst 1990

Tortillas

A round, thin, pancake-shaped bread, the *tortilla* has an ancient tradition originating with the Aztecs. In the Nahuatl language it was called *tlaxcalli*. The original *tortilla* was made from ground corn shaped into a thin, flat round and was cooked on a hot greaseless griddle called a *comal*. Today's corn *tortilla* is made the same way it was hundreds of years ago. The corn kernels are soaked in a solution of lime and water to soften them enough so they can be ground into a smooth dough called *masa*. From this dough are shaped small round forms, or a *tortilla* press can be used to more easily flatten many perfectly round, thin cakes. *Tortilla* machines, found all over Mexico and the Southwest, can produce hundreds of *tortillas* per hour.

Fray Bernardino de Sahagún, in his well-known history of Mexico, *General de las Cosas de Nueva España*, describes the *tortillas* of a vendor from the sixteenth century: "Some are round, some long, some rolled up and round. Some are filled with cooked or uncooked bean paste and are fluffy, and some are filled with *chile* or meat. There are folded-over *tortillas*, those that are covered with *chile* and rolled into balls between the hands, those that are rolled and covered with '*chilmole*,' and yellow ones and white ones." Corn *tortillas* are still a basic staple of the Mexican diet eaten with all meals and often with just beans or *chile*. The *tortilla* folded in half and stuffed with any filling such as beans, *chile*, or potatoes is called a *taco*.

The corn *tortilla* is so versatile that hundreds of dishes can be made from it. In fact an old *tortilla* is never thrown away. Freshly made *tortillas* are delicious with butter, eaten like bread, used to scoop beans and *chile*, and act as edible spoons. Slightly stale *tortillas* are fried for *tacos* and *tostadas* and dipped in *mole* for *enchiladas*. Very stale and dried *tortillas* can be cut into pieces, fried crisp, and alternately layered in a dish with shredded cheese and *chile*, called *chilaquiles* (meaning "pieces of broken-up sombrero"). Everyone has a name for every dish made with *tortillas*. Pieces of *tortilla* scrambled with eggs for a breakfast dish are called *migas con huevos*. A tightly rolled-up *tortilla*, filled with meat or cheese and fried, is called a *flauta* (flute) or *taquito* and is served with a glob of guacamole on top. A *quesadilla* is a *tortilla* with melted cheese in it, folded over, sometimes fried, or just heated enough to melt the cheese. Strips of fried corn tortillas are called *tortilla* chips and are used for dipping into sauces and *guacamole*.

Tortillas made from flour, *tortillas de harina*, were introduced into northern Mexico sometime in the late nineteenth century and have become a staple of the diet of the Southwest. Wheat-flour *tortillas* are made with lard or shortening, salt, baking soda, and water, kneaded together to form a dough that can be handled without sticking to the hands. Small balls are formed and rolled out with a rolling pin to form circular flat pancakes, and then cooked on a greaseless *comal*. Before commercial flour *tortillas* were available, that is, before the 1970s, many Chicano mothers made their own flour *tortillas* every morning and evening for each meal. It was very common for a mother to rise at 4:00 or 5:00 in the morning and *amasar*, or make the dough for five or six dozen *tortillas*. These were eaten for breakfast, put in lunches, snacked on in the afternoon, and were usually gone by dinnertime, so another batch had to be made. The flour *tortilla* is not as versatile as the corn *tortilla*, but is still enjoyed in many different ways. A freshly made, warm *tortilla* spread with butter and salt and rolled into a *taco* was sometimes called *tortilla con manteca de rana* (tortilla with frog lard). When white bread is scarce a kid can make a sandwich with two *tortillas*: spread them with mayonnaise and layer with bologna, lettuce, and tomato, and the result is an innovative sandwich. For dessert a flour *tortilla* may be deep-fried, which puffs it up, sprinkled with cinnamon-sugar, and called a *sopapilla*, although these can mostly be found in New Mexico. Since the *burrito*, made with flour *tortillas*, is served everywhere, including college campuses, flour *tortillas* are extremely popular in the United States and are sold in most supermarkets.

See also Burritos; Tacos
References Kennedy 1975; Peyton 1994; Sewell Linck and Roach 1989

A Traitor
See Tío Taco

Tripe Stew
See Menudo

The Twelve Truths
See Las Doce Verdades

Quetzalcoatl.

U

Urban Youth (1940s)
See Pachucos

Urban Youth (1990s)
See Cholos

Urrea, Teresa (1873–1906)

Known as *La Niña de Cabora* (the Daughter of Cabora) and *La Santa de Cabora* (the Saint of Cabora), Teresa Urrea was a *curandera* or *sanadora* (healer), and somewhat of a psychic and mystic. Her brief life touched many lives in Mexico and the Southwest. She was born in 1873 in Sinaloa, Mexico, but lived about half of her life in the United States. As an adolescent she suffered an illness, a type of epilepsy with high fevers, that once left her in a trance or coma for several days. During this coma she heard voices that told her to minister to the ill. She believed this was her mission, and she devoted her life to healing others. Before she became ill she had already learned some healing rituals and remedies by working with an Indian *curandera*. She lived on a ranch in Cabora, Sonora, where she acquired a large following, especially among the Yaqui Indians, and became known as *La Santa de Cabora*. The government became suspicious of her influence over the Indians and President Porfirio Díaz had Teresa and her father arrested, exiling them to Nogales, Arizona. Between 1892 and 1900 they moved several times within Arizona, moving to El Paso for a brief period and then back, settling in Clifton, Arizona. In 1896, while Teresa and her father lived in Nogales, a group of Yaqui and Tomochi Indians, followers of her and calling themselves *Teresitas*, stormed the Mexican customhouse. The Mexican president blamed this attack on Teresa, accusing her of inciting a revolution.

Wherever Teresa lived she healed the sick, treating up to 200 people a day while in El Paso. Her method of healing was through prayer, using herbal medicines, yet never charging for her services. There are many accounts by those whom she healed. At one point in her life she joined a medical company that toured the United States giving medical advice and other services. She married twice and had two children by her second husband, whom she married in 1900. Apparently disillusioned with the theatrics of the medical company, she returned to Arizona, where she had a large house built that she used as a medical facility. She died of tuberculosis at the age of thirty-two in 1906. The Yaqui Indians of Arizona loved her, and legends about her great healing powers continue to be narrated.

See also Curanderismo
References De Leon 1982; Domecq 1998; Holden 1978; Jiménez 1994

Quetzalcoatl

Vaqueros (Cowboys)

The *vaquero* was the early Hispano cowboy and the antecedent of the Hollywood cowboy. Horses and cattle were brought to New Spain by the Spaniards. When Hernán Cortés landed on the eastern shore of Mexico, he had with him sixteen horses and at least three breeds of cattle. Cattle breeding was a tradition hundreds of years old in Spain, and Cortés brought this tradition to Mexico and eventually to the Southwest. The Spaniards introduced the system of *el rancho*, with *vaqueros* being the workers who herded the cattle and conducting cattle drives. *Vaca* means "cow" and a *vaquero* is "one who works with cows." The Spanish mission *padres* recognized this labor and conscripted *mestizos* (mixed-race people), Indians, and Mexicans to take care of the cattle. It was these individuals who developed the system, equipment, practices, and traditions that have lasted these past few hundred years. The Anglo cowboy learned everything about cattle from the *vaquero*.

The Mexican *vaquero* was a laborer, a peon who was used by the missionaries to ride the horses and take care of the cattle. So it was the culture of the *vaquero* that became the basis for the romantic cowboy of Hollywood. The ensemble, equipment, and clothing of the *vaquero* evolved through the years as a combination of Spanish leather and regional indigenous fabrics. He always wore a sombrero with a wide brim, a leather *chaqueta* (jacket), tight-fitting knee-length *sotas* (breeches), and *botas* (leather leggings) for protection. The *vaquero* also wore iron spurs, like those worn by the *Conquistadores*, which are still worn to this day. The various styles of saddles, from the Moorish to the Spanish war saddle, eventually changed when the *vaqueros* began making their own saddles, more suitable for riding hard and for quick mounting and dismounting.

The early *vaqueros*, those of the sixteenth and seventeenth centuries, were *mestizos*, Indians, Negroes, and mulattos. When Anglo Americans moved into Texas and bought enormous tracts of land, they established huge ranches and hired Mexican *vaqueros* to work them. They recruited and moved whole families from Mexico to work and live on their ranches. The King and Kennedy ranches of east Texas are contemporary examples of this tradition and have many generations of Mexican *vaqueros* still living on their

The early vaqueros, those of the sixteenth and seventeenth centuries, were mestizos, Indians, Negroes, and mulattos. When Anglo Americans moved into Texas and bought enormous tracts of land, they established huge ranches and hired Mexican vaqueros to work them. (North Wind Picture Archive)

ranches. A social historical study of the *vaquero* life on the King and Kennedy ranches, from the early nineteenth century to the present, has been written by Monday and Colley.

The *vaquero* from California also worked on very large ranches, such as the Tejon ranch in the lower San Joaquin Valley. This way of life has been memorialized in the work of Arnold Rojas, who was a *vaquero* and has written about his life in California in the twentieth century. Rojas makes a distinction between the cowboy, the *vaquero*, and the buckaroo. The *vaquero* was originally Hispanic or Mexican, or Indian, and herded cattle in the Far West in the states of California, Nevada, Oregon, Arizona, Utah, and Washington, whereas the cowboys who herded cattle in the southern states were usually Negro or Anglo. The *vaquero* or buckaroo is a westerner and the cowboy is a southerner. The definition is a territorial one, with the cowboy working east of the Rockies and the *vaquero* west of the Rockies. It is this difference that Rojas writes about in his three-volume memoir of the California *vaquero*. Anglos coined the word buckaroo, meaning *vaquero*, because they disliked the word cowboy and did not want to call themselves by that name. Somehow when they pronounced *vaquero*, it came out of their mouths as "buckaroo." The California Indians were trained by the Spanish missionaries to herd cattle, and they were the primary *vaqueros* until the mid-1800s. Mexicans from Sonora took over as *vaqueros* when they started migrating into California in the nineteenth century. The style of horse riding instituted by the Spaniards was called *la jinete*, a term that relates to the equipment used in riding. It not only includes the bits, spurs, and the saddles, but also the length of the stirrups, how the reins are held, and the amount of pressure of the knees on the horse. Rojas was born in California, as was his mother, who as a child had a pleasant encounter with the bandit Tiburcio Vásquez. He spent his whole life working as a *vaquero* and he states, "I speak as a *vaquero*—and I know whereof I speak" (Rojas, 1979, 119).

References Graham 1990, 1991, 1993; Mather 1992; Monday and Colley 1997; Rojas 1958, 1979; Verti 1990

Vásquez, Tiburcio (1835–1875)

A legendary Chicano folk hero who roamed through California's San Joaquin Valley during the late nineteenth century. He came from an old *Californio* family who owned extensive property and a large ranch. But he also lived during a time when Anglo Americans were becoming dominant in the state, when overt discrimination against Mexicans who were considered foreigners was on the rise, and he fell into a life of crime. Compared heroically to Joaquín Murrieta, Tiburcio Vásquez is regarded as a proud man who resisted social domination and fought to maintain and preserve his culture. He actually lived fairly long but was eventually captured, tried, and hanged at the age of forty.

He was born in Monterey County in 1835 or 1837, where he was raised and attended school, becoming fluent in both English and Spanish. His career of flight and lawlessness started in 1851 when, with several other men at a *fandango*, he witnessed or was involved in the death of a constable named Hardimount. Not expecting to be treated justly, he fled to the hills, and from then on, Vásquez led a life of horse stealing, robbery, and hiding out in the foothills of California. The legend states that he shared his stolen goods with the poor Mexicans of the Salinas Valley. He was well liked and depended on the local people to hide him from the posses that were continually after him. He was captured several times and actually spent almost nine years in San Quentin prison, on two different occasions, first in 1857, then again in 1867. After being released in January of 1870, Vásquez spent the next four years in a life of banditry but also one of romance. Women were attracted to him and he frequently fell in love, and he had a special weakness for married women. He claimed to have never killed a single person, and when he robbed people in stores and stagecoaches, he'd tie them up and lay them face up on the ground, a tactic he used often during this period. One source refers to his "hog-tied" captives. He was shot and survived several times but was finally caught in May of 1874. While awaiting trial in the San Jose jail, Vásquez appealed for funds for his defense. Thousands of people came to visit him in jail, bringing flowers, food, and other gifts. With the funds raised he was able to hire two well-qualified lawyers. Even so, he was found guilty by a jury and sentenced to death. He was publicly hanged on March 19, 1875, in San Jose, California.

There are many stories recounting the legendary exploits of Vásquez, especially those dealing with his romantic life, as he was considered a true Don Juan. On several occasions it was a lady that saved him from the legal authorities by helping to hide him. Once, at a party or *fandango*, a woman hid him under her great hooped dress, where he crouched silently until the constable gave up his search of the premises. Another anecdote of narrow escape tells the tale of Vásquez being hidden in the bed, under the covers, of a newly birthed mother. His friends offered to hide him by letting him crawl under the covers at the foot of the bed while the mother showed off her newborn to the sheriff.

Luis Valdez wrote and directed a play about Vásquez titled *Bandido!*, performed at the Mark Taper Forum in Los Angeles in 1994. Valdez stated, "All I'm doing is raising Tiburcio Vásquez to his appropriate mythic status in the mythology of the Old West."

See also Murrieta, Joaquín
References Burciaga 1993; Castillo and Camarillo 1973; Greenwood 1966; Jackson 1939; MacLean 1977; Siegal 1994

Vato Loco (Crazy Dude)
See Bato

La Vida Loca (The Crazy Life)

An expression that describes the urban gang life of Chicanos in large cities, such as Chicago and Los Angeles. *La vida loca* alludes to a way of life of thousands of young Chicano men and women who are submerged in a fast drug-using life, depending mostly on their friends and gangs for support and loyalty.

The dress style of the young men, sometimes called *batos locos*, usually teenagers, is a Pendleton shirt; perfectly pressed, loose khaki pants; a bright white undershirt; and shiny shoes. The girls, *rucas* (Indian girls) or *cholas* (mestizo girls), may wear the same khaki pants or short tight skirts, highly teased long hair, and lots of eye makeup. *La vida loca* is often romanticized, but it is the hard life of survival in an economically depressed environment and relying on a drug culture and gang members for support.

In the novel *Maravilla*, Laura Del Fuego shows *la vida loca* of the 1960s in the *barrio* of Maravilla in Los Angeles. Oscar "Zeta" Acosta, in his *Autobiography of a Brown Buffalo*, shows the life of *batos locos* in the *barrios* of Los Angeles, also during the 1960s and 1970s. Luis Rodriguez has written a wonderful memoir, dedicated to his son, that depicts the crazy life he led in Los Angeles in the 1970s. Gus Frias presents a much more somber picture of the violent way of life led by those in *la vida loca*.

A film titled *Mi Vida Loca*, produced in 1993, depicts the life of a group of homegirls, *las locas*, in the Echo Park area of Los Angeles. Teenage single mothers are portrayed as independent and strong, struggling with boyfriends involved in drugs, but also the friendships and strong relations among the girls are presented realistically. Several of the actresses in the movie were actual gang members. In 1999 the Latino singer Ricky Martin popularized the expression in American popular culture by using it as the title of a song.

See also Bato; Cholos
References Acosta 1972; Del Fuego 1989; Fregoso 1995; Frias 1982; Mirandé 1985; Rodriguez 1993

La Vieja Inés y Los Listones (The Old Mother Game)

A very old game played by little girls that is known by various names. It is called *Los Colores* (the colors), *Los Listones* (the ribbons), and *Tan Tan*. The main players are *la mamá* and "Saint Inez," who may also be called *La Vieja Inés* (Old Lady Inés) or *La Virgen Inés* (Old Maid Inés). All of the other players are given a color by the *mamá*: red, yellow, green, blue, or they may choose their own color. *La Vieja Inés* comes and pretends to knock on the door, *Tan, tan*. The mother asks, *"Quién es?"* (Who is it?) and the answer is *"La Vieja Inés."* The mother asks, *"Que quieres?"* (What do you want?). *"Quiero colores"* is the answer. *"Que color quieres?"* (What color do you want?) *"Quiero verde"* (I want green), or any color is mentioned. The little girl whose color is mentioned runs away and *La Vieja Inés* tries to catch her before she reaches a spot designated as home base. The game goes on until all of the colors have been chosen and all of the girls are caught. In some versions the girls carry ribbons, each of a different color. Scholars who have analyzed the game point to the socialization of gender roles for little girls, and the game serves as a lesson in the inevitable eventual separation from the safety of home. This was one of the games collected by the Federal Writers' Program in New Mexico during the 1930s. Although there were many games played by Hispano and Mexican children, this one appears to be one with a long historical tradition.

Jose Limón has written about a version found in Texas. It is an ancient game that can be traced to medieval Spain, to a place called Zafra. In the version from Zafra two teams are involved, one representing evil, the other goodness. One team is led by the devil, *el demonio,* and the other by an angel, *ángel de la guarda* (angel of the guard). Each player is named a color, and the two leaders, the devil and the angel, try to gain the most players. In this version it is a battle between good and evil to see who can win the most souls.

See also Hilitos de Oro; Naranja Dulce
References Cardozo-Freeman 1975; Ebinger 1993; Limón 1980b; Robe 1972; Writer's Program of New Mexico 1976

La Virgen de Guadalupe

Also commonly known as *Nuestra Señora de Guadalupe,* she is the Virgin Mary who appeared to Juan Diego, a Mexican Christian Indian, on December 9, 1531. Historical documents verify the story of her apparitions. She identified herself as the Virgin Mary, the Mother of God, and speaking in Nahuatl, she asked Juan Diego to go to the Spanish bishop and ask that a temple be built there where she appeared, the mount of Tepeyac. To Juan Diego she was a beautiful woman who spoke his language, so after much difficulty he sought to speak to the bishop, but his story was not heard, and he was asked to return another day. The beautiful woman appeared to Juan Diego a second time, and he was asked to seek the bishop's audience again. On the second try Juan Diego saw the bishop, his story was heard and questioned, but was not believed. The bishop wanted a sign from the Great Lady so that he would know it was really she who was sending Juan Diego. Diego intended to go back to Tepeyac and inform the beautiful woman, but when he returned home he found that his uncle Juan Bernardino was extremely ill. The next morning, on December 12, as he walked to Tlatelolco to call a priest to come to his uncle's side, the beautiful woman came to him a third time asking what was wrong. Diego told her of his sick uncle and of the request from the bishop. She told him his uncle was now well and would not die and sent him to the top of a hill to cut fresh flowers that he was to take to the bishop as proof of her existence. Diego followed her instructions and

La Virgen de Guadalupe is depicted on tiles in the garden of Mission San Gabriel in southern California. (Richard Cummins/Corbis)

at the top of the hill he found beautiful roses of Castile, still covered with dew. He cut them and The Lady, the Mother of God, arranged them in his *tilma* (cloak) and sent him to the bishop, with the proof requested. When Diego unfolded his *tilma* in front of the bishop, the roses fell to the floor, and there on the *tilma* was an image of the Virgin Mary. Now the Spanish bishop believed, and as the beautiful woman requested, a church was built right on the mount of Tepeyac. The *tilma* with the image of the Virgin Mary still hangs in the temple called Guadalupe. The name that the beautiful Lady gave herself was Tlecuauhtlacupeuh, but to the Spaniards it sounded like Guadalupe, which they instantly recognized as "Our Lady of Guadalupe" from Estremadura, Spain. But the Aztecs understood that in the Nahuatl language the name Tlecuauhtlacupeuh meant *"la que viene volando de la luz como el águila de fuego"* (she who comes flying from the region of light like an eagle of fire).

Tonantzin was an Aztec goddess, literally called Our Holy Mother, also known as Tonan. *Guadalupe* appeared at what was once the temple of Tonantzin at the mount of Tepeyac. Even today in Mexico, *La Virgen María* is often called Tonantzin. The acceptance of *La Virgen de Guadalupe* by the indigenous population of Mexico was the beginning of Mexican Christianity and the conversion of the Aztecs to Catholicism. Guadalupe became the symbol of Indian Catholicism, different from the European Catholicism of the Spaniards. As the Aztecs adapted the Catholic religion to their indigenous beliefs, they created a religion that met their own needs and own way of life. She was declared the "Patroness of the Mexican Nation" in 1737, and in 1754 Pope Benedict XIV canonized Guadalupe as an official saint. She was crowned "Queen of Mexico" in 1895, showing how strong a symbol of Mexican nationalism she had become. Today she continues as the country's strongest symbol of Mexican identity. The cathedral built in her honor can no longer be used because of structural damage, but a new one was built in the early 1970s. Masses are held every hour of the day and the church is constantly filled to capacity.

Faith in *La Virgen de Guadalupe* is one of the strongest convictions in Mexican and Chicano culture. Guadalupe has become a powerful cultural image. Her appearance was crucial in restoring dignity and humanity to a conquered people. Eric Wolf refers to Guadalupe as a "master symbol," "a symbol which seems to enshrine the major hopes and aspirations of an entire society" (34). She is the mother of the *mestizo* race, *La Raza* (The People), and a political symbol for the oppressed and powerless. She is affectionately referred to as *La Morenita, Virgencita, Lupita, Madrecita, Madre de Dios*, and *Nuestra Señora*. Virgil Elizondo, a Chicano theologian, states, "Guadalupe is the key to understanding the Christianity of the New World and the Christian consciousness of the Mexicans and the Mexican Americans of the United States" (26).

Belief in her power as a mediator for the oppressed has prompted faithful followers to carry her image into battle for over 400 years. Father Hidalgo, during the Mexican War of Independence; Emiliano Zapata, during the Mexican

Revolution; and César Chávez, during his battle for farmworkers' rights against California agribusiness, all carried the emblem of *La Virgen de Guadalupe*. The image of Guadalupe provides support for those who believe in her divine power as the deliverer from oppression.

El Teatro Campesino has created a cultural piece titled *La Virgen de Tepeyac* (The Virgin of Tepeyac). For many years now it has been performed during the early part of December in the mission church of San Juan Bautista, California. It has become a Bay Area Christmas tradition to make the two-hour journey to the small mission town to experience the miracle of Guadalupe, although all Mexican American churches throughout the United States organize elaborate church ceremonies for December 12, the day of her appearance, so there are literally hundreds of celebrations one can choose from to commemorate the day.

Contemporary Chicanas continuously look toward Guadalupe and reevaluate her influence in their mothers' and grandmothers' lives and in their own lives. Although she is the preeminent representation of womanhood, she has become an icon for women's subjugation and oppression. In the 1970s the artist Yolanda Lopez created a memorable image of working mothers by painting a garment worker at a sewing machine within the recognizable blue shield background that is easily acknowledged as the emblem of *La Virgen de Guadalupe*. In New Mexico a young Chicana created a dance theater piece titled *Apariciones de la Madre,* which incorporated modern ideas of women into the traditional images of the Aztec Guadalupe.

Chicano muralists have painted images of Guadalupe in her traditional Aztec setting on *barrio* walls since the late 1960s, and often other cultural symbols, such as a low-rider car, are added to emphasize the Chicano experience. *La Virgen de Guadalupe* is revered religiously, candles are lit for her, flowers are left at the church for her, and yet she is very much a part of popular culture. Her image is found on T-shirts, key rings, low-rider car hoods, and tattooed across adult male chests. Her face and form are frequently deciphered on *tortillas,* shadows on walls, and the trunks of trees. When such an image is found, thousands of people, whether in Mexico or the United States, flock to see and pray before the image. The influence of Guadalupe is as powerful today as it was 450 years ago.

See also El Teatro Campesino

References Alarcon 1989; Brundage 1979; Demarest and Taylor 1956; Elizondo 1977; Johnston 1981; Lafaye 1983; Lea 1953; Quirarte 1992; Rodriguez, J., 1994; Vigil 1994, 1998; Wolf 1958

Quetzalcoatl

W

Water Spirits
See Chanes

Wedding Customs

Chicano wedding rituals vary from state to state in the Southwest and the Midwest, often incorporating emerging American customs, but there are still common traditions that originate with Catholicism and the Spanish heritage that are shared from community to community. The Spanish word for a wedding is *boda*, meaning "nuptials," and often Chicanos will call a wedding celebration *La Boda*. The southwestern region with the most researched and documented wedding customs is New Mexico, because the descendents of the early Hispanos have been conscious of describing and writing down their traditions. For instance Fabiola Cabeza de Baca, Cleofas Jaramillo, and Nina Otero all wrote about the weddings of northern New Mexico. In her book *The Good Life*, Fabiola Cabeza de Baca has a brief chapter on wedding traditions, including recipes and a detailed description of the preparation of the food.

When a couple married, three main ceremonies took place. These were initiated after the groom and his family had asked the girl's family for her hand in marriage. If the girl or her family refused the offer, she would send a letter to her suitor with her negative response. This was termed as giving *calabazas* (squash or pumpkin) and was a great insult to the wooer. Of the ceremonies, first there was *el día del prendorio* (day of the engagement), when the bride and groom came together publicly for the first time. A great celebration would take place, usually in the home of the bride, with food, drinks, and music. This festivity would be equivalent to an engagement party. The day of the wedding was called *el día del casorio* and could last from two to three days. The upper classes held lavish wedding ceremonies that would last for days with lots of music and food for their many guests; the poorer folks also followed many of the same traditions, although in a more modest fashion. It was the tradition that the bridegroom's family hosted the celebration after the church service. There was always an orchestra that played while the guests

Family members accompany the bride in a wedding ceremony in Cholula, Mexico. (Nik Wheeler/Corbis)

ate, and a big dance on the eve of the wedding day. After the dance, or at the conclusion of the feast, there was the *entrega de novios* (delivery of the wedding couple), when the wedding couple was formally returned to their parents and placed under their guidance. Songs from this ritual were collected by Juan Rael and reveal the solemnity of the ceremony.

The Hispano folklore does not specify the actual religious sacramental rituals, but more recent publications do describe church ceremonies that are still observed today. In very traditional weddings, the *arras*, thirteen coins or pieces of silver, are given by the groom to his bride as a symbol of security. After the wedding vows are stated during the Mass, a *lazo*, a cord with two connected loops, is draped over the couple, to symbolize the union of bride and groom. Just before the couple leaves the church, the bride, or sometimes a designated child, will pay tribute to *La Virgen de Guadalupe* by placing flowers at the foot of her statue or picture. There are always lots of *padrinos* (godfathers) and *madrinas* (godmothers), bridegrooms and bridesmaids, and of course *Mariachi* music.

Frances Toor's classic book on Mexican folklore, *A Treasury of Mexican Folkways*, relates wedding customs of the various regions and indigenous groups of Mexico. A not-so-typical Chicano wedding from southern California in the 1950s is depicted in the novel *The Wedding* by Mary Helen Ponce.

References Cabeza de Baca 1982; Espinosa 1985; Fernandez Mines 1977; Haralson 1980; Rael 1942, 1975; Rivera 1976; Sawin 1985; Toor 1947

Wetback
See Alambrista; Mojado

Witchcraft
See Brujería

With His Pistol in His Hand

The title of a book by the eminent professor Américo Paredes that has become a classic in American folklore and Chicano studies. *With His Pistol in His Hand: A Border Ballad and Its Hero*, published in 1958 by the University of Texas Press, is not only one of the most important academic works on the history of the Chicano, but it is also respected as major scholarship in the field of folklore studies, and specifically on the genre of the ballad. It is a study of a border ballad, "El Corrido de Gregorio Cortez," which looks at the history of the Texas-Mexican border and the life of Gregorio Cortez, and presents an analysis of the man as a ballad hero. As stated by Paredes himself in the introduction, "It is an account of the life of a man, of the way that songs and legends grew up about his name, and of the people who produced the songs, the legends, and the man" (1958, 1). It was in this work that Paredes proposed his theory of the production of Chicano folklore, and especially the border ballad, as a result of a process of border conflict generated by the invasion of Anglo culture and values into the Texas region in the early nineteenth century. The balladry of the Rio Grande border was "one of resistance against outside encroachment" (1958, 244). There was an "inner need" for the people to compose ballads that sang of the deeds of a man standing up for his rights, who in the process is transformed into a hero. Often, the man is nonviolent, but is coerced through persecution or abuse into killing his enemy, often a Texas Ranger, and must escape to the border. "His defeat is assured; . . . often he is killed or captured. But whatever his fate, he has stood up for his right" (149).

When the book was published it caused quite a stir in Texas because of its negative portrayal of the Texas Rangers. The chief editor at the University of Texas Press asked Paredes to delete his critical references to Walter Prescott Webb, J. Frank Dobie, and the Texas Rangers. The book was eventually published in spite of his refusal to make any changes. The timing of its publication was crucial, in 1958, for its powerful influence on Chicano students and intellectuals, since it came out just before the start of the Chicano movement of the 1960s. Its intellectual and political impact on a whole generation of Chicano scholars cannot be overstated. Almost all publications on Chicanos and *Mexicanos* up to that date had been written by Anglo American sociologists or anthropologists, and the few published Hispano scholars, such as Aurelio Espinosa and Arthur Campa, were only known within a narrow circle of folklore specialists. Gregorio Cortez, the border hero, and Américo Paredes, the scholar hero, both became figures that young Chicano students could respect and emulate.

See also "El Corrido de Gregorio Cortez"; Corridos; Paredes, Américo; Los Rinches
References Limón 1980a, 1986, 1990, 1992; Paredes 1958

Quetzalcoatl.

Yard Shrines

The creation of yard displays, as shrines or *ofrendas* (offerings), or *nacimientos* (nativity scenes) during Christmas, is an important way to commemorate many holidays such as Halloween, *Día de los Muertos* (Day of the Dead), *Cinco de Mayo* (Fifth of May), and even the Fourth of July. A yard shrine may be a permanent display in the form of a small chapel, a *nicho* (niche), or a *gruta* (grotto or shrine), set up in the front yard of a home. It may contain one or more holy images, of saints or the Virgin Mary, especially *La Virgen de Guadalupe*, flowers or potted plants, colorful garlands, and votive candles. These shrines are often just called *nichos*, and the word shrine is not even mentioned. During special holidays such as Christmas or on a saint's feast day, a shrine may be lighted up for the community to share. It is a common practice to make the sign of the cross or recite a short prayer when walking past a religious yard shrine.

In many families the shrine is erected as the result of a *promesa* or *manda* (promise or vow) made to a particular saint, or in memory of a family member who has died. A yard shrine, whether called a *nicho* or a *gruta*, can be decorated in various ways. There are always plants and flowers, sometimes seashells decorate the outside if it is constructed of cement, and the decorations will reflect the holiday season of the year. At Christmas, there may be lights, tinsel, and poinsettias. During Lent there may be lilies and pastel paper chains. Yard shrines demonstrate that religion is integrated into the life of a family, and they are considered to be sacred sites for prayer and devotion. There is no division between the public life and the religious and devotional life of a Chicano family. A yard shrine is a public exhibition of a family's religion and their devotion to a particular saint, as well as a display of an artistic sensibility, that emerges unconsciously from the family's beliefs.

A related form of yard folk art, not necessarily religious, is the yard *asamblea* (assemblage). A well-known man in Los Angeles, referred to as *"El Hombre de las Banderas"* (The Man of the Flags), created spectacular scenes up until his death in 1992. Art created in the yard of one's home serves to draw in the community and make it a participant. These yard sculptures are created from bits and pieces of contemporary life and popular culture, drawn from many different sources.

This Christmas nativity scene near the front steps of a home in Salinas, California, is a type of Mexican American yard shrine. (Stephanie Maze/Corbis)

See also Folk Art; Grutas; Nacimiento; Nichos; Ofrenda; La Virgen de Guadalupe
References Boyer 1988; Griffith 1992, 1995; Husband 1985; Kitchener 1994; Ramos 1991; Vidaurri 1991; West 1991

Yardas (Gardens)

Although the Spanish word for garden is *jardín*, many Chicano families favor the term "yard" while referring to their gardens, pronouncing it in Spanish as *yarda*. Although *yarda* appears to be a *pochismo* (Chicano slang), it can be found in *Cassell's Spanish Dictionary*. The layout and organizational aesthetics of Chicano *yardas* are unique enough that folklorists and cultural geographers have written about them. Many *yardas* can aesthetically constitute yard art, even though it does not appear that this is the intent of the creator. Besides planting shrubs, flowers, and sometimes grass, the gardener will bring into play the creativity that goes into decorating a yard unconsciously, with the result being a folk art display. Invariably, a yard will contain many potted flowers arranged in a patterned manner. The central focus of many yards is often a devotional shrine set up in memory of a family member, with a *nicho* housing a saint or Madonna, and the design of the yard's plants and flowers is laid out in reference to the shrine. Some *yardas* may not have planted grass, but instead hard-packed dirt that is kept free of weeds, swept frequently, and kept prepared for family gatherings. But trees, preferably fruit trees, abound to make shade for family gatherings and outdoor cooking.

A common practice among many working-class Mexican Americans is to recycle as much as possible, although the concept that recycling is an environmentally correct thing to do is not always known. Common recycled objects that can be found in yards are tables, kitchen pots, painted tin cans, and car tires used as planters. Tires are cut across the width, making two containers, opened up and cut with a scalloped design around the edges. After being painted and filled with flowers and plants, these plant containers do not even resemble their original form. Recycled tire planters can line a driveway or establish the boundaries of a large yard. The practice of reusing objects that have lost their original purpose, such as kitchen pitchers and pots, is a means of keeping something familiar, something associated with a memory, alive and finding a new use for it. This practice probably originates from poverty, but the historical result has been that it creates its own aesthetic in adding adornment to one's home and life. These "yardscapes," as they've come to be called, are composed of bits and pieces of one's personal life and as such can add visual charm and historical value to a home. A family's religious and cultural values, as well as the special identity of being Mexican American, can be found in *yardas*.

See also Folk Art; Nichos; Yard Shrines
References Kitchener 1987; Ramos 1991

Yo Soy Joaquin
See *I Am Joaquin/Yo Soy Joaquin*

Quetzalcoatl.

Zoot Suit

A style of suit worn by African Americans, Filipino Americans, and Mexican Americans during the 1930s and 1940s. In Chicano culture this style of dress is primarily associated with the *pachucos* of the 1940s. The fashion at that time was to wear very baggy pants with pegged legs, long jackets with high and sharp shoulder pads, thick-soled shoes, and long watch chains dangling from the belt. An addition to the whole style common to Chicanos was a particular haircut, long with a ducktail and a wide-brimmed hat.

The word zoot was known within the urban jazz culture of Harlem, and it meant something either exaggerated in performance or in style. Many African Americans wore an extravagant style of clothing, the baggy pegged pants and jackets with padded shoulders, that later became known as the zoot suit. In the novel *Invisible Man* by Ralph Ellison, he describes the zoot-suiters' style, "walking slowly, their shoulders swaying, their legs swinging from their hips in trousers that ballooned upward from cuffs fitting snug about their ankles; their coats long and hip-tight with shoulders far too broad to be those of natural western men" (1947, 380). In the late-night jazz scenes of Harlem this style was "a killer-diller coat with a drape-shape, reat-pleats and shoulders padded like a lunatic's cell" (380). Tyler makes the point that the zoot suit was an extremely symbolic costume, which gave the wearer the look of a child in adult clothing. The broad square shoulders gave a macho look to the youth, and the finger-tipped coat was made for fun and leisure. The long baggy pants were made for dancing, especially the jitterbug, and the wide Panama hats were another sign of adulthood. "The business of fun, dancing and dating were the key characteristics displayed by Zoot-Suiters. It was an escape from drudgery and futile labor to the bliss of free-wheeling movement in the city among youths in the new youth culture" (Tyler, 23). Prominent black entertainers wore the zoot suit, such as Cab Calloway, Sammy Davis Jr., and Duke Ellington. Ellington performed at the Orpheum in Los Angeles in 1941 and 1942 with a musical called *Jump for Joy* in which the performers wore zoot suits, also known as *Gone with the Wind* suits, after the style worn by Clark Gable in the movie by the same name.

Even though the zoot suit was worn by the young men of several different races and ethnicities, it is primarily identified with the *pachucos* of Los

The zoot suit from the 1940s was an ensemble of very baggy pants with pegged legs, long jackets with high and sharp shoulder pads, thick soled shoes, and long watch chains dangling from the belt. The word zoot was known within the urban jazz culture of Harlem and it meant something exaggerated either in performance or in style. (Bettmann/Corbis)

Angeles. *Pachucos* were mostly second-generation Mexicans, the sons of migrant laborers and working-class immigrants. *Pachucos* created their own subculture, an arrogant style of dressing, a bilingual secret argot, and for some individuals membership in petty criminal gangs. The zoot suit became a symbolic disguise that identified the zoot-suiter as neither a Mexican nor an American. It was not a bicultural or binational position, but rather a position between cultures, a "hanging in space" position. The overly confident, slow swagger of the *pachuco*, today exemplified by the *cholo*, made it appear in fact as if the zoot-suiter were walking on air.

During the summer of 1943 the attention of the whole country was on Los Angeles when gangs of sailors and zoot-suiters battled with each other in the streets of the city. It is unclear if this was a race riot or a riot of patriotic sailors who attacked, beat, and stripped young Mexican Americans whom they perceived to be unpatriotic zoot-suiters. Between the third and thirteenth of June zoot-suiters were open targets. Much has been written about these riots from both literary and historical perspectives.

During the late 1970s the zoot suit received wide recognition and popularity with the production of a successful play by Luis Valdez. In 1981 a film by the same name, *Zoot Suit*, was produced and directed by Luis Valdez, with performances by actors Daniel Valdez and Edward James Olmos.

See also Cholos; Pachucos
References Barker 1950; Cosgrove 1989; Ellison, 1947; Mazon 1984; Orona-Cordova 1992; Sanchez 1978; Stone 1990; Tyler 1994; Valdez 1992; *Zoot Suit* 1981

Zozobra

A giant, forty-foot effigy in the form of a puppet, which is burned during the annual Santa Fe Fiesta held in Santa Fe, New Mexico. The word *Zozobra* translates to "gloom" or "worry" or "anguished." The *Zozobra* is ritualistically burned at the beginning of the fiesta, which symbolizes the end of destructiveness, gloom, and worry, setting the tone for a successful fiesta. The creation of *Zozobra* was introduced into the fiesta in 1926 by Will Shuster, who felt that the fiesta had become "dull and commercialized." Throughout the years the image of *Zozobra* changed from a simple twenty-foot puppet to the elaborate forty-foot figure with animated eyes, arms, and mouth that he is today. In 1969 Shuster turned over the responsibility and copyright of *Zozobra* to the Kiwanis Club of Santa Fe. He is hung on a tall pole on a hill, outside the city, where the burning can be seen by the thousands of people who come to watch. The death of gloom is supposed to resurrect happiness.

In response to the tradition of the burning of *Zozobra*, a group of New Mexico Chicanos started a tradition of burning *El Kookoóee*, a figure known by many Chicanos as the bogeyman, during the *Festival de Otoño*.

See also El Kookoóee; Santa Fe Fiesta
References Cohen 1985; Grimes 1976; Weigle and White 1988

Quetzalcoatl

Bibliography

Abernethy, Francis Edward. *Folk Art in Texas*. Dallas, TX: Methodist University Press, 1985.

Aceves, J. Jesus Rodriguez. *Danzas de Moros y Cristianos*. Guadalajara, Jalisco, Mexico: Gobierno de Jalisco, Secretaria General Unidad Editorial, 1988.

Acosta, Oscar Zeta. *The Autobiography of a Brown Buffalo*. San Francisco, CA: Straight Arrow Books, 1972.

Acuña, Rodolfo. *Occupied America: A History of Chicanos*. 3d ed. New York: Harper-Collins Publishers, 1988.

Ahlborn, Richard Eighme. *The Penitente Moradas of Abiquiu*. Washington, DC: Smithsonian Institution Press, 1986. [Reprint of original edition of 1968.]

Alarcon, Norma. "*Traddutora, Traditora:* A Paradigmatic Figure of Chicana Feminism." *Cultural Critique* 13 (1989): 57–87.

Alvarez, Robert R. "The Mexican-U.S. Border: The Making of an Anthropology of Borderlands." *Annual Review of Anthropology* 24 (9) (1995): 447–470.

Amaya Topete, Jesus. *Aventuras de un Bracero*. 2nd ed. Mexico: Editora Grafica Moderna, 1961.

Anaya, Rudolfo A. *The Legend of La Llorona*. Berkeley, CA: Tonatiuh-Quinto Sol International, Inc., 1984.

———. *The Farolitos of Christmas*. New York: Hyperion Books, 1995a. [Juvenile literature.]

———. "*La Llorona, El Kookoóee,* and Sexuality." In *The Anaya Reader*. New York: Warner Books, 1995b.

Anaya, Rudolfo, Denise Chaves, and Juan Estevan Arellano. *Descansos: An Interrupted Journey, Tres Voces*. Photographs by Juan Estevan Arellano. Albuquerque, NM: Academia/El Norte Publications, 1995.

Anaya, Rudolfo A., and Francisco A. Lomelí, eds. *Aztlán: Essays on the Chicano Homeland*. Albuquerque, NM: Academia/El Norte Publications, 1989.

Ancona, George. *Fiesta U.S.A.* New York: Lodestar Books, 1995.

Anderson, Reed. "Early Secular Theater in New Mexico." In *Paso por Aqui: Critical Essays on the New Mexican Literary Tradition, 1542–1988*, edited by Erlinda Gonzales-Berry. Albuquerque: University of New Mexico, 1989.

Andrede, A. Rolando. "Machismo: A Universal Malady." *Journal of American Culture* 15 (1992): 33–41.

Applegate, Frank G. *Native Tales of New Mexico.* Philadelphia: J. B. Lippincott Co., 1932.

Applewhite, Steven Lozano. "*Curanderismo*: Demystifying the Health Beliefs and Practices of Elderly Mexican Americans." *Health and Social Work* 20 (1995): 247–254.

Aranda, Charles. *Dichos: Proverbs and Sayings from the Spanish.* Santa Fe, NM: Sunstone Press, 1977.

Arellano, Anselmo F., and Julian Josue Vigil, eds. *Arthur L. Campa.* Las Vegas, NM: Editorial Telarana, 1980.

Arellano, Estevan. "*Descansos.*" *New Mexico Magazine,* February 1986, 42–45. [Photographs.]

Arias, Ron. *The Road to Tamazunchale: A Novel.* Reno, NV: West Coast Poetry Review, 1975.

Armas, Jose. "*Machismo.*" *De Colores Journal* 2 (1975): 52–65.

Arnold, Charles August. *The Folklore, Manners, and Customs of the Mexicans in San Antonio, Texas.* San Antonio: University of Texas, 1928. [Thesis reprinted in 1971 by R. and E. Research Associates.]

Arora, Shirley L. "Some Spanish Proverbial Comparisons from California." *Western Folklore* 20 (1966): 229–237.

———. "La Llorona: The Naturalization of a Legend." *Southwest Folklore* 5 (1981): 23–40.

———. "A Critical Bibliography of Mexican American Proverbs." *Aztlán: International Journal of Chicano Studies Research* 13 (1982a): 71–80.

———. "Proverbs in Mexican American Tradition." *Aztlán: International Journal of Chicano Studies Research* 13 (1982b): 43–69.

Arrizón, Alicia. "Soldaderas and the Staging of the Mexican Revolution." *The Drama Review* 42 (Spring 1998): 90–113.

Arteaga, Alfred. "The Chicano Mexican Corrido." *Journal of Ethnic Studies* 13 (Summer 1985): 75–105.

Awalt, Barbe. *Our Saints among Us/Nuestros Santos entre Nosotros: 400 Years of New Mexican Devotional Art.* Albuquerque, NM: LPD Press, 1998. [Essays by Thomas J. Steele and Charles M. Carrillo.]

Awalt, Barbe, and Paul Rhetts. *Charlie Carrillo: Tradition and Soul/Tradición y Alma.* Albuquerque, NM: LPD Enterprises, 1995. [Photographs.]

Axtell, Roger E. *Gestures: The Do's and Taboos of Body Language around the World.* New York: Wiley, 1991.

Baca Zinn, Maxine. "Chicano Men and Masculinity." *Journal of Ethnic Studies* 10 (Summer 1982): 29–44.

Bacigalupa, Andrea. *Santos and Saints' Days.* Santa Fe, NM: Sunstone Review and Press, Inc., 1972. [Glossary of saints.]

Baer, Roberta D., and Marta Bustillo. "Susto and Mal Ojo among Florida Farmworkers: Emic and Etic Perspectives." *Medical Anthropology Quarterly* 7 (1993): 90–100.

La Bamba. Produced and directed by Luis Valdez. Columbia Pictures. 103 min. Burbank, CA: 1987.

Bandini, Arturo. *Navidad, A Christmas Day with the Early Californians. Pastorela, A Shepherds' Play.* Translated by Gladys Louise Williams. San Francisco: California Historical Society, 1958.

Barakat, Robert A. "Aztec Motifs in 'La Llorona'." *Southern Folklore Quarterly* 5 (1965): 289–296.

Barber, Russell J. "The Agua Mansa Cemetery: An Indicator of Ethnic Identification in a Mexican-American Community." In *Ethnicity and the American Cemetery*, edited by Richard E. Meyer. Bowling Green, OH: Bowling Green State University Popular Press, 1993.

Barker, George Carpenter. *Pachuco: An American Spanish Argot and Its Social Functions in Tucson, Arizona*. Tucson: University of Arizona Press, 1974. [First printing 1950.]

Barrera, Alberto. "Mexican-American Roadside Crosses in Starr County." In *Hecho en Texas: Texas-Mexican Folk Arts and Crafts*, edited by Joe S. Graham. Denton: University of Texas Press, 1991.

Barrera, Mario. *Beyond Aztlán: Ethnic Autonomy in Comparative Perspective*. New York: Praeger, 1988.

———. "Story Structure in Latino Feature Films." In *Chicanos and Film: Representation and Resistance*, edited by Chon A. Noriega. Minneapolis: University of Minnesota, 1992.

Barriga, Miguel Diaz. "The Culture of Poverty as Relajo." *Aztlán: International Journal of Chicano Studies Research* 22 (Fall 1997): 43–65.

Bascom, William R. "Four Functions of Folklore." In *The Study of Folklore*, edited by Alan Dundes. Englewood Cliffs, NJ: Prentice-Hall, 1965.

Batchen, Lou Sage. *Las Placitas: Historical Facts and Legends*. Santa Fe, NM: Tumbleweed Press, 1972.

Bauman, Richard, and Roger D. Abrahams. *"And Other Neighborly Names": Social Process and Cultural Image in Texas Folklore*. Austin: University of Texas Press, 1981.

Bauml, Betty J. *A Dictionary of Gestures*. Metuchen, NJ: Scarecrow Press, 1975.

Beeson, Margaret, Marjorie Adams, and Rosalie King. *Memories for Tomorrow: Mexican American Recollections of Yesteryear*. Detroit, MI: Blaine Ethridge Books, 1983.

Bell, Major Horace. *Reminiscences of a Ranger; or Early Times in Southern California*. Illustrations by James S. Bodrero. Santa Barbara, CA: Wallace Hebberd, 1927.

Bennett, Wendell C., and Robert M. Zingg. *The Tarahumara: An Indian Tribe of Northern Mexico*. Chicago: University of Chicago Press, 1935. [Photographs.]

Berkenfield, Barbara. "Santeros Join in Historic Reredos Project." *Spanish Market*, July 1994.

Bierhorst, John. *The Mythology of Mexico and Central America*. New York: William Morrow and Company, Inc., 1990.

Blea, Irene I. "*Brujería*: A Sociological Analysis of Mexican American Witches." In *Sex Roles, Language: Selected Papers 1979*. Berkeley, CA: Tonatiuh-Quinto Sol, 1980.

Boatright, Mody C., ed. *Mexican Border Ballads and Other Lore*. Publications of the Texas Folklore Society No. 21. Dallas, TX: Southern Methodist University Press, 1946.

Bourke, John G. "The Folk-Foods of the Rio Grande Valley and of Northern Mexico." *Journal of American Folklore* 8 (1895). Also published in *Southwestern Lore*, ed. J. Frank Dobie, Dallas, TX: Texas Folklore Society, 1931: 85–117.

Boyd, E. *Saints and Saint Makers of New Mexico*. Santa Fe, NM: Laboratory of Anthropology, 1946. [Bibliography; appendices.]

———. *Popular Arts of Colonial New Mexico*. Santa Fe, NM: Museum of International Folk Art, 1959. [Photography by Eliot Porter and Laura Gilpin.]

———. *Popular Arts of Spanish New Mexico*. Santa Fe, NM: Museum of New Mexico Press, 1974. [Illustrations; bibliography.]

Boyer, Edward J. "Holidays Bring out His Urge to Create Spectacular Yard Displays." *Los Angeles Times*, November 24, 1988: Metro, sec. 2, p. 1.

Braddy, Haldeen. "The Pachucos and Their Argot." *Southern Folklore Quarterly* 24 (December 1960): 255–271.

———. *Mexico and the Southwest: People, Palaver, Places*. Port Washington, NY: Kennikat Press, 1971.

Brenner, Anita. *Idols Behind Altars: The Story of the Mexican Spirit*. Boston, MA: Beacon Press, 1929, reprint 1970.

Briggs, Charles L. *The Wood Carvers of Cordova, New Mexico: Social Dimensions of an Artistic Revival*. Knoxville: University of Tennessee Press, 1980.

———. "The Role of Mexicano Artists and the Anglo Elite in the Emergence of a Contemporary Folk Art." In *Folk Art and Art Worlds*, edited by John Michael Vlach and Simon J. Bronner. Ann Arbor, MI: UMI Research Press, 1986.

———. *Competence in Performance: The Creativity of Tradition in Mexicano Verbal Art*. Philadelphia: University of Pennsylvania Press, 1988.

Briggs, Charles L., and Julian Josue Vigil. *The Lost Gold Mine of Juan Mondragon: A Legend from New Mexico Performed by Melaquias Romero*. Tucson: University of Arizona Press, 1990.

Bright, Brenda Jo. *Mexican American Low Riders: An Anthropological Approach to Popular Culture*. Houston, TX: Rice University, 1994. [Dissertation.]

———. "Remappings: Los Angeles Low Riders." In *Looking High and Low: Art and Cultural Identity*, edited by Brenda Jo Bright and Liza Bakewell. Tucson: University of Arizona, 1995.

Bright, William. *A Coyote Reader*. Berkeley, CA: University of California Press, 1993.

Brito, Aristeo. *The Devil in Texas/El Diablo en Texas*. Translated from the Spanish by David William Foster. Tempe, AZ: Bilingual Press, 1990.

Brown, Lorin W. *Hispano Folklife of New Mexico: The Lorin W. Brown Federal Writers' Project Manuscripts*. Albuquerque: University of New Mexico, 1978.

Brown, M. H. de la Peña. "Una Tamalada: The Special Event." *Western Folklore* 40 (1981): 64–71.

Broyles-Gonzalez, Yolanda. *El Teatro Campesino: Theater in the Chicano Movement*. Austin: University of Texas Press, 1994.

Brundage, Burr Cartwright. *The Fifth Sun: Aztec Gods, Aztec World*. Austin: University of Texas Press, 1979. [Bibliography; illustrations.]

Brunvand, Jan Harold. *The Vanishing Hitchhiker, American Urban Legends and Their Meanings*. New York: W. W. Norton & Co., 1981.

Buckley, Daniel. "Lyrics to Live By." *Tucson Citizen*, March 19, 1996a, sec. D.

———. "Familiar Music." *Tucson Citizen*, April 25, 1996b, sec. D.

Bullock, Alice. *Living Legends of the Santa Fe Country*. Santa Fe, NM: The Sunstone Press, 1972. [First edition 1970.]

Bunting, Bainbridge. *Taos Adobes: Spanish Colonial and Territorial Architecture of the Taos Valley*. Publication No. 2. Santa Fe: Fort Burgwin Research Center, Museum of New Mexico Press, 1964. [Illustrations by Jean Lee Booth and William R. Sims, Jr.]

———. *Of Earth and Timbers Made: New Mexico Architecture*. Albuquerque: University of New Mexico Press, 1974. [Photographs by Arthur LaZar.]

Burciaga, José Antonio. *Drink Cultura*. Santa Barbara, CA: Joshua Odell Editions, Capra Press, 1993.

Burma, John H. "Self-Tattooing among Delinquents, A Research Note." In *Dress, Adornment and the Social Order*, edited by Mary Ellen and Joanne Bubolz Roach. New York: John Wiley & Sons, Inc., 1965.

Buss, Fran Leeper. *La Partera: Story of a Midwife*. Ann Arbor: University of Michigan Press, 1980.

Cabello-Argandoña, Roberto. *Brief History of Cinco de Mayo*. Encino, CA: Floricanto Press, 1993.

Cabeza de Baca, Fabiola. *We Fed Them Cactus*. Albuquerque: University of New Mexico Press, 1954.

———. *The Good Life: New Mexico Traditions and Food*. Santa Fe: Museum of New Mexico Press, 1982. [Glossary.]

Calvillo, Jaime Dario. *Between Heaven and Earth: "Actos" of El Teatro Campesino*. Minneapolis: University of Minnesota, 1981. [Dissertation.]

Campa, Arthur Leon. *Bibliography of Spanish Folklore in New Mexico. University of New Mexico Bulletin*, Language Series 2(3). Albuquerque, NM: University of New Mexico, 1930.

———. *The Spanish Folksong in the Southwest. University of New Mexico Bulletin*, Language Series 5 (1). Albuquerque: University of New Mexico Press, 1933.

———. *Spanish Religious Folktheatre in the Southwest. University of New Mexico Bulletin*, Language Series 5 (1, 2). Albuquerque: University of New Mexico Press, 1934.

———. *Sayings and Riddles in New Mexico. University of New Mexico Bulletin*, Language Series 313. Albuquerque: University of New Mexico Press, 1937.

———. *Los Comanches: A New Mexican Folk Drama. The University of New Mexico Bulletin*, 376. Albuquerque: University of New Mexico Press, 1942.

———. *Treasure of the Sangre de Cristos: Tales and Traditions of the Spanish Southwest*. Norman: University of Oklahoma Press, 1963.

———. *Hispanic Folklore Studies of Arthur L. Campa*. New York: Arno Press, Inc., 1976. [Introduction by Carlos E. Cortes.]

———. "The Spanish Language in the Southwest." In *Humanidad: Essays in Honor of George I. Sanchez*, edited by Américo Paredes. Los Angeles: Chicano Studies Center Publications, University of California, 1977.

———. *Hispanic Culture in the Southwest*. Norman: University of Oklahoma Press, 1979. [Bibliography.]

———. *Arthur L. Campa*. Edited by Anselmo F. Arellano and Julian Josue Vigil. Las Vegas, NM: Editorial Telerana, 1980.

Campos, Anthony John, ed. and trans. *Mexican Folk Tales*. Illustrated by Mark Sanders. Tucson: University of Arizona Press, 1977.

Campos, Ruben M. *El Folklore Literario de Mexico: Investigación Acerca de la Producción Literaria Popular 1525–1925*. Mexico: Publicaciones de la Secretaría de Educación Pública, 1929.

Candelaria, Cordelia. *Arroyos to the Heart*. Santa Monica, CA: Santa Monica College Press, 1993a.

———. "Letting La Llorona Go: Re/reading History's Tender Mercies." *Heresies* 7 (1993b): 111–115.

Cantú, Norma. "Costume as Cultural Resistance and Affirmation: The Case of a South Texas Community." In *Hecho en Tejas: Texas Mexican Folk Arts and Crafts*, edited by Joe S. Graham. Denton: University of North Texas Press, 1991a.

———. "The Mexican-American Quilting Traditions of Laredo, San Ygnacio, and Zapata." In *Hecho en Tejas: Texas-American Folk Arts and Crafts*, edited by Joe S. Graham. Denton: University of Texas Press, 1991b.

———. "*Los Matachines de la Santa Cruz de la Ladrillera*: Notes Toward a Socio-literary Analysis." In *Feasts and Celebrations in North American Ethnic Communities*, edited by Ramón A. Gutiérrez and Genevieve Fabre. Albuquerque: University of New Mexico Press, 1995.

Cardenas, Daniel N. "Mexican Spanish." In *El Lenguaje de los Chicanos: Regional and Social Characteristics Used by Mexican Americans*, edited by Eduardo Hernandez-Chavez, Andrew D. Cohen, and Anthony F. Beltramo. Englewood, NJ: Center for Applied Linguistics, 1974.

Cardenas, Jose Angel. *My Spanish-Speaking Left Foot*. San Antonio, TX: Intercultural Development Research Association, 1997.

Cardozo-Freeman, Inez. "Games Mexican Girls Play." In *Women and Folklore*, edited by Claire R. Farrer. Austin: University of Texas Press, 1975.

———. "Serpent Fears and Religious Motifs among Mexican Women." *Frontiers* 3 (1978): 10–13.

Carmichael, Elizabeth, and Chloe Sayer. *The Skeleton at the Feast: The Day of the Dead in Mexico*. London: British Museum Press, 1991. [Color plates; photographs.]

Carrasco, David. *Quetzalcoatl and the Irony of Empire: Myths and Prophecies in the Aztec Tradition*. Chicago: University of Chicago Press, 1992.

Carson, Xanthus. *Treasure! Worth a Billion Bucks*. San Antonio, TX: Naylor, 1974.

Cash, Marie Romero. *Living Shrines: Home Altars of New Mexico*. Santa Fe: Museum of New Mexico Press, 1998. [Photographs by Siegfried Halus.]

———. *Santos: Enduring Images of Northern New Mexican Village Churches*. Niwot: University Press of Colorado, 1999.

Castañeda, Carlos E. "Maria de Agreda, the Jumano, and the Tejas, 1620–1665." In *The Mission Era: The Finding of Texas 1519–1693*, edited by Carlos E. Castañeda. Austin, TX: Von Boeckmann-Jones Company, 1936.

Castillo, Ana. *Massacre of the Dreamers: Essays on Xicanisma*. Albuquerque: University of New Mexico, 1994.

Castillo, Pedro, and Albert Camarillo, eds. *Furia y Muerte: Los Bandidos Chicanos*. Monograph No. 4. Los Angeles, CA: Aztlán Publications, UCLA Chicano Studies Research Center, 1973.

Castro, Rafaela. "Mexican Women's Sexual Jokes." *Aztlán: International Journal of Chicano Studies Research* 13 (1982): 275–293.

Cerda, Gilberto, Berta Cabaza, and Julieta Farias. *Vocabulario Español de Texas*. Austin: University of Texas Press, 1953.

Cervantes Saavedra, Miguel de. *Comedia Famosa de Pedro de Urdemalas*. New York: Las Americas Pub. Co., 1965.

Cesaretti, Gusmano. *Street Writers: A Guided Tour of Chicano Graffiti*. Los Angeles, CA: Acrobat Books, 1975. [Photographs.]

Chabat, Carlos G. *Diccionario de Caló: El Lenguaje del Hampa en Mexico*. Guadalajara, Jalisco, Mexico: Carlos G. Chabat, 1956.

Chabran, Richard, and Rafael Chabran, eds. *The Latino Encyclopedia*. 6 vols. New York: Marshall Cavendish, 1996.

Champe, Flavia Waters. *The Matachines Dance of the Upper Rio Grande: History, Music, and Choreography*. Lincoln: University of Nebraska Press, 1983.

"Chanes." Anonymous. Ernest Baughman Collection, Zimmerman Library, University of New Mexico, 1974.

Chavez, Fray Angelico. *Our Lady of the Conquest*. Santa Fe: The Historical Society of New Mexico, 1948.

———. *My Penitente Land*. Albuquerque: University of New Mexico, 1974.

———. *La Conquistadora: The Autobiography of an Ancient Statue*. Santa Fe, NM: Sunstone Press, 1983.

———. "Our Lady of the Conquest." *El Palacio* 91 (Spring 1985): 19–29. [Bibliography.]

Chavez, John R. *The Lost Land: The Chicano Image of the Southwest*. Albuquerque: University of New Mexico Press, 1984. [Bibliography.]

Chavéz, Tomas Jr. *Quinceañera: A Liturgy in the Reformed Tradition*. San Angelo, TX: Presbytery of Tres Rios, 1983.

Chicano Pinto Research Project. *Community Variations in Chicano Ex-Convict Adaptations: Final Report*. Los Angeles: University of Southern California, 1975.

CHICLE. *Chicano Literature and Culture*. University of New Mexico: Listserv @UNM.EDU. [An electronic listserv that discusses folklore, literature, novels, culture, research, and other aspects of Chicano culture.]

Chulas Fronteras. Directed by Les Blank. El Cerrito, CA: Brazos Films, 1976. [Spanish/English.]

Clark, Margaret. *Health in the Mexican American Culture*. Berkeley: University of California Press, 1959.

Cobos, Rubén. "The New Mexican Game of '*Valse Chiquiao*'." *Western Folklore* 15 (1956): 95–101.

———. *A Dictionary of New Mexico and Southern Colorado Spanish*. Santa Fe: Museum of New Mexico Press, 1983. [Bibliography.]

———. *Refranes: Southwestern Spanish Proverbs*. Santa Fe: Museum of New Mexico Press, 1985.

———. *Music in the Rubén Cobos Collection of Spanish New Mexican Folklore: A Descriptive Catalogue*, edited by Victoria Lindsay Levine and Amanda Chace. Colorado Springs, CO: The Hulbert Center Press of the Colorado College, 1999.

Cockcroft, Eva Sperling. "The Story of Chicano Park." *Aztlán: International Journal of Chicano Studies Research* 15 (Spring 1984): 79–103. Reprinted in *Chicano Border Culture and Folklore*, edited by Jose and Arturo Ramirez Villarino. San Diego, CA: Marin Publications, Inc., 1992.

Cockcroft, Eva, John Weber, and Jim Cockcroft. *Toward a People's Art: The Contemporary Mural Movement*. New York: E. P. Dutton & Co., 1977. [Illustrated; bibliography.]

Cohen, Judy Chiba. "Zozobra: Our Favorite Monster." *El Palacio* 91 (1985): 38–34.

Colahan, Clark. *The Visions of Sor María de Agreda: Writing Knowledge and Power*. Tucson: University of Arizona Press, 1994. [Bibliography.]

Cole, M. R. *Los Pastores: A Mexican Play of the Nativity*. Boston, MA: Houghton Mifflin and Company, 1907. [Published for the American Folklore Society; illustrations and music.]

Collier, Margarite. Archives. Margarite Collier Collection, 1930s–1970s. Southwest Folklore Archives, University of Arizona Library, Tucson.

Coltharp, Lurline H. *The Tongue of the Tirilones: A Linguistic Study of a Criminal Argot*. Birmingham: University of Alabama Press, 1965. [Glossary; bibliography.]

———. "Invitation to the Dance: Spanish in the El Paso Underworld." In *Texas Studies in Bilingualism*, edited by Glenn G. Gilbert. Berlin, Germany: Walter de Gruyter & Co., 1970.

Cordova, Gilberto Benito. *Abiquiu and Don Cacahuate: A Folk History of a New Mexico Village*. Los Cerrito, NM: San Marcos Press, 1973.

———. *The 3 1/2 Cultures of Espanola*. Albuquerque, NM: El Norte Publications/ Academia, 1990. [Photography by Juan Estevan Arellano.]

Cortes, Carlos E. "*The Greaser's Revenge* to *Boulevard Nights*: The Mass Media Curriculum on Chicanos." In *History, Culture, and Society: Chicano Studies in the*

1980s, edited by Mario Francisco Lomeli et al. National Association for Chicano Studies. Ypsilanti, MI: Bilingual Press/Editorial Bilingüe, 1983.

Cosgrove, Stuart. "The Zoot Suit and Style Warfare." In *Zoot Suits and Second-Hand Dresses: An Anthology of Fashion and Music*, edited by Angela McRobbie. London: Macmillan, 1989.

Coulter, Lane. *New Mexican Tinwork, 1840–1940*. Albuquerque: University of New Mexico Press, 1990.

Cruz, Yolanda A. "Santos, Santeros, and a Different Kind of Muerte." *The New Mexican*, November 15, 1973, p. 31.

"La Cucaracha." In *Aztlán: An Anthology of Mexican American Literature*, edited by Luis Valdez and Stan Steiner. New York: Vintage Books, 1972.

Cummings, Scott T. "Guillermo Gomez-Peña: True Confessions of a Techno-Aztec Performance Artist." *American Theater* 11 (November 1994): 50–52.

Cunningham, Keith K. "Ethnocuisine: Arizona Mexican American." *Southwest Folklore* 21 (1980): 58–60.

Darley, Alex M. *The Passionists of the Southwest, or the Holy Brotherhood*. Glorieta, NM: Rio Grande Press, 1968. [First published in 1893; bibliography.]

Davalos, Karen Mary. "'La Quinceañera': Making Gender and Ethnic Identities." *Frontiers* 16 (Spring and Summer 1996): 101–128.

Davidson, R. Theodore. *Chicano Prisoners: The Key to San Quentin*. New York: Holt, Rinehart & Winston, 1974. [Case Studies in Cultural Anthropology Series.]

Day, Mark. *Forty Acres: César Chávez and the Farm Workers*. New York: Praeger, 1971.

De Cordova, Lorenzo. *Echoes of the Flute*. Santa Fe, NM: Ancient City Press, 1972. [Illustrated by Eliseo Rodriguez; notes by Marta Weigle; glossary.]

De Leon, Arnoldo. "The Rape of Tío Taco: Mexican Americans in Texas, 1930–1935." *Journal of Mexican American Studies* 1 (Fall 1970): 4–15.

———. "Las Fiestas Patrias." In *Biographical Notes on the Hispanic Presence in San Angelo, Texas*. San Antonio, TX: Caravel Press, 1978.

———. *The Tejano Community, 1836–1900*. Albuquerque: University of New Mexico Press, 1982. [Bibliography.]

———. *They Called Them Greasers: Anglo Attitudes Toward Mexicans in Texas, 1821–1900*. Austin: University of Texas Press, 1983. [Bibliography.]

de Onís, Jose. *The Hispanic Contribution to the State of Colorado*. Boulder, CO: Westview Press, 1976.

DeBaca, Elba C. "The Lady in Blue." In *Las Mujeres Hablan: An Anthology of Nuevo Mexicana Writers*, edited by Erlinda Gonzales-Berry, Teresa Marquez, and Tey Diana Rebolledo. Albuquerque, NM: El Norte Publications, 1988.

Del Castillo, Adelaida R. "Malintzin Tenépal: A Preliminary Look into a New Perspective." In *Essays on La Mujer*, edited by Rosaura and Rosa Martinez Cruz Sanchez. Chicano Studies Center Publications, Anthology No. 1. Los Angeles: University of California, 1977.

Del Fuego, Laura. *Maravilla*. Encino, CA: Floricanto Press, 1989.

Delgado, Edmundo R. *Witch Stories of New Mexico, Folklore of New Spain/Cuentos de Brujas de Nuevo Mexico, Folklore de la Nueva España*. Collected by the Works Progress Administration. Santa Fe, NM, 1994.

Demarest, Donald, and Coley Taylor. *The Dark Virgin: The Book of Our Lady of Guadalupe*. Freeport, ME: Coley Taylor Inc., 1956.

Demello, Margo. "The Convict Body: Tattooing among Male American Prisoners." *Anthropology Today* 9 (1993): 10–13.

Devine, Lottie C. *Es Verdad, or It Is True: The Story of a Family and Early-Day Life in Arizona*. Coolidge, AZ: Coolidge Shopper Printing & Publishing Co., 1964.

Día de los Muertos: An Illustrated Essay and Bibliography. Santa Barbara, CA: Center for Chicano Studies and Colección Tloque Nahuaque, University Library, 1983.

Diamond, Betty Ann. *"Brown-eyed Children of the Sun": The Cultural Politics of El Teatro Campesino*. Madison: University of Wisconsin Press, 1977. [Dissertation.]

Dickey, Dan William. *The Kennedy Corridos: A Study of the Ballads of a Mexican American Hero*. Austin: Center for Mexican American Studies, University of Texas, 1978. [Bibliography; photographs.]

Dobie, J. Frank. *Some Part of Myself*. Austin: University of Texas Press, 1980. [Reprint of 1964 edition.]

Dobie J. Frank, ed. *Legends of Texas*. Hatboro, PA: Folklore Associates, Inc., 1964. [Publications of the Texas Folklore Society No. 3; reprint of 1924 edition.]

Dolan, Jay P., and Allan Figueroa Deck, S.J., eds. *Hispanic Catholic Culture in the U.S.: Issues and Concerns*. Notre Dame, IN: University of Notre Dame Press, 1994.

Dolan, Jay P., and Gilberto M. Hinojosa, eds. *Mexican Americans and the Catholic Church, 1900–1965*. Notre Dame, IN: University of Notre Dame Press, 1994.

Domecq, Brianda. *The Astonishing Story of the Saint of Cabora*. Translated from Spanish by Kay S. Garcia. Tempe, AZ: Bilingual Press, 1998.

Dominguez, Miguel. "Coplas from East Los Angeles." *Southwest Folklore* 5 (1981): 41–54.

Dorson, Richard M. *American Folklore*. Chicago, IL: University of Chicago Press, 1959.

———. "Latino Folklore in the Region." In *Forging a Community: The Latino Experience in Northwest Indiana, 1919–1975*, edited by James B. Lane and Edward J. Escobar. Chicago, IL: Cattails Press, 1987.

Drescher, Timothy W. *San Francisco Murals: Community Creates Its Muse 1914–1994*. San Francisco, CA: Pogo Press, 1994. [Photographs.]

Duffy, Karen M. "Tracing the Gift: Aurelio M. Espinosa, 1880–1958." *The Folklore Historian* 12 (1995): 39–53.

Dundes Alan. *Analytic Essays in Folklore*. The Hague: Mouton, 1975.

Dundes, Alan, ed. *The Evil Eye: A Casebook*. Madison: University of Wisconsin Press, 1992.

Dunitz, Robin J. *Street Gallery*. Los Angeles, CA: RJD Enterprises, 1993. [Photographs.]

Dunne, John Gregory. *Delano: The Story of the California Grape Strike*. New York: Farrar, Straus & Giroux, 1967.

Duran, Gustavo. *14 Traditional Spanish Songs from Texas*. Washington, DC: Pan American Union, 1942. [From recordings made in Texas, 1934–1939, by John A., Ruby T., and Alan Lomax.]

Durand, Jorge, and Douglas S. Massey. *Doy Gracias: Iconografía de la Emigración Mexico–Estados Unidos*. Guadalajara, Jalisco, Mexico: Programa de Estudios Jaliscienses, Universidad de Guadalajara, 1990. [Photographs; bibliography.]

———. *Miracles on the Border: Retablos of Mexican Migrants to the United States*. Tucson: University of Arizona Press, 1995. [Plates; bibliography.]

Ebinger, Virginia Nylander. *Niñez: Spanish Songs, Games, and Stories of Childhood*. Santa Fe, NM: Sunstone Press, 1993. [Bibliography.]

Echevarria, Evelio, and Jose Otero, eds. *Hispanic Colorado: Four Centuries of History and Heritage*. Ft. Collins, CO: Centennial Publications, 1976.

Egan, Martha. *Milagros: Votive Offerings from the Americas*. Santa Fe: Museum of New Mexico Press, 1991. [Photographs.]

Elizondo, Virgil. "Our Lady of Guadalupe as a Cultural Symbol: 'The Power of the Powerless.'" In *Liturgy and Cultural Religious Traditions*, edited by Herman Schmidt and David Power. New York: Seabury Press, 1977.

Ellison, Ralph. *The Invisible Man*. New York: New American Library, 1947.

Elsasser, Nan, Kyle MacKenzie, and Yvonne Tixier y Vigil. *Las Mujeres: Conversations from a Hispanic Community*. New York: Feminist Press, 1980. [Photographs by Susan Trowbridge.]

Enciclopedia Universal Sopena: Diccionario Ilustrado de la Lengua Española, vol. 4. Barcelona: Sopena, 1972.

Engh, Michael S.J. "Companion of the Immigrants: Devotion to Our Lady of Guadalupe among Mexicans in the Los Angeles Area, 1900–1940." *Journal of Hispanic Latino Theology* 5 (1997): 37–43.

Erevia, Angela. *Quinceañera*. San Antonio, TX: Mexican American Cultural Center, 1980.

Ernest Baughman Collection. Zimmerman Library, University of New Mexico, Albuquerque, 1974.

Escalera, Jose. "Curanderos in Our Time." In *Chicano Border Culture and Folklore*, edited by Jose Villarino and Arturo Ramirez. San Diego, CA: Marin Publications, 1992.

Espinel, Luisa. *Canciones de Mi Padre*. Tucson: University of Arizona Press, 1946.

Espinosa, Aurelio Macedonio. "New Mexico Spanish Folklore: Myths, Superstitions, and Beliefs." *Journal of American Folklore* 23 (1910): 395–418.

———. *The Spanish Language in New Mexico and Southern Colorado*. Historical Society of New Mexico Series No. 16. Santa Fe, NM: New Mexican Printing Company, 1911.

———. *Cuentos Populares Españoles Recogidos de la Tradición Oral de España y Publicados con una Introducción y Notas Comparativas*. Stanford University Publications, University Series. Language and Literature 3 (1). Stanford, CA: Stanford University Press, 1923.

———. "*Los Romances Tradicionales en California*." In *Homenaje a Menéndez Pidal* series no. 3: 299–313. Madrid, Spain: Impreta de los Sucesores de Hernando, 1925.

———. *Folklore de California*. Palma, Mallorca: "Circulo de Estudios," 1930.

———. "The Field of Spanish Folklore in America." *Southern California Quarterly* 5 (March 1941): 29–35.

———. *The Folklore of Spain in the American Southwest: Traditional Spanish Folk Literature in Northern New Mexico and Southern Colorado*. Edited by J. Manuel Espinosa. Norman: University of Oklahoma Press, 1985.

Espinosa, Aurelio Macedonio, ed. *Los Comanches: A Spanish Heroic Play of the Year Seventeen Hundred and Eighty*. University of New Mexico Language series 1 (1). Albuquerque: University of New Mexico Press, 1907.

Espinosa, Aurelio M., and Jose Manuel Espinosa. "Los Tejanos, A New Mexican Spanish Popular Dramatic Composition of the Middle of the Nineteenth Century." *Hispania* 27 (October 1944): 291–314.

Espinosa, Aurelio Macedonio, Jr. "Spanish-American Folklore." *Journal of American Folklore* 60 (1947): 373–377.

Espinosa, Carmen. *Shawls, Crinolines, Filigree*. El Paso: University of Texas at El Paso, 1970.

Espinosa, Gilberto. "New Mexico Santos." *New Mexico State Magazine* 13 (March, April, May 1935).

———. *Heroes, Hexes, and Haunted Halls*. Albuquerque, NM: Calvin Horn Publisher, Inc., 1972.

Espinosa, Jose E. *Saints in the Valleys: Christian Sacred Images in the History, Life, and Folk Art of Spanish New Mexico.* Albuquerque: University of New Mexico Press, revised edition, 1967. [First edition 1960.]

Espinosa, Jose Manuel. *Spanish Folk-Tales from New Mexico.* New York: American Folklore Society, 1937.

———. "Spanish Folklore in the Southwest: The Pioneer Studies of Aurelio M. Espinosa." *The Americas* 35 (1978): 219–237.

Estrada, Francisco Guero. "Prison Culture and the Chicano." *La Raza* 1 (1971): 54–57.

Farr, Marcia. "*Echando Relajo:* Verbal Art and Gender among Mexicanas in Chicago." In *Cultural Performances: Proceedings of the Third Berkeley Women and Language Conference, April 8, 9, 10, 1994,* edited by Mary Bucholtz, A. C. Liang, Laurel A. Sutton, and Caitlin Hines. Berkeley: Berkeley Women and Language Group, University of California, 1994.

Fernandez Mines, Rosa. "Hispanic Wedding Customs in New Mexico: Yesterday and Today." *Selected Proceedings of the 3rd Annual Conference on Minority Studies,* Vol. 3, April 1975. In *Essays on Minority Folklore.* La Crosse: University of Wisconsin Press, 1977, pp. 129–140.

Ferriss, Susan, and Ricardo Sandoval. *The Fight in the Fields: César Chávez and the Farm Workers Movement.* New York: Harcourt Brace, 1997. [Photographs.]

Fisher, Nora. *Rio Grande Textiles.* Santa Fe: Museum of New Mexico Press, 1994. [Photographs.]

Fisher, Reginald Gilbert. *The Way of the Cross: A New Mexico Version.* Santa Fe, NM: School of American Research, 1958.

Flores, Arturo Conrado. *El Teatro Campesino de Luis Valdez.* Tucson: University of Arizona, 1986. [Dissertation.]

Flores, Richard R. "The Corrido and the Emergence of Texas-Mexican Social Identity." *Journal of American Folklore* 105 (1992): 166–182.

———. *Los Pastores: History and Performance in the Mexican Shepherd's Play of South Texas.* Washington, DC: Smithsonian Institution Press, 1995. [Bibliography.]

Florescano, Enrique. *The Myth of Quetzalcoatl.* Translated by Raul Velazquez. Baltimore, MD: Johns Hopkins University Press, 1999.

Flores-Turney, Camille, "La Muerte: Oscar Lozoya Embraces the Many Shades of Death." *New Mexico Magazine,* October 1996, 42–46.

Ford, Karen Cowan. *Las Yerbas de la Gente: A Study of Hispano-American Medicinal Plants.* Anthropological Papers No. 60, Museum of Anthropology. Ann Arbor: University of Michigan Press, 1975.

Foster, George M. "Cofradía and Compadrazgo in Spain and Spanish America." *Southwestern Journal of Anthropology* 9 (Spring 1953): 1–28.

———. "Relationships between Spanish and Spanish-American Folk Medicine." *Journal of American Folklore* 66 (1953): 201–217.

Foster, Nellie. *The Corrido: A Mexican Culture Trait Persisting in Southern California.* Los Angeles: University of Southern California, 1939. [Thesis.]

Foster, Nelson, and Linda S. Cordell. *Chiles to Chocolate: Food the Americas Gave the World.* Tucson: University of Arizona Press, 1992.

Frank, Larry. *New Kingdom of the Saints: Religious Art of New Mexico, 1780–1907.* Santa Fe, NM: Red Crane Books, 1992. [Photographs; appendices; bibliography.]

Freedman, Samuel G. "Los Lobos: Hot North-of-the-Border Mexican Rock." *Utne Reader* 22 (July–August 1987): 92–98.

Fregoso, Rosa Linda. *The Bronze Screen: Chicana and Chicano Film Culture.* Minneapolis: University of Minnesota Press, 1993.

———. "Homegirls, Cholas, and Pachucas in Cinema: Taking Over the Public Sphere." *California History* 3 (Fall 1995): 317–327.

Freud, Sigmund. *Jokes and Their Relation to the Unconscious.* New York: Norton, 1960.

Frias, Gus. *Barrio Warriors: Homeboys of Peace.* Los Angeles, CA: Diaz Publications, 1982.

Fusion, Robert H. "The Origin of the Word Gringo." In *Singers and Storytellers,* edited by Mody C. Boatright et al. Publications of the Texas Folklore Society No. 30. Dallas, TX: Southern Methodist University Press, 1961.

Galarza, Ernesto. *Merchants of Labor: The Mexican Bracero Story: An Account of the Managed Migration of Mexican Farm Workers in California, 1942–1960.* San Jose, CA: Rosicrucian Press, 1964.

———. *Barrio Boy.* Notre Dame, IN: University of Notre Dame Press, 1971.

Galindo, Letticia D. "Dispelling the Male-Only Myth: Chicanas and *Caló.*" *The Bilingual Review/La Revista Bilingüe* 17 (1992): 3–35.

———. "The Language of Gangs, Drugs, and Prison Life among Chicanas." *Latino Studies Journal* (September 1993): 23–43.

Gallegos, Esperanza. "The Piñata-Making Tradition in Laredo." In *Hecho en Tejas: Texas-Mexican Folk Arts and Crafts,* edited by Joe S. Graham. Denton: University of Texas Press, 1991.

Galván, Roberto A., and Richard V. Teschner. *El Diccionario del Español Chicano/The Dictionary of Chicano Spanish.* Lincolnwood, IL: National Textbook Company, 1985. [Includes proverbs and sayings; bibliography.]

García, Nasario. *Recuerdos de los Viejitos: Tales of the Rio Puerco.* Albuquerque: University of New Mexico Press, 1987. [Portraits by Isabel A. Rodriguez; bilingual.]

———. *Abuelitos: Stories of the Rio Puerco Valley.* Albuquerque: University of New Mexico Press, 1992. [Photographs.]

———. *Tata: A Voice from the Rio Puerco.* Albuquerque: University of New Mexico Press, 1994. [Photographs.]

———. *Comadres: Hispanic Women of the Rio Puerco Valley.* Albuquerque: University of New Mexico Press, 1997a. [Glossary.]

———. *Mas Antes: Hispanic Folklore of the Rio Puerco Valley.* Santa Fe: Museum of New Mexico Press, 1997b.

García, Richard A. "César Chávez: A Personal and Historical Testimony." *Pacific Historical Review* 63 (May 1994): 225–234.

Garza-Falcon, Leticia. *Gente Decente: A Borderland Response to the Rhetoric of Dominance.* Austin: University of Texas Press, 1998.

Gavin, Robin Farwell. *Traditional Arts of Spanish New Mexico: The Hispanic Heritage Wing at the Museum of International Folk Art.* Santa Fe: Museum of New Mexico Press, 1994.

Genz, Fred W. *El Baile de los Cascarones (Cascarones Ball).* Davis: Department of Avian Sciences, University of California, 1970. [Bibliography.]

Gil, Carlos B. "Lydia Mendoza: Houstonian and First Lady of Mexican American Song." In *Chicano Border Culture and Folklore,* edited by Jose Villarino and Arturo Ramirez. San Diego, CA: Marin Publications, Inc., 1992.

Gilbert, Fabiola Cabeza de Baca. *Historic Cookery.* Las Vegas, NM: La Galería de los Artesanos, 1970.

Glantz, Margo, ed. *La Malinche, Sus Padres y Sus Hijos.* Mexico: Faculdad de Filosofía y Letras, Universidad Nacional Autónoma de Mexico, 1994.

Glazer, Mark. "La Muerte: Continuity and Social Organization in a Chicano Legend." *Southwest Folklore* 4 (Winter 1980): 1–13.

——. "The Rio Grande Folklore Archive: A Summary of Methods of Collection, of Classification, and of Holdings." *Southwest Folklore* 5 (1981a): 16–23.

——. "*La Sirena del Mar:* An Interpretation of Symbolism, Disobedience, and Transformation in a Mexican-American Example." *Southwest Folklore* 5 (1981b): 55–69.

——. "Continuity and Change in Legends: Two Mexican American Examples." In *Perspectives on Contemporary Legend: Proceedings of the Conference on Contemporary Legend.* Conference Papers Series No. 4, edited by Paul Smith. Sheffield, UK: Center for English Cultural Tradition and Language (CECTAL), 1984.

——. "The Mexican American Legend in the Rio Grande Valley: An Overview." *Borderlands* 10 (Fall 1986): 143–160.

——. *A Dictionary of Mexican American Proverbs.* New York: Greenwood Press, 1987a.

——. "Mexican-American Culture and Urban Legend: The Case of the Vanishing Hitchhiker." *Urban Resources* 4 (1987b): 31–36.

——. *Flour from Another Sack and Other Proverbs, Folk Beliefs, Tales, Riddles, and Recipes.* Rev. ed. Edinburg, TX: Pan American University Press, 1994. [Bibliography.]

Goldberg, Julia. "Rita Younis: The Next Generation in the Delgado Tin Tradition." *Spanish Market* (July 1994): 20–21.

Goldman, Dorie S. "Down for La Raza: Barrio Art T-shirts, Chicano Pride, and Cultural Resistance." *Journal of Folklore Research* 34 (May–August 1997): 123–139.

Goldman, Shifra M. "Mexican Muralism: Its Social-Educative Roles in Latin America and the United States." *Aztlán: International Journal of Chicano Studies Research* 13 (1982): 111–134.

——. "How, Why, Where, and When It All Happened: Chicano Murals of California." In *Signs from the Heart: California Chicano Murals,* edited by Holly Barnet-Sanchez with an introduction by Eva Sperling Cockcroft. Venice, CA: Social and Public Art Resource Center, 1990a.

——. "The Iconography of Chicano Self-Determination: Race, Ethnicity, and Class." *Art Journal* (Summer 1990b): 167–173.

Gomez, Antonio. "Barriology Exam." *Con Safos: Reflections of Life in the Barrio* 2 (1970a): 34–35. [Answers on page 44.]

——. "Barriology Exam #3." *Con Safos: Reflections of Life in the Barrio* 6 (Summer 1970b): 18–19. [Answers on page 47.]

——. "Barriology Exam." In *The Chicanos: Mexican American Voices,* edited by Ed Ludwig and James Santibanez. Baltimore, MD: Penguin Books, 1971.

Gomez-Peña, Guillermo. *Warrior for Gringostroika: Essays, Performance Texts, and Poetry.* St. Paul, MN: Graywolf Press, 1993.

——. *The New World: Prophecies, Poems, and Loqueras for the End of the Century.* San Francisco, CA: City Lights, 1996.

——. "Mexican Beasts and Living Santos." *The Drama Review* (Cambridge, MA) 41 (Spring 1997): 135–147.

Gomez-Peña, Guillermo, and Roberto Sifuentes. *Temple of Confessions: Mexican Beasts and Living Santos.* New York: PowerHouse Books, 1996.

Gonzales, Alicia Maria. "Murals—Fine, Popular, or Folk Art?" *Aztlán: International Journal of Chicano Studies Research* 13 (1982): 149–163.

Gonzáles, Dolores, ed. *Canciones y Juegos de Nuevo Mexico/Songs and Games of New Mexico.* Writers' Program of the Works Progress Administration, New Mexico. South Brunswick, NJ: A. S. Barnes, 1974.

Gonzales, Rodolfo. *I Am Joaquin/Yo Soy Joaquin*. New York: Bantam Books, Inc., 1972. [Copyright 1967.]

Gonzales-Berry, Erlinda, ed. *Paso por Aqui: Critical Essays on the New Mexican Literary Tradition*. Albuquerque: University of New Mexico Press, 1989.

González, Jovita. *Social Life in Cameron, Starr, and Zapata Counties*. Austin: University of Texas, 1930a. [Master's thesis.]

————. "Tales and Songs of the Texas-Mexicans." In *Man, Bird, and Beast*, edited by J. Frank Dobie. Dallas, TX: Southern Methodist University Press, 1930b.

González, Jovita, and Eve Raleigh. *Caballero: A Historical Novel*. Edited by José Limón and María Cotera. College Station: Texas A&M University Press, 1996.

Gonzalez, Maria del Refugio. *The Spanish Folklore of Webb and Zapata Counties*. Austin: University of Texas, 1952. [Master's thesis.]

Gonzalez Obregon, Luis. *Las Calles de Mexico: Leyendas y Sucedidos*. Mexico: Ediciones Botas, 1947.

Gosnell, Lynn, and Suzanne Gott. "San Fernando Cemetery: Decorations of Love and Loss in a Mexican-American Community." In *Cemeteries and Gravemarkers: Voices of American Culture*, edited by Richard E. Meyer. Logan: Utah State University Press, 1992.

Govenar, Alan. "The Variable Context of Chicano Tattooing." In *Marks of Civilization: Artistic Transformations of the Human Body*, edited by Arnold Rubin. Los Angeles: Museum of Cultural History, University of California at Los Angeles, 1988. [Illustrations.]

Gradante, William. "Low and Slow, Mean and Clean." *Natural History* 91 (1982): 28–39.

————. "Mexican Popular Music at Mid-Century: The Role of José Alfredo Jimenez and the Canción Ranchera." *Studies in Latin American Popular Culture* 2 (1983): 99–114.

————. "Art among the Low Riders." In *Folk Art in Texas*, edited by Francis Edward Abernethy. Dallas, TX: Southern Methodist University Press, 1985, 71–77.

Graham, Joe S. "The Caso: An Emic Genre of Folk Narrative." In *And Other Neighborly Names: Social Process and Cultural Image in Texas Folklore*, edited by Richard Bauman and Roger D. Abrahams. Austin: University of Texas Press, 1981.

————. "Folk Medicine and Intracultural Diversity among West Texas Mexican Americans." *Western Folklore* 49 (1985): 168–193.

————. *Hispanic-American Material Culture: An Annotated Directory of Collections, Sites, Archives, and Festivals in the United States*. New York: Greenwood Press, 1989.

————. *Tejano Folk Arts and Crafts in South Texas/Artesania Tejana*. Kingsville, TX: John E. Conner Museum, 1990.

————. "The Jacal in South Texas: The Origins and Form of a Folk House." In *Hecho en Tejas: Texas-Mexican Folk Arts and Crafts*, edited by Joe S. Graham. Denton: University of North Texas Press, 1991.

————. *El Rancho in South Texas: Continuity and Change from 1750*. Denton: University of North Texas Press, 1993. [Bibliography; photographs.]

Graham, Joe S., ed. *Hecho en Tejas: Texas-Mexican Folk Arts and Crafts*. Denton: University of North Texas Press, 1991. [Photographs; bibliography.]

Greenwood, Robert. *The California Outlaw: Tiburcio Vásquez*. Los Gatos, CA: Talisman Press, 1966.

Grider, Sylvia Ann. "*Con Safos*: Mexican American Names and Graffiti." *Journal of American Folklore* 88 (1975): 132–142. [Illustrations.]

Griffith, Beatrice. *American Me*. Boston: Houghton Mifflin Co., 1948.

Griffith, James S. *Respect and Continuity: The Arts of Death in a Border Community*. Nogales, AZ: Pimeria Alta Historical Society, 1985.

———. *Southern Arizona Folk Arts*. Tucson: University of Arizona Press, 1988.

———. "Quetzalcoatl on the Border? Mestizo Water Serpent Beliefs of the Pimeria Alta." *Western Folklore* 49 (October 1990): 391–400.

———. *Beliefs and Holy Places: A Spiritual Geography of the Pimeria Alta*. Tucson: University of Arizona Press, 1992.

———. "Cascarones: A Folk Art Form of Southern Arizona." *International Folklore Review: Folklore Studies from Overseas* 9 (1993): 34–40.

———. *A Shared Space: Folklife in the Arizona-Sonora Borderlands*. Logan: Utah State University Press, 1995. [Bibliography; illustrations.]

Grimes, Ronald L. *Symbol and Conquest: Public Ritual and Drama in Santa Fe, New Mexico*. London: Cornell University Press, 1976. [Bibliography.]

Griswold del Castillo, Richard. *The Los Angeles Barrio, 1850–1890: A Social History*. Berkeley: University of California Press, 1979. [Bibliography.]

Griswold del Castillo, Richard, and Richard A. García. *César Chávez: A Life of Struggle and Sacrifice*. Norman: University of Oklahoma Press, 1995.

Griswold del Castillo, Richard, and Rita Sanchez. "The Corrido de César Estrada Chávez: A Need to Remember." In *Aztlán Chicano Culture and Folklore: An Anthology*, edited by Jose Pepe Villarino and Arturo Ramirez. New York: McGraw-Hill Companies, Inc., 1997.

Griswold del Castillo, Richard, Teresa McKenna, and Yvonne Yarbro-Bejarano, eds. *Chicano Art: Resistance and Affirmation, 1965–1985*. Los Angeles: Wight Art Gallery, University of California at Los Angeles, 1991.

Guerra, Fermina. *Mexican and Spanish Folklore and Incidents in Southwestern Texas*. Austin: University of Texas, 1941. [Master's thesis.]

Guevara, Ruben. "The View from the Sixth Street Bridge: The History of Chicano Rock." In *The First Rock & Roll Confidential Report*, edited by Dave Marsh. New York: Pantheon Books, 1985.

Guillen, Claudio. *Literature as System: Essays Toward a Theory of Literary History*. Princeton, NJ: Princeton University Press, 1971.

Gutierrez, David G. *Walls and Mirrors: Mexican Americans, Mexican Immigrants, and the Politics of Ethnicity*. Berkeley: University of California Press, 1995. [Bibliography.]

Gutierrez, Jose Angel. *A Gringo Manual on How to Handle Mexicans*. Crystal City, TX: Wintergarden Publishing House, 1973.

Gutiérrez, Ramón A. "The Politics of Theater in Colonial New Mexico." In *Reconstructing a Chicano/a Literary Heritage: Hispanic Colonial Literature of the Southwest*, edited by Maria Herrera-Sobek. Tucson: University of Arizona Press, 1993.

———. "*El Santuario de Chimayo*: A Syncretic Shrine in New Mexico." In *Feasts and Celebrations in North American Ethnic Communities*, edited by Ramón A. Gutiérrez and Genevieve Fabre. Albuquerque: University of New Mexico Press, 1995.

Gutiérrez, Ramón A., and Genevieve Fabre, eds. *Feasts and Celebrations in North American Ethnic Communities*. Albuquerque: University of New Mexico Press, 1995.

Hague, Eleanor. *Spanish-American Folk-Songs*. Memoirs of the American Folklore Society, vol. 10. Lancaster, PA: The American Folklore Society, 1917.

Hall, Douglas Kent. "*Los Matachines*: Dancers Keep Old World Tradition Alive." *New Mexico Magazine*, December 1986, 42–47. [Photographs.]

Hallenbeck, Cleve, and Juanita H. Williams. *Legends of the Spanish Southwest*. Ann

Arbor, MI: Gryphon Books, 1971. [First published in 1938 by Arthur H. Clark & Company.]

Hand, Wayland D. "The Evil-Eye in Its Folk Medical Aspects: A Survey of North America." In *The Evil Eye: A Folklore Casebook*, edited by Alan Dundes. New York: Garland Publishing, Inc., 1981.

Haralson, Marianne. "Joyful Customs Reign at Mexican Weddings." *San Antonio Express News*, June 15, 1980.

Harpole, Patricia. *Los Mariachis! An Introduction to Mexican Mariachi Music*. Danbury, CT: World Music Press, 1990. [Audiotape.]

Harris, Mary G. *Cholas: Latino Girls and Gangs*. New York: AMS Press, 1988. [Bibliography.]

———. "Cholas, Mexican-American Girls, and Gangs." *Sex Roles* 30 (1994): 289–301.

Harris, Max. "Muhammed and the Virgin: Folk Dramatizations of Battles between Moors and Christians in Modern Spain." *The Drama Review* (Cambridge, MA) 38 (Spring 1994): 45–62.

———. "Moctezuma's Daughter: The Role of La Malinche in Mesoamerican Dance." *Journal of American Folklore* 109 (Spring 1996): 149–177.

———. "The Return of Moctezuma: Oaxaca's 'Danza de la Pluma' and New Mexico's 'Danza de los Matachines'." *The Drama Review* (Cambridge, MA) 41 (Spring 1997): 106–135.

Harris, Pauline Beatrice. *Spanish and Mexican Folklore as Represented in Two Families in the Detroit Area*. Wayne State University, Dept. of Spanish & Italian, 1949. [Master's thesis.]

Harwell, Thomas Meade. *Studies in Texan Folklore, Rio Grande Valley Lore: Twelve Folklore Studies with Introductions, Commentaries and a Bounty of Notes*. Lewiston, ID: E. Mellen Press, 1997.

Hattersley-Drayton, Karana, Joyce M. Bishop, and Tomás Ybarra-Frausto, eds. *From the Inside Out: Perspectives on Mexican and Mexican-American Folk Art*. San Francisco, CA: The Mexican Museum, 1989.

Hawes, Bess Lomax. "La Llorona in Juvenile Hall." *Western Folklore* 27 (1968): 153–170.

Heisley, Michael. "Lummis and Mexican-American Folklore." In *Chas. F. Lummis: The Centennial Exhibition Commemorating His Tramp across the Continent*, edited by Daniela P. Moneta. Los Angeles, CA: Southwest Museum, 1985.

Heisley, Michael, and Mary MacGregor-Villarreal. *More Than a Tradition: Mexican American Nacimientos in Los Angeles*. Los Angeles, CA: Southwest Museum, 1991. [Glossary.]

Henderson, Alice Corbin. *Brothers of Light: The Penitentes of the Southwest*. New York: Harcourt, Brace & Company, 1937. [Illustrated by William Penhallow Henderson; bibliography.]

Heredia, Christopher. "Hombres: Latinos Tackle Macho Image." *Los Angeles Times*, November 8, 1992.

Hernandez, Guillermo. *Canciones de La Raza*. Berkeley, CA: El Fuego de Aztlán, 1978.

Hernández-Chavez, Eduardo, Andrew D. Cohen, and Anthony F. Beltramo. *El Lenguaje de los Chicanos: Regional and Social Characteristics Used by Mexican Americans*. Arlington, VA: Center for Applied Linguistics, 1975.

Herrera-Sobek, Maria. *The Bracero Experience: Elitelore versus Folklore*. Los Angeles: University of California Press, 1979. [Bibliography.]

———. "Chicano Literary Folklore." In *Chicano Studies: A Multi-disciplinary Approach*, edited by Eugene Francisco A. Lomeli and Isidro Ortiz Garcia. New York: Teachers College Press, 1984.

———. "The Discourse of Love and Despecho: Representations of Women in the Chicano Décima." *Aztlán, International Journal of Chicano Studies Research* 18 (Spring 1987): 69–82.

———. "The Devil in the Discotheque: A Semiotic Analysis of a Contemporary Legend." In *Monsters with Iron Teeth: Perspectives on Contemporary Legend*, vol. 3, edited by Gillian and Paul Smith Bennett. Sheffield, UK: Sheffield Academic Press, for the International Society for Contemporary Legend Research in Association with the Centre for English Cultural Tradition and Language, 1988.

———. *The Mexican Corrido: A Feminist Analysis*. Bloomington: Indiana University Press, 1990. [Bibliography.]

———. "Corridos and Canciones of Mica, Migra, and Coyotes: A Commentary on Undocumented Immigration." In *Creative Ethnicity: Symbols and Strategies of Contemporary Ethnic Life*, edited by Stephen Stearn and John Allan Cicala. Logan: Utah State University Press, 1991.

———. "Toward the Promised Land: La Frontera as Myth and Reality in Ballad and Song." *Aztlán: International Journal of Chicano Studies Research* 21 (1–2) (1992–1996): 227–261.

———. "The *Comedia de Adan y Eva* and Language Acquisition." In *Reconstructing a Chicano/a Literary Heritage: Hispanic Colonial Literature of the Southwest*, edited by Maria Herrera-Sobek. Tucson: University of Arizona Press, 1993a.

———. *Northward Bound: The Mexican Immigrant Experience in Ballad and Song*. Bloomington: Indiana University Press, 1993b. [Bibliography; discography; index.]

———. "The Mexican/Chicano Pastorela: Toward a Theory of the Evolution of a Folk Play." In *Feasts and Celebrations in North American Ethnic Communities*, edited by Ramon A. Gutiérrez and Genevieve Fabre. Albuquerque: University of New Mexico Press, 1995a.

———. "Social Protest, Folklore, and Feminist Ideology in Chicana Prose and Poetry." In *Folklore, Literature, and Cultural Theory: Collected Essays*, edited by Cathy Lynn Preston. New York: Garland Publishing, Inc., 1995b.

———. "The Corrido as Hypertext: Undocumented Mexican Immigrant Films and the Mexican/Chicano Ballad." In *Culture across Borders: Mexican Immigration and Popular Culture*, edited by David R. Maciel and Maria Herrera-Sobek. Tucson: University of Arizona Press, 1998.

Heyman, Josiah. "The Oral History of the Mexican American Community of Douglas, Arizona, 1901–1942." *Journal of the Southwest* 35 (1993): 186–206.

Hinckle, Catherine J. "The Devil in New Mexican Spanish Folklore." *Western Folklore* 8 (1949): 123–125.

Hinojosa, Francisco G. "Notes on the Pachuco: Stereotypes, History, and Dialect." *Atisbos: Journal of Chicano Research* (Summer 1975): 53–65.

Hispanic Culture Foundation. *The Flow of the River/Corre el Rio*. Albuquerque, NM: Hispanic Culture Foundation, 1991. [Photographs.]

Holden, William. *Teresita*. Owings Mills, MD: Stemmer House, 1978.

Holscher, Louis M., Celestino Fernandez, and Laura L. Cummings. "From Local Tradition to International Phenomenon: La Bamba." *Renato Rosaldo Lecture Series Monograph Series 1989–1990*, no. 7. Tucson: Mexican American Studies and Research Center, University of Arizona, 1991. [Bibliography.]

Homenaje a Nuestras Curanderas/Honoring Our Healers. Ed. Luz Alvarez. Oakland, CA: Latina Press, 1996.

Horcasitas, Fernando, and Douglas Butterworth. "La Llorona." *Tlalocan* 4 (1963): 204–224.

Horka-Follick, Lorayne Ann. *Los Hermanos Penitentes: A Vestige of Medievalism in Southwestern United States*. Los Angeles, CA: Westernlore Press, 1969. [Bibliography.]

Horowitz, Ruth. "The Power of Ritual in a Chicano Community: A Young Woman's Status and Expanding Family Ties." *Marriage and Family Review* 19 (Winter 1993): 257–281.

Horvath, Steven M., Jr. *The Social and Political Organization of the Genízaros of Plaza de Nuestra Señora de los Dolores de Belén, New Mexico, 1740–1812*. Providence, RI: Brown University Press, 1979. [Dissertation.]

Howe, Charles E. B. "Joaquín Murieta de Castillo." In *California Gold-Rush Plays*, edited with an introduction by Glenn Loney. New York: Performing Arts Journal Publications, 1983. [Play originally published in 1859.]

Hudson, Wilson M. *The Healer of Los Olmos and Other Mexican Lore*. Dallas, TX: Southern Methodist University Press, 1951.

———. "The Twelve Truths in the Spanish Southwest." In *Mesquite and Willow*, edited by Mody C. Boatright. Publications of the Texas Folklore Society No. 27. Dallas, TX: Southern Methodist University Press, 1957. [Bibliography.]

Huerta, Jorge A. *A Bibliography of Chicano and Mexican Dance, Drama, and Music*. Oxnard, CA: Colegio Quetzalcoatl, 1972.

———. *Chicano Theater: Themes and Forms*. Ypsilanti, MI: Bilingual Press, 1982.

Hurt, Wesley R. "The Spanish-American Comanche Dance." *Journal of Folklore Institute* 3 (1966): 116–132.

Husband, Eliza. *Geography of a Symbol: The Hispanic Yard Shrines of Tucson, Arizona*. Tucson: University of Arizona, 1985. [Master's thesis.]

Igo, John N., Jr. "Los Pastores: A Triple Tradition." *Journal of Popular Culture* 19 (Winter 1985): 131–138.

Ingalls, Zoe. "Studying New Mexico's 'Saddest Songs.'" *Chronicle of Higher Education*, September 13, 1996, B11.

Jackson, Joseph Henry. *Bad Company: The Story of California's Legendary and Actual Stage-robbers, Bandits, Highwaymen and Outlaws from the Fifties to the Eighties*. New York: Harcourt, Brace and Co., 1949.

Jaramillo, Cleofas M. *Romance of a Little Village Girl*. San Antonio, TX: Naylor Co., 1955.

———. *Shadows of the Past; Sombras del Pasado*. Santa Fe, NM: Ancient City Press, 1972. [First edition 1941; illustrated by the author.]

———. *The Genuine New Mexico Tasty Recipes*. Santa Fe, NM: Ancient City Press, 1981.

Jasper, Pat, and Kay Turner, eds. *Art among Us/Arte entre Nosotros: Mexican American Folk Art of San Antonio*. San Antonio, TX: San Antonio Museum of Art, 1986.

Jiménez, Carlos M. *The Mexican American Heritage*. Berkeley, CA: TQS Publications, 1992.

Johnston, Francis W. *The Wonder of Guadalupe: The Origin and Cult of the Miraculous Image of the Blessed Virgin in Mexico*. Chulmleigh, Devon, UK: Augustine Pub. Co., 1981.

Jordan, Rosan A. "Ethnic Identity and the Lore of the Supernatural." *Journal of American Folklore* 88 (1975): 370–382.

———. "Tension and Speech Play in Mexican-American Folklore." In *And Other Neighborly Names: Social Process and Cultural Image in Texas Folklore*, edited by Richard Bauman and Roger D. Abrahams. Austin: University of Texas Press, 1981.

———. "The Vaginal Serpent and Other Themes from Mexican-American Women's Lore." In *Women's Folklore, Women's Culture*, edited by Rosan A. Jordan and Susan J. Kalcik. Publications of the American Folklore Society, New Series. Philadelphia: University of Pennsylvania Press, 1985, pp. 25–44.

Jordan, Terry G. *Texas Graveyards: A Cultural Legacy*. Austin: University of Texas Press, 1982.

Jordan de Caro, Rosan. "A Note about Folklore and Literature (The Bosom Serpent Revisited)." *Journal of American Folklore* 86 (1973): 62–65.

———. *The Folklore and Ethnic Identity of a Mexican American Woman*. Indianapolis: Indiana University, 1975. [Dissertation.]

Kalb, Laurie Beth. *Crafting Devotions: Tradition in Contemporary New Mexico Santos*. Albuquerque: University of New Mexico Press, 1994. [Photographs; bibliography.]

Kanellos, Nicolas. *A History of Hispanic Theatre in the United States: Origins to 1940*. Austin: University of Texas Press, 1990.

Kanellos, Nicolas, ed. *Mexican American Theatre: Then and Now*. Houston, TX: Arte Público Press, 1983.

———. *Mexican American Theater: Legacy and Reality*. Pittsburgh, PA: Latin American Literary Review Press, 1987.

Kaplan, Lawrence, and Lucille N. Kaplan. "Beans of the Americas." In *Chilies to Chocolate: Food the Americas Gave the World*, edited by Nelson and Linda S. Cordell Foster. Tucson: University of Arizona Press, 1992.

Katz, Linda Fine. *The Evolution of the Pachuco Language and Culture*. Los Angeles: University of California Press, 1974. [Master's thesis in English as a Second Language.]

Kay, Margarita Artschwager. "Health and Illness in a Mexican American Barrio." In *Ethnic Medicine in the Southwest*, edited by Edward H. Spicer. Tucson: University of Arizona Press, 1977.

Kearney, Michael. "A World-View Explanation of the Evil Eye." In *The Evil Eye*, edited by Clarence Maloney. New York: Columbia University Press, 1976. [Bibliography.]

Keller, Gary D., ed. *Chicano Cinema: Research, Reviews, and Resources*. Binghamton, NY: Bilingual Review/Press, 1985. [Filmography.]

Keller, Randall G. "The Past in the Present: The Literary Continuity of Hispanic Folklore in New Mexico and the Southwest." *Bilingual Review* 16 (1991): 99–157.

Kennedy, Diana. *The Tortilla Book*. New York: Harper & Row, 1975. [Drawings by Sidonie Coryn.]

Kim, Sojin. *Chicano Graffiti and Murals: The Neighborhood Art of Peter Quezada*. Jackson: University Press of Mississippi, 1995. [Color plates.]

Kitchener, Amy V. "Windows into the Past: Mexican American Yardscapes in the Southwest." Tucson, AZ: Small Manuscripts Collection, Southwest Folklore Center, University of Arizona Library, December 19, 1987. [Unpublished paper.]

———. *The Holiday Yards of Florencio Morales: El Hombre de Las Banderas*. Jackson: University Press of Mississippi, 1994. [Photographs; bibliography.]

———. "La Cadena Que no Se Corta: Las Artes Tradicionales de la Comunidad Mexico-Americana de Tucson/The Unbroken Chain: The Traditional Arts of Tucson's Mexican-American Community." *Journal of American Folklore* 110 (1997): 320–323.

Klette, Ernest. *The Crimson Trail of Joaquín Murieta*. Los Angeles, CA: Wetzel Publishing Co., 1928.

Lafaye, Jacques. *Quetzalcóatl y Guadalupe: La Formación de la Consciencia en Mexico 1531–1813*. Mexico: Fondo de Cultura Económica, 1983.

Lamadrid, Enrique R. "*Entre Cíbolos Criado:* Images of Native Americans in the Popular Culture of Colonial New Mexico." In *Reconstructing a Chicano/a Literary Heritage: Hispanic Colonial Literature of the Southwest,* edited by Maria Herrera-Sobek. Tucson: University of Arizona Press, 1993.

———. *Tesoros del Espíritu: A Portrait in Sound of Hispanic New Mexico*. Embudo, NM: El Norte/Academia Publications, 1994.

———. "The Rogue's Progress: Journeys of the Picaro from Oral Tradition to Contemporary Chicano Literature of New Mexico." *Multi-Ethnic Literature of the United States* 20 (Summer 1995): 15–35.

Lane, James B., and Edward J. Escobar, eds. *Forging a Community: The Latino Experience in Northwest Indiana, 1919–1975.* Chicago, IL: Cattails Press, 1987. [Anthology.]

Larcombe, Samuel. "Pioneer Project Explores the Meaning of Roadside Crosses." *Hispanic Market,* July 1994.

Laval, Ramon A. *Cuentos de Pedro Urdemales*. Santiago de Chile: Cruz del Sur, 1943.

LaWare, Margaret R. "Encountering Visions of Aztlán: Arguments for Ethnic Pride, Community Activism and Cultural Revitalization in Chicano Murals." *Argumentation and Advocacy* 34 (Winter 1998): 140–154.

Lea, Aurora Lucero-White. *Literary Folklore of the Hispanic Southwest*. San Antonio, TX: Naylor Company, 1953.

Leal, Luis. "Américo Paredes and Modern Mexican American Scholarship." *Ethnic Affairs* 1 (Fall 1987): 1–11.

———. *No Longer Voiceless*. San Diego, CA: Marin Publications, 1995.

———. "Joaquín Murrieta in Literature." In *Aztlán: Chicano Culture and Folklore: An Anthology,* edited by Jose Pepe Villarino and Arturo Ramirez. New York: McGraw-Hill Companies, Inc., 1997.

Leander, Birgitta. *In Xochitl in Cuicatl. Flor y Canto: La Poesía de los Aztecas*. Mexico: Instituto Nacional Indigenista, 1972.

Leddy, Betty. "La Llorona in Southern Arizona." *Western Folklore* 7 (1948): 272–277.

Leon Portilla, Miguel. *Los Antiguos Mexicanos: A Través de Sus Crónicas y Cantares*. Mexico: Fondo de Cultura Economica, 1961.

Levy, Jacques E. *César Chávez: Autobiography of La Causa*. New York: Norton, 1975.

Limón, Jose E. "*El Folklore y Los Mexicanos en Los Estados Unidos: Una Perspectiva Cultural Marxista*." In *La Otra Cara de Mexico: El Pueblo Chicano,* compiled by David R. Maciel. Mexico: Ediciones "El Caballito," 1977.

———. *Expressive Culture of a Chicano Student Group at the University of Texas at Austin, 1967–1975*. Austin: University of Texas, 1978. [Dissertation.]

———. "Américo Paredes: A Man from the Border." *Revista Chicano-Riqueña* 8 (1980a): 1–5.

———. "'La Vieja Inés': A Mexican Folkgame—A Research Note." In *Twice a Minority: Mexican American Women,* edited by Margarita B. Melville. St. Louis, MO: C. V. Mosby Company, 1980b.

———. "The Folk Performance of 'Chicano' and the Cultural Limits of Political Ideology." In *And Other Neighborly Names: Social Process and Cultural Image in Texas Folklore,* edited by Richard Bauman and Roger D. Abrahams. Austin: University of Texas Press, 1981.

———. "History, Chicano Joking, and the Varieties of Higher Education: Tradition and Performance as Critical Symbolic Action." *Journal of the Folklore Institute* 19 (2–3) (1982): 141–166.

———. "Texas-Mexican Popular Music and Dancing: Some Notes on History and Symbolic Process." *Latin American Music Review* 4 (1983): 229–246.

———. *The Return of the Mexican Ballad: Américo Paredes and His Anthropological Text as Persuasive Political Performance*. Working Paper Series No. 16. Stanford, CA: Stanford Center for Chicano Research, 1986.

———. "Agringado Joking in Texas Mexican Society." *Perspectives in Mexican American Studies* 1 (1988a): 109–127.

———. "La Llorona, the Third Legend of Greater Mexico: Cultural Symbols, Women, and the Political Unconscious." In *Between Borders: Essays on Mexicana/ Chicana History*, edited by Adelaida R. Castillo. Los Angeles, CA: Floricanto Press, 1988b.

———. "Oral Tradition and Poetic Influence: Two Poets from Greater Mexico." In *Redefining American Literary History*, edited by A. Lavonne Brown and Jerry W. Ward Jr. New York: Modern Language Association of America, 1990.

———. *Mexican Ballads, Chicano Poems: History and Influence in Mexican American Social Poetry*. Berkeley: University of California Press, 1992. [Bibliography.]

———. "Folklore, Gendered Repression, and Cultural Critique: The Case of Jovita González." *Texas Studies in Literature and Language* 35 (Winter 1993): 453–473.

———. *Dancing with the Devil: Society and Cultural Poetics in Mexican-American South Texas*. Madison: University of Wisconsin Press, 1994.

———. *American Encounters: Greater Mexico, the United States, and the Erotics of Culture*. Boston, MA: Beacon Press, 1998.

Lipsitz, George. *Time Passages: Collective Memory and American Popular Culture*. Minneapolis: University of Minnesota Press, 1990.

Lockpez, Inverna, ed. *Chicano Expressions: A New View in American Art*. New York: INTAR Latin American Gallery, 1986.

Lomas, Juan. *Teoria y Practica del Insulto Mexicano/Pueblo Mexicano: Una Recopilación de Juan Lomas*. Mexico: Posada, 1974.

Lomas Garza, Carmen. *Making Magic Windows: Creating Papel Picado/Cut-Paper Art with Carmen Lomas Garza*. San Francisco, CA: Children's Book Press/Libros para Niños, 1999.

Lopez, Ella T. *Make Mine Menudo: Chicano Cook Book*. La Puente, CA: Sunburst Enterprises, 1976.

Lopez-Stoppard, Gloria. *A Place in El Paso: A Mexican American Childhood*. Albuquerque: University of New Mexico Press, 1996.

Loza, Steven Joseph. "Origins, Form, and Development of the Son Jarocho: Veracruz, Mexico." *Aztlán, International Journal of Chicano Studies Research* 13 (1982): 257–274.

———. *The Musical Life of the Mexican/Chicano People in Los Angeles, 1945–1985: A Study in Maintenance, Change, and Adaptation*. Los Angeles: University of California, 1985. [Dissertation.]

———. *Barrio Rhythm: Mexican American Music in Los Angeles*. Urbana: University of Illinois Press, 1993. [Bibliography.]

Lucero-White, Aurora. *Folk-Dances of the Spanish-Colonials of New Mexico*. Santa Fe, NM: Examiner Publishing Co., 1940. [Music transcribed by Eunice Hauskins. Patterns and descriptions of dances by Helene Mareau.]

———. *The Folklore of New Mexico*, vol. 1. Santa Fe, NM: Seton Village Press, 1941.

———. *Los Hispanos: Five Essays on the Folkways of the Hispanos as Seen through the Eyes of One of Them*. Denver, CO: Sage Books, Inc., 1947.

Lucero-White, Aurora, ed. and trans. *Coloquios de Los Pastores*. Santa Fe, NM: Santa Fe Press, 1940.

Luckenbill, Dan. *The Pachuco Era: Catalog of an Exhibit*. Los Angeles: Department of Special Collections, University Research Library, University of California, 1990. [Photographs.]

Lummis, Charles F. *Spanish Songs of Old California*. Los Angeles, CA: Charles F. Lummis, 1923a.

———. *Stand Fast Santa Barbara!: Save the Centuried Romance of Old California in This, Its Last and Most Romantic Stronghold: Sense, Sentiment, Business*. Santa Barbara, CA: Community Arts Association, 1923b.

MacAulay, Suzanne. *Colcha Embroidery along the Northern Rio Grande: The Aesthetics of Cultural Inversion in San Luis, Colorado*. Philadelphia: University of Pennsylvania, 1992. [Dissertation.]

MacGregor-Villarreal, Mary. "Celebrating Las Posadas in Los Angeles." *Western Folklore* 39 (1980): 71–105.

Macias, Ysidro Ramon. "The Evolution of the Mind." *El Pocho Che* 1 (1969): 13–20.

Maciel, David R. "Pochos and Other Extremes in Mexican Cinema: or, El Cine Mexicano Se Va de Bracero, 1922–1963." In *Chicanos and Film: Representation and Resistance*, edited by Chon A. Noriega. Minneapolis: University of Minnesota Press, 1992.

Macklin, June. "'All the Good and Bad in This World': Women, Traditional Medicine, and Mexican American Culture." In *Twice a Minority: Mexican American Women*, edited by Margarita B. Melville. St. Louis, MO: Mosby, 1980.

MacLean, Angus. *Legends of the California Bandidos*. Fresno, CA: Pioneer Publishing, 1977. [Illustrations.]

Madrid-Barela, Arturo. "In Search of the Authentic Pachuco: An Interpretive Essay." *Aztlán: Chicano Journal of the Social Sciences and the Arts* 4 (Spring 1973): 31–60. [Bibliography.]

———. "Alambristas, Braceros, Mojados, Norteños: Aliens in Aztlán, An Interpretative Essay." *Aztlán: International Journal of Chicano Studies Research* 6 (Spring 1975): 27–42.

———. "Pochos: The Different Mexicans, An Interpretive Essay, Part I." *Aztlán: International Journal of Chicano Studies Research* 7 (Spring 1976): 51–64.

Madsen, William. "The Alcoholic Agringado." *American Anthropologist* 66 (1964): 356–357.

Marks, Susan Tosaw. "Low Riding: One Road to an Ethnic Identity." *Southwest Folklore* 4 (Winter 1980): 40–50.

Martin, Patricia Preciado. *Images and Conversations: Mexican Americans Recall a Southwestern Past*. Tucson: University of Arizona Press, 1983. [Photographs by Louis Carlos Bernal.]

———. *Days of Plenty, Days of Want*. Tempe, AZ: Bilingual Press/Editorial Bilingüe, 1988.

———. *Songs My Mother Sang to Me: An Oral History of Mexican American Women*. Tucson: University of Arizona Press, 1992.

———. *El Milagro and Other Stories*. Tucson: University of Arizona Press, 1996.

Martinez, Cervando, and Harry W. Martin. "Folk Diseases among Urban Mexican-Americans: Etiology, Symptoms, and Treatment." *Journal of the American Medical Association* 196 (April 11, 1966): 147–150.

Martinez, Thomas M. "Chicanismo." *Epoca* (National Concilio for Chicano Studies) 1 (Winter 1971): 35–39.

Martinez, Yleana. "Cracking Cascarones." *Hispanic* (March 1996): 49–50. [Photographs.]

Martinez-Chavez, Diana. "Quinceañeras." *Hispanic* (October 1989): 11–12.

Mather, Christine. *Colonial Frontiers*. Santa Fe, NM: Ancient City Press, 1983. [Color plates.]

———. *True West: Arts, Traditions, and Celebrations*. New York: C. Potter, 1992. [Photographs by Jack Parsons.]

Mazon, Mauricio. *The Zoot-Suit Riots: The Psychology of Symbolic Annihilation*. Austin: University of Texas Press, 1984. [Bibliography.]

McDowell, John Holmes. *Children's Riddling*. Bloomington: Indiana University Press, 1979.

McNutt, James Charles. *Beyond Regionalism: Texas Folklorists and the Emergence of a Post-Regional Identity*. Austin: University of Texas, 1982. [Dissertation.]

McWilliams, Cary. *North from Mexico: The Spanish-Speaking People of the United States*. New York: Greenwood Press, 1968. [Copyright 1948.]

Medina, Frank. *Once Upon a Cotton Picking Time*. New York: Vantage Press, 1975.

Meed, Douglas V. *Bloody Border: Riots, Battles, and Adventures along the Turbulent U.S.-Mexican Borderlands*. Tucson, AZ: Westernlore Press, 1992.

Meléndez, Theresa. "Coyote: Towards a Definition of a Concept." *Aztlán: International Journal of Chicano Studies Research* 13 (1982): 295–307. [Bibliography.]

———. "The Coyote." In *American Wildlife in Symbol and Story*, edited by Angus K. Gillespie and Jay Mechling. Knoxville: University of Tennessee Press, 1987.

Melville, Margarita B. "The Mexican American and the Celebration of the Fiestas Patrias: An Ethnohistorical Analysis." *Grito del Sol* 3 (1978): 107–116.

Mencken, H. L. *The American Language: An Inquiry into the Development of English in the United States*, Supplements 1 and 2. New York: Knopf, 1945–1948.

Mendoza, Vicente T. "Some Forms of the Mexican Canción." In *Singers and Storytellers*, edited by Mody C. Boatright. Dallas, TX: Southern Methodist University Press, 1961a.

———. *La Canción Mexicana: Ensayo de Clasificación y Antología*. Mexico: Universidad Nacional Autónoma de Mexico, 1961b.

Mendoza-Denton, Norma. "Gender and Ideology in Gang-Girls' Discourse about Makeup." *Ethnos* 61 (1996): 47–63.

———. *Chicana/Mexicana Identity and Linguistic Variation: An Ethnographic and Sociolinguistic Study of Gang Affiliation in an Urban High School*. Stanford, CA: Stanford University, 1997. [Dissertation.]

Meo Zilio, Giovanni. *Diccionario de Gestos; España e Hispanoamérica*. Bogota, Colombia: Instituto Caro y Cuervo, 1980–1983.

Mesa-Bains, Amalia. "'Domesticana': The Sensibility of Chicana Rasquache." *Aztlán: Chicano Journal of the Social Sciences and the Arts* 24 (Fall 1999): 157–167.

Miller, Elaine K. *Mexican Folk Narratives from the Los Angeles Area*. Publications of the American Folklore Society, Memoir series 5, no. 56. Austin: University of Texas Press, 1973.

Mills, George. *The People of the Saints*. Colorado Springs, CO: Taylor Museum of the Colorado Springs Fine Arts Center, 1967.

Mintz, Sidney W., and Eric R. Wolf. "An Analysis of Ritual Co-Parenthood (Compadrazgo)." *Southwestern Journal of Anthropology* 6 (1950): 341–368.

Mirandé, Alfredo. *The Chicano Experience: An Alternative Perspective*. Notre Dame, IN: University of Notre Dame Press, 1985. [Bibliography.]

———. "Que Gacho es Ser Macho: It's a Drag to Be a Macho Man." *Aztlán: International Journal of Chicano Studies Research* 17 (1986): 63–89.

———. *Hombres y Machos: Masculinity and Latino Culture*. Boulder, CO: Westview Press, 1997. [Bibliography; photographs.]

Mireles, Jovita Gonzalez. *Dew on the Thorn*. Edited and introduced by José E. Limón. Houston, TX: Arte Público Press, 1997.

Monday, Jan Clements, and Betty Bailey Colley. *Voices from the Wild Horse Desert*. Austin: University of Texas Press, 1997.

Monreal, David. *Cinco de Mayo: An Epic Novel*. Encino, CA: Floricanto Press, 1993.

Monsalvo, Sergio C. *La Canción del Inmigrante: De Aztlán a Los Lobos*. Mexico: Tinta Negra Editores, 1989.

Monsiváis, Carlos. "The Culture of the Frontier: The Mexican Side." In *Views across the Border: The United States and Mexico*, edited by Stanley R. Ross. Albuquerque: University of New Mexico Press, 1978.

Montano, Mario. *The History of Mexican Folk Foodways of South Texas: Street Vendors, Offal Foods, and Barbacoa de Cabeza*. Pittsburgh: University of Pennsylvania Press, 1992. [Dissertation.]

Montoya, Jose. *Jose Montoya's Pachuco Art: A Historical Update*. Sacramento, CA: Royal Chicano Air Force, 1977.

Montoya, Lori J. "El Kookoóee Destroys Fear at Festival de Otoño." *New Mexico Daily Lobo*, "In Sync," October 12, 1994.

Moore, Joan W. *Going down to the Barrio*. Philadelphia, PA: Temple University Press, 1991.

Moore, Joan, James Diego Vigil, and Josh Levy. "Huisas of the Street: Chicana Gang Members." *Latino Studies Journal* 6 (January 1995): 27–48. [Bibliography.]

Moore, Michael. *Los Remedios: Traditional Herbal Remedies of the Southwest*. Santa Fe, NM: Red Crane Books, 1990. [Illustrated by Mimi Kamp.]

Mora, Carl J. *Mexican Cinema: Reflections of a Society 1896–1980*. Berkeley: University of California Press, 1982. [Bibliography; photographs.]

Morrison, Suzanne Shumate. *Mexico's "Day of the Dead" in San Francisco, California: A Study of Continuity and Change in a Popular Religious Festival*. Berkeley, CA: Graduate Theological Union, 1992. [Dissertation.]

Muñoz, Carlos Jr. "Reclaiming Our Heritage: Carlos Muñoz, Jr. Discusses Cinco de Mayo and the Politics of Identity." *CrossRoads* 10 (May 1991): 2–4.

Muñoz Camargo, Diego, ca. 1529–1599. *Descripción de la Ciudad y Provincia de Tlaxcala de las Indias y del Mar Oceano para el Buen Gobierno y ennoblecimiento dellas*. Ed. facsimil del ms. de Glasgow, con un estudio preliminar de Rene Acuna, 1a ed. Mexico: Instituto de Investigaciones Filológicas, Universidad Nacional Autónoma de Mexico, 1981.

Museum of International Folk Art. *Spanish Textile Tradition of New Mexico and Colorado*. Series in Southwestern Culture. Santa Fe: Museum of New Mexico Press, 1979. [Photographs.]

Myal, Suzanne. *Introduction to Tucson's Mexican Restaurants*. Tucson, AZ: Fiesta Publications, 1997.

Myers, Joan. *Santiago: Saint of Two Worlds*. Albuquerque: University of New Mexico, 1991. [Photographs by Joan Myers; essays by Marc Simmons, Donna Pierce, and Joan Myers.]

Najera-Ramirez, Olga. "Greater Mexican Folklore in the United States: An Annotated Bibliography." *Ethnic Affairs* 1 (Fall 1987): 64–115.

———. "Social and Political Dimensions of Folklorico Dance: The Binational Dialectic of Residual and Emergent Culture." *Western Folklore* 48 (January 1989): 15–32.

———. "Engendering Nationalism: Identity, Discourse, and the Mexican Charro." *Anthropological Quarterly* 67 (1994a): 1–14.

———. "Fiestas Hispanicas: Dimensions of Hispanic Festivals and Celebrations," in

Handbook of Hispanic Cultures in the United States, edited and introduced by Thomas Weaver; general editors, Nicolas Kanellos and Claudio Esteva-Fabregat. Houston, TX: Arte Público Press. Madrid: Instituto de Cooperación Iberoamericana, 1994b, pp. 328–338.

———. "The Racialization of a Debate: The Charreada as Tradition or Torture." *American Anthropologist* 98 (September 1996): 505–511.

———. "La Charreada! Rodeo a la Mexicana." San Jose, CA: UCSC/KTEH Production, 1997.

Nelson, Eugene. *The Bracero, A Novel*. Berkeley, CA: Thorp Springs Press, 1971.

Neruda, Pablo. *Fulgor y Muerte de Joaquín Murrieta, Bandido Chileno Injusticiado en California el 23 de Julio de 1853*. Santiago de Chile: Zig-Zag, 1966.

The New Handbook of Texas. 6 vols. Ron Tyler, editor in chief; Douglas E. Barnett, managing editor. Austin: Texas State Historical Association, 1996.

Nieto-Gomez, Anna. "Women in Mexican History: 'Cinco de Mayo.'" SOMOS 2 (May 1979): 16–20.

Niggli, Josephina. *Mexican Folk Plays*. Chapel Hill: University of North Carolina, 1938.

Noriega, Chon A., ed. *Chicanos and Film: Representation and Resistance*. Minneapolis: University of Minnesota Press, 1992.

Nuiry, Octavio Emilio. "Ban the Bandito!" *Hispanic* (July 1996): 26–32.

Oktavec, Eileen. *Answered Prayers: Miracles and Milagros along the Border*. Tucson: University of Arizona, 1995. [Photographs; bibliography.]

Ord, Angustias de la Guerra. *Occurrences in Hispanic California*. Translated and edited by Francis Price and William E. Ellison. Washington, DC: Academy of American Franciscan History, 1956.

Ornelas, Richard Garnica. *Folk Tales of the Spanish Southwest*. Los Angeles: University of Southern California, 1962. [Dissertation.]

Orona-Cordova, Roberta. "Zoot Suits and the Pachuco Phenomenon: An Interview with Luis Valdez." In *Chicano Border Culture and Folklore*, edited by Jose and Arturo Ramirez Villarino. San Diego, CA: Marin Publications, Inc., 1992.

Ortega, Adolfo. *Caló Tapestry*. Berkeley, CA: Editorial Justa Publications, Inc., 1977.

———. *Caló Orbis: Semiotic Aspects of a Chicano Language Variety*. American University Studies, Series 13, Linguistics, vol. 21. New York: P. Lang, 1991.

Ortega, Pedro Ribera. *Christmas in Old Santa Fe*. Santa Fe, NM: Sunstone Press, 1973. [Illustrated by Orlando Padilla; first edition 1961.]

Ortiz, Almudena. *Fiesta de Quinceañera: Queen for a Day*. Berkeley: University of California, 1992. [Master's thesis.]

Ortiz de Monetllano, Bernard. "Caída de Mollera: Aztec Sources for a Mesoamerican Disease of Alleged Spanish Origin." *Ethnohistory* 34 (Fall 1987): 381–399.

Ortiz y Pino, Yolanda. *Original Native New Mexican Cooking*. Santa Fe, NM: Sunstone Press, 1993.

Ortiz y Pino de Dinkel, Reynalda, and Dora Gonzales de Martinez, comps. *Una Colección de Adivinanzas y Diseños de Colcha/A Collection of Riddles and Colcha Designs*. Santa Fe, NM: Sunstone Press, 1988.

Otero, Miguel Antonio. *Otero, An Autobiographical Trilogy*. 3 vols. New York: Arno Press, 1974.

Otero-Warren, Nina. *Old Spain in Our Southwest*. New York: Harcourt, Brace & Company, 1936.

Pacheco, Luz. "La Paz: A Tale of Two Cities (Bolivia). *UNESCO Courier* (March 1997): 28–31. [Includes Short Article on Cholos.]

Padilla, Genaro. "Imprisoned Narrative? Or Lies, Secrets, and Silence in New Mexico Women's Autobiography." In *Criticism in the Borderlands: Studies in Chicano Literature, Culture, and Ideology*, edited by Hector Calderon and Jose David Saldivar. Durham, NC: Duke University Press, 1991.

Paredes, Américo. *With His Pistol in His Hand: A Border Ballad and Its Hero*. Austin: University of Texas Press, 1958.

———. "On Gringo, Greaser, and Other Neighborly Names." In *Singers and Storytellers*, edited by Mody C. Boatright et al. Publications of the Texas Folklore Society, No. 30. Dallas, TX: Southern Methodist University Press, 1961.

———. "Ancestry of Mexico's Corridos: A Matter of Definitions." *Journal of American Folklore* 76 (1963): 231–235.

———. "The Anglo-American in Mexican Folklore." In *New Voices in American Studies*, edited by Ray B. Browne, Donald M. Winkelman, and Allen Hayman. Lafayette, IN: Purdue University Press, 1966a, pp. 113–128.

———. "*El Folklore de los Grupos de Origen Mexicano en Estados Unidos.*" *Folklore Americano* 14 (1966b): 146–163.

———. "Mexican Legendry and the Rise of the Mestizo: A Survey." In *American Folk Legend: A Symposium*, edited, with a preface, by Wayland D. Hand. Berkeley: University of California Press, 1971, pp. 97–107.

———. *A Texas-Mexican Cancionero: Folksongs of the Lower Border*. Urbana: University of Illinois Press, 1976.

———. "Ethnographic Work among Minority Groups: A Folklorist's Perspective." In *New Directions in Chicano Scholarship*, edited by Ricardo and Raymund Paredes Romo. La Jolla: Chicano Studies Center, University of California, San Diego, 1978.

———. "Folklore, Lo Mexicano, and Proverbs." *Aztlán: International Journal of Chicano Studies Research* 13 (1982): 1–11.

———. *Folklore and Culture on the Texas-Mexican Border*. Austin: Center for Mexican American Studies, University of Texas, 1993a. [Bibliography.]

———. *Uncle Remus con Chile*. Houston, TX: Arte Público Press, 1993b.

Paredes, Américo, ed. and trans. *Folktales of Mexico*. Chicago: University of Chicago Press, 1970.

Paredes, Américo, and George Foss. "The Décima Cantada on the Texas-Mexican Border: Four Examples." *Journal of the Folklore Institute* 3 (1966): 91–111.

Parsons, Jack. *Straight from the Heart: Portraits of Traditional Hispanic Musicians*. Essay by Jim Sagel. Albuquerque: University of New Mexico Press, 1990. [Photographs.]

———. *Low 'n Slow: Lowriding in New Mexico*. Text by Carmella Padilla; poetry by Juan Estevan Arellano. Santa Fe: Museum of New Mexico Press, 1999.

"La Pastorela/The Shepherds' Tale." Video. Written and directed by Luis Valdez, produced by Richard D. Soto. San Juan Bautista, CA: El Teatro Campesino, 1991.

Paz, Octavio. *The Labyrinth of Solitude: Life and Thought in Mexico*. New York: Grove Press, 1961.

Pearce, T. M. "The New Mexican Shepherds' Play." *Western Folklore* 16 (1957): 263–280.

Pearlman, Steven Ray. *Mariachi Music in Los Angeles*. Los Angeles: University of California, 1988. [Dissertation.]

Peña, Manuel. "Ritual Structure in a Chicano Dance." *Latin American Music Review* 1 (1980): 47–73.

———. "The Emergence of Conjunto Music, 1935–1955." In *And Other Neighborly Names: Social Process and Cultural Image in Texas Folklore*, edited by Richard Bauman and Roger D. Abrahams. Austin: University of Texas Press, 1981.

———. *The Texas-Mexican Conjunto: History of a Working Class Music*. Austin: University of Texas Press, 1985a. [Bibliography.]

———. "From Ranchero to Jaitón: Ethnicity and Class in Texas-Mexican Music (Two Styles in the Form of a Pair)." *Ethnomusicology* 29 (Winter 1985b): 29–55.

———. "Notes Toward an Interpretive History of California-Mexican Music." In *From the Inside Out: Perspectives on Mexican and Mexican-American Folk Art*, edited by Karana Hattersley-Drayton, Joyce M. Bishop, and Tomás Ybarra-Frausto. San Francisco, CA: The Mexican Museum, 1989.

———. "Class, Gender, and Machismo: The 'Treacherous-Woman' Folklore of Mexican Male Workers." *Gender and Society* 5 (1991): 30–46.

———. "*Musica Fronteriza*/Border Music." *Aztlán: International Journal of Chicano Studies Research* 21 (1992–1996): 191–226.

Perez, Soledad. "Susto." In *Texas Folk and Folklore*, edited by Mody Coggin Boatright. Dallas, TX: Southern Methodist University Press, 1954.

Perl, Lila. *Piñatas and Paper Flowers*. Translated by Alma Flor Ada. New York: Clarion Books, 1983.

Perrigo, Lynn. *Hispanos: Historic Leaders in New Mexico*. Santa Fe, NM: Sunstone Press, 1985.

Perrone, Bobette. *Medicine Women, Curanderas, and Women Doctors*. Norman: University of Oklahoma Press, 1989.

Perry, Ann. "Tejano Festivals: Celebrations of History and Community." In *Hispanic Texas: A Historical Guide*, edited by Helen Simons and Cathryn A. Hoyt. Austin: University of Texas Press, 1992.

Peyton, James W. *La Cocina de la Frontera: Mexican-American Cooking from the Southwest*. Santa Fe, NM: Red Crane Books, 1994.

Phillips, Susan A. *Wallbaggin': Graffiti and Gangs in L.A.* Chicago, IL: University of Chicago Press, 1999.

Pierce, Donna, ed. "Santa Fe's Fiesta." *El Palacio* 91 (Spring 1985): 7–17. [Bibliography.]

Pilcher, Jeffrey M. *Que Vivan los Tamales!: Food and the Making of Mexican Identity*. Albuquerque: University of New Mexico Press, 1998.

"Los Pintos de America." *De Colores Journal* 3 (1) (1976): 4.

Pitt, Leonard. *The Decline of the Californios: A Social History of the Spanish-Speaking Californians, 1846–1890*. Berkeley: University of California Press, 1966. [Bibliography.]

Plascencia, Luis F. "Low Riding in the Southwest: Cultural Symbols in the Mexican Community." In *History, Culture, and Society: Chicano Studies in the 1980s*, edited by Mario Garcia et al. Ypsilanti, MI: Bilingual Press/Editorial Bilingüe, 1983.

Ponce, Mary Helen. *The Wedding*. Houston, TX: Arte Público Press, 1989.

———. *Hoyt Street*. Albuquerque: University of New Mexico Press, 1993.

Ponce, Merrihelen. *The Lives and Works of Five Hispanic New Mexican Women Writers, 1878–1991*. Albuquerque: Southwest Hispanic Research Institute, University of New Mexico, 1992.

Portilla, Jorge. *Fenomenología del Relajo, y Otros Ensaysos*. Mexico: Edicione Era, 1966.

Portillo, Lourdes, and Susana Muñoz. *La Ofrenda: The Days of the Dead*. 50-min. videorecording. San Francisco, CA: Xochitl Films, 1990.

Powell, Philip Wayne. *Tree of Hate: Propaganda and Prejudices Affecting United States Relations with the Hispanic World*. New York: Basic Books, 1971.

Quintana, Patricia. *The Taste of Mexico*. Photography by Ignacio Urguiza. New York: Stewart, Tabori & Chang, 1986.

Quirarte, Jacinto. "Sources of Chicano Art: Our Lady of Guadalupe." *Explorations in Ethnic Studies* 15 (1992): 13–26.

Rael, Juan B. "New Mexican Spanish Feasts." *California Folklore Quarterly* 1 (1942): 83–90.

———. *The New Mexican Alabado.* Language and Literature Series, vol. 9, no. 3. Stanford, CA: Stanford University Press, 1951.

Rael, Juan B., and Reyes Martinez. *Cuentos Españoles de Colorado y de Nuevo Méjico.* 2 vols. Stanford, CA: Stanford University Press, 1957. [Reprinted by Arno Press, 1977.]

———. *The Sources and Diffusion of the Mexican Shepherds' Plays.* Guadalajara, Mexico: Librería la Joyita, 1965.

———. "Arroyo Hondo, Penitentes, Weddings, Wakes." *El Palacio* 81 (1975): 3–19. [Includes excerpts from WPA files; excerpted from an article in the *California Folklore Quarterly,* 1940 by Juan B. Rael.]

Rafael, Hermes. *Origen e Historia del Mariachi.* Mexico: Editorial Katún, 1983.

Ramirez, Emilia Schunior. *Ranch Life in Hidalgo County after 1850.* Edinburg, TX: New Santander Press, 1971.

Ramirez, Marc. "Rockin' Teacher Speaks the Language of Youth." *Seattle Times,* May 17, 1997, p. A6.

Ramos, Art. "Mexican-American Yard Art in Kingsville." In *Hecho en Tejas: Texas-Mexican Folk Arts and Crafts,* edited by Joe S. Graham. Denton: University of North Texas Press, 1991.

Ramos, Charles. "Spanish American Devil Lore in Southern Colorado." *Western Folklore* 9 (January 1950): 50–55.

Ramos, Samuel. *Profile of Man and Culture in Mexico.* Austin: University of Texas Press, 1962.

Rebolledo, Tey Diana. "Las Escritoras: Romances and Realities." In *Paso por Aqui: Critical Essays on the New Mexico Literary Tradition,* edited by Erlinda Gonzales-Berry. Albuquerque: University of New Mexico Press, 1989.

———. "Y Donde Estaban las Mujeres?: In Pursuit of an Hispana Literary and Historical Heritage in Colonial New Mexico, 1580–1840." In *Reconstructing a Chicano/a Literary Heritage,* edited by Maria Herrera-Sobek. Tucson: University of Arizona Press, 1993.

———. "Introduction." In *We Fed Them Cactus,* edited by Fabiola Cabeza de Baca. Albuquerque: University of New Mexico Press, 1994.

Rebolledo, Tey Diana, and Eliana S. Rivero. *Infinite Divisions: An Anthology of Chicana Literature.* Tucson: University of Arizona Press, 1993.

"Rekindling the Flame." *New Mexico Magazine,* December 1986, pp. 35–39. [Photographs.]

Reyna, Jose Reynaldo. *Mexican American Prose Narrative in Texas: The Jest and Anecdote.* Los Angeles: University of California Press, 1973. [Dissertation.]

———. *Folklore Chicano del Valle de San Luis, Colorado.* San Antonio, TX: Penca Books, 1980a.

———. *Modismos de Tejas.* San Antonio, TX: Penca Books, 1980b.

Reyna, Jose R., and Maria Herrera-Sobek. "Jokelore, Cultural Differences, and Linguistic Dexterity: The Construction of the Mexican Immigrant in Chicano Humor." In *Culture across Borders: Mexican Immigration and Popular Culture,* edited by David R. Macial and Maria Herrera-Sobek. Tucson: University of Arizona, 1998.

Ridge, John Rollin. *The History of Joaquín Murieta: The King of California Outlaws,*

Whose Band Ravaged the State in the Early Fifties. Hollister, CA: Evening Free Lance, 1927.

Riedel, Johannes. *Dale Kranque: Chicano Music and Art in South Texas*. St. Paul: University Media Resources, Dept. of Independent Study, Continuing Education and Extension, University of Minnesota, 1982.

Riley, Michael. "The Dangerous Mime: Historical Photographs, Narratives, and Cultural Representations." In *Collectanea: Papers in Folklore, Popular, and Expressive Culture*. Austin: Center for Intercultural Studies in Folklore and Ethnomusicology, University of Texas, 1990.

Rivera, Rick P. *A Fabricated Mexican*. Houston, TX: Arte Público Press, 1995.

Rivera, Rowena A. "New Mexican Colonial Poetry: Tradition and Innovation." In *Paso por Aqui: Critical Essays on the New Mexico Literary Tradition*, edited by Erlinda Gonzales-Berry. Albuquerque: University of New Mexico Press, 1989.

Rivera, Susan Madrid. *The Traditional Spanish Wedding Reflecting the Life Styles of a Spanish-Speaking Community*. University of Northern Colorado, 1976. [Dissertation.]

Rivera, Tomas. *Y No Se lo Trago la Tierra*. 2d ed. Translated by Evangelina Vigil-Piñon. Houston, TX: Arte Público Press, 1992.

Roach, Joyce Gibson. "The Legends of El Tejano, the Texan Who Never Was." *Western Folklore* 27 (1968): 33–42.

Robb, John Donald. *Hispanic Folk Songs of Hispanic New Mexico*. Albuquerque: University of New Mexico Press, 1954. [Arranged for piano and voice.]

———. "The Matachines Dance—A Ritual Folk Dance." *Western Folklore* 20 (1961): 87–101. [Music score.]

———. *Hispanic Folk Music of New Mexico and the Southwest: A Self-Portrait of a People*. Norman: University of Oklahoma Press, 1980.

Robe, Stanley L. "Four Mexican Exempla about the Devil." *Western Folklore* 10 (1951): 310–315.

———. "The Relationship of 'Los Pastores' to Other Spanish-American Folk Drama." *Western Folklore* 16 (1957): 281–289.

———. *Antología del Saber Popular: A Selection from Various Genres of Mexican Folklore across Borders*. Monograph No. 2. Los Angeles: Chicano Studies Center Publications, University of California, 1971.

———. "Problems in Mexican American Folk Tradition: The Southern California Scene." In *Contemporary Mexico: Papers of the Fourth International Congress of Mexican History*, edited by James Wilkie. Los Angeles: University of California Press, 1976.

Robe, Stanley, ed. *Hispanic Legends from New Mexico: Narratives from the R. D. Jameson Collection*. University of California Publications. Folklore and Mythology Studies, no. 31. Los Angeles: University of California Press, 1980.

Robertiello, Jack. "All Wrapped up in Tamales." *Americas* (English Edition) 48 (March–April 1996): 58–60.

Robinson, Willard B. "Colonial Ranch Architecture in Spanish-Mexican Tradition." *Southwestern Historical Quarterly* (October 1979): 123–150.

Rodriguez, Jeanette. *Our Lady of Guadalupe: Faith and Empowerment among Mexican-American Women*. Austin: University of Texas Press, 1994. [Bibliography.]

Rodriguez, Luis J. *Always Running, La Vida Loca: Gang Days in L.A.* New York: Touchstone Press, 1993.

Rodríguez, Mariángela. *Mito, Identidad y Rito*. Mexico: CIESAS, 1998.

Rodriguez, Roberto. *The X in La Raza: An Anti-Book*. Albuquerque, NM: Roberto Rodriguez, 1996.

Rodriguez, Sylvia. "Defended Boundaries, Precarious Elites: The Arroyo Seco Matachines Dance." *Journal of American Folklore* 107 (Spring 1994): 248–267.

———. *The Matachines Dance: Ritual Symbolism and Interethnic Relations in the Upper Rio Grande Valley*. Albuquerque: University of New Mexico Press, 1996. [Bibliography; photographs.]

Roeder, Beatrice A. *Chicano Folk Medicine from Los Angeles, California*. Folklore and Mythology Studies vol. 34. Berkeley: University of California Press, 1988.

Rojas, Arnold R. *Lore of the California Vaquero*. Fresno, CA: Academy Library Guild, 1958.

———. *Vaqueros and Buckeroos*. Bakersfield, CA: Hall Letter Shop, 1979.

Romano, Octavio. *Don Pedrito Jaramillo: The Emergence of a Mexican-American Folk-Saint*. Berkeley: University of California, 1964. [Dissertation.]

———. "Charismatic Medicine, Folk-Healing, and Folk Sainthood." *American Anthropologist* 67 (1965): 1151–1173.

Romero, Brenda. *The Matachines Music and Dance in San Juan Pueblo and Alcalde, New Mexico: Context and Meanings*. Los Angeles: University of California, 1993. [Dissertation.]

Romero, Jose Ruben. *La Vida Inútil de Pito Perez*. 2d ed. Mexico: Editorial Mexico Nuevo, 1938.

Romero, Orlando, and David Larkin. *Adobe: Building and Living with Earth*. New York: Houghton Mifflin Co., 1994. [Photographs.]

Romero Salinas, Joel. *La Pastorela Mexicana: Origen y Evolución*. Mexico: Cultura Fondo Nacional para el Fomento de las Artesanas, Fonart, 1984.

Romo, Ricardo. "Borderland Murals: Chicano Artifacts in Transition." *Aztlán: International Journal of Chicano Studies Research* 21 (1992–1996): 125–190.

Romotsky, Jerry, and Sally R. Romotsky. *Los Angeles Barrio Calligraphy*. Los Angeles, CA: Dawson's Book Shop, 1976. [Photographs.]

Rosaldo, Renato. *Culture and Truth: The Remaking of Social Analysis*. Boston, MA: Beacon Press, 1989.

Rosales, Francisco Arturo. *Chicano!: The History of the Mexican American Civil Rights Movement*. Houston, TX: Arte Público Press, 1996.

———. *Pobre Raza!: Violence, Justice, and Mobilization among Mexico Lindo Immigrants, 1900–1936*. Austin: University of Texas Press, 1999.

Rosensweig, Jay B. *Caló: Gutter Spanish*. New York: E. P. Dutton & Co., 1973.

Ross, Fred. *Conquering Goliath: César Chávez at the Beginning*. Keene, CA: United Farm Workers, 1989. Distributed by El Taller Grafico.

Rubel, Arthur J. "The Mexican-American Palomilla." *Anthropological Linguistics* 4 (1965): 92–97.

———. *Across the Tracks: Mexican-Americans in a Texas City*. Austin: University of Texas Press, 1966. [Bibliography.]

Rubel, Arthur J., Carl W. O'Neill, and Rolando Collado-Ardón. *Susto, A Folk Illness*. Berkeley: University of California Press, 1984. [Bibliography.]

Sagel, Jim. "La Comadre Sebastiana: The Flip Side of Death." *New Mexico Magazine* 70 (September 1992): 78–83.

Sagel, Jim, ed. "Caló Supplement." *Puerto del Sol* 27 (1992): 65–273.

Salas, Elizabeth. *Soldaderas in the Mexican Military: Myth and History*. Austin: University of Texas Press, 1990. [Bibliography.]

Salcedo, Michele. *Quinceañera! The Essential Guide to Planning the Perfect Sweet Fifteen Celebration*. New York: Henry Holt and Company, 1997. [Photographs; recipes.]

Salinas, Raúl. "A Trip through the Mind Jail (for Eldridge)." *La Raza* 1 (1970): 80.

Salinas-Norman, Bobbi. *Indo-Hispanic Folk Art Traditions: A Book of Culturally-based, Year-round Activities with an Emphasis on the Day of the Dead.* Oakland, CA: Piñata Publications, 1988. [Illustrated.]

Samora, Julian, Joe Bernal, and Albert Peña. *Gunpowder Justice: A Reassessment of the Texas Rangers.* Notre Dame, IN: University of Notre Dame, 1979.

Sanborn, Laura Sue. "Camposancos: Sacred Places of the Southwest." *Markers VI: The Journal of the Association for Gravestone Studies* 6 (1989): 158–179.

Sanchez, George J. *Becoming Mexican American: Ethnicity, Culture, and Identity in Chicano Los Angeles, 1900–1945.* New York: Oxford University Press, 1993.

Sanchez, Joseph P. *The Spanish Black Legend/La Leyenda Negra Española: Origins of Anti-Hispanic Stereotypes/Origenes de los Estereotipos Antihispánicos.* Series No. 2. Albuquerque, NM: Spanish Colonial Research Center, National Park Service, 1990.

Sanchez, Louis. "Some Unclassic Myths of California." *California Folklore Quarterly* 4 (1945): 58–63.

Sanchez, Rosaura. "Spanish Codes in the Southwest." In *Modern Chicano Writers: A Collection of Critical Essays,* edited by Joseph Sommers and Tomás Ybarra-Frausto. Englewood Cliffs, NJ: Prentice-Hall, Inc., 1979.

Sanchez, Thomas. *Zoot-suit Murders: A Novel.* New York: Dutton, 1978.

Sanchez-Tranquilino, Marcos. "Space, Power, and Youth Culture: Mexican American Graffiti and Chicano Murals in East Los Angeles, 1972–1978." In *Looking High and Low: Art and Cultural Identity,* edited by Brenda Jo Bright and Liza Bakewell. Tucson: University of Arizona, 1995.

Sandburg, Carl. *The American Songbag.* New York: Harcourt Brace Jovanovich, Inc., 1955.

Sanders, Clinton R. *Customizing the Body: The Art and Culture of Tattooing.* Philadelphia, PA: Temple University Press, 1989.

Sandoval, Annette. *Homegrown Healing: Traditional Home Remedies from Mexico.* New York: Berkley Books, 1998.

Sandoval, Ruben. *Games, Games, Games/Juegos, Juegos, Juegos: Chicano Children at Play—Games and Rhymes.* Garden City, NY: Doubleday & Co., Inc., 1977. [Photographs.]

Sands, Kathleen M. *Charrería Mexicana: An Equestrian Folk Tradition.* Tucson: University of Arizona Press, 1993.

———. "Charreada: Performance and Interpretation of an Equestrian Folk Tradition in Mexico and the United States." *Studies in Latin American Popular Culture* 13 (1994): 77–100.

Santamaria, Francisco Javier. *Diccionario de Mejicanismos, Razonado: Comprobado con citas de Autoridades, Comparado con el de Americanismos y con los Vocabularios Provinciales de los Mas Distinguidos Diccionaristas Hispano-Americanos.* Mexico: Ed. Porra, 1978.

Sawin, Patricia. *La Entrega de los Novios: Ritual and Resistance in 19th Century New Mexico.* Austin: University of Texas, 1985. [Master's thesis.]

Schander, Mary Lea. *Songs in the Air: Music of Early California.* Pasadena, CA: Hammers and Picks Publications, 1994. [Music score.]

Schmidt, Henry C. *The Roots of Lo Mexicano: Self and Society in Mexican Thought, 1900–1934.* College Station: Texas A&M University Press, 1978. [Bibliography.]

Sedillo, Mela. *Mexican and New Mexican Folkdances.* 2d ed. Albuquerque: University of New Mexico Press, 1950.

Señoras of Yesteryear: Mexican American Harbor Lights—Pictorial History. Indiana Harbor, IN: Señoras of Yesteryear, 1992. [Photographs.]

Seriff, Suzanne, and Jose E. Limón. "Bits and Pieces: The Mexican-American Folk Aesthetic." In *Art Among Us/Arte Entre Nosotros: Mexican American Folk Art of San Antonio*, edited by Pat Jasper and Kay Turner. San Antonio, TX: San Antonio Museum of Art, 1986.

Sewell Linck, Ernestine, and Joyce Gibson Roach. *Eats: A Folk History of Texas Foods*. Fort Worth: Texas Christian University Press, 1989. [Recipes.]

Shay, Anthony. "Fandangos and Bailes: Dancing and Dance Events in Early California." *Southern California Quarterly* 64 (Summer 1982): 99–113.

Sheehy, Daniel Edward. *The Son Jarocho: The History, Style, and Repertory of a Changing Musical Tradition*. Los Angeles: University of California, 1979. [Dissertation.]

Sheridan, Thomas E. *Los Tucsonenses: The Mexican Community in Tucson, 1854–1941*. Tucson: University of Arizona Press, 1986.

Sheridan, Thomas E., and Joseph Noriega. "From Luisa Espinel to Lalo Guerrero: Tucson's Mexican Musicians before World War II." In *Frontier Tucson: Hispanic Contributions*. Tucson: Arizona Historical Society, 1987.

Siegal, Nina. "Reclaiming Vasquez's West (Luis Valdez's 'Bandido!')." *American Theater* 11 (July–August 1994): 10.

Silverthorne, Elizabeth. *Christmas in Texas*. College Station: Texas A&M University Press, 1990. [Bibliography.]

Simmons, Marc. "Witchcraft and Black Magic: An Interpretive View." *El Palacio* 80, 1974a, pp. 5–11.

———. *Witchcraft in the Southwest: Spanish and Indian Supernaturalism on the Rio Grande*. Flagstaff, AZ: Northland Press, 1974b. [Bibliography.]

———. "La Mano Negra." *Santa Fe Reporter*, August 9–15, 1989, p. 2.

———. *Coronado's Land: Essays on Daily Life in Colonial New Mexico*. Albuquerque: University of New Mexico Press, 1991. [Bibliography.]

Simmons, Merle Edwin. *The Mexican Corrido as a Source for Interpretive Study of Modern Mexico, 1870–1950*. New York: Kraus Reprint Co., 1969.

Simons, Helen, and Cathryn A. Hoyt. *Hispanic Texas: A Historical Guide*. Austin: University of Texas Press, 1992. [Texas Historical Commission.]

Siporin, Steve. *American Folk Masters: The National Heritage Fellows*. New York: Harry N. Abrams, Inc., 1992.

Siporin, Steve, ed. *Folk Art of Idaho: "We Came to Where We Were Supposed to Be."* Boise: Idaho Commission on the Arts, 1984. [Photographs.]

Smethurst, James. "The Figure of the 'Vato Loco' and the Representation of Ethnicity in the Narratives of Oscar Z. Acosta." *Multi-Ethnic Literature of the United States* 20 (Summer 1995): 119–133.

Soloman, Madelyn Loes. *Some Mexican Folk Dances Found in Los Angeles*. Los Angeles: University of California, 1941. [Master's thesis.]

Sommers, Laurie Kay. "Symbol and Style in 'Cinco de Mayo.'" *Journal of American Folklore* 98 (October–December 1985): 476–482.

———. *Fiesta, Fe, y Cultura: Celebrations of Faith and Culture in Detroit's Colonia Mexicana*. Detroit: Casa de Unidad Cultural Arts and Media Center and Michigan State University, 1995. [Photographs.]

Sonnichsen, Philip. "Lalo Guerrero: Pioneer in Mexican American Music." *La Luz* 6 (May 1977): 11–14.

Soto, Shirlene. *"Tres Modelos Culturales: La Virgen de Guadalupe, La Malinche y La Llorona."* *Fem* 48 (October–November 1986): 13–16.

Spanish Colonial Arts Society. *Spanish New Mexico: The Spanish Colonial Arts Society Collection*. 2 vols. Edited by Donna Pierce and Marta Weigle; foreword by Anita Gonzales Thomas; photographs by Jack Parsons. Santa Fe: Museum of New Mexico Press, 1996.

Spicer, Edward H. *Ethnic Medicine in the Southwest*. Tucson: University of Arizona Press, 1977.

Spielberg, Joseph. "Humor in Mexican-American Palomilla: Some Historical, Social, and Psychological Implications." *Revista Chicano-Riqueña* 2 (1974): 41–50.

Sprott, Robert O. F. M. *Making up What Is Lacking: Towards an Interpretation of the Penitentes*. Working Paper Series No. 110. Albuquerque: Southwest Hispanic Research Institute, University of New Mexico, 1984. [Bibliography.]

Stark, Louisa R. "The Origin of the Penitente 'Death Cart.'" *Journal of American Folklore* 84 (1971): 305–307.

Stark, Richard Boies. *Music of the Spanish Folk Plays in New Mexico*. Santa Fe: Museum of New Mexico Press, 1969.

Starr, Frederick. *Catalogue of a Collection of Objects Illustrating the Folklore of Mexico*. London: The Folklore Society, 1899.

Steele, Thomas J., S.J. *Santos and Saints: Essays and Handbook*. Albuquerque, NM: Calvin Horn Publisher, Inc., 1974. [Appendices.]

———. *Hispanic Los Aguelos and Pueblo Tsave-Yohs*. Working Paper Series No. 120. Albuquerque: Southwest Hispanic Research Institute, University of New Mexico, 1992.

Steele, Thomas J., S.J., and Rowena A. Rivera. *Penitente Self-Government: Brotherhoods and Councils, 1797–1947*. Santa Fe, NM: Ancient City Press, 1985. [Appendices.]

Stewart, Marcus A. *Rosita: A California Tale*. San Jose, CA: Mercury Steam Print, 1882.

Stoller, Marianne L. "Traditional Hispanic Arts and Crafts in the San Luis Valley of Colorado." In *Hispanic Crafts of the Southwest: An Exhibition Catalogue*, edited by William Worth. Colorado Springs, CO: The Taylor Museum of the Colorado Springs Fine Arts Center, 1977.

———. "The Hispanic Women Artists of New Mexico: Present and Past." *El Palacio* 92 (Summer/Fall 1986): 21–25.

Stone, Michael Cutler. "Bajito y Sauvecito (Low and Slow): Low Riding and the 'Class' of Class." *Studies in Latin American Popular Culture* 9 (1990): 85–126.

Sturmberg, Robert. *History of San Antonio and the Early Days in Texas*. San Antonio, TX: St. Joseph's Society, 1920. [Photographs.]

Swenson, Ed. "Mexican-American Tent Shows on Permanent Exhibit at Hertzberg Collection in San Antonio." *The White Tops* 71 (July/August 1998): 15.

Tales Told in Our Barrio. Tucson, AZ: Carrillo School, 1984.

Taylor, Archer. "Folklore and the Student of Literature." In *The Study of Folklore*, edited by Alan Dundes. Englewood Cliffs, NJ: Prentice-Hall, 1965.

El Teatro Campesino: The Evolution of America's First Chicano Theatre Company, 1965–1985. San Juan Bautista, CA: El Teatro Campesino, 1985.

Thomas, Irene Middleman. "Shake, Rattle, and Roll." *Hispanic* (July 1994): 14–17.

Thompson, Stith. *Motif-Index of Folk-Literature: A Classification of Narrative Elements in Folktales, Ballads, Myths, Fables, Mediaeval Romances, Exempla, Fabliaux, Jestbooks, and Local Legends*. Rev. and enl. ed. Bloomington: Indiana University Press, 1989.

Tijerina, Andres. *Tejano Empire: Life on the South Texas Ranchos*. College Station: Texas A&M University Press, 1998. [Illustrations by Ricardo M. Beasley.]

Tinker, Edward Larocque. *Corridos & Calaveras*. With notes and translations by Américo Paredes. Austin: University of Texas Press, 1961. [From a collection made by the author in Mexico, and now belonging to the Hall of the Horsemen of the Americas, the University of Texas.]

Tinkle, Lon. *J. Frank Dobie: The Makings of an Ample Mind*. Austin, TX: Encino Press, 1968.

———. *An American Original: The Life of J. Frank Dobie*. New York: Little, Brown and Co., 1978.

Toor, Frances. *A Treasury of Mexican Folkways*. New York: Crown, 1947. [Photographs.]

———. *Mexican Popular Arts*. Detroit, MI: Blaine Ethridge Books, 1973. [Photographs.]

Torres, Eliseo. *The Folk Healer: The Mexican American Tradition of Curanderismo*. Kingsville, TX: Nieves Press, 1983a.

———. *Green Medicine: Traditional Mexican American Herbal Remedies*. Kingsville, TX: Nieves Press, 1983b.

Trotter, R. T., II, and J. A. Chavira. *Curanderismo: Mexican American Folk Healing System*. Rev. ed. Athens: University of Georgia Press, 1997.

Trotter, Robert T., Bernard Ortiz de Montellano, and Michael H. Logan. "Fallen Fontanelle in the American Southwest: Its Origin, Epidemiology, and Possible Organic Causes." *Medical Anthropology* 10 (1989): 211–221.

Tully, Marjorie F. *An Annotated Bibliography of Spanish Folklore in New Mexico and Southern Colorado*. University of New Mexico Publications in Language and Literature, no. 3. Albuquerque: University of New Mexico Press, 1950.

Turner, Kay F. "La Vela Prendida: Mexican American Women's Home Altars." *Folklore Women's Communication* 25 (1981): 5–6.

———. "Mexican American Home Altars: Toward Their Interpretation." *Aztlán: International Journal of Chicano Studies Research* 13 (1982): 309–327.

———. *Mexican American Home Altars: The Art of Relationship*. Austin: University of Texas, 1990. [Dissertation.]

———. *Beautiful Necessity: The Art and Meaning of Women's Altars*. London: Thames & Hudson, 1999.

Turner, Kay F., and Pat Jasper. "La Casa, la Calle y la Esquina: A Look at the Art among Us." In *Art among Us/Arte entre Nosotros: Mexican American Folk Art of San Antonio*, edited by Pat Jasper and Kay F. Turner. San Antonio, TX: San Antonio Museum Association, 1986.

Turner, Ralph H., and Samuel J. Surace. "Zoot-Suiters and Mexicans: Symbols in Crowd Behavior." *American Journal of Sociology* 62 (1956): 14–20.

Tushar, Olibama López. *The People of El Valle: A History of the Spanish Colonials in the San Luis Valley*. Pueblo, CO: El Escritorio, 1992.

Tyler, Bruce. "Zoot-Suit Culture and the Black Press." *Journal of American Culture* 17 (Summer 1994): 21–33. [Bibliography.]

Ulibarri, Savine R. *Mi Abuela Fumaba Puros/My Grandma Smoked Cigars*. Berkeley, CA: Quinto Sol Publications, 1977.

Utley, Francis Lee. "Folk Literature: An Operational Definition." In *The Study of Folklore*, edited by Alan Dundes. Englewood Cliffs, NJ: Prentice Hall, 1965.

Valdez, Luis. *Zoot Suit and Other Plays*. Houston, TX: Arte Público, 1992.

Valdez, Luis, and Stan Steiner. *Aztlán: An Anthology of Mexican American Literature*. New York: Alfred A. Knopf, 1972.

Valdez, Margarita. *Tradiciones del Pueblo: Traditions of Three Mexican Feast Days in Southwest Detroit*. Detroit, MI: Casa de Unidad Cultural Arts and Media Center, 1990.

Valero Silva, Jose. *El Libro de la Charrería*. Mexico: Ediciones Gacela, S.A., 1987.

Varley, James F. *The Legend of Joaquín Murrieta: California's Gold Rush Bandit*. Twin Falls, ID: Big Lost River Press, 1995.

Vasquez, Dr. Librado Keno. *Regional Dictionary of Chicano Slang*. Austin, TX: Jenkins Book Publishing Company, Inc., 1975.

Velasquez-Treviño, Gloria. *Cultural Ambivalence in Early Chicana Prose Fiction*. Stanford, CA: Stanford University, 1985. [Dissertation.]

———. "Jovita González, Una Voz de Resistencia Cultural en la Temprana Narrativa Chicana." In *Mujer y Literatura Mexicana y Chicana: Culturas en Contacto*. Mexico: Colegio de la Frontera Norte, 1988.

Venegas, Daniel. *Las Aventuras de Don Chipote, o, Cuando los Pericos Mamen*. Introducción by Nicolas Kanellos. Mexico: Secretaría de Educación Pública, Centro de Estudios Fronterizos del Norte de Mexico, 1984.

Venegas, Sybil. *The Day of the Dead in Aztlán: Chicano Variations on the Theme of Life, Death and Self Preservation*. Los Angeles: University of California, 1993. [Thesis.]

Vento, Arnoldo Carlos. *Mestizo: The History, Culture and Politics of the Mexican and the Chicano, The Emerging Mestizo-Americans*. Lanham, MD: University Press of America, 1998.

Verti, Sebastian. *Mexican Traditions*. Mexico: Editorial Diana, 1993.

Vidaurri, Cynthia L. "Texas-American Religious Folk Art in Robstown, Texas." In *Hecho en Tejas: Texas-American Folk Arts and Crafts*, edited by Joe S. Graham. Denton: University of North Texas Press, 1991.

Vigil, Angel. *The Corn Woman: Stories and Legends of the Hispanic Southwest*. Translated by Jennifer Audrey Lowell and Juan Francisco Marin. Englewood, CO: Libraries Unlimited, Inc., 1994.

———. *Una Linda Raza: Cultural and Artistic Traditions of the Hispanic Southwest*. Golden, CO: Fulcrum, 1998.

Vigil, James Diego. "Chicano Gangs: One Response to Mexican Urban Adaptation in the Los Angeles Area." *Urban Anthropology* 12 (1983): 45–75. [Bibliography.]

———. *Barrio Gangs: Street Life and Identity in Southern California*. Austin: University of Texas Press, 1988.

———. "Car Charros: Cruising and Low-Riding in the Barrios of East Los Angeles." *Latino Studies Journal* 2 (May 1991): 71–79.

———. "Street Baptism: Chicano Gang Initiation." *Human Organization* 55 (1996): 149–153.

Villanueva, Tino. "*Sobre el Termino 'Chicano.'*" *Cuadernos Hispano-Americano* (June 1978): 387–410.

Villarino, Jose Pepe, and Arturo Ramirez. *Chicano Border Culture and Folklore*. San Diego, CA: Marin Publications, Inc., 1992.

———. *Aztlán, Chicano Culture, and Folklore: An Anthology*. New York: McGraw-Hill Companies, Inc., 1997.

Villarreal, Jose Antonio. *Pocho*. Garden City, NY: Doubleday, 1959.

Villaseñor, Edmund. *Macho! A Novel*. New York: Bantam Books, 1973.

Wallis, Michael, and Craig Varjabedian. *En Divina Luz: The Penitente Moradas of New Mexico*. Essay by Michael Wallis; photographs by Craig Varjabedian. Albuquerque: University of New Mexico Press, 1994. [Bibliography.]

Wallrich, William J. "Spanish-American Devil Lore in Southern Colorado." *Western Folklore* 9 (1950): 50–55.

———. "The Santero Tradition in the San Luis Valley." *Western Folklore* 10 (1951): 153–161.

Wardropper, Bruce W. "Fictional Prose, History, and Drama: Pedro de Urdemalas." In *Essays on Narrative Fiction in the Iberian Peninsula in Honour of Frank Pierce*, edited by R. B. Tate. Oxford, UK: The Dolphin Book Co., Ltd., 1982.

Waterbury, Archie Francis. *Dona Rutilia: The Folk Belief System of a Mexican Herbalist.* Berkeley: University of California, 1974. [Dissertation.]

Watkins, Frances E. "He Said It with Music: Spanish-California Folk Songs Recorded by Charles F. Lummis." *California Folklore Quarterly* 1 (1942): 359–367.

Waugh, Julia Nott. *The Silver Cradle*. Austin: University of Texas Press, 1955. [Drawings by Bob Winn.]

Weber, David J. *New Spain's Far Northern Frontier: Essays on Spain in the American West, 1540–1821.* Albuquerque: University of New Mexico, 1979.

Weigle, Marta. *The Penitentes of the Southwest*. Santa Fe, NM: Ancient City Press, 1970. [Illustrated by Eli Levin; bibliography.]

———. *Brothers of Light, Brothers of Blood*. Albuquerque: University of New Mexico Press, 1976. [Bibliography.]

———. "Ghostly Flagellants and Doña Sebastiana: Two Legends of the Penitente Brotherhood." *Western Folklore* 36 (1977): 135–147.

———. *Two Guadalupes: Hispanic Legends and Magic Tales from Northern New Mexico.* Santa Fe, NM: Ancient City Press, 1987.

Weigle, Marta, and Claudia Larcombe, eds. *Hispanic Arts and Ethnohistory in the Southwest: New Papers Inspired by the Work of E. Boyd.* Santa Fe, NM: Ancient City Press, 1983.

Weigle, Marta, and Peter White. *The Lore of New Mexico*. Albuquerque: University of New Mexico Press, 1988. [Photographs; appendices; bibliography.]

West, John O. *Mexican American Folklore: Legends, Songs, Festivals, Proverbs, Crafts, Tales of Saints, of Revolutionaries, and More.* Little Rock, AR: August House, 1988.

———. "Grutas in the Spanish Southwest." In *Hecho en Tejas: Texas-Mexican Folk Arts and Crafts*, edited by Joe S. Graham. Denton: University of North Texas Press, 1991.

Whaley, Charlotte. *Nina Otero-Warren of Santa Fe*. Albuquerque: University of New Mexico Press, 1994.

Wilder, Mitchell A., and Edgar Breitenback. *Santos: The Religious Folk Art of New Mexico*. Colorado Springs, CO: Taylor Museum of the Colorado Springs Fine Arts Center, 1943. [Photographs.]

Williams, Brett. "Why Migrant Women Feed Their Husbands Tamales: Foodways as a Basis for a Revisionist View of Tejano Family Life." In *Ethnic and Regional Foodways in the United States*, edited by Linda Keller Brown and Kay Mussell. Knoxville: University of Tennessee, 1984.

Wolf, Eric. "The Virgin of Guadalupe: A Mexican National Symbol." *Journal of American Folklore* 71 (1958): 34–39.

Woodward, Dorothy. *The Penitentes of New Mexico*. New York: Arno Press, 1974. [Dissertation, Yale University, 1935.]

Wright, Corinne King. *Los Pastores: The Mystery Play in California*. Los Angeles: University of Southern California, 1920. [Dissertation.]

Writer's Program of New Mexico. *The Spanish-American Song and Game Book*. Compiled by workers of the Writers' Program, Music Program, and Art Program of the Works Progress Administration in the state of New Mexico. New York: AMS Press, Inc., 1976. [Published from the 1942 edition; illustrations.]

Wroth, William. *Christian Images in Hispanic New Mexico*. Colorado Springs, CO: The

Taylor Museum of the Colorado Fine Arts Center, 1982. [Color plates; bibliography; glossary of saints.]

———. *Weaving and Colchas from the Hispanic Southwest*. Santa Fe, NM: Ancient City Press, 1985. [Illustrations.]

Wroth, William, ed. *Hispanic Crafts of the Southwest: An Exhibition Catalogue*. Colorado Springs, CO: The Taylor Museum of the Colorado Fine Arts Center, 1977.

Ybarra-Frausto, Tomás. "Arte Chicano: Images of a Community." In *Signs from the Heart: California Chicano Murals*, edited by Holly Barnet Sanchez, with an introduction by Eva Sperling Cockcroft. Venice, CA: Social and Public Art Resource Center, 1990.

———. "The Chicano Movement/The Movement of Chicano Art." In *Exhibiting Cultures: The Poetics and Politics of Museum Display*, edited by Ivan Karp and Steven D. Lavine. Washington, DC: Smithsonian Institution Press, 1991a.

———. "Rasquachismo: A Chicano Sensibility." In *Chicano Art: Resistance and Affirmation, 1965–1985*, edited by Richard Griswold del Castillo, Teresa McKenna, and Yvonne Yarbro-Bejarano. Los Angeles: Wright Art Gallery, University of California, 1991b.

———. "Interview with Tomás Ybarra-Frausto: The Chicano Movement in a Multicultural/Multinational Society." In *On Edge: The Crisis of Contemporary Latin American Culture*, edited by Juan Flores, Jean Franco, and George Yudice. Minneapolis: University of Minnesota Press, 1992.

Zavala, Adina de. *History and Legends of the Alamo and Other Missions in and around San Antonio*. San Antonio, TX: Adina de Zavala, 1917. [Illustrated.]

Zavala, Bertha. *La Cocina Mexicana*. Mexico: Bertycel, 1990.

Zelayeta, Elena. *Elena's Secrets of Mexican Cooking*. Englewood Cliffs, NJ: Prentice-Hall, Inc., 1958.

Zinam, Oleg, and Ida Molina. "The Tyranny of the Myth: Doña Marina and the Chicano Search for Ethnic Identity." *Mankind Quarterly* 32 (Fall–Winter 1991): 3–18.

Zoot Suit. Written and directed by Luis Valdez; produced by Peter Burrell, 103 min. Los Angeles: Universal Pictures, 1981.

Zopf, Dorothy R. "The Hispanic Tradition of Quiltmaking in Taos County, New Mexico." In *On the Cutting Edge: Textile Collectors, Collections, and Traditions*, edited by Celia Oliver and Jeannette Lasansky. Lewisburg, PA: Oral Traditions Project of Union County Historical Society, 1994.

Quetzalcoatl

Index

Rafaela G. Castro has worked as a librarian at the University of Oregon, Contra Costa College, and the University of California, Davis, and has lectured in Chicano Studies at the University of California, Berkeley.